Equality and the British Left

Manchester University Press

Critical Labour Movement Studies

Series editors
John Callaghan
Steven Fielding
Steve Ludlam

Equality and the British Left

A study in progressive political thought, 1900–64

Ben Jackson

Manchester University Press
Manchester and New York
distributed exclusively in the USA by Palgrave

The right of Ben Jackson to be identified as the author of this work has been asserted by her in accordance with the Copyright, Designs and Patents Act 1988.

Published by Manchester University Press
Oxford Road, Manchester M13 9NR, UK
and Room 400, 175 Fifth Avenue, New York, NY 10010, USA
www.manchesteruniversitypress.co.uk

Distributed in the United States exclusively by
Palgrave Macmillan, 175 Fifth Avenue,
New York, NY 10010, USA

Distributed in Canada exclusively by
UBC Press, University of British Columbia, 2029 West Mall,
Vancouver, BC, Canada V6T 1Z2

British Library Cataloguing-in-Publication Data is available

Library of Congress Cataloging-in-Publication Data is available

ISBN 978 0 7190 7307 6 paperback

First published by Manchester University Press in hardback 2007

This paperback edition first published 2011

Printed by Lightning Source

Everybody does not suffer misery from boots.

One person I know . . . can testify to that . . . A stroke of luck, aided perhaps by a certain alacrity on his own part, lifted him out of the class in which one buys one's boots and clothes out of what is left over from a pound a week, into the class in which one spends seventy or eighty pounds a year on clothing. Sometimes he buys shoes and boots at very good shops; sometimes he has them made for him; he has them stored in a proper cupboard, and great care is taken of them; and so his boots and shoes and slippers never chafe, never pinch, never squeak, never hurt nor worry him, never bother him; and, when he sticks out his toes before the fire, they do not remind him that he is a shabby and contemptible wretch, living meanly on the dust heaps of the world. You might think from this that he had every reason to congratulate himself and be happy seeing that he has had good follow after evil; but, such is the oddness of the human heart, he isn't contented at all. The thought of the multitudes so much worse off than himself in this matter of foot-wear, gives him no sort of satisfaction. Their boots pinch *him* vicariously . . . In one respect the thought of boots makes him even more viciously angry now, than it used to do. In the old days he was savage with his luck, but hopelessly savage; he thought that bad boots, ugly, uncomfortable clothes, rotten houses, were in the very nature of things. Now, when he sees a child sniffing and blubbering and halting upon the pavement, or an old country-woman going painfully along a lane, he no longer recognises the pinch of destiny. His rage is lit by the thought, that there are fools in this world who ought to have foreseen and prevented this. He no longer curses fate, but the dullness of statesmen and powerful responsible people who have neither the heart, nor courage, nor capacity, to change the state of mismanagement that gives us these things.

H. G. Wells, This Misery of Boots, 1907, 14–16

Contents

Series editors' foreword

The start of the twenty-first century is superficially an inauspicious time to study labour movements. Political parties once associated with the working class have seemingly embraced capitalism. The trade unions with which these parties were once linked have suffered near-fatal reverses. The industrial proletariat looks both divided and in rapid decline. The development of multi-level governance, prompted by 'globalisation' has furthermore apparently destroyed the institutional context for advancing the labour 'interest'. Many consequently now look on terms such as the 'working class', 'socialism' and 'the labour movement' as politically and historically redundant.

The purpose of this series is to give a platform to those students of labour movements who challenge, or develop, established ways of thinking and so demonstrate the continued vitality of the subject and the work of those interested in it. For despite appearances, many social democratic parties remain important competitors for national office and proffer distinctive programmes. Unions still impede the free flow of 'market forces'. If workers are a more diverse body and have exchanged blue collars for white, insecurity remains an everyday problem. The new institutional and global context is moreover as much of an opportunity as a threat. Yet, it cannot be doubted that, compared with the immediate post-1945 period, at the beginning of the new millennium, what many still refer to as the 'labour movement' is much less influential. Whether this should be considered a time of retreat or reconfiguration is unclear – and a question the series aims to clarify.

The series will not only give a voice to studies of particular national bodies but will also promote comparative works that contrast experiences across time and geography. This entails taking due account of the political, economic and cultural settings in which labour movements have operated. In particular this involves taking the past seriously as a way of understanding the present as well as utilising sympathetic approaches drawn from sociology, economics and elsewhere.

John Callaghan
Steven Fielding
Steve Ludlam

Acknowledgements

In the course of writing this book I have acquired numerous debts. The earliest version of this work was submitted as a DPhil thesis at Nuffield College, Oxford. I am grateful to Oxford University's Pirie-Reid fund for their financial support during the writing of the thesis, and to Nuffield College for electing me to a Nuffield studentship. After completing my doctorate, I was fortunate to be awarded a post-doctoral research fellowship at Mansfield College, Oxford; I thank the Principal and Fellows of Mansfield for electing me to this position and for providing such a congenial setting in which to complete my work on this book.

My greatest academic debt is to Michael Freeden, who was a wise and generous supervisor of my doctoral thesis, and who has been an unstinting supporter of this project in all of its guises. As will become apparent in the following pages, I have learned a great deal from his important work on the political thought of the British Left. David Miller, my college supervisor at Nuffield, was also immensely helpful, and he generously read many early drafts. I have benefited from the comments of many other outstanding scholars during my work on this book. I am grateful to Michael Kenny, Gregg McClymont, Marc Stears and Stuart White, all of whom read and commented on earlier drafts of some or all of this material. I am particularly grateful to Gregg and Stuart, who had the dubious honour of reading multiple drafts, starting with my very earliest and sketchiest musings. I would also like to thank the following friends and colleagues for comments and discussions that have shaped my thinking during the book's gestation: Christopher Brooke, Daniel Butt, Clare Chambers, Simon Cox, John Davis, Brian Gibson, Ewen Green, Jose Harris, Martin McIvor, Karma Nabulsi, Paul Segal, Derek Sloan, Nicholas Stargardt, Ryszard Stemplowski, Adam Swift and Sam Taylor.

While researching this book I received expert assistance from the staff at various libraries and archives, especially the Bodleian Library, Oxford; the British Library of Political and Economic Science; and Nuffield College Library, Oxford. I am also grateful to John Callaghan, Steven Fielding and Steve Ludlam, the editors of the series this book appears in, and to the staff at Manchester University Press, for their interest in this project, and for their helpful advice as I brought it to completion.

The following people and institutions have very kindly granted me permission to quote from private papers: the British Library of Political and Economic Science; the Fabian Society; Nuffield College Library; Ann Oakley; University College London Library; and Seymour J. Weissman. Earlier versions of material in Chapters 3 and 5 previously appeared in articles I published in the *Journal of Political Ideologies*, 8 (2003), 83–110 and in *History of Political Thought*, 25 (2004), 508–35 respectively. A few sentences in Chapters 2 and 7 are drawn from articles previously published in *Public Policy Research*, 12 (2005), 140–7 and in *Twentieth Century British History*, 16 (2005), 416–40 respectively. Thanks are due to the editors and publishers of these journals for their permission to reproduce this material here.

My greatest debt is to my parents, Edward and Jacqueline Jackson, whose unfailing support has been essential to this project from the very start. My brother, Daniel Jackson, kindly contributed constant solicitousness about when, exactly, the book would be finished. I am very grateful to Zofia Stemplowska, who has read this book in all of its various drafts almost as many times as I have, but with considerably greater enthusiasm. Her comments on the text were indispensable, and have greatly improved the clarity and coherence of my arguments; her advice, support and encouragement were just as essential.

I am sorry that I will not be able to show this book to my grandparents, John and Mary McGavin. They lived through the period it discusses, and I would have liked to talk to them again about what I have learned. Their generosity was crucial, and it remained with me during my work on this book. I dedicate the book to their memory.

Ben Jackson
Oxford, August 2006

Abbreviations

CPGB	Communist Party of Great Britain
EJ	*Economic Journal*
FT	*Fabian Tract*
GO	P. Davison (ed.), *The Complete Works of George Orwell Volumes 1–20* (London, 1998).
HCD	*House of Commons Debates*
IJE	*International Journal of Ethics*
ILP	Independent Labour Party
JMK	D. E. Moggridge and E. S. Johnson (eds), *The Collected Writings of John Maynard Keynes Volumes 1–30* (London, 1971–89).
LL	*Labour Leader*
LM	*Labour Monthly*
LN	*Left News*
LPACR	*Labour Party Annual Conference Report*
LPRD	Archives of the Labour Party Research Department
MG	*Manchester Guardian*
NEC	Labour Party National Executive Committee
NFRB	New Fabian Research Bureau
NL	*New Leader*
NLR	*New Left Review*
NS	*New Statesman*
PQ	*Political Quarterly*
SC	*Socialist Commentary*
SR	*Socialist Review*

Introduction

Critics of capitalism have long argued that the market, if left to its own devices, will inevitably generate unacceptable inequality in the distribution of wealth, opportunities and work. While the history of attempts to substantiate this criticism is partly a story about ever increasing sophistication in the marshalling of appropriate empirical evidence, it is also necessarily a story about the shifting political concepts and ideological strategies that have been pressed into service in order to justify the superiority of a more egalitarian distribution. Since the demands of political argument require egalitarians to describe the disadvantages of a capitalist distributive pattern and to specify a more attractive alternative, to argue against economic inequality is to draw upon a range of complex and contested theoretical concepts. Inevitably, then, the history of the egalitarian critique of capitalism is a history of political thought, charting the multitude of theoretical variations that have been built around egalitarian ideals, and the complicated interaction between these distributive theories and political action more generally.

This book examines the egalitarian ideals advocated by the British Left. More precisely, it focuses on some fundamental questions about the development of the Left's egalitarianism during the rise of British social democracy. What, for example, did theorists and political actors on the British Left mean when they said they were committed to 'equality'? How did they argue for a more egalitarian society? Which policies did they think could best advance their egalitarian ideals? And how did the answers to these questions change across the first six decades of the twentieth century? I have two main aims in addressing these questions. First, I hope to deepen our understanding of the ideological influences on Britain's political trajectory in the twentieth century. This book provides a systematic analysis of an egalitarian tradition that played an important role in British politics, but has come to be neglected or caricatured by politicians and historians alike. Second, I also hope to contribute to the history of egalitarian political theory. This book demonstrates that the British Left developed an innovative and sophisticated body of egalitarian thought that is inaccurately presented in, or even excluded from, other accounts of the historical formation of the idea of equality.

Intellectual history and the British Left

Although I therefore see this book as offering a distinctive, and in some respects revisionist, set of arguments, it is of course indebted to important work already accomplished in this field. In particular, the book draws on the now substantial scholarship on the intellectual framework of modern British politics. While commentators have long criticised the neglect of political thought by historians of twentieth-century Britain,[1] a number of studies has at least begun to remedy this deficiency. Much of this research has focused on the political thought of the British Left, which is now the subject of an exceptionally detailed and complex historiography. Following a number of pioneering books on the new liberalism published in the late 1970s,[2] there has been a steady accumulation of research built on these foundations, providing fresh insights into the ideas that influenced progressive social reforms. While the nature and influence of British liberalism has been a continuing source of interest,[3] a great deal has also been written on related questions such as the political application of idealist philosophy;[4] the political theory of the welfare state;[5] and debates about heterodox economic policies in the 1930s and afterwards.[6] Much of this work can be read as an attempt to correct earlier, and inflated, claims that the most important ideological influence on the British Left was Fabian socialism, but scholars have also contributed to a more nuanced account of the trajectory of British socialism, focusing in particular on the late nineteenth and early twentieth centuries and on the 1940s and 50s.[7]

Inevitably, some important issues remain unresolved by this burgeoning historiography. While one widely discussed theme to emerge from this scholarship has been the pattern of mutual ideological influence between the left of the new liberalism and moderate socialists, these theoretical overlaps have principally been explored in the context of the early twentieth century, and it remains to be established how this shared 'progressivism' fared from the 1930s onwards. More generally, the specifically political theory of the Left after the 1930s has not been the subject of much sustained analysis, since most of the research on this period focuses on the development of economic theory, or the evolution of particular policy proposals, without considering in detail the more abstract philosophical shifts that took place in parallel with the policy discussions.

This book contributes new perspectives on these issues by tracking the development of one crucial political theme, the ideal of equality, from its use in British progressive ideologies in the early twentieth century to the decades following the Second World War. Equality is clearly an idea of considerable importance to the politics of the Left, yet it has been an elusive and somewhat intractable topic in the voluminous writings on the history of the British Left. There has been no systematic attempt to delineate how British egalitarians understood their commitment to a more equal society. A number of brief, small-scale treatments offer helpful initial orientation, but are far from providing the in-depth discussion that this subject deserves.[8] Exceptionally, Nicholas Ellison's *Egalitarian Thought and Labour Politics* has considered the history of the Left's egalitarianism in greater detail.[9] This is a valuable work that contains many important insights, and I will refer to it on a number of occasions in the following pages. However, it is not a historical study of the kind that I have tried to write here. Since Ellison follows the trajectory of the Labour Party's egalitarianism from 1931, he excludes from consideration the period that is examined in the first part of this book. In my view, this earlier period is of crucial importance for understanding the genesis and subsequent development of the British Left's egalitarianism, and in particular for exploring the relationship between the egalitarian thought of left liberals and socialists. In contrast, Ellison takes the thought of the Labour Party as his subject matter, and does not consider the way in which Labour's view of equality interacted with the distributive theories of other groups on the Left. Indeed, although Ellison's study makes some useful observations about the conceptual evolution of Labour's egalitarianism, he is principally concerned with policy-making, and the differing policy proposals that Labour developed in order to promote equality.[10] In this book, the order of priority is reversed. Most attention will be accorded to the conceptual history, with the links between egalitarian ideals and egalitarian policies discussed as a secondary concern.

Method and scope of the book

These comments raise an important question of method: how should we study the history of abstract concepts such as 'equality'? For the purposes of this book, I will be extracting two crucial insights from the complex literature on this question.[11]

First, I take as my starting point the now familiar observation that a history of an ideal such as equality will also require an understanding of the various historical situations faced by the agents who employ it. The meaning of a political term can shift or take on radically different connotations according to the situation in which it is deployed. As Quentin Skinner has famously argued, historians interested in characterising the meaning of a political idea in a particular historical setting should therefore be wary of focusing their attention on a reified concept at the expense of concentrating on 'the various agents who used the idea, and on their varying situations and intentions in using it'.[12]

Second, this book also aims to recognise the complexity of political ideologies by examining the multiple ways in which the concept of equality relates to, and conditions, the interpretation of other political concepts. As Michael Freeden has argued, political ideologies are flexible intellectual frameworks that aggregate and prioritise a number of political concepts. Ideologies possess a cluster of core concepts alongside adjacent and peripheral ones, but it is by no means the case that a given ideology must always maintain the same internal conceptual config-uration. On the contrary, not only can the relative importance and membership of the core cluster vary, but the non-specific nature of the core concepts means that they are also subject to diverse interpretations, depending on which adjacent and peripheral concepts are then attached to them.[13] Since this book is a study of egalitarianism within one particular political tradition, it will therefore examine the ways in which equality has been related to other core ideals in progressive ideologies, notably social justice, liberty and community, and trace how these relationships have in turn shaped the Left's understanding of its egalitarian objectives.

I have determined the scope of the book, and selected its sources, with these considerations in mind. I will analyse the thought of a wide range of figures, rather than a few 'great men', and make use of various media of political opinion, including books, pamphlets, periodicals, speeches, private papers and party documents. The historical significance of the thought of particular individuals can only be understood when compared with that of their contemporaries, and it is in any case misleading to see political ideology as the product of isolated theorists when it usually emerges from the collaborative efforts of groups aiming to influence public policy and public opinion. Accordingly, I will examine the egalitarian ideas produced by a series of intellectually productive and politically influential groups on the British Left, including well-known intellectual formations such as the new liberals and the Labour Party revisionists of the 1950s, along with less celebrated groups such as the British Marxists of the 1930s. Obviously, the use of intellectual productivity as a criterion for inclusion means that this book does not encompass all levels of political opinion on the British Left in this period, but rather focuses on the elite who were the principal theorists of equality. In the absence of a more satisfactory term, I will sometimes describe these figures as 'intellectuals', although this should not be taken to indicate that they were all necessarily professional political theorists or even academics. I also include reflective journalists, politicians and apparatchiks within this category, and indeed all those who have contributed to the development of the Left's egalitarian ideas.[14] This approach will enable me to reassess the egalitarianism of famous individuals, for example J. A. Hobson, R. H. Tawney, George Orwell and Anthony Crosland, by examining their ideas historically, in the context of the specific debates and political initiatives that they participated in.

There is of course no disguising the fact that this is a work about a relatively elevated level of political discussion. I therefore make no claims about mass opinion on the Left, and restrict myself to commenting on the views of a theoretically inclined minority. As an elite-level study, however, this book does show that the most influential intellectuals on the British Left, running roughly from the Fabians and the new liberals to the revisionists and the early New Left, thought seriously about egalitarian ideals, and developed patterns of egalitarian argument that were widely used in British political debate to legitimate a range of redistributive public policies.

As should be clear from my earlier remarks, the unit of analysis in this study will not be a particular political party or organisation but rather a specific ideological constellation, namely the Left.[15] Ideological influences stretch beyond party boundaries, and rival political organisations can even be embedded in broadly similar ideological positions. This point was well put by the leading new liberal theorist Leonard Hobhouse in 1924. Reviewing a book on socialism for the *Manchester Guardian*, Hobhouse drew attention to the chapter written by a certain Major Clement Attlee, praising Attlee's recognition that state intervention was necessary to promote 'the revolutionary trinity – liberty, equality, and fraternity'. This understanding of the purposes of state intervention, thought Hobhouse, 'gave rise to the social liberalism of recent times and to its twin, the ethical socialism described by Major Attlee. Between these there is really no quarrel, though he who takes the one label will probably find himself in a Liberal committee room perhaps appealing for votes against his brother who has adopted the alternative label. But the true divisions of political thought often wander far from the lines dividing parties'.[16] This book endorses Hobhouse's remark, and considers the ideas of figures affiliated to various political organisations, but who were nonetheless united by, among other things, their opposition to class-based inequality. Indeed, not only will supporters of the Liberal and Labour Parties be discussed, but also elements of the radical Left, notably Marxist writers of the 1930s and 50s, all of whom demand collective consideration because they shared certain important political assumptions and exchanged ideas about egalitarian objectives and strategies. Although my approach is ecumenical, I do draw on a distinction, first made by Michael Freeden, between a leftist and a centrist strand within British liberalism in this period.[17] For the most part, I will document two different perspectives on inequality in liberal political thought: a meritocratic, centrist liberal approach and an egalitarian analysis that was constitutive of left liberalism. However, the importance of certain centrist liberals to egalitarian thought is certainly acknowledged in the following pages. In particular, I will discuss in some detail the Left's reception of the work of that inescapable duo, William Beveridge and John Maynard Keynes.

By tracking the movement of political ideas across different generations, this book will establish the existence of a relatively coherent egalitarian tradition on the British Left. I will show that certain core egalitarian ideas were transmitted from one generation of progressives to the next, and were adapted by successive cohorts to suit their own political circumstances. Although my analysis will include both radical and moderate factions on the Left, it is the egalitarian tradition associated with left liberals and gradualist socialists that emerges as the dominant ideological force in the period covered by this book. I will refer to this tradition as 'progressive' or 'social democratic', since its leading exponents sought to distinguish their egalitarianism from the principles of social justice defended by both the radical Left and the Right.[18]

One final limit to the scope of this book should be noted. Although this is a study of egalitarian political thought, I only discuss gender equality briefly, when it arises in debates about economic egalitarianism, and I do not mention racial equality or supra-national egalitarianism at all. Instead, the focus of the book is specifically on the Left's critique of class-based inequality in Britain. It would be unfair to suggest that this focus simply reflects the limitations of this egalitarian tradition, since a few of the figures I will discuss were passionate advocates of gender equality, and offered powerful criticisms of racial prejudice and the exploitation of developing nations. Nonetheless, class inequality in Britain was certainly the Left's dominant concern in this period, sometimes to the exclusion of any other form of injustice,[19] and I have elected to focus solely on this dimension of their thought. I should stress, however, that this by no means indicates a judgement about the relative importance of this form of inequality; my only claim is that the investigation of the Left's beliefs about class inequality in Britain is in itself a legitimate and fruitful area of study.

Arguing about equality: concepts and context

Arguments about equality, as I noted at the outset, draw on complex and contested political concepts. Three will be particularly important in this book: equality itself; social justice; and community. How were these terms understood at the beginning of the twentieth century?

The history of political thought is replete with a variety of suggestions about how equality might be defined, but modern reform movements have character-istically taken as their starting point the 'equality' of the revolutionary trinity mentioned by Hobhouse: a claim about the mutual concern and respect shared between human beings, which declares any differences in social background or individual capacity to be irrelevant to the equal social status owed to every member of the community. This can be contrasted with the hierarchical understanding of the proper relationship between human beings that stresses a natural or socially authorised inequality of status between different categories of person, such as in the relationship between slaves and their master, or between different social groups which are recognised as being ranked according to a vertical scale.[20]

This form of equality emerged into western political thought slowly and inconsistently. For most of European history, claims about the fundamental equality of status of all human beings were considered to be deeply provocative and inflammatory. One of the earliest expressions of these radical views came during the English Civil War, in the political thought of the radical movement dubbed the 'Levellers'. The Levellers' famous assertion of the fundamental equality of all humans before God, and their commitment to popular sovereignty, was seen by the egalitarians discussed in this book as an important precursor, and even anticipation, of the modern struggle for political and economic equality. The oft-quoted words of Colonel Rainsborough in the Putney debates in 1647 were thought to have crystallised the basic idea at the core of modern egalitarianism: 'For really I think that the poorest he that is in England has a life to live as the greatest he; and therefore truly, sir, I think it's clear that every man that is to live under a government ought first by his own consent to put himself under that government'.[21]

The short-lived egalitarianism of the English Civil War primarily addressed political rather than economic inequality. The shattering event that directly placed both political and economic equality at the heart of modern politics was of course the French Revolution, although this was itself the pre-eminent example of a broader cultural shift that began in nations like France and Britain during the latter half of the eighteenth century. As Gareth Stedman Jones and Samuel Fleischacker have argued, this period saw the first expressions of a more egalitarian perception of economic relations. Rather than regarding the main objective of social policy as containing the vice and criminality of an inherently inferior lower class, radical critics now argued that the poor should be seen as the equals of the wealthy and as the victims of social structures that significantly shaped the prospects and resources available to different groups in society. In the influential words of Robert Burns, which were very familiar to many of the egalitarians discussed in the following pages, it could now be said that 'a man's a man for a' that', since 'the honest man, tho' e'er sae poor/ Is king o' men for a' that'.[22] The philosophical groundwork for such ideas had been laid by Locke, Rousseau, Kant and even Adam Smith, but they were given their most explicit political presentation after the French Revolution in the so-called 'Conspiracy of the Equals' led by Gracchus Babeuf, and in the writings of Thomas Paine. 'Nature has given to every man an equal right to the enjoyment of all goods', proclaimed the Babeuvist manifesto.[23] The radical discourses that gradually developed in the wake of this egalitarian breakthrough, most notably the diverse ideological currents that were to become collectively known as 'socialism', powerfully articulated the need for both wider political participation and the reduction of economic inequality if the ideals of the French revolutionary trinity were to be realised.

In making this case, radicals began to use another important concept: social justice. This was a novel use of the term 'justice', intended to rebut the notion that the provision of economic resources to the poor was a matter of charity, of discretionary private benevolence, and to defend the contrary position that a certain resource share was owed to each citizen as a matter of right. This was not how the concept of justice was understood prior to the late eighteenth century. Classical political theory, in the texts of Plato and Aristotle and the later writings of Roman lawyers, furnished subsequent generations with a basic definition of justice as rendering to individuals what they are due. This was conventionally taken to mean that the legal procedures of the state should treat individuals in a non-arbitrary manner and rectify any injuries inflicted by one person on another. The category of 'distributive justice' developed by Aristotle did prescribe principles for the just distribution of certain goods, but by this Aristotle meant distribution in proportion to individual excellence rather than any substantively egalitarian attempt to redistribute social benefits and burdens. The new idea of 'social justice' therefore differed from earlier theories of justice on two main grounds. First, social justice was seen as a virtue that applied to a society and not simply to individual behaviour: social institutions that distributed material resources and social positions were now subject to assessment as just or unjust. For Aristotle and other classical and medieval authors, it would have been odd to see distributive justice as giving the state a role in shaping the pattern of resource distribution in society. Second, social justice had a substantive political content that was also absent from classical ideas about justice, namely the claim that the alleviation of poverty and the diminution of economic inequality were matters of justice rather than charity. Instead of seeing distribution according to merit as the definitive principle of justice, theorists of social justice now prioritised the satisfaction of individual needs. Underlying these conceptual shifts was a growing conviction that the elimination of need was for the first time a practical objective: the economic growth unleashed by industrialisation demonstrated that sufficient resources were now available to end poverty, while the earliest social scientific studies detected social structures, rather than lax individual behaviour, as the cause of economic hardship. This new conceptualisation of justice began to enter political discourse from the late eighteenth century onwards, and can be found, for example, in the writings of Paine, who demanded old-age pensions and a universal cash endowment for every 21 year old as 'not charity but a right – not bounty but justice'.[24]

These new ideals of equality and justice were slowly taken up and deployed by radical movements opposed to the economic inequality generated by capitalism. However, for most of the nineteenth century, these views remained very far from the mainstream of British political debate. Malthus's pessimistic predictions about the impact of redistribution on population growth held the field, as did the more general belief that poverty represented the outcome of immutable economic (or even divine) laws that could only be challenged with grave consequences for economic efficiency and social stability.[25] Radical energies were in any case directed towards the widening of the franchise, possibly, as the Chartists argued, as the very means to secure a decent share of economic resources for all social classes.[26] It was only in the late nineteenth century that a serious ideological counter-offensive began to be made against the prevailing perception of economic inequality as both inevitable and just. Concerns about the social consequences of industrialisation acquired political urgency with the gradual widening of the franchise and the diffusion of socialist ideas and movements around Europe. With the democratisation of Britain now underway, the threat to social stability posed by working-class and radical political movements meant that 'the affronting contrasts of riches and poverty' moved to the heart of political debate.[27] The actual term 'social' or 'economic' justice seems to have been first used in British political debate at this time, without fanfare, as Victorian social philosophers grappled with the ethical implications of industrialisation and competing conceptions of a just distribution of wealth.[28] By the early twentieth century, both socialists and radical liberals wrote of the 'injustice of poverty', and argued that, across various forms of social activism, such as 'the labour movement, the women's movement' and 'the national uprisings', 'a passion for justice' was 'the inspiring principle which has not only stirred the wronged to seek redress but has inspired the sympathy of those possessed of imagination and understanding in the classes or peoples that had no wrong to complain of'. Justice was therefore considered 'a better word even than liberty to overturn the obsolete conception of "charity" and "being kind to the poor" as a reason for social activity'.[29]

Nineteenth-century critics of capitalism added one further important point to these demands for 'social justice'. Various ideological currents, for example both 'utopian' and Marxist socialism, as well as the romantic critique of capitalism associated with writers such as Thomas Carlyle and John Ruskin, saw capitalism as problematic not simply because it distributed material goods inequitably, but also because it fostered selfish behaviour and created antagonistic and competitive social relationships. These criticisms indicated that egalitarian aspirations need not be restricted to a demand for fairer shares of resources or opportunities, but could also invoke an ideal of community. On this view, a community of equals should be characterised by mutual co-operation rather than the competitive self-interest fostered by capitalism. In spite of its material benefits, socialists and romantics argued, the advent of capitalism had destroyed certain morally desirable kinds of social relationships that had characterised pre-industrial communities and that it would be desirable to re-introduce into any putative post-capitalist order. For example, it was argued that the members of a genuine community ought to be increasingly motivated to work out of a spirit of mutual service or civic duty rather than on the basis of the morally dubious motives of greed and fear employed by capitalism. This change in the character of individual motivation would there-fore eliminate the need for unequal material rewards as incentives; a qualitative shift to a co-operative community would in turn have implications for the principles governing the production and distribution of material resources.[30]

This brief summary of the early historical trajectory of egalitarianism has necessarily been somewhat stylised, but it gives an indication of the ideological resources available to egalitarians by the end of the nineteenth century, as they grappled with the relevance of a political vocabulary inherited from different historical circumstances to an industrialised and class-stratified society.[31]

The structure of the book

This book examines the ways in which the Left in Britain appropriated and devel-oped the nascent economic egalitarianism of the late nineteenth century, including a few episodes in which these theoretical debates exercised some influence over political decision-making or the formulation of party policy. The following pages track egalitarian ideals from their elaboration by the early new liberal and socialist writers, and their role in the acrimonious distributive conflicts precipitated by the Liberal government of 1905–15, through to the interwar period and the eventual apotheosis of egalitarianism during the Second World War. It concludes with the reassessment of socialist thought that succeeded the 1945–51 Labour government.

The book is structured in a way that is thematic but roughly chronological. Part I focuses on the years running from 1900–31, and charts the theoretical structure of the arguments for equality shared, or so I will argue, by both left liberals and socialists in this period. In spite of the ideological diversity on the Left in the early twentieth century, these chapters emphasise a significant degree of agreement amongst progressives both on a broadly egalitarian under-standing of social justice and on the ambition to create a more co-operative and harmonious community. Part II examines two new theoretical perspectives on inequality that rose to prominence, and clashed, in progressive discourse during the period 1931–45: Marxism and economic theory. In the face of depression and the rise of fascism, Marxist and Marx-influenced socialists popularised a pessimistic analysis of the compatibility of egalitarian objectives with the private ownership of the means of production, and of the plausibility of a gradualist egalitarian strategy. At the same time, social democrats began to supplement the egalitarian case made in the early twentieth century with the claim that an egalitarian distribution would enhance both productive and distributive efficiency, using the new analytical tools of Keynesian theory and welfare economics to justify these claims. Part III discusses the revisions in egalitarian political thought that took place from 1945–64, as the Left came to terms with the legacy of the Second World War and the arrival of the so-called 'welfare state'. Significantly, although egalitarians of this period used a similar discourse of social justice to that employed by their counterparts earlier in the twentieth century, ambitious visions of a co-operative community now appeared much more controversial and were the source of perceptible ideological division.

While the overall historical trajectory of the egalitarian thought surveyed in this book shows the shifting deployment of a variety of arguments and policies, there should be no doubt that the British Left was characterised by a serious egalitarian purpose that was located at the very heart of its political thought. The claim of this study, then, is that ideologically the British Left has principally been distinguished from its competitors on the Centre or the Right by a commitment to economic egalitarianism and, moreover, that this egalitarian tradition is apt to be misunderstood if we do not take the trouble to acquaint ourselves with the political thought of its leading exponents.

Notes

1 P. Clarke, 'The progressive movement in England', *Transactions of the Royal Historical Society*, Fifth Series, 24 (1974), 159; M. Freeden, 'The stranger at the feast: ideology and public policy in twentieth-century Britain', *Twentieth Century British History*, 1 (1990), 9–34. For the most influential argument that historians of modern Britain should integrate political language into their explanations of social change, see G. Stedman Jones, 'Rethinking Chartism', in his *Languages of Class* (Cambridge, 1982), 90–178; but see also Stedman Jones's cautionary words in his 'The determinist fix: some obstacles to the further development of the linguistic approach to history in the 1990s', *History Workshop Journal*, 42 (1996), 19–35.

2 P. Clarke, *Liberals and Social Democrats* (Cambridge, 1978); M. Freeden, *The New Liberalism: An Ideology of Social Reform* (Oxford, 1978); S. Collini, *Liberalism and Sociology: L. T. Hobhouse and Political Argument in England 1880–1914* (Cambridge, 1979).

3 E.g. G. Gaus, *The Modern Liberal Theory of Man* (London, 1983); M. Freeden, *Liberalism Divided: A Study in British Political Thought 1914–1939* (Oxford, 1986); R. Bellamy, *Liberalism and Modern Society* (Cambridge, 1992); A. Simhony and D. Weinstein (eds), *The New Liberalism* (Cambridge, 2001).

4 E.g. R. Plant and A. Vincent, *Philosophy, Politics and Citizenship* (Oxford, 1984); S. den Otter, *British Idealism and Social Explanation* (Oxford, 1996); P. Nicholson, *The Political Philosophy of the British Idealists* (Cambridge, 1990). See also the earlier study by M. Richter, *The Politics of Conscience: T. H. Green and his Age* (London, 1964).

5 E.g. J. Harris, 'Political ideas and the debate on state welfare, 1940–45', in H. Smith (ed.), *War and Social Change* (Manchester, 1986), 233–63; J. Harris, 'Political thought and the welfare state, 1870–1940: an intellectual framework for British social policy', *Past and Present*, 135 (1992), 116–41; J. Harris, 'Political thought and the state', in

S. Green and R. Whiting (eds), *The Boundaries of the State in Modern Britain* (Cambridge, 1996).

6 E.g. E. Durbin, *New Jerusalems: The Labour Party and the Economics of Democratic Socialism* (London, 1985); P. Clarke, *The Keynesian Revolution in the Making 1924–36* (Oxford, 1988); N. Thompson, *Political Economy and the Labour Party: The Economics of Democratic Socialism, 1884–1995* (London, 1996), 87–133.

7 E.g. M. Bevir, 'Fabianism and the theory of rent', *History of Political Thought*, 10 (1989), 313–27; M. Bevir, 'Sidney Webb: utilitarianism, positivism, and social democracy', *Journal of Modern History*, 74 (2002), 217–52; D. Tanner, 'The development of British socialism, 1900–18', in E. H. H. Green (ed.), *An Age of Transition: British Politics 1880–1914* (Edinburgh, 1997), 48–66; M. Stears, *Progressives, Pluralists and the Problems of the State* (Oxford, 2002); K. Morgan, *The Webbs and Soviet Communism* (London, 2006); S. Brooke, *Labour's War* (Oxford, 1992), 269–302; S. Brooke, 'Evan Durbin: reassessing a Labour "revisionist"', *Twentieth Century British History*, 7 (1996), 27–52; M. Francis, *Ideas and Policies Under Labour 1945–51* (Manchester, 1997); M. Kenny, *The First New Left: British Intellectuals After Stalin* (London, 1995). See also the important earlier study by A. M. McBriar, *Fabian Socialism and English Politics 1884–1918* (Cambridge, 1962); and the overview in W. H. Greenleaf, *The British Political Tradition, Volume 2: The Ideological Heritage* (London, 1983), 347–539.

8 Compare H. Drucker, *Doctrine and Ethos in the Labour Party* (London, 1979), 44–67; A. Gutmann, *Liberal Equality* (Cambridge, 1980), 69–95; R. Plant, 'Democratic socialism and equality', in D. Lipsey and D. Leonard (eds), *The Socialist Agenda: Crosland's Legacy* (London, 1981), 135–55; Freeden, *Liberalism Divided*, 247–57, 306–7, 316–18; D. Miller, 'Equality and market socialism', in P. Bardhan and J. Roemer (eds), *Market Socialism: The Current Debate* (New York, 1993), 300–4; G. Foote, *The Labour Party's Political Thought* (London, 1997), 76–9; J. Harris, 'Labour's political and social thought', in D. Tanner *et al.* (eds), *Labour's First Century* (Cambridge, 2000), 31–6; K. Hickson, 'Equality', in R. Plant *et al.* (eds), *The Struggle for Labour's Soul: Understanding Labour's Political Thought Since 1945* (London, 2004), 120–36.

9 N. Ellison, *Egalitarian Thought and Labour Politics: Retreating Visions* (London, 1994).

10 See the introductory discussion in Ellison, *Egalitarian Thought*, 2–27.

11 See e.g. J. G. A. Pocock, *Politics, Language and Time* (London, 1972); R. Koselleck, *Futures Past* (Cambridge, MA, 1985); W. Connolly, *The Terms of Political Discourse* (Princeton, NJ, third edition, 1993); M. Freeden, *Ideologies and Political Theory* (Oxford, 1996); Q. Skinner, *Visions of Politics, Volume 1: On Method* (Cambridge, 2002).

12 Q. Skinner, 'Meaning and understanding in the history of ideas', in J. Tully (ed.), *Meaning and Context: Quentin Skinner and his Critics* (Cambridge, 1988), 56. For the same point from a different philosophical starting point, see R. Koselleck, 'Begriffsgeschichte and social history', in his *Futures Past*, 80. The parallels between Skinner's and Koselleck's approaches have been persuasively set out in M. Richter, *The History of Political and Social Concepts* (Oxford, 1995).

13 Freeden, *Ideologies*, 75–91.

14 For a powerful exposition and defence of this expansive understanding of the term 'intellectual' in the context of British political culture, see S. Collini, *Absent Minds: British Intellectuals in the Twentieth Century* (Oxford, 2006), 45–65.

15 For an important discussion of the ideological distinction between Left and Right, which I follow here, see N. Bobbio, *Left and Right: The Significance of a Political Distinction* (Cambridge, 1996).

16 L. T. Hobhouse, 'What is socialism?', *MG*, 10.6.1924, 6.

17 Freeden, *Liberalism Divided*, 12–14, 127–8 and *passim*.
18 The definition of a political tradition is taken from S. Hazareesingh, *Political Traditions in Modern France* (Oxford, 1994), 5–6; see also A. MacIntyre, *After Virtue* (London, 1985), 220–2. For an indication of the British social democratic or progressive tradition I have in mind, see P. Clarke, 'The social democratic theory of the class struggle', in J. Winter (ed.), *The Working Class in Modern British History* (Cambridge, 1983), 3–18.
19 Indeed, the universal use of the male pronoun in my quotations from the texts of this period shows that some very elementary present-day concerns about gender equality simply did not occur to these egalitarians at all.
20 The previous two sentences draw on the illuminating discussion in S. White, *The Civic Minimum: An Essay on the Rights and Obligations of Economic Citizenship* (Oxford, 2003), 27–9.
21 A. Sharp (ed.), *The English Levellers* (Cambridge, 1998), xviii–xi, 103. For a discussion of Leveller egalitarianism by a celebrated British socialist, see H. N. Brailsford, *The Levellers and the English Revolution* (London, 1961), 59, 119–20, 274–5, 462.
22 R. Burns, 'A man's a man for a' that' [1795], in *Poetical Works of Robert Burns*, ed. W. Wallace (Edinburgh, 1990), 444.
23 S. Fleischacker, *A Short History of Distributive Justice* (Cambridge, MA, 2004), 53–79; G. Stedman Jones, *An End to Poverty? A Historical Debate* (London, 2004), 16–63; J. Waldron, *God, Locke and Equality* (Cambridge, 2002); G. D. H. Cole, *A History of Socialist Thought, Volume 1: The Forerunners* (London, 1959), 11–22, quote at 21.
24 This paragraph draws on the discussions of the origins of entitlements to economic resources in Fleischacker, *Short History*, 1–79; Stedman Jones, *End to Poverty*; D. Miller, *Principles of Social Justice* (Cambridge, MA, 1999), 2–6; D. D. Raphael, *Concepts of Justice* (Oxford, 2001), 233–6. For a comparative discussion of these works, see B. Jackson, 'The conceptual history of social justice', *Political Studies Review*, 3 (2005), 356–73. Paine's argument for redistribution on grounds of justice is in T. Paine, *Agrarian Justice* [1796], in his *Rights of Man, Common Sense and Other Political Writings*, ed. M. Philp (Oxford, 1995), 409–33, quote at 425.
25 Stedman Jones, *End to Poverty*, 64–109, 171–98.
26 Stedman Jones, 'Rethinking Chartism', 102–10, 168–78.
27 The Editor, 'The *Socialist Review* outlook', *SR*, 10 (1913), 324.
28 Miller, *Principles*, 3; e.g. J. S. Mill, *Principles of Political Economy* [1848], in *The Collected Works of J. S. Mill, Volume 2*, ed. J. M. Robson (Toronto, 1965), 199–234; J. S. Mill, *Utilitarianism* [1863], in J. S. Mill and J. Bentham, *Utilitarianism and Other Essays*, ed. A. Ryan (London, 1987), 318–19, 331–2, 335–7; J. S. Mill, *Autobiography* (London, 1989 [1873]), 175–7; H. Sidgwick, *Principles of Political Economy* (London, third edition, 1901 [1883]), 498–543; T. H. Green in *Oxford Chronicle*, 14.1.1882, quoted in Nicholson, *Political Philosophy*, 164.
29 '*Socialist Review* outlook', 325; L. T. Hobhouse, 'An apostle of peace', *MG*, 16.12.1916, 5; C. D. Burns, 'Review of *Principles of Social Reconstruction*', *IJE*, 27 (1916–17), 387.
30 This paragraph draws on D. Miller, 'In what sense must socialism be communitarian?', *Social Philosophy and Policy*, 6 (1989), 52–60; G. A. Cohen, 'Back to socialist basics', *NLR*, 207 (1994), 3–16. Influential historical examples of this idea of community can be found in R. Owen, *An Address to the Inhabitants of New Lanark* [1816], in G. Claeys (ed.), *Selected Works of Robert Owen, Volume 1: Early Writings* (London, 1993); J. Ruskin, *Unto This Last* (London, 1862); W. Morris, *News From Nowhere* (Cambridge, 1995 [1891]), especially 94–102. On the broader implications of this emphasis on qualitative transformation, and especially its instantiation in the political culture of British

socialism, see S. Yeo, 'A new life: the religion of socialism in Britain, 1883–96', *History Workshop Journal*, 4 (1977), 5–56.

31 It should be noted, however, that theorists and activists of this period saw the canon of political theory as an important source of insights into modern social problems. The writings of Plato, Aristotle, Rousseau and Kant, as well as Biblical texts, were regularly invoked in debates about economic inequality. See Harris, 'Political thought and the welfare state', 126–31; den Otter, *British Idealism*, 19–51; E. Barker, *Political Thought in England, 1848–1914* (London, second edition, 1928 [1915]), 24–5. For examples, see J. S. MacKenzie, *A Manual of Ethics* (London, third edition, 1897), 311–13; B. Glasier, 'Socialism and the wrong of ages: in reply to the Liberal pamphlet', *LL*, 1.1.1909, 1; L. T. Hobhouse, *Elements of Social Justice* (London, 1922), 97–9.

Part I

1900–31: Foundations

1

Riches and poverty

1.1 Introduction: class conflict and political thought

The decades surrounding the First World War raised a testing question for the British political system: on what terms could the working class be integrated into a stable social settlement? Manual workers and their families constituted an overwhelming, but severely disadvantaged, majority of the British population in this period, and both their industrial strength and political power were on the increase. Over 70 per cent of the British workforce was drawn from the working class; trade unions had begun to tap into this potential support after a long period of quiescence, with the percentage of union members in the total labour force peaking at around 45 per cent in the early 1920s.[1] The gradual expansion of the franchise to include the male working class ensured that, for the first time, the workers were equal with other social classes in the civic realm. The minds of rational office-seeking politicians were now concentrated on how to craft a platform that could win working-class electoral support. The creation of autonomous Labour representatives in Parliament and the eventual emergence of a separate 'Labour Party' in 1918 pressed home the point.

Against this background of industrial instability, rapid political change and widespread concern about the 'social problem', politicians in the Liberal Party seized the initiative. The Liberal government of 1905–15, in alliance with the infant Labour Party, introduced fiscal and social policies that placed heavier financial burdens on the rich, while creating significant benefits targeted at relieving poverty. This 'new liberalism' aroused fierce opposition from the Conservatives and their upper-class supporters, who saw these policies as tantamount to the declaration of class war. The First World War exacerbated this social tension, since wartime Britain's unprecedented collective social mobilisation generated starkly opposed perceptions of a fair distribution of sacrifice. Indeed, for a few brief years after 1917, socialist revolutions seemed to be sweeping across Europe. This offered the more alarmist members of the upper class an unappetising intimation of the most extreme resolution possible to class conflict in Britain. The post-war replacement of the Liberal Party by the Labour Party as the principal party of the

Left apparently confirmed the arrival of an era of acrimonious distributive conflict and significant political controversy about state intervention in the economy.[2]

Although this class conflict clearly reflected important material grievances, it would be a mistake to suppose that these clashes of economic interest straightforwardly translated into political action without first being mediated through political discourse and, ultimately, relatively complex forms of political thought.[3] On the contrary, British political debate in the late nineteenth and early twentieth centuries was riven by conflicting theories about the nature of the social settlement that could best accommodate working-class aspirations and eliminate the distributive conflict that had engulfed British society. Important research has documented a variety of influential theoretical languages in this period, most of them organised around the question of whether poverty, unemployment and class stratification should be regarded as an individual or a social responsibility. Advocates of social reform argued that social (and hence state) responsibility should be extended to include distributive matters that had previously been regarded as the province of individual initiative and private benevolence. Drawing on contemporary intellectual currents, such as idealist philosophy or evolutionary theory, social reformers claimed that social structures, rather than character and will-power, wielded a decisive influence over the economic fate of individuals, and argued that state provision of material resources or employment opportunities would enhance rather than detract from the flourishing of the individual. This was clearly a theoretical innovation of the first importance, and it has rightly absorbed the attention of many scholars working in this field.[4]

Yet there is a related topic that has remained largely implicit within this scholarly discussion, and which this book aims to bring to the surface and to discuss in some detail. While the crucial first ideological step towards a state that provided for social welfare was the claim that citizens were vulnerable to many contingencies outside of the control of the individual, this still left undefined the precise distributive pattern that was thought to realise this new understanding of social responsibility. Of course, there was little question that this conceptual shift would in practice legitimate policies that redistributed economic resources from the rich to the poor, but the more important theoretical issue, at least as far as intellectuals on the Left were concerned, was to identify distributive principles that could guide such policies by describing an ideal division of wealth, opportunities and work. Only once such a theory had been elaborated would the larger ethical purpose of redistribution become clear.

The first three chapters of this book provide a detailed discussion of the distributive principles debated and endorsed by the Left in the period that begins roughly at the turn of the century and concludes with the fall of the second Labour government in 1931. In particular, they show that a dual commitment to an egalitarian view of social justice and a more co-operative community united the otherwise diverse gradations of progressive ideology. Left liberals and socialists replied to the meritocratic or libertarian ideals espoused by rival ideological camps with a political discourse that emphasised the moral arbitrariness of market outcomes; the extent to which economic success was a collective rather than an individual achievement; and the need to condition economic rewards on productive effort. Strongly egalitarian principles were then derived from these commitments and applied to the formulation of public policy.

In order to reconstruct this egalitarian ideology, these chapters call on a familiar cast-list and range of sources: the leading progressive publicists of the time and the numerous books, pamphlets, speeches, newspapers and periodicals in which left-wingers debated the issues of the day. Particular attention is paid to the ideological overlap and mutual influence between three groups that played a central role in the production of the Left's political ideas. First, the prolific new liberal theorists Leonard Hobhouse and John Hobson (and their allies), who articulated the most radical version of British liberalism and also wielded some influence over the formulation of British socialism. Second, the leading socialist thinkers of the early twentieth century: Fabian intellectuals such as George Bernard Shaw and Beatrice and Sidney Webb, as well as the key theorists and politicians of the Independent Labour Party (ILP): Bruce Glasier, Keir Hardie, Ramsay MacDonald and Philip Snowden. Third, the younger generation of socialist academics and publicists who first rose to prominence immediately before the First World War, notably G. D. H. Cole, Harold Laski and R. H. Tawney. Although the political thought of many of these figures has been well discussed elsewhere, only in the case of Tawney has there been a specific study of egalitarian themes,[5] and there has as yet been no systematic attempt to investigate the overlaps between the ideals of social justice advocated by all three groups.[6]

This chapter begins my account of their shared egalitarian outlook by considering the Left's objections to class inequality. Progressive writers and politicians employed a variety of arguments against inequality; by documenting the range of these arguments I will give an initial indication of the character of the Left's egalitarian vision. I then ask whether progressives saw the aims of social mobility and meritocratic equal opportunity as able to satisfy their concerns about class inequality. I maintain that a meritocratic distribution was seen as an insufficient realisation of the Left's understanding of social justice, and this lays the groundwork for the more substantively egalitarian position discussed in subsequent chapters.

1.2 Why inequality mattered

'Justice is a name to which every knee will bow', wrote Hobhouse in 1922. In contrast, 'equality is a word which many fear and detest'.[7] While the postulation of some dimension of substantive equality as a legitimate social goal generated an outraged response from one social constituency, it was also apparent to the Left that equality was able to draw on certain bases of social support that lent it considerable rhetorical power. It was widely believed that the central demand of the working class was for equal treatment across a variety of dimensions, and the ethic of mutual co-operation and solidarity that was thought to characterise working-class communities and political organisations served as a concrete instantiation of the egalitarian social norms that should be extended across the nation. This polarity in public opinion was frequently discussed during the upsurge in industrial unrest that both preceded and succeeded the First World War, and during the related disruption to social and economic relationships created by the War itself.[8] 'To the great mass of the earners', argued a typical post-war *New Statesman* editorial, 'the War has enormously precipitated the growth of the conviction that, as between man and man in modern society, justice means, fundamentally, equality'.[9]

Against this background, egalitarian objectives were highlighted as central to the political contest between Left and Right. 'Socialism implies the inherent equality of all human beings', argued Keir Hardie, declaring that the 'inward meaning of the rise of the Labour Party' was the extension of the old radical principle of political equality to the economic sphere.[10] As Hobson noted, an egalitarian spirit could also be seen as the most important factor differentiating the old liberalism from the new. New liberals, he wrote, sought to give 'positive significance to the "equality" which figured in the democratic triad of liberty, equality, fraternity'.[11] Both socialists and liberals took as a starting point the modern view of democratic equality discussed in the Introduction, asserting that, in spite of the obvious differences in capacity or character between individuals, all were 'equally entitled as human beings to consideration and respect' because they possessed an underlying common humanity that should trump inequalities of talent or wealth. Each individual shared a basic similarity; any differences were only 'those of degree and lie as it were on the surface of that deep-seated identity which is common human nature'.[12]

Why did the Left argue that class-based inequality infringed this ideal of equality of respect? While on the face it the answer might seem obvious, it is nonetheless worth pursuing this question in more detail. Progressive publicists and politicians voiced diverse objections to inequality, and their criticisms drew on a number of prestigious political ideals and important sociological claims. In order to make sense of the egalitarian commitments that were central to progressive ideologies in this period, the full extent of the Left's revulsion at the inequalities of British society must first be recalled.

Left-wing critics of British society in the early twentieth century usually began their indictments with a very striking observation: the co-existence of terrible and widespread poverty with the enormous riches concentrated in the hands of a minority. This was not simply a rhetorical or anecdotal claim; it was buttressed by compelling evidence drawn from the first serious empirical studies of poverty and inequality in the United Kingdom. The celebrated social surveys of Charles Booth and Seebohm Rowntree were eagerly consumed by left-leaning (and indeed centrist) social critics, along with other early investigations of both the poverty of the working class and the vastly larger incomes enjoyed by the upper class. Booth and Rowntree had both calculated that roughly a third of the populations of London and York respectively lived under or just above an exceptionally austere poverty line. They also demonstrated that a major problem faced by poor families in these cities was that the wages they earned were simply too low to meet a very basic set of subsistence needs.[13] Statistics collected by the Inland Revenue or other official bodies were used to monitor the scale of incomes at the other end of the distribution. In his widely read book *Riches and Poverty*, the radical liberal journalist and future MP Leo Chiozza Money drew on these figures to point out that about one-half of the aggregate income of the United Kingdom accrued to just over 10 per cent of the population, while over one-third of the national income went to roughly 3 per cent. In Money's view, all of this empirical evidence demonstrated that Britain contained 'a great multitude of poor people, veneered with a thin layer of the comfortable and the rich'. Ramsay MacDonald added that such research should 'shatter with the rudest indifference' complacent social attitudes based on 'figures showing the astounding totals of national wealth, or the satisfactory averages of personal income'.[14]

Poverty and insecurity

Unsurprisingly, these stark economic divisions were thought to have a number of unjust social consequences. The first and perhaps most straightforward of these was the material suffering endured by the poor themselves. The vast productive potential of capitalism and the great aggregate wealth of the nation were frequently contrasted with the abject deprivation endured by the working class. As the studies of Booth and Rowntree had demonstrated, in 'the richest country in the world' around a third of the population lacked or were only barely able to obtain 'food and house-room for an average family', so that 'insufficient food, and bad, unhealthy dwellings' fostered 'ill-fed, undersized children' and spread debilitating diseases. Among this section of the population, parents had 'no surplus for any other object of expenditure' and their children bore 'every sign of privation and neglect'.[15] This poverty was seen as the result of social and economic structures rather than the inadequate characters of the poor. An economic system that permitted a dramatically unequal distribution of the product of industry, it was argued, had created a class that simply lacked the basic means to support themselves. In Hardie's evocative image (borrowed from Carlyle), the worker was like Midas: 'reduced to the point of starvation surrounded by the wealth which his own touch has called into being'. Surplus food, clothing and fuel could be seen across Britain, 'and he is suffering from lack of all three', but these needs were left unsatisfied by the capitalist system.[16]

A second, and related, problem was the economic insecurity that was endemic to working-class life, and absent from the lives of those able to draw on large incomes or who owned large amounts of property. Even if working-class incomes were able to scrape above the poverty line determined by Rowntree, the fluctuating demand for most manual labour meant that there was no guarantee that working-class families would maintain their standard of living in the medium to long term. The constant threat of unemployment placed a dreadful burden on wage-earners, since any interruption of earnings left them reliant on limited, and spartan, state support. As a result, said G. D. H. Cole, workers were 'driven to the factories by sheer economic necessity', with fear used as a key weapon in industrial relations: 'fear of hunger, fear of unemployment, fear of submersion in the hopeless strata of society'.[17] Even when incomes were consistent and provided just about enough for a family's subsistence needs, it was still hard to find savings that could be put aside for more difficult periods or to provide for old-age. As the future Labour Party leader George Lansbury put it, there was 'no certainty as to whence tomorrow's daily bread will come', leaving working families to suffer from 'the horror of sickness and the dread of physical breakdown'.[18] This made a stark contrast with the safety-net enjoyed by the wealthy, who could call on their greater financial reserves to avoid the fear and exploitation experienced by the workers, and were therefore able to extricate themselves from a day-to-day struggle for material survival and make long-term life plans.[19]

Freedom

In addition to the material suffering and insecurity inflicted on the working class, egalitarians further suggested that economic inequalities created unfair differences between the freedoms enjoyed by different social classes. Freedom (or liberty) can of course be construed in various senses, and there were at least three ways in which egalitarians insisted that individual liberty was unfairly distributed by economic inequality. First, they claimed that members of the working class were forced into dependence on the will of employers and the wealthy. Building on the observation that workers faced acute insecurity and vulnerability as a result of their reliance on the owners of property for employment, egalitarians argued that this made workers dependent on decisions taken by others, preventing them from exercising any control over central dimensions of their lives and leaving them open to arbitrary and exploitative action on the part of employers. Since workers were 'dependent for the opportunity to earn wages' on finding 'a master' willing to give them work, this placed them in a weak bargaining position: 'no master will employ you unless he can see his way to make a profit out of your labour'.[20] While prominent defenders of the capitalist system drew on the notion of liberty of contract to justify employment agreements as freely consented to by workers,[21] egalitarians saw this line of argument as implausible. As Hobhouse put it, a 'starving man may be free by the law of the land, but is not free by the law of the facts to reject the only bargain which enables him to obtain food', since the 'weaker man consents as one slipping over a precipice might consent to give all his fortune to one who will throw him a rope on no other terms'. Equality was therefore a necessary pre-condition for a fair and free bargain.[22]

From this perspective, inequality placed serious constraints on both freedom of contract and liberty understood in a wider sense, as the republican objective of becoming free through active self-rule. Elements of this discourse are arguably residues of older republican views of liberty that contrasted freedom with the slavery suffered by those dependent on the arbitrary desires of a monarch.[23] In the debates of the early twentieth century, however, the primary concern of radicals was transferred from political to economic despotism. The economic dominance of capitalists was responsible for 'a far more genuine loss of liberty, and a far keener sense of personal subjection, than the official jurisdiction of the magistrate, or the far-off, impalpable rule of the king'.[24] The phrase 'wage-slavery' was widely employed, suggesting an analogy between the character of proletarian life and an existence at the mercy of a chattel slave-owner or feudal chieftain.[25] Since 'the owners of the means of life' were able to 'dictate the terms on which all who are not owners are to be permitted to live', the course of working-class lives was 'dependent' on 'the goodwill or caprice of a private employer'. The aristocratic character of the capitalist meant that, as Tawney suggested, some still 'live, in effect, at the will of a lord'.[26]

A second way in which individual freedom was said to be undermined by inequality was through its suppression of opportunities for self-development on the part of the disadvantaged. As has been discussed elsewhere, progressive ideologies of this period often emphasised a developmental understanding of liberty, where freedom was thought to consist in the individual realising to the full certain capacities or characteristics. The precise nature of these capacities, and the exact role of the state in bringing them to fruition, were issues that sometimes divided progressives, but all agreed that this freedom to develop one's 'best self' depended on certain material pre-conditions.[27] The severe poverty and stark educational inequality that characterised Britain in the early twentieth century were seen as obvious impediments to the self-development of members of the working class. 'Poverty and ignorance benumb the faculties and depress the energies of men', wrote Harold Laski, leaving them with a 'sense of inferiority' that 'deprives them of that hope which is the spur of effort. They remain contented with a condition in which they cannot make the best of themselves.'[28] Access to education, and to important cultural goods, remained the preserve of the better-off, since they were treated as commodities to be purchased like any other. It therefore seemed highly plausible to argue that, in the absence of a more egalitarian distribution of economic resources and educational opportunities, the development of the workers' potential would remain unfulfilled.[29]

Another fetter on individual self-development, stressed particularly by ILP socialists like Hardie and Glasier, was the lack of personal fulfilment and self-realisation experienced in the workplace. This concern was to some extent derived from the influence of the romantic critique of capitalism on early British socialists (and some liberals), and the widely revered texts of Ruskin and Morris were a powerful source of inspiration for a scathing analysis of the dehumanising character of much manual work.[30] According to this analysis, manual labourers were generally put to work at a repetitive task; had little say over their workplace conditions; owned neither the tools with which they worked nor the product of their labour; and were in general unable to express their pride, individuality or creativity in their productive tasks. This state of affairs was often contrasted with the greater self-realisation that was thought to have been possible in the work of artisans and craftsmen before the arrival of mechanisation and capitalism.[31]

In addition to limiting self-development and breeding dependence, economic inequality constrained individual freedom in a third, more straightforward sense: it prevented workers from effectively exercising those liberties to act nominally granted to all citizens by law. In complex industrial societies like Britain, personal freedom was 'necessarily bound up with the ability to obtain commodities and services produced by other persons', and consequently required material resources to enable even the most elementary forms of free action. If greater economic resources were granted to the working class, or minimum workplace standards enforced by legislation, it would result in 'an enormous growth in practical freedom of action', since it would now be possible for workers to act across a range of dimensions previously inhibited by poverty or the coercion of employers.[32] As Hobson pointed out, in this sense even 'the right to move unhindered from one place to another' could only become 'effective liberty to travel' if the state ensured that public transport was accessible to all social classes.[33] From this perspective, the distribution of leisure time could be seen as more significant to individual freedom than the character of the tasks undertaken in the workplace. 'Liberty cannot begin until leisure begins', declared George Bernard Shaw, since it was only outside of the factory that workers would at last be free to pursue their own desires (as well as, on some accounts, to further their self-development).[34]

Of course, the identification of these three distinct senses in which inequality constrained working-class freedom does not mean that every egalitarian of this period would necessarily have signed up to all three lines of argument. The relevant point for present purposes is that egalitarians frequently argued that an important reason to reduce economic inequality was precisely to emancipate the working class from various forms of unfreedom. Progressives were determined to wrest the rhetoric of liberty from the Right by demonstrating that redistribution would in fact expand individual freedom. 'The disinherited and propertyless people are learning that Socialism and freedom "gang thegither"', claimed Hardie, 'and will use the state as the means whereby property, and the freedom which its possession ensures, shall become the common inheritance of every citizen'.[35]

Democracy

Related to these worries about individual freedom was the argument that economic inequality distorted democratic procedures and prevented the worst-off from exercising their rights as citizens. Progressive ideologies of the early twentieth century endorsed a basic set of equal civil and political freedoms as non-negotiable components of a just society. Progressive thought was also, by the standards of the time, strongly democratic, in the sense that it generally recognised the authority of popular sovereignty, and welcomed widespread political participation.[36] This did not necessarily mean a wholesale commitment to a radical participatory democracy (a broadly representative system was usually considered more plausible), but it nonetheless involved a belief that law determined by only one section of the community represented an arbitrary imposition: 'Law is slavery only when the law is inflicted by a class upon another class. When all submit to law imposed by all for the common good, then law is not slavery, but true liberty.'[37] The expansion of the franchise to include male members of the working class and (eventually) women raised the possibility that universal civic participation would make the state an instrument of the common good rather than particular sectional interests. But could these formal rights of citizenship be made effective in a polity fragmented by deep-seated economic and social inequality? Egalitarians generally concluded that they could not.

Democratic decision-making, they argued, was meaningless if a whole class of the people was effectively excluded from the process because it lacked the resources (material or educational) to participate on the same terms as the more advantaged members of the community. As a result, 'democracy is unattainable while wealth remains so unequally divided'.[38] Advocates of industrial democracy also argued that, in addition to the damaging impact of material inequality, political equality was likewise vitiated by the existence of hierarchical workplace relationships that fostered domination and subordination, since this inequality of status would have a knock-on effect on the assertion of formal political rights. If in industry one person 'enjoys riches and gives commands and the other has only an insecure subsistence and obeys orders', stressed Cole, 'no amount of purely electoral machinery on a basis of "one man, one vote" will make the two really equal socially or politically'.[39] A bare right to vote and participate in democratic politics was not, in itself, sufficient to guarantee that each individual would be given their due hearing, nor to cultivate the independence of mind required by a democratic citizen.

The inequalities of capitalism were therefore thought to produce a political system in which there was an unfair correlation between those who exercised greatest influence on the democratic process and those who possessed the bulk of the community's wealth. Harold Laski, for example, drew attention to the fact that the notionally democratic systems of both Britain and the USA were in practice dominated by the rich. The less fortunate found to their detriment that 'the engines of government' were controlled by the prosperous, with the legislature, media and legal system all biased in favour of the wealthy. In short, 'it is only when no man merely by virtue of his possessions can influence the course of affairs that the equal interest of men in the results of the political process can secure validation'. Great economic inequality meant that those who dominate the state 'will make the fulfillment of their private desires the criterion of public good'.[40]

Status and self-respect

Egalitarians of this period employed one other major criticism of inequality: the claim that the economic distance between rich and poor fostered an unacceptable hierarchy of social status, undermining social solidarity and the self-respect of the disadvantaged. As we have seen, the basic principle underlying the Left's egalitarianism was an ideal of equal respect or democratic mutual regard that envisaged each individual as entitled to the same consideration as any other, and rejected any attempt to rank social groups according to a vertical scale. One of the features of British society that most disturbed egalitarian critics was the extent to which economic inequality generated distinct social groups, defined by their wealth and the kind of work they performed, segregated from one another in everyday social interaction, and each possessing (according to dominant norms) sharply differing levels of social prestige.

These social divisions of the early twentieth century have been well described by Alan Bullock:

> Employers and management still largely held to the view summed up in that phrase of the early industrial revolution 'masters and hands.' They were the masters, the men who took the decisions, who hired and fired as they thought fit, without any need to give a reason or to consider how their decisions might affect the men they employed. In their eyes, their employees were 'hands' to whom they repudiated either obligation or relationship other than to pay a wage, and that at the lowest rate possible.

This was, Bullock added, an underlying cause of the profound antagonism that characterised British industrial relations. The workers felt that they did not deserve to be treated as 'creatures of a lower order, without rights or status'.[41] As Glasier suggested, 'the great wrong of existing social conditions does not lie in the mere circumstances that many are poor while many are rich, but in the injustice and degradation, in the assertion of superiority and inferiority, in the denial of brotherhood, which these conditions imply'.[42]

This aspect of the egalitarianism of this period has been widely discussed by political theorists, since it reveals an apparent concern with equal respect and egalitarian social relationships that some commentators have seen as absent from or in tension with present-day egalitarian political theory.[43] This may indeed prove to be a useful point of contact between contemporary concerns and the historical issues pursued in this book, although it should be noted that these two egalitarian objectives – an equal distribution of economic resources and a community composed of citizens of equal social standing – were seen as entirely complementary in the early twentieth century. According to egalitarians of this period, it was the socio-economic position of individuals that determined their place in the hierarchy of social esteem, and separated them from social interaction with others placed elsewhere in this hierarchy. The Left saw occupational status, and the relative share of wealth and economic security attached to it, as governing the relationships that individuals had with other members of the community, and as ultimately determining whether or not they were treated with respect.[44]

As the quote from Bullock suggests, an important dimension of this inequality manifested itself in the commodification of labour in industry. Manual workers, progressives argued, were denied the status of human beings in the workplace, counting only 'as a "commodity"' to be 'bought for the purpose of realising a profit' and treated 'as a thing instead of a number of persons'. The worker was 'still in industry what even the bourgeois was in an autocratic or aristocratic state, a subject and not a citizen, called to obedience but denied self-government'.[45] The injunction to treat the individual as an end and not merely as a means was employed, and sometimes explicitly attributed to Kant, to signify that the industrial system treated the worker as a means to the pursuit of profit, rather than as a citizen who was equal in status to any other.[46] The problem here was not only managerial autocracy, but also the resulting division of the product of industry. Both liberal and socialist political commentators repeatedly returned to this issue in the progressive journalism of this period, particularly in the aftermath of the First World War, when it was widely believed that enormous capital gains had fallen into the laps of property owners. Much social antagonism, it was argued, was due to the fact that while the ordinary worker had been called 'to make unprecedented sacrifices', the state 'quietly permitted thousands of his richer neighbours to make unprecedented fortunes'. The nominally egalitarian ethos of wartime Britain was seized on as having peacetime applications: 'a philosophy of equality that was good enough to defeat one enemy of the human race ought to be good enough to defeat another. There is much to be said for following up the defeat of Prussianism with the defeat of poverty.'[47]

Criticism of the social attitudes of employers, and more generally of the rich, was widespread and uninhibited on the Left: egalitarians detected snobbery, selfishness and a lack of sympathy with the plight of the working class. As Tawney noted, many employers developed 'an extraordinarily overbearing, tyrannous, and irresponsible habit of mind', regarding workers 'as "servants"', and promulgating 'the idea that the mass of the people are "productive" tools'.[48] The upper classes were chastised for their arrogance and 'the subtle insolence that is involved in the conception that other persons with whom you habitually consort are social inferiors'.[49] An associated worry was that these hierarchical social attitudes, and the economic injustice they were founded on, would have injurious consequences for the self-respect of the working class, fostering feelings of inferiority and subordination. The 'privilege and tyranny' generated by class inequalities created 'a spirit of domination and servility, which produces callousness in those who profit by them, and resentment in those who do not, and suspicion and contention in both'.[50]

Acknowledging the range and depth of all of these diverse objections to inequality goes some way towards heading off any casual assumptions about the character of the British Left's egalitarianism. The Left's arguments for equality did not exhibit an envious or purely symbolic obsession with the advantages enjoyed by the rich, nor did progressives preach a narrow economic egalitarianism focused only on the 'details of the counting house'.[51] Rather they employed a cluster of objections to the unequal distribution of work and wealth in British society, and to the social and political injustices that this inequality created. Egalitarians wanted to foster a community characterised by 'fellowship', in which citizens of equal social standing treated one another with mutual respect, free from 'invidious comparisons of superior and inferior', and fairly shared the fruits of their collective labour.[52] The redistribution of economic resources, educational opportunities and productive obligations was therefore the means to the achievement of a wider set of civic goals. Justice was the value that linked together these diverse concerns. A fair distribution was a necessary condition for social relationships of solidarity and mutual regard, and would safeguard citizens from poverty, insecurity and economic constraints on their liberty. Accordingly, egalitarian writers of this period stressed the need to implement principles of just distribution as a means of promoting the various social goals discussed in the preceding pages.[53] Of course, this raises a further cluster of complex issues about the character of the principles of justice endorsed by the Left. The remainder of this chapter will begin to address these issues by examining the role of equality of opportunity in the Left's thinking about social justice.

1.3 Equality of opportunity and its limits

The ideal of equality of opportunity has a consensual and uncontroversial connotation that makes it a tempting objective to cite when discussing social justice. Yet on closer examination it is also an exceptionally malleable concept, susceptible to an extraordinary range of interpretations. Understandings of equality of opportunity can range from a minimal absence of formal legal restrictions on occupational choice to a more substantial attempt to equalise the environmental factors that prevent individuals from realising their talents, and could even entail a radical commitment to equalise the capacity of individuals to live a fulfilling life regardless of their natural endowments. On the most radical interpretation of the concept, the distinction between equalising opportunities and equalising economic outcomes becomes somewhat blurred.[54] This section discusses the approach to equality of opportunity taken by progressives in the early twentieth century, and, in particular, their clear perception of the limits of a minimalist interpretation of this concept.

Meritocratic liberalism
The advocates of the minimal ideal of equality of opportunity in this period were usually centrist liberals. The split between meritocratic and egalitarian strands of the new liberalism had been implicit within the movement from its inception, and it was noticeable that front-rank new liberal politicians like Winston Churchill placed greater emphasis on the provision of a basic minimum to the exclusion of the more egalitarian principles defended by leading new liberal theorists. As Churchill put it: 'We want to draw a line below which we will not allow persons to live and labour, yet above which they may compete with all the strength of their manhood.'[55] The divergence between centrist and left liberals became more explicit after the War, and one manifestation of this was an increasingly explicit endorsement by centrists of a meritocratic interpretation of the ideal of equality of opportunity.[56] Ramsay Muir, a journalist and leading publicist for the post-war Liberal Party, stressed that a liberal state would not 'establish an artificial equality among men who are naturally unequal and different. The only forms of equality which it will pursue will be equality before the law, and equality of opportunities for all citizens to make the most of their varying powers.' A cardinal principle of liberalism was simply 'belief in the open career, so that the fittest men may fill the posts of leadership'.[57] Charles Masterman, the influential writer and sometime Liberal politician, made a similar point: 'For liberalism the race must still be to the swift, and the battle to the strong.' Liberals, he argued, aspired to 'government by an aristocracy of intelligence; of energy; of character'.[58] Such writers advocated what would later be called a 'meritocracy'. Their rhetoric drew on the familiar imagery associated with this belief: life as a race with prizes accruing to the 'winners', or the need for a ladder to enable the 'talented' to climb out of poverty. These meritocrats assumed that any substantive belief in social and economic equality inevitably neglected the vastly different tastes and capacities of human beings, and unjustly constrained the liberty of talented individuals.[59]

As Churchill had indicated, though, such liberals did want to constrain the most egregious inequalities created by a meritocratic distribution by furnishing citizens with a minimum level of resources to ensure that their basic subsistence needs were met.[60] They were also clear that access to education and jobs should be allocated on the basis of merit, a criterion that was recognised to mandate substantial changes to existing social practices.[61] It was therefore possible for centrist liberals and egalitarians to agree on the necessity of certain redistributive policies from different theoretical starting points, and it would be a mistake to regard centrists as simply endorsing existing property entitlements. Indeed, as I will discuss later, it was to be just such an overlap between the two positions that would later help to generate such strong cross-party support for the Beveridge Report.

The meritocratic ideal clearly drew on claims about personal responsibility and rewarding excellence that held a wide appeal. It was therefore necessary for egalitarians to explain whether this version of equality of opportunity offered a satisfactory realisation of their vision of a classless society. Their immediate response to this challenge was to urge that, rather than rejecting the idea of equality of opportunity outright, it ought to be treated with greater seriousness than it had been in the analysis of meritocratic liberals and other defenders of economic inequality. As Tawney observed, equality of opportunity was a political principle that was intuitively acceptable to a wide range of people, 'one to which homage is paid today by all, including those who resist most strenuously attempts to apply it'.[62]

Opportunities and outcomes

The text that offered the most influential treatment of this theme was indeed Tawney's own celebrated book *Equality*:

> But opportunities to rise are not a substitute for a large measure of practical equality, nor do they make immaterial the existence of sharp disparities of income and social condition. On the contrary, it is only the presence of a high degree of practical equality which can diffuse and generalise opportunities to rise. Their existence in fact, and not merely in form, depends, not only upon an open road, but upon an equal start.[63]

Tawney's case rested on the important point that equal opportunities could not be realised as long as significant material inequalities had the effect of placing citizens in different social classes with unequal starting positions. 'If the metaphor of the ladder is to continue to be employed', he argued, 'its reality obviously depends on the social and educational conditions surrounding its base, not less than its worth and weight'.[64] As long as privileged families were capable of greatly advantaging their offspring in terms of education, financial assets and general cultural background, it was obvious that equality of opportunity would remain a sham. In Tawney's memorable phrase, it was 'the impertinent courtesy of an invitation offered to unwelcome guests, in the certainty that circumstances will prevent them from accepting it'.[65] Although Tawney's work was the most famous version of this argument, similar points were frequently made by other left-wing publicists, who stressed that the typical social experiences of a working-class childhood, involving poverty, insecurity and limited access to education, would pose significant barriers to class mobility. The possibility of developing a 'best self' was severely constrained by inadequate nutrition, poor housing and the need to enter the labour market as early as possible to bolster the family income. Poverty entailed 'not only starvation, but the stunting of the mind'; a hungry child could not 'profit by education in like degree to those who are well fed'. The minimal interpretation of equal opportunity simply neglected that 'the opportunity offered the child varies directly with the income of its parent'.[66] In this way, the charge that the pursuit of equality would impose uniformity rather than respecting individual diversity could be reversed: a certain amount of material similarity was required precisely to foster the unique development of each individual and to break the uniform correlation between individual life chances and social class.[67]

The empirical study of social mobility was at this stage only in its infancy, but this radical appropriation of meritocratic ideals did reveal a growing awareness of the complexity of the causal mechanisms that generated economic and social inequality. Although egalitarians were conscious of the influence of subtle, intangible factors on the transmission of intergenerational advantage, such as the varying cultural resources or emotional support provided by families, two mechanisms were singled out as exercising decisive structural constraints on the development of individual talent: education and inherited wealth. As Hugh Gaitskell later recalled after he became leader of the Labour Party, the work of Tawney and Hugh Dalton was particularly influential in shaping the thinking of later egalitarians on this issue.[68] Dalton, a socialist economist and future Labour Chancellor, provided a pioneering discussion of the role of inherited wealth in perpetuating the class system, while Tawney's *Equality* masterfully synthesised the existing research on the determinants of inequality, drawing particular attention to inequalities of wealth and educational access.[69] Along with similar texts of this period, the writings of Tawney and Dalton had an agenda-setting role. They identified the distribution of wealth and education as of crucial importance to any policy interventions designed to dampen or, more ambitiously, eliminate inequalities in the intergenerational transmission of advantage. Their writings forcefully demonstrated that the full development of the potential said to be latent within the working class would require a significant degree of economic redistribution and educational reform.

Eugenics and equal opportunity
But this focus on equalising opportunities through redistribution and widening educational access raised a difficult question for the egalitarians of this period. To what extent were the natural endowments of individuals fixed by hereditary rather than environmental factors, and what did this imply for public policy? As I will discuss in the final chapter of this book, egalitarians after the Second World War faced a similar question. Influenced by the latest sociological research, they robustly argued that environmental factors were of decisive importance in shaping the developed capacities of the individual.[70] In the decades around the First World

War, however, the influence of eugenics on public debate remained palpable.[71] Although this meant that some egalitarians kept unlikely intellectual company, we should be careful about taking their remarks on this topic out of context. Given what was thought to be the state of scientific research on this subject, it could not be straightforwardly reported that expert knowledge regarded environmental influences as decisive for the development of individual ability. Nonetheless, there was still scope for egalitarians to draw radical implications from this more conservative premise, since if the claim of eugenicists was that there was a natural inequality between human beings, formed primarily by hereditary influences, this was still vulnerable to a powerful counter-attack.

As both Hobhouse and Tawney argued, even ardent partisans of the primacy of hereditary influences had to concede that the social context was relevant to the development of individual capacities, since it was obvious that abilities could only fully emerge through interaction with certain social institutions, perhaps most obviously the education system and the family. As Tawney put it, 'if grapes will not grow on thorns, or figs on thistles, neither, without soil, sunshine and rain, will grapes grow on vines, or figs on fig trees'.[72] It was therefore somewhat eccentric to argue that Britain in the early twentieth century, scarred as it was by manifest inequality in educational access, was stratified according to naturally given capacities. This enabled egalitarians to call the eugenicists' bluff, for if their ambition was, as Hobhouse summarised, 'to discover whether wastrels are men of degenerate stock, and if we are ultimately to take measures to prevent the degenerate stock from breeding', it was necessary to 'first know that the stocks that we are dealing with are in reality hopeless'. In order to accomplish this discrimination, then, it was surely important to 'have our social conditions so adjusted that all men who are in reality capable of adapting themselves to a well-ordered social organisation shall have the opportunity of proving what is in them'.[73] It followed that, even if hereditary factors were thought to be decisive for individual development, it was necessary to reduce environmental inequalities in order to achieve a more accurate discrimination between natural capacities.[74]

Beyond class mobility

But these arguments were generally made in the conditional tense, since the objective of these remarks was to exploit the limited egalitarian implications of these basically hierarchical theories. As well as stressing that the existing distribution of marketable talent and wealth did not reflect underlying natural inequality, progressives also made it clear that a theory of justice that focused purely on a fairer distribution of the capacity to rise up the social ladder did not fully capture their political objectives. While there was certainly support for the view that jobs should be allocated in a transparent, meritocratic fashion that took into account only the relevant competencies of candidates,[75] the Left remained sceptical of the unequal economic rewards and conditions attached to different occupations. Accordingly, they explained that their advocacy of a more substantive form of equality of opportunity should not be taken as exhausting their understanding of the ideals of equality and social justice. As the *New Statesman* put it in response to Winston Churchill's advocacy of equality as '*la carrière ouverte aux talents*', this 'gambler's chance is no evidence of the reign of equality. One might as well pretend to make men equal by the institution of government lotteries.' Social privilege remained objectionable, noted Tawney, whether or not 'the members of the privileged class vary from time to time' or 'sometimes include persons who have been drawn from the unprivileged classes'.[76] 'What is needed', said Hobson, 'is not an educational ladder, narrowing as it rises, to be climbed with difficulty by a chosen energetic few'; rather, the goal should be 'a broad, easy stair . . . which will entice everyone to rise' and be made 'for general and not for selected culture'.[77]

This was a crucial dividing line between the meritocracy favoured by centrist liberals and the more egalitarian position developed by left liberals and socialists. As Cole put it, his aim was emphatically not 'an equal chance for all to get the better of others', since this would result 'not in the fullest chance of self-expression for everyone, but in the crushing out of the individuality of the unsuccessful many under the heal of the successful few'.[78] Such a society was 'only a modified form of devil take the hindmost'.[79] An exclusive concern with individual mobility and self-advancement was not only seen as infringing the equal respect owed to every citizen, but also as conflicting with the Left's communitarian ideals. The long-term project harboured by the Left was in fact the replacement of a social ethos that emphasised 'selfish' individual economic maximisation with one that prioritised public service and mutual co-operation. As Hobhouse put it: 'We want a new spirit in economics – the spirit of mutual help, the sense of a common good. We want each man to feel that his daily work is a service to his kind, and that idleness or anti-social work are a disgrace.'[80]

Equality of opportunity was therefore a concept employed by the Left in this period, but in progressive discourse it meant something rather different from the equality of opportunity recommended by more centrist figures. This 'Left equality of opportunity' suggested that securing a meritocratic allocation of social positions would itself require as a pre-condition a substantial reduction in material and educational inequality. In any case, such a distribution was said to be only a partial realisation of the ideal of social justice. A single-minded focus on improving the class mobility of talented individuals was thought to neglect the importance of securing a broader, collective mobility that lessened the economic and social distance between social classes. The Left wanted 'to narrow the space between valley and peak',[81] so that both the 'talented' and their more modestly endowed fellow citizens had the opportunity to develop their personalities and to contribute to the flourishing of the community they shared. However, this emphasis on the importance of citizens making a social contribution does raise a further question of great importance to the social reform debates of this period: what would constitute a just distribution of labour within an egalitarian community? This question is taken up in the next chapter, which begins to discuss the more substantively egalitarian position held on the Left by focusing on the obligation to work, and the egalitarian conclusions that progressives drew from their endorsement of this social duty.

Notes

1 D. Gallie, 'The labour force', in A. H. Halsey and J. Webb (eds), *Twentieth Century British Social Trends* (Basingstoke, 2000), 288; D. Butler and G. Butler, *British Political Facts 1900–2000* (Basingstoke, 2000), 396.

2 For overviews of the distributive conflicts in this period, see W. G. Runciman, *Relative Deprivation and Social Justice: A Study of Attitudes to Social Inequality in Twentieth Century Britain* (Harmondsworth, 1972 [1966]), 65–91; J. Cronin, *Labour and Society in Britain 1918–79* (London, 1984), 19–48. Specifically on the decades before the War, see J. Harris, *Private Lives, Public Spirit: A Social History of Britain, 1870–1914* (Oxford, 1993), 96–149; and her 'The transition to high politics in English social policy 1880–1914', in M. Bentley and J. Stevenson (eds), *High Politics and Low Politics in Modern Britain* (Oxford, 1983), 58–79.

3 For a crisp statement of this point, see G. Stedman Jones, 'Why is the Labour Party in a mess?', in his *Languages of Class*, 241–3.

4 For a representative text from the period, see R. H. Tawney, 'Poverty as an industrial problem' [1913], in J. Winter (ed.), *R. H. Tawney: The American Labour Movement and Other Essays* (Brighton, 1979), 111–28. Varying interpretations of this ideological development include S. Collini, 'Hobhouse, Bosanquet and the state: philosophical idealism and political argument in England 1880–1918', *Past and Present*, 72 (1976), 86–111; his *Liberalism and Sociology*, 13–146; Freeden, *New Liberalism*, 26–116; J. Harris, *Unemployment and Politics* (Oxford, 1972), 7–50, 211–72; Harris, 'Political thought and the welfare state'; Plant and Vincent, *Philosophy, Politics and Citizenship*, 34–94. For comparison of the British case with other major industrialised nations, see M. Freeden, 'The coming of the welfare state', in T. Ball and R. Bellamy (eds), *The Cambridge History of Twentieth-Century Political Thought* (Cambridge, 2003), 7–44.

5 S. J. Robinson, 'R. H. Tawney's theory of equality: a theological and ethical analysis' (PhD thesis, Edinburgh University, 1989).

6 There has of course been more general discussion of the ideological links between these groups: see Clarke, *Liberals and Social Democrats*; Freeden, *Liberalism Divided*, 177–222, 294–328; D. Tanner, *Political Change and the Labour Party, 1900–18* (Cambridge, 1990), 19–43.

7 Hobhouse, *Elements*, 94.

8 On the social impact of the War, see Runciman, *Relative Deprivation*, 65–71; R. McKibbin, *The Ideologies of Class* (Oxford, 1990), 297–300.

9 'The precipice', *NS*, 14.9.1918, 465; also 'The vision at North Salford', *NS*, 10.11.1917, 125–6; 'Thoughts on the present discontents', *NS*, 5.10.1918, 10; 'The passion of labour', *NS*, 23.11.1918, 152–3; 'The state of the nation', *NS*, 15.2.1919, 413.

10 J. K. Hardie, *From Serfdom to Socialism* (London, 1907), 10, 77–8.

11 J. A. Hobson, *Confessions of an Economic Heretic* (London, 1938), 52. See also L. T. Hobhouse, 'Liberal and humanist', in *C. P. Scott 1846–1932: The Making of the 'Manchester Guardian'* (London, 1946), 85–6.

12 R. H. Tawney, *Equality* (London, 1931), 47; L. T. Hobhouse, 'Aristocracy' [1930], in his *Sociology and Philosophy: A Centenary Collection of Essays and Articles* (London, 1966), 203; also Hobhouse, *Elements*, 95; his *Liberalism* (Cambridge, 1994 [1911]), 58. For discussion of Tawney's conception of equality of respect and its possible origins in his Christian faith, see R. Terrill, *R. H. Tawney and his Times* (London, 1974), 124–8; A. Wright, *R. H. Tawney* (Manchester, 1987), 70–5; Robinson, 'Tawney's theory of equality', 6–13, 52–76 and *passim*. Note that in my view Tawney's view of equality was

not substantially different from that of other progressives of this period (contrast with Foote, *Labour Party's Political Thought*, 76–7; Robinson, 'Tawney's theory of equality', 174–87).

13 C. Booth, *Life and Labour of the People in London* (London, 1891–1903); B. S. Rowntree, *Poverty: A Study of Town Life* (London, 1901); A. Briggs, *Social Thought and Social Action: A Study in the Work of Seebohm Rowntree 1871–1954* (London, 1961), 16–45; D. Englander and R. O'Day (eds), *Retrieved Riches: Social Investigation in Britain 1840–1914* (Aldershot, 1995); B. Webb, *My Apprenticeship* (London, 1926), 186–220. Another influential study was A. L. Bowley and A. R. Burnett-Hurst, *Livelihood and Poverty* (London, 1915).

14 L. G. Chiozza Money, *Riches and Poverty* (London, 1905), 41–3; J. R. MacDonald, *Socialism and Society* (London, 1905), 1. See also e.g. J. A. Hobson, *The Crisis of Liberalism* (Brighton, 1974 [1909]), 160–1; Hobhouse, *Liberalism*, 78–9, 106; J. R. MacDonald, *The Socialist Movement* (London, 1911), 31–3; P. Snowden, *The Living Wage* (London, 1912), 27–8.

15 'Poverty and the state', *Nation*, 4.7.1908, 477; D. Lloyd George, speech, London, 17.10.1910, in his *Better Times* (London, 1910), 332.

16 Hardie, *Serfdom to Socialism*, 83.

17 G. D. H. Cole, *Chaos and Order in Industry* (London, 1920), 20. For an influential literary characterisation of this insecurity, see R. Tressell, *The Ragged Trousered Philanthropists* (London, 2004 [1914]).

18 G. Lansbury, *Your Part in Poverty* (London, 1917), 19; see also Hardie, *Serfdom to Socialism*, 56; V. Grayson, *HCD*, 186, 13.3.1908, cols 60–1; Hobson, *Crisis*, 106–7; D. Lloyd George, *HCD*, 25, 4.5.1911, cols 611–12.

19 Tawney, *Equality*, 207–8; Lansbury, *Your Part in Poverty*, 34.

20 P. Snowden, *Socialism Made Plain* (London, 1920), 4; also J. R. MacDonald, *Socialism and Government* (London, 1910), 154.

21 E.g. H. Spencer, *The Man Versus The State* (Harmondsworth, 1969 [1884]), 174–9, 181–2.

22 L. T. Hobhouse, *Morals in Evolution* (London, 1956 [1906]), 335; his *Liberalism*, 43; also his *Social Development* (London, 1924), 280.

23 Q. Skinner, *Liberty Before Liberalism* (Cambridge, 1998); S. White, 'Rediscovering republican political economy', *Imprints*, 4 (2000), 213–35.

24 S. and B. Webb, *Industrial Democracy* (London, second edition, 1902), 841–2, quote at 841.

25 E.g. H. M. Hyndman, *Social Democracy: The Basis of its Principles and the Cause of its Success* (London, 1904), 11; MacDonald, *Socialist Movement*, 134–5; R. Hunter, 'What is wage slavery?', *LL*, 11.2.1910, 86; C. R. Attlee, 'History: socialist and liberal', *NL*, 12.1.1923, 8; D. Irving, *HCD*, 166, 16.7.1923, col. 1934.

26 Hardie, *Serfdom to Socialism*, 9; P. Snowden, *Twenty Objections to Socialism* (London, 1920), 2–3; R. H. Tawney, *The Acquisitive Society* (London, 1937 [1921]), 77–8, quote at 78; also his *Equality*, 241–8; H. N. Brailsford, *Socialism For To-day* (London, 1925), 28–9.

27 Collini, *Liberalism and Sociology*, 28–32; Gaus, *Modern Liberal Theory*, 244–6; Freeden, *Ideologies*, 181–8, 201–3, 206–8; Stears, *Progressives*, 28–44, 102–4, 118–21.

28 H. Laski, 'A plea for equality', in his *The Dangers of Obedience and Other Essays* (London and New York, 1930), 213; also his 'Socialism and freedom', *FT No. 216* (London, 1925), 8. See also section 3 of this chapter for further discussion of this point in the context of debates about social mobility.

29 Webb and Webb, *Industrial Democracy*, 847–9; Hobson, *Crisis*, 109–11; Brailsford, *Socialism*, 43–5; Tawney, *Equality*, 201–7.

30 D. Howell, *British Workers and the Independent Labour Party 1888–1906* (Manchester, 1983), 352, 354; M. Bevir, 'William Morris: the modern self, art, and politics', *History of European Ideas*, 24 (1998), 175–94; J. A. Hobson, 'The new industrial revolution', *Contemporary Review*, 118 (1920), 644; B. Glasier, *William Morris and the Early Days of the Socialist Movement* (London, 1921), 146–9.

31 Hardie, *Serfdom to Socialism*, 50–5; MacDonald, *Socialist Movement*, 83–7; B. Glasier, *The Meaning of Socialism* (Manchester, 1919), 94–5. Whether this was a view of working-class labour that was actually shared by the bulk of the working class is open to question: see R. McKibbin, *Classes and Cultures: England 1918–51* (Oxford, 1998), 127–37.

32 S. Webb and B. Webb, *The Decay of Capitalist Civilisation* (London, 1923), 45–6, quote at 45; S. Webb and B. Webb, *The Prevention of Destitution* (London, 1911), 321.

33 Hobson, *Crisis*, 99–100, quotes at 99.

34 G. B. Shaw to B. Webb, 5.7.1928, Passfield Papers 2/4/I/41. See also G. B. Shaw, *The Intelligent Woman's Guide to Socialism and Capitalism* (New York, 1928), 320–30. The importance of leisure to those engaged in unpaid work was somewhat neglected in these debates.

35 Hardie, *Serfdom to Socialism*, 9. The nested quote is adapted from Robert Burns's famous line: 'freedom and whisky gang thegither', in 'The author's earnest cry and prayer', *Poetical Works of Robert Burns*, 140.

36 This was true even of those progressives sometimes labelled as 'elitists' or 'bureaucratic': McBriar, *Fabian Socialism*, 71–95; R. Harrison. *The Life and Times of Sidney and Beatrice Webb, 1858–1905: The Formative Years* (Basingstoke, 2000), 235–51; Bevir, 'Sidney Webb', 242–4. For the range of views on democracy within the labour movement in this period, see L. Barrow and I. Bullock, *Democratic Ideas and the British Labour Movement* (Cambridge, 1996).

37 P. Snowden, *The Individual Under Socialism* (London, n.d. [c.1910]), 13; also Hobhouse, *Elements*, 58, 88–9.

38 'Equality of income', *Nation*, 10.5.1913, 223; also C. D. Burns, *Government and Industry* (London, 1921), 283; Brailsford, *Socialism*, 28–32; J. A. Hobson, 'Towards social equality', Hobhouse Memorial Lecture 1931, in *Hobhouse Memorial Lectures 1930–40* (London, 1948), 4.

39 G. D. H. Cole, *Guild Socialism Restated* (London, 1920), 15. This argument was not restricted to partisans of guild socialism: see also Hobhouse, *Liberalism*, 120.

40 H. Laski, *A Grammar of Politics* (London, 1970 [1925]), 161–2, 153; see also Laski, 'Plea for equality', 219. Laski offered empirical verification of this in an influential survey of the class background of members of the British Cabinet: H. Laski, 'The personnel of the English Cabinet, 1801–1924', *American Political Science Review*, 22 (1928), especially 27–31; this study was then used in Tawney, *Equality*, 92. For similar theoretical points, see L. T. Hobhouse, *The Labour Movement* (London, third edition, 1912), 125; G. B. Shaw, *The Case for Equality* (London, 1913), 9–11; J. A. Hobson, *Problems of a New World* (London, 1921), 19; Tawney, *Acquisitive Society*, 77.

41 A. Bullock, *The Life and Times of Ernest Bevin Volume 1* (London, 1960), 253.

42 Glasier, *Socialism*, 226–7.

43 See Miller, 'Equality and market socialism', 298–304; Miller, *Principles*, 239–44; J. Wolff, 'Fairness, respect and the egalitarian ethos', *Philosophy and Public Affairs*, 27 (1998), 103–4; W. Kymlicka, *Contemporary Political Philosophy: An Introduction* (Oxford, second edition, 2002), 195–9. For historical treatments along the same lines, see Wright, *Tawney*, 71–2; Robinson, 'Tawney's theory of equality', 10–13.

44 Webb and Webb, *Decay*, 40; Hobson, 'Towards social equality', 22; Tawney, *Equality*, 41, 69–73 and *passim*.

45 Cole, *Chaos and Order*, 42; 'The cause of strikes', *NS*, 14.6.1919, 252; 'The future of industry', *Nation*, 11.10.1919, 26; also Lansbury, *Your Part in Poverty*, 34–5.

46 MacDonald, *Socialist Movement*, xi, 28; H. Roberts, *England: A National Policy for Labour* (London, 1923), 26; C. Pipkin, *The Idea of Social Justice* (New York, 1927), 541; H. Laski, *The Recovery of Citizenship* (London, 1928), 11.

47 'How to counter revolution', *NS*, 8.2.1919, 391; also 'The revolt of labour', *NS*, 25.1.1919, 340; 'The future of industry', *Nation*, 11.10.1919, 26.

48 *R. H. Tawney's Commonplace Book*, ed. J. Winter and D. Joslin (Cambridge, 1972), 22, entry dated 30.6.1912.

49 Webb and Webb, *Decay*, 37–8, quote at 38; also J. A. Hobson, *Work and Wealth* (London, 1914), 153–5; J. R. MacDonald, *Socialism: Critical and Constructive* (London, 1921), 18–20; Shaw, *Intelligent Woman's Guide*, 71.

50 Tawney, *Equality*, 118.

51 Tawney, *Equality*, 155.

52 G. D. H. Cole, 'Why I am a socialist', in his *Economic Tracts for the Times* (London, 1932), 326; G. D. H. Cole, 'Another sort of freedom', *Worksop Guardian*, 1.3.1940, copy in Cole Papers A1/38/1.

53 L. T. Hobhouse, *The Metaphysical Theory of the State* (London, 1918), 87–8; Hobson, *Problems of a New World*, 202–13; MacDonald, *Socialism: Critical and Constructive*, 1–11; Tawney, *Acquisitive Society*, 10–14; Laski, 'Socialism and freedom', 8, 13–14; Pipkin, *Idea of Social Justice*, 552. This argument was not the exclusive preserve of the Left: centrist liberals also emphasised the need for a principled basis for the distribution of burdens and benefits, though they differed from the Left over precisely what the content of those principles should be. See B. S. Rowntree, 'Labour unrest and the need for a national ideal', *Contemporary Review*, 116 (1919), 496–8; and his 'Industrial unrest', in R. Hogue (ed.), *British Labour Speaks* (New York, 1924), 107.

54 For discussion of these different interpretations of equality of opportunity, see G. A. Cohen, 'Socialism and equality of opportunity', in M. Rosen and J. Wolff (eds), *Political Thought* (Oxford, 1999), 354–8; A. Swift, *Political Philosophy: A Beginners' Guide for Students and Politicians* (Cambridge, 2001), 98–106.

55 W. S. Churchill, 'Liberalism and socialism', in his *Liberalism and the Social Problem* (London, 1909), 82. See also 'The social policy of liberalism', *Nation*, 27.11.1909, 354–5. Clarke attributes this article to Hobson (in his *Liberals and Social Democrats*, 117, 310), and it is notable that the article only endorses Churchill's attack on existing property entitlements and his advocacy of a national minimum. The author maintains a tactful silence on the principles of justice that should operate above the minimum. The other leading new liberal politician, David Lloyd George, was vaguer than Churchill on this issue, but he was also relaxed about individuals becoming wealthy 'by their industry, by their skill, by their energy, by their enterprise': speech, Newcastle, 9.10.1909, in his *Better Times*, 160.

56 Freeden, *Liberalism Divided*, 127–76, 246–7, 251–2 and *passim*. For further discussion of the centrist liberal position on equality, see M. Stears and S. White, 'New liberalism revisited', in H. Tam (ed.), *Progressive Politics in the Global Age* (Cambridge, 2001), 41–3, 46–50.

57 R. Muir, *Politics and Progress* (London, 1923), 32, quoted in Freeden, *Liberalism Divided*, 251; R. Muir, *The New Liberalism* (London, n.d. [1923]), 27.

58 C. F. G. Masterman, *The New Liberalism* (London, 1920), 30, 213.

59 Muir, *New Liberalism*, 27, 28.

60 Masterman, *New Liberalism*, 30–1; Muir, *New Liberalism*, 9.

61 Rowntree, 'Labour unrest', 497.

62 Tawney, *Equality*, 138.

63 Tawney, *Equality*, 143.

64 R. H. Tawney, 'Lectures on the finance and economics of public education', Cambridge University, 1935, Tawney Papers 17/6, lecture 2, 44.

65 Tawney, *Equality*, 150.

66 Brailsford, *Socialism*, 43–5, quote at 43; Laski, *Grammar*, 154; Chiozza Money, *Riches and Poverty*, 175; also Hobson, *Crisis*, 165, 204–6; Snowden, *Living Wage*, 50–2; Lansbury, *Your Part in Poverty*, 59–61; E. D. Simon, *The Inheritance of Riches* (London, 1925), 19, 37–8; Shaw, *Intelligent Woman's Guide*, 93–4; G. D. H. Cole, 'Historical foundations of ideas of equality', typescript, *c*.1955, Cole Papers E3/17/3, 24–5; his 'How much equality do we want?', lecture notes, *c*.1955, Cole Papers E3/17/6, 2.

67 C. D. Burns, *The Philosophy of Labour* (London, 1925), 61, 65; W. Robson, 'Socialism and the standardised life', *FT No. 219* (London, 1926), 5–6; J. A. Hobson, *Wealth and Life* (London, 1929), 65; Laski, 'Plea for equality', 226–9.

68 H. Gaitskell, *Recent Developments in British Socialist Thinking* (London, n.d. [*c*.1956]), 18–23.

69 See H. Dalton, *Some Aspects of the Inequality of Incomes in Modern Communities* (London, 1920), 281–343; Tawney, *Equality*, 63–98. See also Tawney's review of Dalton: 'The inequality of incomes', *Highway*, February 1921, 58–9.

70 See section 7.4 in this book.

71 On the relationship between progressive thought and eugenics in this period, see M. Freeden, 'Eugenics and progressive thought: a study in ideological affinity', in his *Liberal Languages* (Princeton, NJ, 2005), 144–72; D. Paul, 'Eugenics and the Left', *Journal of the History of Ideas*, 45 (1984), 567–90.

72 Tawney, *Equality*, 194; also L. T. Hobhouse, *Social Evolution and Political Theory* (New York, 1913 [1911]), 56–7; Tawney, 'Lectures on the finance and economics of public education', Tawney Papers 17/6, lecture 2, 2–6. The importance of environmental influences was acknowledged by most sympathisers to eugenics: Freeden, 'Eugenics', in his *Liberal Languages*, 145–7; Harris, *Private Lives*, 242–4.

73 Hobhouse, *Social Evolution*, 74; also Tawney, 'Poverty as an industrial problem', 125. This argument was used to justify the Webbs' famous proposals to reform the Poor Law: Hobhouse, *Social Evolution*, 73–4; S. Webb, 'Eugenics and the Poor Law: the Minority Report', *Eugenics Review*, 2 (1910), 235–7, quoted in Freeden, 'Eugenics', in his *Liberal Languages*, 146.

74 Another egalitarian argument that drew on eugenics was that class inequality was genetically inefficient, since it limited one's choice of mate to members of the same class. See Shaw, *Case for Equality*, 14–17; Webb and Webb, *Decay*, 41–4.

75 E.g. Cole, *Guild Socialism*, 75.

76 'Revolution', *NS*, 11.12.1920, 300–1; *R. H. Tawney's Commonplace Book*, 73, entry dated 8.1.1914.

77 Hobson, *Crisis*, 110.

78 G. D. H. Cole, *A Guide Through World Chaos* (New York, 1934 [1932]), 495. See also Tawney's famous condemnation of 'the tadpole philosophy' underlying certain interpretations of equality of opportunity: *Equality*, 142–3.

79 'Seven members of the Labour Party', *The Labour Party's Aim* (London, 1923), 57.

80 Hobhouse, *Labour Movement*, 75.

81 Tawney, *Equality*, 141.

2

From each according to their ability

2.1 Introduction: rights and responsibilities

A traditional criticism of policy measures that transfer resources to the disadvantaged is that the recipients are effectively the beneficiaries of state-sponsored largesse, since they are in receipt of benefits that they have not personally earned and that are issued to them regardless of the productive contribution they have made. In short, the recipients of welfare benefits are given someone else's rightfully earned money, for which they do nothing in return. This was a common rhetorical manoeuvre used against social reform measures in the early twentieth century, and was given a distinctive period appeal by the supplementary claim that under such circumstances state action was likely to corrode the 'character' of the recipients. As we have seen, egalitarians on the British Left rejected this type of claim because they regarded economic redistribution as a matter of justice; egalitarians invoked rights that belonged to every citizen and were sceptical of the discretionary character of charitable giving. But the view of public assistance as 'doles' was deeply entrenched in public sentiment and anti-egalitarian ideology, and it followed that any persuasive account of social justice would have to address both the distribution of productive obligations and the justifiability of existing entitlements to income and wealth.

This aspect of the history of progressive thought has retained considerable political interest, since latter-day portrayals of classical social democratic ideology have tended to assert that it focused on the distribution of benefits to the exclusion of burdens. Commentators sometimes claim that earlier social democrats simply wanted to hand out money to the poor without reflecting on the plausibility of existing individual property entitlements or the productive contributions that ought to be required in return.[1] Indeed, even some present-day egalitarians have been wary of claiming that economic rights incur productive responsibilities, seeing this idea as 'symptomatic of an overly defensive turn' in egalitarian thought 'first taken in the early 1980s'.[2] In this chapter, I argue that these charges are inaccurate. The claim that income should be related to productive effort was actually a staple of the Left's ideological arsenal in the early twentieth century, and it played a crucial role in justifying economic redistribution in this period. This point is explored in some detail in sections 2 and 3 of this chapter. In the final section of the chapter, I show that leading progressives also discussed justifications of inequality based on perceptions of individual entitlement and desert. However, these arguments were treated sceptically: the Left saw economic prosperity as the product of the collective efforts of the whole community rather than as the result of the heroic dynamism of isolated wealth-creators. Although progressives therefore thought that it was fair to make income conditional on some form of social contribution, they did not believe that income should be proportionate to the market value of that contribution.

2.2 The duty to contribute I: sources and structure

Central to progressive discourse about social justice in this period was the claim that every citizen was bound by a norm of reciprocity to make a contribution to the productive labour of the community as a return for a fair share of the benefits of social membership. This relatively straightforward idea generated a powerful rhetoric of redistribution that was to prove crucial to the public justification of social reforms until well into the second half of the twentieth century. Before examining in more detail precisely how this argument was elaborated in progressive political theory, and how it influenced popular political rhetoric, it is worth asking why egalitarians were so committed to this idea of reciprocity. One important consideration was obviously the strategic imperative to neutralise the 'free-rider' objection frequently made by the opponents of redistribution. However, this does not in itself account for the remarkable degree of agreement, across various currents of progressive ideology, that the correct response to this criticism was to emphasise a principle of reciprocity. From a philosophical perspective, there are certainly other kinds of response that might be made, drawing on, for example, claims about unconditional natural rights to resources. Instead, two important contextual factors pushed egalitarians towards an emphasis on productive contribution: their sociological circumstances and the dominant forms of political theory in the early twentieth century.

Sources

First, the social environment in which these egalitarian ideals were developed was obviously one that was dominated by the plight of a large *working* class whose productive contribution was tangible and impressive. Indeed, working men and women themselves often subscribed to 'a kind of folk-Marxism' that stressed 'their own work was the source of all value', in contrast to the intangible and yet much more highly rewarded non-manual work performed by other classes.[3] This striking sociological perception, given uncompromising ideological expression in the labour theory of value, filtered into working-class political culture from the early nineteenth century onwards, generating an emphasis among trade unionists, working-class radicals and early socialists on the dignity and importance of manual labour, and a corresponding scepticism about the contribution made by the wealthy.[4] The political force of this contrast was such that it became increasingly remarked upon in the discussions of the most advanced progressive intellectuals of the late nineteenth century. In words often quoted by later egalitarians, John Stuart Mill noted that under capitalism 'reward, instead of being proportioned to the labour and abstinence of the individual, is almost in an inverse ratio to it: those who receive the least, labour and abstain the most'. As an alternative, Mill aspired to a time 'when the rule that they who do not work shall not eat, will be applied not to paupers only, but impartially to all'.[5] The social observations implicit in Mill's words give an important insight into the sociological starting point of egalitarian political discourse in this period, and indicates why there was a particularly receptive audience for a redistributive rhetoric grounded on the idea of material reward as a return for social service.

Second, at the level of elite political theory, the dominant intellectual languages of late Victorian, Edwardian and post-Edwardian Britain all strongly emphasised social duty and the reciprocal obligations incurred by membership of a complex, functionally differentiated community. As Collini has suggested, a characteristic theoretical move in Victorian and post-Victorian moral and political thought was to confront moral agents with a stark ethical polarity: either they performed their assigned social duty or they lapsed into morally discreditable selfishness. This dichotomy established the 'unreflective Kantianism of Victorian moral common-places',[6] and produced a common style of thinking across a variety of intellectual idioms influential on progressive thought. Idealist political philosophy, particularly as espoused by T. H. Green and his followers (notably D. G. Ritchie), stressed that individual rights were derived from social membership and related to service to the common good, explicitly criticising the abstract natural rights claims made by the social contract tradition.[7] Idealism, along with the ubiquitous influence of evolutionary theory on progressive ideologies, generated a powerful analogy between 'society' and a biological organism. This suggested that the complex interdependence of members of a community had an organic quality, with each member performing distinct social functions essential to the survival and flour-ishing of the whole.[8] The doctrines of positivism, as expressed in the writings of August Comte, influenced this organic language; and Comte's work was also important to progressives as an independent affirmation of the importance of social service. As Beatrice Webb famously recalled, in mid-Victorian Britain 'the impulse of self-subordinating service was transferred, consciously and overtly, from God to man', with Comte's advocacy of altruistic service to humanity offering an important vehicle for this transformation.[9] This is not to say, of course, that Christianity itself did not persist as a resource for left-wing thought. For example, Christian ideals of service were seen as having profound implications for the distribution of social duties.[10] Classical political theory also remained widely read in this period, and progressives used writers such as Plato, Aristotle and Rousseau as key reference points in the discussion of social policy. An ideal of active citizenship was one lesson derived from these texts, suggesting that members of a community should find fulfilment in mutual service and the exercise of civic virtue, while the form of functional interdependence in the ideal Platonic state, although by no means egalitarian, nonetheless stressed the importance of every section of the community undertaking some productive burdens or discharging some useful social function.[11] In spite of the obvious diversity of these philosophical currents, it is clear that they all strongly emphasised a duty to contribute to society. Taken collectively, these ideological sources all characterised individuals as embedded within a community that not only conferred entitlements on its members, but also made demands on them.

Structure

Both the social and the intellectual environments inhabited by the progressive publicists and politicians of the early twentieth century made the distribution of the obligation to work an important issue in debates about the fairness of social arrangements. The Left's treatment of this question drew on these influences to stress that individuals owed some sort of 'functional' contribution to the community. As Tawney noted in an early manuscript, progressives saw justice as 'associated with' the 'idea of "function." Its opposite seems to be "privilege," i.e. enjoyment without function.'[12] While the concept of 'function' has often been discussed by commentators on the political thought of the Left in this period, there has been some confusion about the extent to which different groups or theorists adhered to contrasting interpretations of the idea. For instance, Anthony Wright has distinguished between the use of the concept by Tawney on the one hand, and its interpretation by Cole and the right-leaning guildsman Ramiro de Maeztu on the other, while Ross Terrill has seen a distinction between the conception used by Laski, Bertrand Russell and Tawney, and the different version deployed by Cole and the pluralist theorist and theologian J. N. Figgis.[13] As with all such complex concepts, it is of course true that 'function' did accrue various connotations according to the ideological framework it was deployed within.[14] However, in the specific context of early twentieth-century left liberal and socialist thought, an understanding of 'Left functionalism' was in fact elaborated that secured general agreement among the key architects of progressive ideologies.[15] Left liberals, Fabians, ILP socialists and socialist pluralists all concurred that every individual had a duty to undertake some form of 'functional' activity as a return for the benefits of social membership, with functional activity generally understood as any form of productive contribution to the necessary work of society, and in particular as participation in paid work (as long as appropriate exemptions were in place for dependants and those physically incapable of working). The performance of other important social tasks, such as raising children, also qualified as functional in this sense, although the latter was usually associated with a gendered division of labour.[16] Laski summarised this view: 'Rights, therefore, are correlative with functions. I have them that I may make my contribution to the social end . . . I have no claim to receive without the attempt, at least, to pay for what I receive.'[17]

2.3 The duty to contribute II: political implications

The political significance of this functional theory of social justice was that the individual's duty to contribute to productive activity was considered to be one side of a reciprocal obligation between the community and the citizen. If individuals upheld their part of the bargain and made a productive contribution to the community, then as a matter of right the community owed them a fair share of the social product. The importance of this formulation was that it offered progressives a principle of justice with a sharp cutting edge in the political disputes of this period. In response to the allegation that economic redistribution unfairly rewarded the idle, and constituted a charitable handout that would breed dependence and passivity, they argued that, on the contrary, such payments had been earned by productive service to the community. It was then open to egalitarians to turn the flank of their opponents by arguing that, in contrast, a major site of distributive injustice under capitalism was that many individuals received large incomes in return for little perceptible functional contribution.

The idle rich

From this latter perspective, the principal target of this emphasis on personal contribution was the idle rich. Those who were thought to have grown wealthy without significant personal effort, such as the owners of capital, land or inherited wealth, were suspected of holding so-called 'functionless wealth'. 'If a system is wrong which maintains an idle man in bare necessaries', wrote Hobhouse, 'a system is much more wrong which maintains an idle man in great superfluity'.[18] For this reason, argued Beatrice Webb, attempts to enforce productive obligations on the poor were hypocritical unless the same demand was made of *any* citizen who managed to live on the labour of others.[19] The social approval garnered by the indolent wealthy was specifically criticised by many left-wing writers as the most immoral feature of British society. The very rich constituted 'an idle class which produces nothing', and were guilty of 'social parasitism'. Since they consumed without contributing in return, they were in essence thieves.[20] Once again, Tawney provided an influential version of this argument in his first book, *The Acquisitive Society*, where he excoriated the 'class of pensioners upon industry', who acquired large fortunes without contributing any productive social service.[21] Although Tawney was not the first to elaborate a functional theory of property rights, his lively prose crystallised the Left's major concerns about functionless wealth. The radical liberal industrialist and politician Ernest Simon even claimed that *The Acquisitive Society* was 'read by thousands of working men', and was 'used on thousands of Labour platforms, and in innumerable talks in the workshops and factories' to persuade the workers that capitalism was 'unjust, and morally indefensible'.[22]

While the image of a crowd of workers thumbing through Tawney's text is an enticing one, it is likelier that the rhetoric of leading radical politicians gave these arguments their widest currency. The speeches of radical Liberal politicians and their Labour counterparts often focused on the parasitic character of landlords, capitalists and aristocrats as a means of justifying redistributive policies that benefited the hard-working poor. Lloyd George's 'People's Budget' in 1909 famously put these issues at the heart of political debate. His subsequent advocacy of new liberal fiscal policy featured some harsh words about the productive contribution of the upper classes. The landlord's 'sole function', Lloyd George argued, 'is stately consumption of wealth produced by others'. Indeed there was a substantial problem of 'unemployment amongst the upper classes', since a large number of them devoted themselves 'to a life of idleness' and lived 'without labour'. The opponents of redistribution, the Lords, were 'ordinary men chosen accidentally from among the unemployed', while 'most of the people who never worked for a living at all belong to the Tory Party'.[23] A similar rhetorical strategy was also used by Labour politicians such as MacDonald, who presented Labour's fiscal policies as designed 'to tax the parasites and not persons who gave service'.[24]

Such fierce rhetorical assaults on functionless wealth raised an important theoretical question for advocates of this model of economic reciprocity. Given their emphasis on the importance of work, did it then follow that a functional theory of property rights demanded the complete abolition of income derived from capital ownership? While this might seem to be a superficially plausible inter-pretation of their arguments, it is clear that for many leading proponents of this view it was the relative size rather than the source of wealth that made an income illegitimate. While some radical socialists may have expressed universal hostility to all forms of capital income, left liberals and many socialists were keen to differentiate their position from these strands of socialist thought by stressing that they did not advocate the complete collective ownership of property, but rather its collective regulation in order to secure both greater public ownership and a wider diffusion of private property among individuals.

In his influential discussion of the nature of property rights in 1913, Hobhouse drew on the Aristotelian idea of private property as necessary for the expression of individual personality. He argued that this position, properly understood, mandated the redistribution of private property, so that every citizen was able to access the personal freedom that was conferred by property ownership.[25] In Hobhouse's view, the morally objectionable form of property that should be subject to collective control was not indeed capital ownership per se, but 'property for power' as contrasted with 'property for use'. With this distinction, Hobhouse sought to differentiate between the ownership of small amounts of property that conferred 'control of things' and hence 'gives freedom and security' for an ordered individual life, and the ownership of larger amounts, which gave 'control of persons through things' and 'gives power to the owner'.[26] According to Hobhouse, the legitimacy of this latter form of property was undermined not only because it endowed the owner with the power to exploit those who owned nothing, but also by the fact that it enabled the rich to avoid work altogether.[27] Similar thoughts were expressed from within the socialist camp at roughly the same time. Like Hobhouse, MacDonald thought 'that individuality requires private property through which to express itself', and he endorsed private property if it enabled the expression of personality. MacDonald also called for the socialisation or redistribution of property that did not reflect 'active service to society' and enabled capitalists to monopolise the ownership of wealth.[28] Similarly, Philip Snowden warmly welcomed Hobhouse's distinction between 'property for power' and 'property for use' as 'a very happy and suggestive phrase', and argued that socialists aimed to make 'property for use' 'accessible to every individual, if he is to enjoy true freedom and to develop his true individuality'.[29]

This distinction between justifiable and socially harmful forms of property was built on by succeeding writers, and was famously replicated in Hobson's distinction between 'property' and 'improperty'.[30] Tawney explicitly drew on Hobson's terminology in *The Acquisitive Society*, where he proposed that not only income from work, but also income from certain forms of property ownership should be regarded as functional. The latter category included productive private property that was used by its owner; income from patents and copyrights held by the original authors and inventors; and a certain amount of income from interest. Tawney agreed that savings could be a genuine sacrifice on the part of the individual and that interest should therefore be paid to recognise the level of sacrifice made.[31] Later socialists such as Tawney therefore joined with Hobhouse and MacDonald in regarding a certain amount of capital income as compatible with a functional theory of property rights. Cole even argued that 'the broadening of the basis of ownership has nothing to do with the conflict between socialism and private enterprise'. A community with a large socialised sector, thought Cole, 'could have as broad a basis of ownership as might be desired', since the safest form of investment for the private savings of individuals would be through collectively organised investment trusts or state and municipal securities.[32] But it also followed that the most flagrantly functionless form of capital income was inherited wealth, since it was quite plainly unrelated to any kind of effort or sacrifice on the part of those who received such income.[33]

The workers' contribution

While the purpose of this argument was partly to question the justifiability of large concentrations of wealth, it was also intended to buttress the redistribution of material resources to the poor by portraying it as a return for social contribution. Did such a notion of productive obligation really unite *all* progressive intellectuals in this period? One reason to answer 'no' to this question has been given by Stefan Collini, who has unfavourably contrasted Hobhouse's functional theory of social justice with George Bernard Shaw's apparently much more straightforward claim that individuals should be paid, unconditionally, an equal income.[34] Shaw's strict egalitarianism, and the reactions it elicited from other progressives, will be discussed in detail in the next chapter. For the moment, though, it is important to stress that Shaw's egalitarianism in fact placed as great an emphasis on productive obligations as did Hobhouse.

The debate between Hobhouse and Shaw on equality in the pages of the *Nation*, which Collini's account is based on, certainly suggests that Shaw was, on that occasion, sceptical of Hobhouse's proposal to make income conditional on productive labour.[35] However, this does not seem to have been Shaw's considered view. In virtually every other presentation of his egalitarianism, he explicitly made the payment of equal incomes conditional on productive service. Indeed, Shaw took this idea of reciprocity in a far more illiberal direction than Hobhouse. 'On the question of incentive', Shaw wrote to the sometime Fabian Graham Wallas,

'I am convinced that we must get rid of the notion that any choice can be tolerated in the obligation to work. Direct unhesitating compulsion should be a matter of course.'[36] The importance of this contributory ethic was such that work was not only a condition of the receipt of income, but also there was in fact to be no option for individuals to choose whether or not to accept the income being paid to them by the state. This was because 'voluntary poverty is just as mischievous socially as involuntary poverty'.[37] Shaw believed that this coercive work requirement was justifiable because it carried with it an equal share of the community's wealth, and because he thought that its illiberal implications would be attenuated by a substantial reduction in the length of the average working day, suggesting 'four hours of necessary duty' as his daily ideal.[38] As Shaw argued in debate with the right-wing publicist Harold Cox, 'it is disgraceful to consume without producing'. In an egalitarian society, 'our debt of work to the community is a just debt. Its enforcement is not slave-driving', since 'slave-driving means compelling honest and industrious men and women to work under wretched conditions to support idlers. And that is exactly what we do at present.'[39]

Other egalitarians were less punitive than Shaw in their presentation of the duties incurred by the least advantaged. But they did consistently argue that the labour of the working class constituted a formidable productive contribution that entitled the workers to a fairer share of material resources. Egalitarians also added that, if fair resource shares were distributed, then certain work or training requirements could legitimately be imposed on free-riders. Progressive social policy measures such as the introduction of pensions, the provision of health insurance, and the specification of minimum wage rates were all defended as a reciprocal obligation incurred by the community as a result of productive contributions.[40] While in political terms there was a well-documented rivalry between the Liberal government's emphasis on compulsory contributive unemployment insurance and the Fabian advocacy of the Minority Report of the Poor Law Commission,[41] both proposals were publicly justified by reference to a principle of reciprocal productive obligation. The use of this principle might seem obvious enough in the case of social insurance, since the entitlement to benefits was established through contribution in a literal sense,[42] but the same argument was also used by the Webbs, who posited a mutual obligation between the community and the individual as the basis of the proposals for the relief of destitution made by Beatrice's Minority Report. 'As a socialist', argued Sidney Webb, 'I cannot feel much sympathy for a man who tries persistently to live on the labour of others, even though he be at the very bottom of the income scale'. The advocates of the Minority Report accordingly stressed that income would be conditional on individuals accepting job offers or opportunities for retraining.[43] As Hobhouse summarised, underlying both the proposals of the Minority Report and the legislation of the Liberal government was a 'newer conception of rights and duties': 'we should seek to render generally available the means of avoiding destitution, though in doing so we should uniformly call on the individual for a corresponding effort on his part'.[44]

This view was not simply a preoccupation of middle-class intellectuals; Labour politicians with closer links to working-class communities agreed. On several occasions before 1914, Labour MPs sponsored the so-called 'Right to Work Bill', which aimed to establish the state as an employer of last resort for those who could not find employment in the private sector.[45] One interesting feature of the rhetoric used to support this Bill was that it did not simply stick to the claim that every individual had a right to work. In fact, Labour politicians often went much further than this by arguing that citizens were actually under a duty to work, moving from a formulation that implied some choice over whether or not to exercise an entitlement to one that suggested that work was in fact morally obligatory. When pressed by opponents about the fate of those who might choose not to work, Labour politicians uncompromisingly claimed that in fact 'a man unwilling to work should be made to work', since everyone should 'do their share of the work of the community'. They denied 'that the Labour Party had any sympathy with the loafer and shirker of work who tried to batten and fatten on public funds'.[46] Of course, this was an obligation that was just as salient to the very wealthiest members of the community as to the poorest. As Lansbury argued, Labour had 'no sympathy either with the rich loafer or with the poor loafer', and indeed the workers carried 'on their backs . . . all those classes which live on rents, profits, etc.'[47] What all of this implied for the design of unemployment policy was not discussed in much detail, although in the course of the parliamentary debate on the 1911 National Insurance Act MacDonald did indicate that he thought 'the state is entitled to lay down certain conditions under which the unemployment benefits are going to be paid'. MacDonald mentioned a requirement to undertake education or training as a plausible form of benefit conditionality.[48] In any case, as a matter of principle, it was clear that senior figures in the Labour Party strongly believed that every citizen owed some form of contribution to the necessary work of society.

The only exception to the Left's firm avowal of productive obligations was a scheme for an unconditional basic income or 'state bonus' proposed by a few social reformers, notably Dennis Milner and Bertrand Russell. However, this idea stayed on the margins of progressive political thought in this period; revealingly, even Russell himself referred to this proposal for a regular unconditional income payment as a 'vagabond's wage'.[49]

To each according to their effort?

As the next chapter will show, Shaw was quite clear that the division of work should bear no relation to the division of income, and that participation in work was simply a pre-condition for an entitlement to an equal income for all. As far as Shaw was concerned, the level of productive effort expended by individuals was irrelevant to the precise share of wealth they were due. However, it was less clear whether other progressives shared this view. They appeared uncertain about whether incomes should, as a matter of justice, track inequalities in individual effort, or whether individual effort qualified as functional merely by dint of any kind of participation in the labour market (or other civic service). Tawney had for instance argued that a functional society would 'proportion remuneration to service', suggesting perhaps that varying levels of effort deserved varying levels of reward, but ultimately leaving this point undeveloped.[50]

Hobhouse did consider the problem of apportioning reward to effort in more detail. He allowed that, as a matter of justice, any increase in effort by a worker deserved to be rewarded with a larger income,[51] and he had earlier suggested that a crude indicator of effort might be hours worked. He explained: 'I think that in a good social order, exertion in directions useful to society would be, except for those who are incapacitated, a condition of obtaining any income at all, and I think that it should be open to men and women to increase their income by increased exertion.'[52] However, as Hobson, Laski and Shaw all pointed out, there was in fact no reliable way of measuring personal effort.[53] Even the indicator of hours worked was too crude to be meaningful, since it took no account of differences between types of work or individual capacity. Formidable practical constraints seemed to militate against such a scheme ever being implemented. Instead, most progressives settled on the conclusion that the demands of reciprocity could be realised simply by applying the injunction that 'no person can be permitted to secure remuneration except on the condition of performing work recognised as useful'.[54] A further issue was whether reward for effort exhausted the demands of functional payments: should rewards should take into account individual productive achievements (as distinct from efforts), or even the need to motivate certain key categories of workers with material incentives? The next section of this chapter begins to address these questions.

2.4 The social determination of values

Since egalitarians proposed to make income conditional on productive contri-bution, did it then follow that reward levels should be proportionate to an individual's productive achievements? This would certainly be one logical development of a theory of social justice grounded on the idea of function, since it could be argued that if rewards are to be related to social functions, then those who perform more important work deserve to receive greater rewards. The progressives of the early twentieth century did not adopt this argument, however, because they thought arriving at a fair metric of productive achievement was problematic, and regarded the most obvious candidate, the market price of skills, as deeply unfair. Economic production, they argued, was complex, the result of the interaction of a whole society, and to attribute individuals' productivity purely to their own native qualities was to ignore the necessary social context for the recognition and exercise of those capacities. The national income was regarded as the result of the co-operative effort of the whole community. 'It is not possible to isolate the contribution of any industry, firm or individual worker.'[55] In the context of the political arguments of the early twentieth century, this was an important claim: if an unprecedented state-sponsored intervention in the distribution of economic resources was to be deemed legitimate, then it was necessary to explain why existing property entitlements lacked persuasive justification. This could partly be done through the social criticism examined in the previous chapter; a compelling case for economic redistribution could be provided by cataloguing the unjust impact of a laissez-faire regime on the life chances of the disadvantaged. But it was also necessary to tackle head-on the anti-egalitarian theoretical premise employed by various currents in British political debate, namely that it was unjust for the state to take away from individuals resources that they had personally earned through purportedly fair market exchanges. This anti-egalitarian claim was elaborated in a number of different ways.

Individualist theories of value: Left, Right and Centre

As we have seen, centrist liberals like Churchill or Muir argued that individuals deserved greater material rewards if they delivered greater productive achievements. Of course, both Churchill and Muir made this claim while acknowledging that some redistribution was necessary to secure a minimum standard for all; far more radical criticisms of state intervention were also made. Avowedly libertarian arguments, of the sort earlier popularised by Herbert Spencer, proclaimed the grave injustice created by any interference with market distributions.[56] For example, the influential conservative writer W. H. Mallock stressed the crucial causal importance of a scarce form of entrepreneurial and managerial ability to the creation of wealth. He argued that the owners of this ability were therefore entitled to the entire increment of wealth generated as a result of placing their talents at the disposal of industry. In practice, this meant that a small minority of wealth-creators could justifiably claim the vast majority of the product of industry.[57] Mallock was also scathing about the possibility of 'equality of opportunity' ever being implemented without extensive state-sponsored constraints to prevent the able from developing their talents.[58] The Conservative politician Hugh Cecil took this point even further, and argued that it was a mistake to identify justice with equality in any substantive sense. On the contrary, fairness was best seen as a procedural matter: 'Justice only requires that no one should be injured or cheated.'[59]

These were obvious and important opponents of redistribution, and considerable attention had to be paid to answering their claims. Crucially, though, progressives saw themselves as fighting on two fronts at this time: in addition to the various defences of inequality on the Right, it was widely assumed that a rival distributive theory on the Left also posed a significant challenge to an egalitarian account of social justice. This rival theory was usually described as 'Marxist', although its relationship to Marx's writings or any explicitly Marxist political organisation was at best unclear. Nonetheless, progressives of this period often assumed that the labour theory of value represented a normative statement to the effect that the members of the proletariat, as the creators of economic value through their productive labour, were morally entitled to be rewarded with the full fruits of that labour. Conversely, since the bourgeoisie made no contribution to the creation of economic value, it was thought that Marxism dictated that the owners of capital (or perhaps even all non-manual workers) were not entitled to any material reward. This theory of 'proletarian self-ownership' is in principle capable of an egalitarian interpretation, since it could simply be understood as asserting the right of workers as a class to the collective product of their labour, with the distribution of the product within the proletariat then based on needs rather than individual productive capacity. In the particular debates under consideration here, however, progressives were instead adamant that 'Marxist' socialism demanded that individual workers received an income that reflected the product of their respective labours. Needless to say, this was not in fact Marx's own position and, if anything, this argument probably owes more to the so-called 'Ricardian socialist' writers of the nineteenth century, who did indeed assert the right of workers to the full value of their product.[60]

This distortion of Marx's position was probably both a reflection of the popularised presentation of Marxist doctrine that was advanced by Marxists themselves, and the result of a (perhaps wilful) misunderstanding on the part of their critics. It was common to find Marxists explaining the theory of surplus value in terms calculated to evoke strong moral reactions, such as the veteran communist William Paul's description of profit as 'unpaid labour. It is a glorified, legalised burgling expedition against the working class.' Similarly, H. M. Hyndman, the founder of the Marx-inspired Social Democratic Federation, estimated that capitalists deprived the workers 'of two-thirds or three-fourths of the value of their day's or week's or year's work'.[61] This style of presentation suited social democratic critics, since they then interpreted the 'Marxist' position as stressing 'the right of each man to the whole produce of his labour', and finding the 'iniquity of the competitive regime to lie in the power of the capitalist to take toll of the worker's product'.[62] This was said to be 'the Marxian doctrine of surplus value': the claim that all value stemmed from labour, so that 'it followed that all wealth was due to the labourer', whereas under capitalism the labourer's product, beyond a subsistence minimum, 'was wrongfully absorbed by the capitalist and landlord, who had done nothing to bring it into existence'.[63]

Seen in the light of the contrasting perceptions of economic justice held by the Right and (allegedly) the radical Left, the significance of a *social* theory of value becomes apparent. As against the widely held view that individuals' productive contributions entitled them to a reward proportionate to that contribution, egalitarians maintained that production was in fact a collective act, and argued that a fair distribution of the social product should recognise the input of every section of the community (both workers by hand and by brain), rather than simply rewarding those who were most productive or possessed skills that were highly valued by the market. While it was fair to condition material rewards on productive contribution, to reward achievement as measured by market or labour value would therefore be unjust.

Production as a collective act

This social theory of value originally made its way into progressive discourse as a derivation of the theory (or theories) of rent that the new liberals and, especially, the Fabians developed from the writings of Ricardo and Mill in the late nineteenth century. Initially, this discussion concerned positive economic theory, and purported to demonstrate the existence of economically unnecessary surplus payments to the owners of land, capital and ability, which consequently could be redistributed or taken into social ownership without altering their supply. Although this proved to be a useful means of reconciling the idea of an economically functionless surplus with certain widely accepted liberal doctrines and the marginal utility theory of value favoured by neo-classical economics, it was open to serious objections as an economic theory, and was not of primary ideological significance for the egalitarian vision subsequently defended by the Left in the early twentieth century. For this purpose, the more important aspect of the notion of rent was its normative implication: individuals could not claim sole responsibility for the economic value of their skills or assets.[64]

In addition to Ricardo and Mill, the writer who gave the greatest political salience to this idea was the American social reformer Henry George. George's book *Progress and Poverty* (and his barn-storming oratory) popularised the notion that increases in land values in the late nineteenth century were principally due to forces outside of the control of landlords, and suggested that they had therefore gained a large increase in wealth through no personal effort. This observation was gradually extended by writers on the Left from the specific question of land ownership to cover other increments in wealth, including capital gains, inherited income, and the excessive rent of ability demanded by the talented to perform social service.[65] According to this analysis, the great aggregate prosperity of Britain was the result of the productive efforts of the entire community, not just the favoured few who had in fact accrued the spoils. Those who had done well from industrialisation had relied on the labour of the working class, and had required a stable, well-regulated social environment in which to conduct business. This new understanding of wealth as socially rather than individually produced was placed at the top of the political agenda by the innovative fiscal policies introduced by the Liberal government in 1909, since the core theoretical defence of its progressive taxation measures was the claim that the community was in fact entitled to a share of what had previously been regarded as both the right and the desert of the individual. The idea that an 'unearned increment' had accrued to landlords and others, instead of being shared with the community as a whole, became a staple of Liberal and Labour political rhetoric,[66] while the experience of the First World War further enhanced the argument's status on the Left, as it was widely believed that a few wealthy individuals had benefited from immense capital gains while the majority of the population had been sacrificing sweat and blood for the common good.[67]

Hobson called this position 'the social determination of values', because it emphasised that under capitalism

> [t]he payment made to any contributor to the productive processes, either as a worker with hand or brain, or as owner of any other factor of production, is not determined to any appreciable extent by the nature of the particular contribution he himself makes, but by an operation of the market in which the contributions of innumerable other persons and processes are taken into account. This may be called the doctrine of the social determination of values. Put simply, it signifies that what anybody gets for what he does depends to a very small degree upon his own effort, skill, or other personal merit, and almost wholly upon the actions of other people who either make what he is making, or make other things wherewith to buy what he is making.[68]

Hobhouse took a similar view: 'What we take at first blush for the contribution of an individual to this growth [of wealth] is not his contribution alone. He absorbs from his society, he comes into a capital of organised knowledge and skill; he adds something to it but does not create it. The most individual production is largely a social production.'[69] Indeed, Hobhouse added, the very existence of property rights was dependent on state regulation; the rights of property-owners would be meaningless 'without the judge and the policeman and the settled order which society maintains'.[70] These arguments were also made by leading socialists.[71] 'Value', wrote Laski, 'is a social product', the 'result not of individual, but of co-operative effort'. In Glasier's analysis, it was 'collective and co-operative labour', combined with 'scientific knowledge' and 'the increment of social and political organisation', that produced 'the vast abundance of wealth which is available in modern states'. Accordingly, concluded Laski, 'we cannot trace the individual contribution of any man to the sum-total of production'.[72] This recognition of the co-operative basis of wealth creation served as an argument against both purely meritocratic or libertarian principles of justice, and the employment of the labour theory of value as a normative principle. Against these rival theories, it was argued that material rewards could not be distributed to particular individuals or classes in proportion to their productive performances, since some account had to be taken of the contribution made by the community to their productivity.[73]

Desert and social justice

While this social theory of value was indispensable to egalitarians as a means of undermining the moral legitimacy of either a market-based distribution of wealth or one justified via the idea of proletarian self-ownership, its implications for the positive distributive proposals of the Left required further clarification. One elaboration of this argument might be described as a revisionist desert principle, which sees the objective of a socially just regime as discriminating between income genuinely produced by the individual and income created by social co-operation. Justice would then consist in giving back to the community (as represented by the state) the wealth that the community as a whole deserved, while simultaneously enabling individuals to earn the income that their personal productive activity merited. This is the interpretation favoured by a number of commentators on the political thought of this period, and it has also been suggested that if this was indeed the position adopted by the Left, then it would be plagued by both 'underlying theoretical ambiguity' and 'practical difficulties', since the distinction between the individual and the communal components of wealth seems conceptually problematic and unlikely to be of much use as a guide to policy.[74] While it is true that certain ideological and rhetorical motifs employed by the Left support this interpretation,[75] there are two reasons to be cautious about imagining that progressives aspired to quantify precisely the social and the individual contributions to the production of wealth.

First, leading progressives generally regarded *any* type of desert principle as inherently suspicious. As Hobson observed, while unreflective public opinion might agree with the idea of desert, on closer examination this type of distributive principle was open to significant objections. 'For, if we put the case of two men who exert themselves each to his utmost, but one being stronger gets a larger output, it does not seem so obviously just that he should be paid more.'[76] Different physical and mental capacities were therefore insufficient to mandate differential rewards. As he had earlier suggested when discussing piece-work,

> [a] weak man may hew one ton of coals while a strong man may hew two. Has not the former 'done his best' equally with the latter? The strength of the strong man, the natural or even acquired skill of a skilful man, cannot be assumed as a personal merit which deserves reward in the terms of payment. If there is merit anywhere, it is in the effort, not in the achievement or product, and piece-wages measure only the latter.[77]

This view was shared by more explicitly socialist writers, who strongly contested the claim that the ultimate goal of socialism was rendering to the worker the full value of their product. Cole saw this latter position as 'pure capitalist morality. Why should a man who produces more be paid more?' The eventual goal of socialists, he argued, was rather that 'the fruits of the common labour of all should be equitably shared', since 'the right of labour to a life of comfort and self-expression is quite independent of whether it creates all wealth or not'.[78] As Glasier suggested, the purportedly 'Marxist' assertion of proletarian self-ownership was in fact an 'individualist' rather than a socialist doctrine, asserting 'the right' of those undertaking 'only one of the functions of organised social life to the whole produce of industry which is essential to the life of all'. Such a narrowly economistic view of productive contribution excluded other forms of social service from consideration, for example 'motherhood', and said nothing about how to accommodate the needs of dependants. The core of socialism was 'not that the workers engaged in the actual production of exchangeable commodities should receive the whole wealth which they are the immediate instruments of creating; but that society collectively should organise the production of all wealth, whether of commodities or services, for the common good of all its members'.[79]

Admittedly, it should be noted that Hobhouse was more circumspect than other progressives in his discussion of desert claims, and, at an abstract level, he strove to retain a certain amount of reward for achievement as a principle of justice, so long as the achievement was of benefit to the community and not solely to the individual, and the differentials were constrained by a minimum and maximum level of income.[80] Nonetheless, it was clear that, for practical purposes, he was extremely cautious about using meritocratic language, since he saw social co-operation as so intimately related to individual achievement as to render ambiguous any attempt to quantify the latter more precisely. It was 'generally impossible to assign any separate value to the product of a single worker'.[81]

Even if these objections were put to one side, though, there was a second difficulty involved in a precise discrimination between 'individual' and 'social' wealth: developing a fair measurement of individual effort and skill was in practice impossible, since apart from anything else it depended on intractably controversial judgements about the relative economic value of different kinds of work. This was the argument usually deployed in less abstract contexts, for example when faced by employers' proposals to introduce piece-work payments in particular industries.[82]

A revisionist desert principle therefore suffered from serious normative problems and practical difficulties. As Hobhouse put it, 'it is not so much a definite portion which the community contributes to increasing wealth, it is rather a condition on which the successes of individuals depend'. As a result, 'we are dealing here with factors so intricately interwoven in their operation that they can only be separated by an indirect process'.[83] An alternative construal of the social theory of value offered the indirect route that Hobhouse alluded to. While conceding that it was impossible to determine accurately the relative influences of individual and social factors on production, this version of the theory instead argued that the wealth available for social appropriation, the 'unproductive surplus', was that which individuals did not require for their functional activity. As Hobhouse argued, each citizen should receive 'such remuneration as would stimulate him to put forth his best efforts and would maintain him in the condition necessary for the life-long exercise of his function'.[84] In other words, the community could take account of the social determination of values by allowing economic inequality only if it enabled greater productive activity or was necessary to cater to the needs of an individual. In particular, this meant that, as in the case of capital incomes, the greater the size of an income, the less likely it was necessary as a stimulus to individual effort: 'where the income is very large, there it is exceedingly probable that the social factor plays a part', or, in a more polemical vein, 'the higher the income, the less the earning'.[85]

This chapter has established that progressives of the early twentieth century based their ideas about social justice on a strong principle of economic reciprocity, and a firm conviction that market rewards took no account of the social character of economic production. The next chapter builds on these relatively abstract theories by examining more specifically their political implications and, in particular, the debates on the Left about which distributive principles would most effectively meet the two criteria for functional incomes just mentioned: eliciting productive contributions and catering for individual needs.

Notes

1 E.g. A. Giddens, *The Third Way and its Critics* (Cambridge, 2000), 5–6. The following account is greatly indebted to Stuart White's important critique of these claims: see his 'Rights and responsibilities: a social democratic perspective', in A. Gamble and A. Wright (eds), *The New Social Democracy* (Oxford, 1999), 166–70; and his *Civic Minimum*, 49–76.

2 J. Wolff, 'Training, perfectionism and fairness', *Journal of Applied Philosophy*, 21 (2004), 288.

3 McKibbin, *Classes and Cultures*, 139.

4 For examples, see Stedman Jones, 'Rethinking Chartism', in his *Languages of Class*; G. Claeys, *Machinery, Money and the Millennium: From Moral Economy to Socialism, 1815–1860* (Princeton, NJ, 1987), 135–9 and *passim*; N. Thompson, *The Real Rights of*

Man: Political Economies for the Working Class 1775–1850 (London, 1998), 25–6, 47, 64, 84–5, 104–5.

5 J. S. Mill, *Chapters on Socialism* [1879], in J. S. Mill, *On Liberty and Other Writings*, ed. S. Collini (Cambridge, 1989), 231; Mill, *Autobiography*, 175; quoted in e.g. H. Dawson Large, 'Who makes the wealth', *LL*, 30.12.1910, 827; MacDonald, *Socialist Movement*, 126; Webb, *My Apprenticeship*, 155.

6 S. Collini, *Public Moralists: Political Thought and Intellectual Life in Britain 1850–1930* (Oxford, 1991), 63–6, quote at 63. Collini does not necessarily claim any causal link between these ideas and Kant's writings.

7 T. H. Green, *Lectures on the Principles of Political Obligation*, ed. P. Harris and J. Morrow (Cambridge, 1986 [1890]), e.g. 159–61; D. G. Ritchie, *Natural Rights* (London, 1894), 101–3 and *passim*; Nicholson, *Political Philosophy*, 83–95; Freeden, *Ideologies*, 185–6; S. den Otter, '"Thinking in communities": late nineteenth-century liberals, idealists and the retrieval of community', in E. H. H. Green (ed.), *An Age of Transition: British Politics 1880–1914* (Edinburgh, 1997), 71–2.

8 Freeden, *New Liberalism*, 94–116; J. Meadowcroft, *Conceptualizing the State: Innovation and Dispute in British Political Thought 1880–1914* (Oxford, 1995), 59–68.

9 Webb, *My Apprenticeship*, 123–30, quote at 123; Bevir, 'Sidney Webb', 223–6 and *passim*.

10 M. Bevir, 'Welfarism, socialism and religion: on T. H. Green and others', *Review of Politics*, 55 (1993), 639–61; Bevir, 'British socialism and American romanticism', *English Historical Review*, 110 (1995), 878–901; Tawney, *Acquisitive*, 179–90.

11 Hobson, *Crisis*, 75–6; Harris, 'Political thought and the welfare state', 126–31; Harris, *Private Lives*, 245–50; den Otter, 'Thinking in communities', 69, 75–8. See also the Introduction to this book, note 31.

12 R. H. Tawney, 'The new Leviathan', manuscript notes, *c*.1920, Tawney Papers 10/10, 9.

13 Wright, *Tawney*, 58–60; Terrill, *Tawney*, 157. Wright also distinguished Cole's conception of function from the Webbs' in his *G. D. H. Cole and Socialist Democracy* (Oxford, 1979), 54–5. For further discussion of de Maeztu, see M. Stears, 'Guild socialism and ideological diversity on the British Left, 1914–26', *Journal of Political Ideologies*, 3 (1998), 295–8; for Figgis, see D. Runciman, *Pluralism and the Personality of the State* (Cambridge, 1997), 124–49; Stears, *Progressives*, 89–96.

14 For a helpful overview of these different interpretations, see den Otter, *British Idealism*, 189–95.

15 The major source of disagreement about the concept at this time in fact concerned the distinct issue of democratic government. 'Pluralists' and 'statists' divided over whether state authority should be disaggregated among a number of self-governing units, each representing a different social function. A key issue here was the desirability of a radical form of industrial democracy. See Wright, *Cole*, 13–101; M. Stears, 'Socialism and pluralism: a study in British inter-war ideology' (DPhil thesis, Oxford University, 1997); Stears, *Progressives*, 88–123, 168–98 and *passim*; C. Laborde, *Pluralist Thought and the State in Britain and France 1900–25* (London, 2000), 69–100.

16 E.g. Hobhouse, *Liberalism*, 87; his 'The state in relation to poverty IV: public control', *MG*, 4.3.1909, 8; for further discussion, see White, *Civic Minimum*, 108–13.

17 Laski, *Grammar*, 94; see also 40–1; J. H. Greenwood, 'The duty to work', *LL*, 29.1.1909, 70; Hobhouse, *Liberalism*, 79, 84–7; Hobson, *Work and Wealth*, 226–7; Tawney, *Acquisitive*, 14–15, 25–6, 31–3.

18 Hobhouse, *Labour Movement*, 16; also Hobson, *Crisis*, 196–7.

19 B. Webb, *The Wages of Men and Women: Should They Be Equal?* (London, 1919), 5–6, 66–7.

20 H. N. Brailsford, *Families and Incomes: The Case for Children's Allowances* (London, n.d. [1926]), 5; Webb and Webb, *Decay*, 29–30.

21 Tawney, *Acquisitive*, 35–6, 84–6, 173–5, quote at 35.

22 Simon, *Inheritance*, 11–12. The influence of *The Acquisitive Society* can be seen in H. Laski, 'The state in the new social order', *FT No. 200* (London, 1922), 8; Laski, *Grammar*, 193–4; Hobson, *Incentives in the New Industrial Order* (London, 1922), 95; Hobson, *Wealth and Life*, 228–30.

23 Lloyd George, speeches at Limehouse, 30.7.1909; London, 17.10.1910; Newcastle, 9.10.1909, all in his *Better Times*, 151, 338–40, 174, 160; also P. Snowden, 'The Lords and the budget', *LL*, 23.7.1909, 473. It should be noted that Liberal politicians like Lloyd George focused on the parasitism of landlords and aristocrats; capitalists were not their principal target: see also note 66 below.

24 J. R. MacDonald, speech, 27.1.1909, *LPACR* 1909, 107.

25 L. T. Hobhouse, 'The historical evolution of property, in fact and in idea' [1913], in his *Liberalism and Other Writings* (Cambridge, 1994), 180–1, 195–6.

26 Hobhouse, 'Historical evolution', 181, 198.

27 Hobhouse, 'Historical evolution', 181, 191; his *Labour Movement*, 17. For further discussion in this vein, see C. Gore (ed.), *Property: Its Duties and Rights* (London, 1913).

28 MacDonald, *Socialist Movement*, 125–32, quotes at 129, 127; also MacDonald, *Socialism and Society*, 180–1; Glasier, *Socialism*, 126–8.

29 P. Snowden, 'Property', *SR*, 12 (1914), 73–7, quotes at 74.

30 J. A. Hobson, *Democracy After the War* (London, 1918), 28–32; Hobson, *Wealth and Life*, 144.

31 Tawney, *Acquisitive*, 58–9; also Brailsford, *Socialism*, 81–2.

32 G. D. H. Cole, 'The diffusion of ownership', *NS*, 24.3.1928, 754; also Laski, *Grammar*, 187–8.

33 P. Snowden, *Labour and National Finance* (London, 1920), 114–23; his *The Rich Man's Budget: Mr Churchill's Proposals Exposed* (London, 1925), 8; Hobhouse, *Elements*, 165–6; L. T. Hobhouse, 'The problem', in J. A. Hobson and M. Ginsberg (eds), *L. T. Hobhouse: His Life and Work* (London, 1993 [1931]), 284–5; Laski, *Grammar*, 525–6; G. D. H. Cole, *The Next Ten Years in British Social and Economic Policy* (London, 1929), 380–1. For discussion of the Left's attitude to capital incomes in the context of a contemporary theory of functional property rights, see White, *Civic Minimum*, 118–24.

34 Collini, *Liberalism and Sociology*, 134–7; see also Stears, *Progressives*, 246.

35 G. B. Shaw, 'Letters to the editor: equality of income', *Nation*, 31.5.1913, 350–1; L. T. Hobhouse, 'Letters to the editor: equality of income', *Nation*, 7.6.1913, 384.

36 G. B. Shaw to G. Wallas, 5.6.1928, Wallas Papers 1/89.

37 Shaw, *Intelligent Woman's Guide*, 72; see also 95, 355–7.

38 G. B. Shaw to G. Wallas, 5.6.1928, Wallas Papers 1/89. Significantly reducing the length of the working day was a widespread ambition on the Left: see Chapter 3, note 125.

39 'Shaw trounces Harold Cox: should the national income be equally divided?', *LL*, 20.3.1913, 4.

40 E.g. Hobhouse, *Labour Movement*, 134–40; Freeden, *New Liberalism*, 222–4.

41 McBriar, *Fabian Socialism*, 263–79; Clarke, *Liberals and Social Democrats*, 118–24; A. M. McBriar, *An Edwardian Mixed Doubles: The Bosanquets Versus the Webbs* (Oxford, 1987), 311–14, 330–3.

42 See *HCD*: D. Lloyd George, 25, 4.5.1911, col. 643; W. S. Churchill, 26, 25.5.1911, col. 502.

43 S. Webb, 'The unemployed and the unemployable', *LL*, 29.7.1910, 473; S. Webb and B. Webb, *English Poor Law Policy* (London, 1910), 270–1, 316–19; Webb and Webb, *Prevention of Destitution*, 320–3; B. Webb, 'Preface', in National Committee for the Prevention of Destitution, *The Case for the National Minimum* (London, 1913), iii–iv; G. Lansbury, in *The Poor Law Minority Report: Report of a Debate on 20–1 September 1910* (London, 1910), 12–13; J. Stapleton, 'Localism versus centralism in the Webbs' political thought', *History of Political Thought*, 12 (1991), 154–5.

44 Hobhouse, *Liberalism*, 86–7; also L. T. Hobhouse, 'The state in relation to poverty III: the break-up of the Poor Law', *MG*, 1.3.1909, 9.

45 K. D. Brown, *Labour and Unemployment* (Newton Abbot, 1971), 68–130; Harris, *Unemployment*, 235–44; *LPACR* 1909, 94–101.

46 *HCD*: W. Crooks, 194, 26.10.1908, col. 1661; G. Lansbury, 21, 10.2.1911, col. 641; J. R. MacDonald, 177, 9.7.1907, col. 1448; see also J. O'Grady, 21, 10.2.1911, col. 590; Tanner, 'Development of British socialism', 61–3.

47 G. Lansbury, *HCD*, 21, 10.2.1911, cols 641, 643.

48 J. R. MacDonald, *HCD*, 25, 4.5.1911, col. 657. See also 'Seven Members . . .', *Labour Party's Aim*, 58.

49 E. and D. Milner, *Scheme for a State Bonus: A Rational Method of Solving the Social Problem* (Darlington, 1918); B. Russell, *Roads to Freedom: Socialism, Anarchism and Syndicalism* (London, 1918), 118–20, 179. On Milner's proposal, see 'A state bonus for all?', *Nation*, 25.5.1918, 195–6. Discussions of basic income proposals in this period have been painstakingly reconstructed in W. Van Trier, 'Everyone a king: an investigation into the meaning and significance of the debate on basic incomes with special reference to three episodes from the British inter-war experience' (PhD thesis, University of Leuven, 1995), 29–142. Basic income proposals will be further discussed in section 3.2.

50 Tawney, *Acquisitive*, 31. Hobson criticised this aspect of Tawney's argument in *Wealth and Life*, 229–30. On the difficulties with Tawney's position, see Gutmann, *Liberal Equality*, 82–3; Robinson, 'Tawney's theory of equality', 98–110; S. Collini, 'Moral mind: R. H. Tawney', in his *English Pasts* (Oxford, 1999), 188–91.

51 Hobhouse, *Elements*, 139; also L. T. Hobhouse, 'The regulation of wages', in R. Cecil *et al.*, *Essays in Liberalism* (London, 1922), 167–8.

52 Hobhouse, 'Letters to the editor: equality of income', *Nation*, 24.5.1913, 312.

53 Shaw, 'Letters to the editor: equality of income', *Nation*, 31.5.1913, 350, and his *Intelligent Woman's Guide*, 22–3; Laski, *Grammar*, 194–5, and his *Communism* (London, 1927), 178; Hobson, *Wealth and Life*, 239.

54 Laski, *Grammar*, 196.

55 H. N. Brailsford *et al.*, *The Living Wage* (London, 1926), 27.

56 M. Taylor, *Men Versus the State: Herbert Spencer and Late Victorian Individualism* (Oxford, 1992), 232–61; D. Weinstein, *Equal Freedom and Utility: Herbert Spencer's Utilitarianism* (Cambridge, 1998), 57–61.

57 See W. H. Mallock, *A Critical Examination of Socialism* (London, 1908); J. N. Peters, 'Anti-socialism in British politics, c.1900–22: the emergence of a counter-ideology' (DPhil thesis, Oxford University, 1992), 124–58.

58 Mallock, *Critical Examination*, 274–5. For critiques of Mallock, see J. A. Hobson, 'Are riches the wages of efficiency?', *Nation*, 9.11.1907, 183–4; G. B. Shaw, 'Socialism and superior brains: a reply to Mr Mallock', *FT No. 146* (London, 1909).

59 H. Cecil, *Conservatism* (London, 1912), 168; Meadowcroft, *Conceptualizing*, 95–7.

60 See K. Marx, *Critique of the Gotha Programme* [1875], in D. McLellan (ed.), *Karl Marx: Selected Writings* (Oxford, 2000), 614–16; S. White, 'Needs, labour and Marx's conception of justice', *Political Studies*, 44 (1996), 91–101; White, *Civic Minimum*, 51–3; Claeys, *Machinery, Money and the Millennium*, 34–129. For a writer from this period who recognised that Marx did aspire to transcend 'bourgeois right', see A. D. Lindsay, *Karl Marx's Capital: An Introductory Essay* (London, 1925), 107–8.

61 W. Paul, 'For you Mr Worker! Where wages and profits come from', *Socialist*, April 1917, quoted in S. MacIntyre, *A Proletarian Science: Marxism in Britain, 1917–33* (Cambridge, 1980), 150, along with other examples, see also 168–9; H. M. Hyndman, *The Economics of Socialism* (London, 1896), 111.

62 Hobhouse, *Labour Movement*, 33. This was also thought to be the position of syndicalists: see G. D. H. Cole, *The World of Labour* (London, 1913), 349.

63 L. T. Hobhouse, 'The ethical basis of collectivism', *IJE*, 8 (1898), 137–8; also B. Glasier, 'Socialism and the theory of Marx', *LL*, 15.1.1909, 33; his 'Final words on Marx', *LL*, 29.1.1909, 65.

64 Compare the different perspectives of McBriar, *Fabian Socialism*, 29–47; and Bevir, 'Fabianism and the theory of rent', 313–27; and see also Gaitskell, *Recent Developments*, 7–9; Durbin, *New Jerusalems*, 32–4. In spite of their differences, both Bevir and McBriar acknowledge that the purely economic aspirations of these ideas had slipped to the background by the early twentieth century and that a moral critique of capitalism was subsequently invoked by leading Fabians.

65 J. A. Hobson, 'The influence of Henry George in England', *Fortnightly Review*, 62 (1897), 835–44; McBriar, *Fabian Socialism*, 29–47; Freeden, *New Liberalism*, 42–4; J. Plowright, 'Political economy and Christian polity: the influence of Henry George in England reassessed', *Victorian Studies*, 30 (1987), 235–52; R. Barker, *Political Ideas in Modern Britain* (London, 1997), 20–1; M. Daunton, *Trusting Leviathan: The Politics of Taxation in Britain, 1799–1914* (Cambridge, 2001), 343–4, 349–51.

66 The liberal weekly the *Nation* was the most important theoretical vehicle for this argument: see ' "Earned" and "unearned" ', 27.4.1907, 334–5; J. A. Hobson, 'Is socialism plunder?', 19.10.1907, 82–3; 'An equitable budget', 30.1.1909, 662–3; 'The principles of the budget', 12.6.1909, 374–6. For its use in political rhetoric, see the parliamentary debate on the 'People's Budget': e.g. *HCD*, 4: D. Lloyd George, 29.4.1909, cols 505–6, 532–6; S. Buxton, 3.5.1909, cols 776–7; L. Chiozza Money, 3.5.1909, cols 821–2; P. Snowden, 5.5.1909, col. 1080. Once again, the use of this rhetoric by Liberal politicians was less radical than that of left liberal theorists or Labour politicians: Daunton, *Trusting Leviathan*, 361–5, 370–1.

67 'Who is getting richer?', *NS*, 2.11.1918, 84; F. W. Pethick-Lawrence, 'Rich and poor: pre-war and post-war', *SR*, 18 (1921), 239–44.

68 Hobson, *Wealth and Life*, xv. See also J. Allett, *New Liberalism: The Political Economy of J. A. Hobson* (Toronto, 1981), 70–95.

69 Hobhouse, *Elements*, 162; see also his *Labour Movement*, 69–71; *Liberalism*, 92–3; 'The problem', 281–2.

70 Hobhouse, *Liberalism*, 91.

71 Indeed, some of the earliest advocates of this view were Sidney Webb, Sydney Olivier and Annie Besant respectively in G. B. Shaw (ed.), *The Fabian Essays in Socialism* (London, 1889), 59, 127, 163–4; see also M. Bevir, 'British socialist thought 1880–1900' (DPhil thesis, Oxford University, 1989), 178. Ruskin has also been identified as an early exponent of a social theory of value: J. Harris, 'Ruskin and social reform', in D. Birch (ed.), *Ruskin and the Dawn of the Modern* (Oxford, 1999), 25.

72 Laski, *Communism*, 121; Glasier, 'Socialism and the theory of Marx', 33. Similar views were expressed across the spectrum of progressive opinion: see e.g. H. Dawson Large, 'Who makes the wealth?', *LL*, 30.12.1910, 827; C. T. Campion, 'Social value and the socialist ideal', *SR*, 11 (1913), 51–9; Snowden, *Socialism Made Plain*, 7–9; Burns, *Government and Industry*, 108–9; C. D. Burns, *Industry and Civilisation* (London, 1925), 140–1; Lindsay, *Karl Marx's Capital*, 105–6; Shaw, *Intelligent Woman's Guide*, 21; Tawney, *Equality*, 157–61; MacIntyre, *Proletarian Science*, 164–8.

73 Of course, complete logical consistency was not always achieved on this point. Labour politicians found it hard to resist the rhetorical power of the labour theory of value in their speeches: e.g. Snowden and P. Curran in *LPACR* 1909, 104, 105; J. R. Clynes, *HCD*, 166, 16.7.1923, cols 1920–1.

74 Collini, *Liberalism and Sociology*, 130–4; quotes from 131; also Plant and Vincent, *Philosophy*, 62, 84–5.

75 See e.g. MacDonald, *Socialism and Society*, 181; his *Socialism and Government*, 34–7.

76 Hobson, *Wealth and Life*, 239.

77 Hobson, *Work and Wealth*, 193; see also 167–8; and Hobson's response to Shaw in Shaw, *Case for Equality*, 18–19.

78 G. D. H. Cole, *The Payment of Wages* (London, second edition, 1928 [1918]), 112; his *World of Labour*, 350.

79 Glasier, 'Final words on Marx', 65; his 'Socialism and the theory of Marx', 33; also H. N. Brailsford, 'Socialism and property', *NL*, 6.3.1925, 4.

80 Hobhouse, *Elements*, 142–4.

81 Hobhouse, *Labour Movement*, 33.

82 'Payment by results', *NS*, 20.9.1919, 609; G. D. H. Cole, 'On payment by results', *NS*, 3.6.1922, 232; his *Payment of Wages*, 108–12 and *passim*. This issue was also clearly one where tensions could emerge between the ambitious theoretical egalitarianism of the intellectuals and the tenacious defence of differentials by many trade unionists.

83 Hobhouse, 'The problem', 286; his *Liberalism*, 93.

84 Hobhouse, *Liberalism*, 93; his *Labour Movement*, 34–5; also J. A. Hobson, *Taxation in the New State* (London, 1919), 70–4.

85 'The principles of the budget', *Nation*, 12.6.1909, 375; 'Mr Bruce Glasier on the budget', *LL*, 16.7.1909, 462; also L. Chiozza Money, *HCD*, 5, 17.5.1909, col. 47; MacDonald, *Socialist Movement*, 160; Hobson, *Taxation*, 234–5; Daunton, *Trusting Leviathan*, 345–6.

3
Fair shares

3.1 Introduction: dividing up

'It is a matter of common agreement among all persons whose opinion is worth considering at all', wrote G. D. H. Cole, 'that wealth is far too unevenly divided'.[1] Since progressives were united on this point, it followed that, as the *Nation* put it, 'all social reformers, to whatever party they belong, are committed to various levelling processes'.[2] As we have seen, the justification for this egalitarian orientation was derived from a desire to efface the numerous social and political harms inflicted by class divisions. Progressives aspired to a community characterised by egalitarian social relationships, equal life chances and active citizenship, objectives that required above all greater fairness in the distribution of social burdens and benefits.

The previous two chapters examined the Left's understanding of a just distribution of opportunities and productive obligations and began to sketch in the implications of the Left's egalitarian vision for the distribution of income and wealth. This chapter turns more systematically to debates about the distribution of income and wealth and is subdivided into three sections, each addressing a concept that was fundamental to progressive thinking about this issue: equality, need and incentive. It shows that the majority of progressives favoured the principles of need and, reluctantly, incentive, leading them to endorse a distributive pattern that was loosely, although not precisely, egalitarian. The final section of the chapter outlines the policies that followed from these theoretical commitments.

3.2 For and against equality of income

Strict equality of incomes was the most uncompromising principle of social justice elaborated in this period. Although it was never more than the preoccupation of a small minority, the simplicity of this basic proposal exerted a powerful imaginative grip over both Left and Right. The Right, of course, insisted that all egalitarians inevitably advocated the levelling of every citizen's income and wealth to the same amount, with disastrous consequences for economic efficiency and moral responsibility.[3] Most intellectuals on the Left, meanwhile, positioned themselves against this doctrine by repeatedly explaining that they advocated no such thing. 'Is there need once more', asked the Webbs wearily, 'to explain that equality is not necessarily identity, and that it carries no implication of uniformity?'[4] As Hugh Dalton stressed, 'absolute equality of incomes, as an ideal of economic justice, has found few weighty advocates'. The only difficulty was that some critics of equality believed that once they 'have disposed of the argument for absolute equality, they have disposed also of all arguments for reducing existing inequalities'.[5]

Nonetheless, these attempts to defend a more nuanced egalitarianism were threatened by George Bernard Shaw's uncompromising advocacy of a strict equality of income. An indefatigable self-publicist, Shaw emerged as the most visible theoretical defender of strict equality from 1910 onwards, eventually summarising his position in his 1928 book, *The Intelligent Woman's Guide to Socialism and Capitalism*. Shaw possessed both a keen sense of irony and a love of mischief-making, and there have always been doubts about the extent to which he genuinely believed in material equality; some commentators have suggested that his theoretical interventions were fundamentally designed to stir things up and cause trouble, rather than make a constructive contribution to political debate.[6] Indeed, Shaw himself later publicly recanted his egalitarianism and, influenced by the apparent economic success of the Soviet Union, endorsed the standard communist line on the continuing necessity of material incentives to maximise productive efficiency.[7]

However, there remain grounds for taking Shaw's position seriously. Although he certainly wanted to create controversy with his proposals, Shaw also saw himself as providing collectivist socialists with a distinctive, agenda-setting position that could be used to differentiate their ideology from the welfarism of left liberals on the one hand and the radicalism of guild socialists and syndicalists on the other. This was a point he made explicit when he first advocated equality of income in a lecture to the Fabian Society in 1910. A commitment to material equality would enable the Fabians to once again be 'making the pace for the general progressive movement', and would 'clear ourselves of that suspicion of bureaucratic oligarchy which attaches to us at present and attaches with good reason'.[8] Unhappily for Shaw, neither the Fabians nor the Labour Party establishment were interested in his suggestion, and his strict egalitarianism did not prove to be widely persuasive. As one reviewer noted, 'there is one only eminent socialist who holds the tenet [of equality of income] – himself'.[9] Nonetheless, Shaw's egalitarianism deserves some attention, because it was usually presented as the extreme interpretation of equality against which more loosely egalitarian writers wanted to position themselves. It is therefore important to be clear about the shortcomings that other progressives detected in a strictly egalitarian position before considering their more constructive proposals.

The debate about strict equality
Shaw claimed that socialism was 'a proposal to divide-up the income of the country in a new way' or, more precisely, 'the complete discarding of the institution

of private property by transforming it into public property and the division of the resultant public income equally and indiscriminately among the entire population'.[10] In order to achieve his favoured distribution, he insisted that the state would have to own all productive assets, since it 'cannot distribute the national income equally until it, instead of the private owners, has the national income to distribute'.[11]

Shaw's substantive distributive proposal was therefore simply that every citizen should be paid the same income, regardless of differences in merit, need or function. In return for this wage, as discussed in the previous chapter, every citizen was expected to perform useful work. In spite of Shaw's firm assertion of productive obligations, one of his principal justifications for his egalitarianism was in fact its beneficial impact on individual autonomy. Shaw took great delight in chastising his purportedly liberal colleagues for relying on the distributive principle of needs, on the grounds that such a view sanctioned paternalistic intervention in the plans of autonomous individuals. In a debate with Hobson at the National Liberal Club in 1913, Shaw claimed that liberal advocates of distribution according to need were, in effect, alleging that people were not equal in making a good use of their income, and demanding that more should go to those who could make a good use of it.[12] For Shaw, this produced a worrying implication:

> He [Hobson], apparently, has not considered who is to decide the remarkable and important point: what is a good use of one's income? If there is anything in liberalism at all, it is the repudiation of the pretension of certain persons to determine for other persons whether they are acting properly or becomingly, or not. My reply on the whole to Mr Hobson is, that he is in the wrong Club, or he would be, if this were a Liberal Club.[13]

The principle of needs was therefore problematic because it depended on some external agent determining for other people the character of their needs. Rather than empowering some central agency to imagine what individuals might want, Shaw argued, a far better course of action was to give people money and then let them buy what they like with it. As Shaw succinctly put it, 'that is the use of money: it enables us to get what we want instead of what other people think we want'.[14]

Shaw indicated that a second virtue of his egalitarianism was its simplicity. He argued that the other major criteria traditionally recommended to guide distribution, those of merit and need, quickly ran into the irresolvable problem of how to determine fairly the amount that should be awarded to each individual. Any attempt to implement these principles would therefore be prone to intractable disagreements and hence administratively unworkable.[15] As the socialist economist Barbara Wootton put it, unequal rewards meant that it was necessary to say not only who ought to be paid more than whom but also 'how much more A should have than B', on which 'none of us can ever agree'.[16] In contrast, a Shavian society would be based on a straightforward principle and, as commentators throughout the years have recognised, the very simplicity of Shaw's proposal placed advocates of inequality on the defensive, since it demanded that they navigate their way through the forbidding complexities of providing an alternative criterion to guide distribution.[17]

Nonetheless, a major weakness of Shaw's proposal was obviously his cavalier dismissal of the problem of incentives.[18] In common with certain other socialist writers, Shaw was optimistic about the possibility of motivating productive work without the need for differentials in pecuniary rewards, and he was critical of those who demanded high levels of remuneration to exercise their scarce talents. In capitalist commerce, Shaw said, it was seen as legitimate for such individuals to 'hold up to ransom those to whom their services are indispensable, and become rich at their expense'. But this use of rent of ability was intolerable to Shaw, and, just as socialists proposed to nationalise land and capital to prevent rent accruing from the ownership of those assets, Shaw demanded that socialists also 'nationalise ability'.[19] This was an unusual point of view, since other progressives broadly accepted that some differential payments would be necessary to mobilise workers into important jobs. Wootton, who was sympathetic to a Shavian conception of equality, claimed that Shaw's failure to address this question left a gaping hole in his theory. As she observed, if incomes ceased to be based on economic values, they would stop allocating individuals to jobs in a way that simultaneously fostered economic efficiency and protected freedom of occupational choice. Wootton by no means endorsed economic inequality as a means of guiding the distribution of labour, but she worried about the consequences if even that crude indicator of demand was absent from an egalitarian society. The onus was therefore on egalitarians to develop a 'more rational and humane' alternative system. But here, thought Wootton, 'we have no help from the Shavian oracle'.[20] This was not completely fair, since Shaw did at least offer a solution to the difficulty of securing the performance of demanding or unpleasant work. His answer was to compensate those who undertook such tasks by granting them greater leisure time and earlier retirement.[21] However, an analysis of Shaw's theory by the socialist economist Henry Dickinson concluded that a regime of strict equality of income (albeit with differential leisure opportunities) would nonetheless ultimately require the abolition of freedom of occupational choice, and accordingly conceded that some level of material inequality would in the end be necessary to prevent this undesirable outcome.[22]

Aside from incentives, many progressives also worried that Shaw's egalitarianism would be unjust because it ignored differences in individual needs, and in particular the requirements of those with varying numbers of dependants.[23] This point was taken particularly seriously because of Rowntree's pioneering finding that working-class families usually fell below the poverty line after they started to have children.[24] Many egalitarians therefore argued that workers were entitled to income in proportion to the number of their dependants, a point that Shaw allegedly neglected in his writings. Although this objection was frequently stated, it should be noted that in Shaw's most extended discussion of his distributive theory he did answer it. His response was the straightforward one that everyone should be granted an individual, equal income from birth, with the income of children placed under the care of their parents.[25]

Socialist pluralists and equality

G. D. H. Cole took a similar view to Shaw. This commitment to equality was not initially placed at the forefront of Cole's socialism, however, since his fundamental concern in his early writings was the lack of freedom and power experienced by individuals in the workplace. Cole's main contention was that an excessive emphasis on material distribution had blinded socialists to the more important evil of capitalism: its failure to enable the active participation of workers in the decision-making of politics and industry. While Fabian theorists proposed a social order with a more equitable distribution of wealth, he argued, they still supported the rule of an elite few. Cole's critique of Fabianism meant that in his proposals for a radically democratic guild socialism he side-stepped distributive questions and focused instead on inequalities in power as the principal theoretical division between his pluralism and what he saw as Fabian statism.[26] As he put it, 'there are economic arguments and moral arguments enough in favour of the adoption of the principle of equality in the economic sphere', and Cole felt no particular need to add to them.[27]

Nonetheless, a commitment to economic equality was implicit in Cole's early writings, since a guild socialist society required both an egalitarian distribution of resources *and* democratic control of industry. As an ultimate goal, Cole indicated that he supported an absolute equality of income.[28] However, Cole stressed that the achievement of this form of equality depended on the emergence of certain psychological pre-conditions that could only develop gradually. In terms reminiscent of Marx's elaboration of the socialist transition in *The Critique of the Gotha Programme*, Cole noted that equal incomes could not simply be implemented by administrative fiat, as Shaw had hinted. In fact, they could only arrive after a lengthy period of transition from capitalism, once the whole idea of remuneration for work done had been abandoned. At that point, membership of the community would be sufficient to grant each citizen an equal share in the national income, 'without regard to any particular work or service'.[29]

Did Cole therefore imagine that under guild socialism the notion of productive responsibility emphasised by other progressives could be relaxed, and income distributed to individuals regardless of their productive contribution? At times, Cole hinted that he did want to dispense with this constraint: 'Shaw's whole point is that the idea of remuneration is in itself wrong, that people . . . ought to be assured of an income by virtue of their citizenship, or by virtue of the fact they are human beings.'[30] Statements such as this, coupled with Cole's later advocacy of a 'social dividend', a regular income paid to individuals by the state as 'a recognition of each citizen's claim as a consumer to share in the common heritage of productive power',[31] have led some proponents of basic income schemes to cite Cole as a pioneering advocate of unconditional income grants.[32] However, this seems to be a misunderstanding of Cole's position. Cole certainly disparaged any attempt to link the precise amount or quality of work performed to the quantity of material reward, for the reasons discussed in the previous chapter. But, as we have seen, this need not rule out making the distribution of material resources conditional on the performance of some form of productive contribution. This is indeed the position that Cole adopted when discussing his social dividend scheme, since he explicitly stated that for citizens 'the only condition for the receipt of this social dividend' is 'a proved readiness to play their part in the common tasks and duties of the whole community'.[33] In short, it would 'be payable . . . only on condition that they were ready to work'. This was because it was 'utopian to suggest that, if all the citizens were entitled to an adequate living income without any obligation to render reasonable service to the community in return, there would be under present conditions none who would fail to pull their weight'.[34] It therefore seems plausible to regard Cole as an advocate of a 'participation income' rather than a basic income, and as someone who held the same norm of reciprocity as other progressives of this period, namely 'an obligation upon all citizens to serve one another according to their capacities in promoting the common well-being'.[35]

More generally, it remained uncertain how Cole and other pluralists or guild socialists proposed to reconcile their strong commitment to self-governing associations with the achievement of an egalitarian distributive pattern. Although Cole suggested that a Guilds Congress would have some power over salary scales, the suspicion persisted that in a society of autonomous associations it would be difficult to prevent the emergence of economic inequality.[36] As critics pointed out, such associational autonomy could in fact be used by particular guilds to take for themselves excessive payments that would ultimately be to the detriment of the community. As Hobson noted, guilds could easily 'divert into the pockets of their members the differentiated rents and monopoly gains to which the whole community has an equal claim'.[37] Such an autonomous association, added the Webbs, was always tempted to take 'advantage of all differential factors in production (such as superiority of soil or site, of machinery or administrative skill) that it controls', in order to exact 'pay above the average, or hours and conditions of work less onerous than those of others'.[38]

Arguably, Laski's intellectual journey away from his pluralist roots was a concession to this criticism, and an explicit acknowledgement that social justice required a relatively strong central state to secure a common level of provision for every citizen.[39] With respect to Cole, it is hard to avoid the conclusion that his critics had the better of the argument here: he offered only a hazy sense of how economic equality might be obtained under guild socialism, and indeed in his later revisionist works he joined Laski in according the state a considerable role in promoting a just distribution of wealth.[40]

The next two sections of this chapter consider the constructive proposals advocated by the majority of progressives in this period, as they sought to distance themselves from strict egalitarianism, and to explain why certain kinds of income and wealth inequalities were permissible. The focus will be on two key issues, both already mentioned as the two principal left-wing objections to Shavian socialism. First, which inequalities were justified by the principle of distribution according to need? Second, to what extent could inequalities in income and wealth be justified by the need for financial incentives?

3.3 Needs, poverty and the civic minimum

As their response to Shavian equality revealed, progressives regarded the principle of distribution according to need as a crucial ethical ideal, and they accorded it a central place in their thinking about social justice. Both left liberals and socialists expressed admiration for the distributive maxim ultimately proposed by Marx in *The Critique of the Gotha Programme*: 'from each according to his ability, to each according to his need'.[41] The satisfaction of need was therefore the most important background condition to be fulfilled before citizens were obliged to render useful social service. However, this did raise the difficult issue of what exactly constituted a 'need': how did the egalitarians of the early twentieth century sift through the different conceptual options?[42]

Utilitarianism and welfare

To answer this question, we must turn our attention to the ubiquitous use of the language of 'welfare' in this period. In mapping this complex conceptual terrain, a helpful starting point is the influential utilitarian argument for equality based on the diminishing marginal utility of income. This argument maintains that the more resources individuals possess, the less additional welfare they receive from each extra unit. Accordingly, from the classical utilitarian perspective of seeking to maximise the welfare that can be produced from a given stock of resources, there seems to be a powerful case for redistributing resources from the rich to the poor. Since the marginal value of an extra pound is far greater to those at the bottom of the income distribution than to those at the top, it can be argued that the poor need that pound more urgently.

Although such 'marginalist' arguments were clearly available to egalitarians in the early twentieth century, and indeed were sometimes used by leading figures on the Left, the utilitarian case for equality did not play a major role in the political vocabulary of British progressivism prior to the 1930s. Utilitarianism was certainly not without its advocates in British political debate. Economists like Alfred Marshall, for example, drew on utilitarian arguments when they argued in support of new liberal fiscal policies.[43] However, given the somewhat austere ethical premises of much of the progressive political thought of this period, the classical Benthamite belief in maximising 'happiness' was usually regarded by the Left as unattractively hedonistic, and liable to mandate the sacrifice of individual interests for the benefit of the majority.[44] In any case, it also seemed strategically maladroit to couch the public justification for the redistribution of wealth in terms of maximising overall happiness. As Collini has argued, the utilitarian case 'could not gain sufficient purchase' on political argument 'to forestall objections grounded in deep-seated notions of the individual's entitlement to the wealth which he had created, nor to legitimate such an unprecedented assertion of the place of the state in arranging a system of distributive justice'.[45] A more persuasive course of action was to claim that a certain distributive pattern would enable the realisation of a thicker moral ideal carrying greater ideological prestige, such as freedom, equality or justice, or preferably all three at once. In fact, utilitarian arguments only began to play a more substantial role in the Left's egalitarian thought with the entry of professional economists such as Evan Durbin, Douglas Jay and Hugh Gaitskell into progressive politics during the 1930s. Their training in neo-classical economics led them to embrace the doctrines of Alfred Marshall and to regard the pursuit of the greatest possible aggregate welfare as an important social objective.[46]

Nonetheless, it was of course recognised in earlier debates that Bentham's uncompromising doctrine was not the only available formulation of utilitarianism. Mill's recasting of the theory was more sympathetically received by important liberal philosophers like Green, Ritchie and Hobhouse, although liberals of this period, influenced by idealist philosophy, still aspired to move beyond even a Millian utilitarianism. The decisive new liberal move in this context was to offer the idea of 'social utility' as the goal of reform, by which was meant a collective social welfare that was only created by an egalitarian distribution of well-being between each member of the community. In this respect, left liberals were consequentialist in their philosophical orientation, but in a sense that paid attention to the needs of each individual rather than simply the overall aggregate welfare of the community as a whole.[47] The *Nation's* initial response to Shaw's advocacy of equality of income offered a suggestive example of this view. It seemed to the leader writer (who may have been Hobson) that a Shavian socialism embodied a dangerous insistence on uniformity, ignoring the vast differences between individual capacities and the distinct social functions that individuals were required to discharge. As the organic analogy suggested, individual components of an organism required different amounts of resources to sustain them. In theory, therefore, 'the maximum equality of use got from each unit of the social income and the maximum aggregate utility of the whole income would require a different rate of income for every person in the community, precisely because no two persons are the same in the amount of their requirements'.[48] As the author of the article subsequently explained, he had wanted to stress that Shaw's emphasis on equal incomes neglected the very different effects that the same quantity of goods could have on different individuals. While Shaw had dismissed this, saying that 'equal enjoyment is not the object of the reform', the leader writer disagreed: 'But what is the object of the reform, if it be not equality, I will not say of enjoyment, but of benefit?'[49]

In this vein, Hobson suggested that he wanted to distribute income according to 'the support it renders to the whole life of the recipients. It should give to each what each is capable of utilising for a full human life.' This meant that he proposed an expansive, threefold categorisation of needs: the payment necessary to enable the citizen to perform his economic function; 'a full, human maintenance fund for a member of a civilised society'; and 'provision for such education, travel, social intercourse, or other opportunities of personal development and human enjoyment' as would raise individuals' value for themselves and society.[50] In a characteristic new liberal move, benefit to the individual and benefit to the community were here presented as mutually reinforcing contributions to the realisation of the common good. Hobhouse was similarly expansive in his interpretation of needs, arguing that the common good required, as an ideal, the satisfaction of every individual need if the harmonious development of the organic whole was to be achieved. The interconnection of the fortunes of the individual and the collective apparently required that the community should make every conceivable effort to cater for individuals' idiosyncratic requirements.[51] Left liberals therefore offered as their ideal theory an expansive interpretation of individual needs, envisaging the realisation of maximum social well-being through the satisfaction of needs understood as both certain attributes common to all, and as the particular requirements for the attainment of each individual's optimal welfare.

Poverty and the national minimum

In spite of the most advanced liberals' theoretical sympathy for such a radical interpretation of distribution according to need, it was recognised that a pure version of this principle had severe political disadvantages. As Laski pointed out, it allowed too much scope for expensive tastes: 'we could not proffer a clerk a reward which enabled him to purchase the quartos of Shakespeare, however urgently he demanded their possession'.[52] In so far as the principle of needs sought to take into account idiosyncratic aspects of citizens' life plans, it was useless for immediate political purposes, since it allowed individuals free rein to press frivolous claims or claims that were incapable of realisation since they demanded a level of material abundance that did not exist. Furthermore, as Hobson himself conceded, it was in practice difficult to ascertain with any accuracy individuals' relative capacities to transform resources into welfare. Hobson admitted that though he would ideally press for an expansive view of needs, it was ultimately inapplicable as a guide to policy. 'The difficulty of entrusting any authority with so difficult a task of discrimination' meant that other options had to be pursued.[53]

This was not thought to be an insuperable objection to an attempt to make sense of distribution according to need. It merely indicated that a more practical version could be developed using a less expansive specification of individual needs. Leaving the theoretical intricacies aside, it seemed a relatively straightforward matter to draw up a schedule of the basic resources required by typical individuals to function effectively. As Hobson confessed, 'the bodies and minds of what we term normal beings are so largely similar in make-up and needs that it is economical and right to treat them as identical'.[54] The implication was, according to Laski, that 'up to the margin of sufficiency' there should be 'identity of response to primary needs'.[55] The crucial point was to ensure that those needs that were common to all were fulfilled in order of their urgency. As Sidney Webb put it: 'In the hard and strenuous times before us there must be no cake for anyone until all have bread'.[56]

From this understanding of needs, social reformers derived the most powerful practical proposal at their disposal in this period: the provision of a minimum level of resources for all citizens. While more egalitarian ideals were widely discussed, it was clear that, in the political environment of the early twentieth century, the most feasible first step towards a just social order would be a floor constraint on the unequal distribution of wealth thrown up by the market. Even Cole, a writer formally committed to strict equality at the level of ideal theory, signed up to this agenda: 'The practical political maxim for the present is not full economic equality, but the recognition of an all-round minimum of human needs below which no human being must on any account be allowed to fall.'[57] As we have seen, the objective of a floor constraint was one that the Left shared with more centrist liberals, and to some extent this was a goal that both could unite around. But there were also differences between the two camps, particularly after the War, since the Left justified this 'national minimum' in more egalitarian terms, and envisaged it ultimately being set at a more generous level.

Centrist liberals generally favoured a set of basic sufficiency needs, and they drew once again on Rowntree's indispensable quantification of the poverty line. In his study of York, Rowntree's definition of poverty had been deliberately spartan and focused on minimal subsistence needs; one commentator said it presupposed 'an almost inhuman thrift'.[58] As a result, the finding that a third of the population of York lived at or below this poverty line was all the more startling and difficult to contest. After the War, Rowntree up-rated his definition of poverty, taking into account shifting social norms, and advocated what he called a 'human needs wage', as opposed to one based on basic subsistence requirements. He glossed this term as 'a wage sufficient to enable a man to marry, to live in a decent house, and to bring up a family of normal size in a state of physical efficiency with a reasonable margin for leisure and recreation'.[59] As has been argued elsewhere, Rowntree was therefore not an undiluted exponent of poverty as an 'absolute' condition, but in fact aimed to set a minimum standard that enabled individuals to participate in certain important social activities.[60] As far as the Left was concerned, satisfying Rowntree's conception of needs was certainly an important and admirable medium-term objective for social policy, and progressives enthusiastically supported any measures designed to raise the disadvantaged to that level.[61]

Nonetheless, beyond this immediate goal left liberals and socialists took a more explicitly relative view of the condition of poverty. They linked poverty to specifically egalitarian concerns, and advocated a 'national minimum' or a 'living wage' as necessary to promote the full social and civic participation of the working class. Centrist discourse about poverty and need focused primarily on the brutal suffering caused by a lack of material resources or the economic inefficiencies caused by a poorly fed or unhealthy workforce. These concerns were echoed on the Left, but in addition egalitarians emphasised a more radical understanding of the condition of poverty, as an experience that not only induced material suffering, but also prevented the poor from fully sharing in social and political life and deprived them of the opportunity for self-realisation. In this sense, being in need was clearly understood as relative to social norms. As Snowden observed, 'the features of our advancing civilisation are always before the eyes of the working classes', with the implication that 'new expenses have come into the category of necessaries': 'People cannot see tramways without wanting to ride sometimes; they cannot see newspapers without at least buying one occasionally; they cannot see others taking a holiday into the country or to the seaside without desiring to do the same.'[62] 'Poverty is a relative term', said the Webbs. 'Any person is poor who has less spending power than is common in the circle in which he lives.'[63]

Progressives therefore believed that the floor to the distribution of wealth should ultimately be determined by referring to the resources and prevailing customs of the community, and should enable individuals to accomplish a wider range of activities than mere material subsistence or even social respectability. The Left's ultimate objective was the institution of a 'civic minimum', rather than a sufficiency minimum, since egalitarians saw the satisfaction of need as intimately related to the exercise of citizenship and the equal status enjoyed by every member of a democratic community. As Hobhouse suggested, each individual should 'be able, as the reward of work, to secure the material conditions, not only of a healthy life but of what we may succinctly call a civic life'.[64] This meant that it was not enough for the individual to 'be a healthy animal'. Instead, as a citizen, the worker had to play his part 'in the higher interests of the society to which he belongs'. 'As this is his duty', continued Hobhouse, 'so the conditions of work and wages which enable him to perform it are his rights'.[65] For democratic citizenship to be adequately exercised by every member of the community it was considered necessary for all citizens to obtain a high threshold of material well-being, and to have access to the opportunities availed by the well-off as a matter of course. The founding ideological statement of the Labour Party, *Labour and the New Social Order*, tapped into these ideas, confidently proclaiming 'the first principle of the Labour Party' as 'the securing to every member of the community, in good times and bad alike (and not only to the strong and able, the well-born or the fortunate), of all the requisites of healthy life and worthy citizenship'.[66] The rights and duties of citizenship were interpreted broadly, including the obvious emphasis on political participation, but also connoting a wider sense of productive service to the community, and a right to access the cultural and educational resources produced by this collective productive endeavour.[67] Individual needs were not only material, but also encompassed psychological and emotional requirements; poverty was not 'merely the lack of the necessaries of a physical existence', but the deprivation 'of the opportunity for the enjoyment of education, culture, refinement and leisure'.[68]

An excellent example of this type of proposal was the Webbs' famous call for a national minimum. Addressing a self-interested or economistic public audience necessarily requires egalitarians to stress the benefits of redistribution for productive efficiency and, like many other progressives, the Webbs sometimes presented their national minimum in these terms, as a means of advancing, in the idiom of Edwardian Britain, 'national efficiency'.[69] However, this should not disguise the extent to which the Webbs also articulated an explicit concern with the social conditions of citizenship (particularly in the stage of their careers covered by these chapters). The passage from *Labour and the New Social Order* quoted earlier provides some evidence of this, since Sidney Webb was the principal author of this document.[70] In other work, the Webbs' specification of a national minimum followed the same basic pattern, encompassing minimum standards of income, education, housing, health and leisure, with the later addition of an entitlement to an environment free from pollution.[71] This threshold was not only defended as a means of making the workforce more efficient, but also as extending to all sections of the community the quality of life currently enjoyed by the wealthy, both as an end in itself, and as a means of enhancing citizenship. The Webbs' aim was 'to stimulate the whole population, and not only the exceptionally gifted or the exceptionally energetic, to the utmost possible exercise of their faculties', while promoting 'throughout the whole mass and not alone in exceptionally altruistic or exceptionally enlightened individuals, the greatest attainable development of public spirit'.[72]

In the idea of a civic minimum, therefore, all sections of the Left had found a powerful and radical principle that sought to meet an ambitious but not utopian perception of individual needs, and to question the grave inequalities that prevented the working class from fully participating in the social and political life of the nation.

Family needs and the endowment of motherhood

One pressing question raised in the course of this debate was how to meet the needs of dependants. As we have seen, progressives were particularly exercised about this issue because of the importance of family responsibilities in pushing workers below Rowntree's poverty line. This seemed to be a case where the principle of distribution according to need could directly guide social policy, but it was also significant because it brought to the surface tensions between the Left's discourse of economic egalitarianism and feminist claims for equality between men and women.

A contested question in this period was whether women should be paid at the same rate as men for similar work, since it was assumed that male workers were supporting families, while female workers were characteristically single, awaiting marriage and domestic responsibilities. This became a particularly controversial issue in British industrial relations during the War as large numbers of women were introduced into the workforce. A common trade union complaint against this practice was that women would undercut men in the labour market since they did not have the family responsibilities that ensured that men's basic wage demands would be much higher.[73] The War Cabinet's Committee on Women in Industry, appointed to investigate the matter in 1918, produced a majority report that was, on the whole, in favour of greater parity between male and female wages, but which shied away from an unequivocal endorsement of equality. However, a fiercely argued minority report from Beatrice Webb made a clear case for parity of wages between men and women, ultimately arguing that the national minimum standards advocated by the Left should apply equally to both genders.[74]

Leading egalitarian theorists had different perspectives on this issue. Hobhouse apparently rejected the notion that women were undercutting men in the labour market, but at the same time assumed that minimum payments ought to embody some differentiation according to gender.[75] This meant that there was no harm in gender wage inequality 'if the man's wage is sufficient to maintain a family and if a woman does not normally maintain a family'. Hobhouse thought that while a woman's wage should not fall below the standard required to satisfy her individual needs, it should still be lower than a male counterpart performing the same work, assuming that the man was maintaining a family of five (the size of family taken by Hobhouse from Rowntree for the purpose of setting the level of average needs).[76] Others, such as Cole, sided with Beatrice Webb and argued that the national minimum ought to be 'a family wage, a wage on which a man could just maintain or a woman could just maintain the average number of dependants under reasonable conditions'.[77] This was a more egalitarian view, but it raised further difficult questions about precisely how wage bargaining could take account of family needs.

Should there have been a more elaborate differentiation of wages according to the specific number of a worker's dependants, for example? For obvious reasons, this position seemed unconvincing. As Cole observed, 'any proposal' to proportion wages according to dependants was 'manifestly unworkable under the existing wage system', since during economic downturns it would result in 'the wholesale dismissal of married workers', and in any case 'such a principle could not possibly be made to fit with the existing variations of payment for varying economic services'.[78] This was problematic, in that a national minimum that met only the average number of dependants seemed unfair, since families with more children would be substantially disadvantaged relative to those with fewer than the average figure. 'Average justice is rough justice', insisted the socialist journalist H. N. Brailsford, calculating that if government policy targeted only the 'average' family with five members then 'six children ... in every ten, by average justice, may possibly have enough, but four are doomed to certain privation'.[79]

A creative solution to this difficulty, ultimately adopted in government policy after the Second World War, was for the state to pay a supplement to families to enable them to cope with the additional costs generated by raising children. This had the advantage of targeting payments precisely in accordance with family size, but without the distorting effects on the labour market noted by Cole. The most influential proponent of this 'family allowance' was the politician and indefatigable social reformer Eleanor Rathbone: her cogent advocacy of the proposal, and vigorous activism on its behalf, has rightly been recognised as critical to its eventual implementation.[80] Yet there was also a revealing difference between the feminist framework in which Rathbone first developed the idea and the eventual acceptance of the plan on the Left as a measure aimed at tackling class inequality. For Rathbone, family allowances were intended as an 'endowment of motherhood' to emancipate women from financial dependence on men, and to reduce inequality between the genders rather than between rich and poor.[81] But as Rathbone's proposal was disseminated into political debate this objective was necessarily blurred in order to appeal to the widest possible political constituency. In particular, as David Howell has argued, debates in the labour movement primarily focused on family allowances as an anti-poverty measure, to be funded out of general taxation in order to redistribute income to the working class. Feminist arguments could make no headway against the dominant trade union 'discourse of the family wage', which pictured the male worker as rightly providing for his whole family through his labour and, with some justification, saw family allowances as a threat to union wage-bargaining, since it was feared that it would simply allow employers leeway to reduce working-class pay packets. Only once family allowances were embedded in the dominant left-of-centre language of social class and economic justice did the policy begin to secure important supporters within Labour and trade union circles.[82] In this respect, a typical (and influential) advocate was H. N. Brailsford. As the editor of the ILP's paper, the *New Leader*, from 1922–6, Brailsford was a leading post-war publicist for the party and played an important role in making the policy of family allowances palatable to economic egalitarians. He presented the measure as an act of vertical redistribution, suggesting that graduated income tax and possibly death duties could fund weekly cash payments to working class families. This was an idea 'as old as Thomas Paine', taking from 'the product of our common labour', and in particular the 'superfluities of the rich', to enable working-class children to 'grow up with a less unequal chance of health and strength and mental growth'.[83]

Even with the introduction of this class-based justification, powerful figures in the labour movement remained strongly opposed to this apparent incursion into trade union territory. Nonetheless, in this period family allowances at least began to take their place in the arguments and writings of leading left-wingers as one prong of a broader attack on economic inequality and poverty, and they famously featured as a component of the ILP's much-discussed 1926 proposals to enshrine a 'living wage'.[84] In these debates there was a close connection between the justification for family allowances and the egalitarian commitment to distribute resources according to need, coupled with a recognition of the important ethical insight that child-rearing was a salient issue for social justice, and not simply a private matter beyond the scope of political intervention.[85] But the debate on family allowances also gave a significant indication of the hegemony of class inequality in the political discourse of the Left: inequalities between men and women were deemed to be secondary (or even unimportant) when compared to the economic divisions that separated the rich from the poor.

3.4 Incentives and the rent of ability

Having established the nature of the floor that the Left wanted to put in place, this section completes the architectural image by investigating how progressives planned to determine an appropriate ceiling to inequality. Given their scepticism about desert as a justification for an unequal distribution, this raises the important question briefly considered in the context of Shaw's strict egalitarianism: did consequentialist considerations about economic efficiency justify inequality?

Equality and efficiency
Although my discussion so far has emphasised that progressives believed redistribution to be mandated by moral principles such as justice and equality, this should not suggest that they neglected altogether the possible impact of such policies on economic efficiency. In order to make a credible case for equality, it was obviously important to show that an egalitarian distribution was at least compatible with productive efficiency. Indeed, egalitarians of this period often argued that capitalist inequality was itself fundamentally inefficient. They regularly

identified mass unemployment, poor living conditions and a lack of educational opportunity as a catastrophic waste of human potential and productive capacity.[86] As has been well discussed elsewhere, Hobson's theory of under-consumption provided a more precise way of arguing that redistributing to the poor, and consequently enhancing working-class purchasing power, would actually benefit economic growth and stability. In Hobson's view, deficient demand for goods created economic downturns, and the way to restore prosperity was to redistribute to those most likely to consume: the working class rather than the wealthy, since the latter would simply save any extra income.[87] Although given a frosty reception by professional economists and radicals committed to a more comprehensively socialist analysis of capitalist crises, Hobson's under-consumptionism was sporadically used as an argument for greater economic equality in both liberal and socialist discourse, and constituted one important attempt to reconcile egalitarian aspirations with concerns about economic efficiency.[88]

In a similar vein, progressives also stressed that the systematic reform of capitalist reward structures in line with principles of justice would in itself create a new social ethos that would facilitate a greater willingness on the part of individuals to contribute productively to the necessary work of the community. This claim acquired its greatest political salience in the immediate aftermath of the War, since at that time it was widely agreed that the major problem facing the British economy was declining production, particularly in heavy industry. This decline in output was believed to be partly due to the substantial post-war industrial unrest, and the unprecedented number of days lost to industrial action.[89] Employers saw this as an example of sectional greed rather than a deep social malaise; they grew increasingly interested in scientific management techniques, and in greater use of payment by results, as methods of maximising productive efficiency.[90] In contrast, the Left offered a different understanding of the causation of the class conflict that was crippling industrial output. Progressives claimed that a crucial motivating factor for this industrial militancy was the effect of the War on the legitimacy of the capitalist system in the eyes of the workers. In an influential passage of his *The Economic Consequences of the Peace*, Keynes noted that the acceptance of the distribution of reward in pre-war Britain had depended on certain psychological characteristics on the part of the workers, namely that they 'accepted from ignorance or powerlessness, or were compelled, persuaded, or cajoled by custom, convention, authority, and the well-established order of society into accepting, a situation in which they could call their own very little of the cake that they and nature and the capitalists were co-operating to produce'.[91] This passivity, Keynes thought, had been destroyed by the experience of the Great War. To the Left, the implication of all this was straightforward: 'An increasing number of people dislike the conditions under which they live and work. The motives, which the whole industrial order assumes will impel them to work, fail to move them, and so they work reluctantly and badly.'[92] In this sense, social justice was itself seen as a pre-condition for improving productivity.

The Left therefore claimed that improving the position of those at the bottom of the income distribution would in fact enable workers to make a greater productive contribution, partly by ensuring that they possessed both a job and the necessary material resources to make them physically and mentally able to work effectively, and partly by the more diffuse consideration of making them feel that they were members of a just system to which they owed certain obligations. As Hobson argued, when a 'fair day's work is not unduly long or onerous, when it is fairly paid, and when each sees that all the others are called upon to do their proper share', this 'general sense of fairness' will 'exercise a compelling influence on each man to keep his output up to a decent level'.[93] However, difficulties arose when progressives analysed the position of those at the upper end of the income and wealth distribution. There was widespread agreement that it was not simply the absolute amount possessed by the poor but also the contrast between rich and poor which made the capitalist system illegitimate in the eyes of the workers. It was therefore necessary for progressives to explain how they could reduce such inequalities without in the process undermining economic efficiency.

Incentives and the Left

As we have seen, the two old allies, Hobson and Hobhouse, disagreed over the feasibility of proportioning reward to effort. In spite of this difference of opinion, there was no doubt that they were at one on the question of inequalities justified on grounds of economic efficiency. Both agreed that the imposition of complete material equality would provide insufficient motivation for individuals to perform socially valuable work. As a consequence, some measure of reward for achievement was necessary to induce citizens to perform important social functions.[94] It is tempting to portray this acceptance of incentives as an illuminating difference between liberal egalitarians on the one hand and socialists on the other. It might be argued that socialists placed greater emphasis than liberals on a qualitative transformation in human psychology, of the kind earlier envisaged by John Ruskin and William Morris, with the result that socialists thought that feelings of social service would in themselves become sufficient to motivate those who discharged key social functions. As we have seen with respect to many other aspects of the egalitarianism of this period, however, matters are rather more complex than this straightforward dichotomy suggests.

It is certainly true that some strands of socialist thought, for example elements of the ILP's ethical socialist discourse, Cole's guild socialism and, according to some interpretations, Tawney's *Acquisitive Society*, suggested that financial gain could ultimately be replaced by an ethic of mutual service as the main motivational driver of productive activity. It was sometimes frankly claimed that socialism would 'change human nature' and 'take away the desire for accumulating riches', allowing industry to draw on new motives of public service.[95] This radical socialist claim was not always straightforwardly that individuals would be motivated to work purely for a collective common good, but rather that once industry had been reconstructed into a participative, democratic enterprise in which every citizen played a valued role, workers would be enthused with new motivational energies. The veteran Christian socialist Charles Gore argued that, if workers in industry felt that they had a stake in the management of their workplaces, 'the stimulus to industry which would be gained by their deepened interest would enormously counterbalance whatever loss was caused by the withdrawal of that stimulus which has been derived from the corrupt motive of the accumulation of a large fortune by the individual'.[96] Once each individual had 'status, responsibility and a voice in controlling his industrial life', added the young Clement Attlee, then this would itself serve as 'a new incentive in industry'.[97]

As numerous critics pointed out, though, even this position appeared to depend on overly optimistic predictions about human psychology.[98] Hobson granted that a 'functional' society, in Tawney's sense, might precipitate some sort of transformation in personal motivation, but doubted whether that in itself would be sufficient to render any reliance on incentives superfluous, since 'weakening the relative importance of the monetary estimate' would be 'slow and insufficient to "socialise" the natures of certain hard, capable, selfish types of men, who will refuse to give their best work unless they are free to take high rents of ability'.[99] The problem with the most radically egalitarian position was therefore that it did not take adequate account of the likely behaviour of those with particularly scarce skills.[100] Crucially, though, this was also a view shared by many socialists. No less an authority than the Webbs had earlier noted that if under socialism 'there is any difficulty in getting all the talent required to fill all the places that exist, the conditions must simply be rendered more attractive in whatever form is found expedient'. This meant that if those with talent refused to work they could 'extract a certain "rent" from the community, over and above the maintenance and other conditions requisite for the fullest and finest use of that talent'.[101] Other socialists, for example Laski, expressed similar views:

> We must also pay wages in such a fashion that we attract into each socially necessary occupation a sufficiency of talent to run them adequately. We need enough miners; but we need also enough judges and enough doctors. Probably no judge works harder, even if he works differently, than a miner in the sea-pits of Durham. If we base our remuneration on effort alone, we should pay miner and judge at equal rates . . . We must, I think, admit that the value to society of a great judge or a great doctor is greater than the value of a miner . . . For us, then, the justification for any difference in reward must lie in the probability that such difference will provide us with the service that we require in greater numbers than would be true were equality of reward to obtain.[102]

Even those leading socialists who endorsed a radical transformation in productive motivation as an ideal goal accepted that in the medium to long term some material incentives would nonetheless be inescapable. Cole remained convinced that citizens could 'be induced to regard the doing of a fair day's work as a duty which they owe to society' without unequal material rewards, but in his later works this was described as an objective for the distant future, and he conceded that he had previously overestimated the extent to which the workplace could be expected to be the primary site of individual self-expression.[103] Both left liberals and socialists therefore conceded that, for the immediate future, some individuals would continue 'to extort rents of ability from society, to which they have no moral right, but which society must pay in order to get the best fruits of such ability'.[104]

But this did not mean that the Left uncritically endorsed inequality of income. There was a general agreement that the defenders of the capitalist status quo greatly exaggerated the significance of financial gain as a motive in productive activity. There was no doubt that it was *a* factor, but progressives typically argued that it was best seen as only one amongst a range of different motives, including the desire for esteem and public recognition; the desire to render service to others; and the intrinsic satisfaction of the task in hand.[105] They were therefore exceptionally unenthusiastic about conceding the case for incentives, and supplemented this concession with the suggestion that current income inequalities were well in excess of the pay differentials necessary to secure peak economic efficiency. As Hobson put it, rents of ability 'are often taken by industrialists, merchants, and professional men, far exceeding the necessary incentives to evoke the use of their special ability'.[106] In such cases, rent of ability had become a kind of functionless wealth, ripe for redistribution.

Inequality and the common good

In the previous chapter, we saw that the theory of social justice proposed by progressives regarded all large incomes as containing a significant 'unearned' component. Although large incomes derived from capital ownership were perhaps more obviously 'unearned' than large incomes derived from the exercise of managerial and entrepreneurial skill, it was nonetheless a cardinal egalitarian principle that so-called 'earned' incomes were no such thing. As Hobson noted, 'the fact that some personal productive effort is put forth in earning' a large salary should not conceal the fact that a portion of it is 'as much unearned as the ground rent of a landowner or the monopoly interest of a trust-magnate'.[107] Payments needed to stimulate the will to work that went over and above a set of basic physical and mental needs were certainly thought to be legitimate if workers required compensation for undertaking arduous or unpleasant work. Indeed, such compensatory payments were themselves usually phrased in the language of needs, since an important dimension of 'need' was thought to be the provision of the resources necessary to elicit the willingness to work at such difficult occupations. However, the possession of scarce 'skill, knowledge, initiative, judgement, organising power' was a different case.[108] This was the main burden of the concept of the rent of ability, an idea introduced into British political debate by the Fabians and subsequently appropriated by the new liberals, which was used to indicate that, as in the case of the despised landlords, the enormous incomes paid to the owners of scarce talents served no economic function and lacked any moral justification.[109] The role of the state was to constrain these unjustified inequalities through policies such as progressive taxation or public ownership. But if concerns about economic efficiency were to be addressed, then the difficult question was how to allow some space for incentives without letting the currently egregious levels of material inequality persist?

Some commentators have argued that the thinking of earlier egalitarians was rather vague on this point, relying on grand moral sentiments rather than clear-minded philosophising. One result of this imprecision, they argue, was that such theories lacked any clear criteria to distinguish between permissible or unjustifiable material inequalities, of the kind later offered by egalitarian philosophers like John Rawls. This has the politically disastrous implication that such writers crudely advocated an inexorable compression of any given distribution of wealth, or else resorted to vague rhetorical phrases that offered little practical guidance.[110] It should be clear from the bulk of the argument of this chapter that this suggestion does an injustice to the rich array of principles debated and advocated by egalitarians in this period. With particular reference to the redistribution of the wealth commanded by those at the top of the class hierarchy, it is interesting to note that the criterion offered by progressive theorists to determine a permissible level of inequality was in fact similar to Rawls's difference principle itself. They argued that inequalities were only justified if they served the common good; that is, if they were necessary as incentive payments to secure productive activity from those who possessed key economic skills and could be justified directly to the disadvantaged on that basis. As Laski observed, 'distinctions of wealth or status must be distinctions to which all men can attain and they must be required by the common welfare'. This meant that 'the inequalities of any social system are justified only as it can be demonstrated that the level of service they procure are obviously higher because of their existence'.[111]

It is likely that Laski picked up this idea from Hobhouse. He had earlier penned a review of Hobhouse's *Elements of Social Justice* for the *Nation*, noting that 'nothing in the book is better than the treatment of equality', and quoting with approval Hobhouse's claim that any difference in what is due to individuals must 'be a difference required by the common good'.[112] As Hobhouse had earlier made explicit, the important theoretical insight contained within his position was that 'whatever inequality of actual treatment, of income, rank, office, consideration, there be in a good social system, it would rest, not on the interest of the favoured individual as such, but on the common good'. If millionaires and paupers were to co-exist, it must be because such a distribution was to the advantage of both, 'the good of the pauper being included therein as well as the good of the millionaire'.[113] Once again, the common good was construed as a distribution-sensitive criterion, since Hobhouse thought that to maximise it was to secure the greatest possible flourishing of each of the individuals that constituted it.[114]

Clearly, these ideas were not as precisely developed as the difference principle finally defended by Rawls, namely that inequalities are only justifiable if they maximise the position of the worst-off in society.[115] Nonetheless, it is not fanciful to see progressive writings of this period as embodying a similar thought about the extent to which inequalities should be tolerated; as legitimate only if they secured the services of talented individuals for tasks that benefited not only those individuals but also all sections of the community. Egalitarians of the early twentieth century consequently made an important connection between resource distribution and the common good, and indeed opposed inequality if it could not be shown to serve the interests of the working class.

The egalitarian ethos

As with Rawls's difference principle, this attempt to draw a theoretical limit to inequality was indeterminate in terms of its practical implications. The precise boundary at which redistribution would impinge on the efficient discharge of social functions was left as an open question, to be determined by experimentation with different reward schedules and models of industrial organisation. Such experiments would ultimately distinguish those economically necessary payments from those that represented functionless wealth.[116] However, it was also recognised that the precise extent of the inequality generated by this distributive principle would be determined by how far individual economic agents were able to internalise an ethic of public service. Although most progressives were sceptical of an ideal of public service as the *only* major incentive for work, they nonetheless saw the growth of a more egalitarian social settlement as likely to bring about a gradual change in prevailing beliefs about the fairness and social desirability of maximising personal wealth. Consequently, the extent of the differentials demanded by the possessors of scarce talents could be significantly reduced in so far as it was possible to cultivate a social ethos that encouraged other forms of productive motivation that were unrelated to material self-interest.[117] Once again, this was a view shared by both left liberals and socialists.

For instance, in his pre-war writings Hobson was particularly optimistic about this issue. He noted that, as social institutions were altered through acts of social reform, individual behaviour would likewise be modified. A growing perception of the extent to which individuals were socially interdependent would mean that the individual 'will come consciously to realise his personal freedom in actions that are a willing contribution to the common good'. It would become more difficult for the individual 'to defend in himself or others economic conduct or institutions in which individual, class or national conflicts are involved'. In short, 'a better social consciousness and a better economic environment will react on one another for further mutual betterment'.[118] Even in his later work, Hobson remained convinced that 'it seems reasonably possible to modify the conscious stress of personal gain-seeking and to educate a clearer sense of social solidarity and service'.[119] The same conviction was shared by the Webbs, who argued that the gradual unfolding of social reform would slowly lead public opinion to 'regard the exceptionally gifted man who insists on extorting from the community the full rent of his ability as a mean fellow – as mean as the surgeon who refuses to operate except for the highest fee that he can extract'.[120] Indeed, this qualitative transformation in social attitudes was itself seen as an important aim of social reform. Lansbury, for example, said that reformers should disseminate the idea that work should be done 'for the service of the whole community', and 'create such a public opinion as will make us all realise that it is just as dishonourable to exploit our neighbours by the use of our brain-power as it would be to exploit them by use of our physical power'.[121]

The development of these social sentiments, and their influence on the preferences of economic actors, was thought to follow from institutional change, but it was also argued that institutions and policies expressive of the common good would in turn be further developed and encouraged by qualitative changes in attitudes and beliefs. A positive feedback loop would occur between institutions and the social ethos, as individuals were gradually persuaded to be less self-interested in their view of economic activity, and to undertake work not only as a way of benefiting themselves, but also as a contribution to the well-being of their community. As Hobhouse argued, the achievement of social justice depended on both legislative action and a change in individual moral attitudes:

> Mere reform of machinery is worthless unless it is the expression of a change of spirit and feeling. If economic reform meant nothing but economic reform, it would leave the nation no happier or better than before. The same dishonesty, the same meanness, the same selfish rapacity would simply find different outlets. But if machinery without moral force is worthless, good intentions without machinery are helpless. A better spirit, if it is to survive, must be incarnated in better institutions, and if there is to be a keener sense of justice, a livelier feeling for the common good, a broader and deeper sense of common responsibility, these qualities must find avenues of expression in the normal working of the social system.[122]

Some might still be troubled by the absence of a definitive statement about the level of inequality that the Left anticipated under a putatively egalitarian regime. Nonetheless, it is important to note that any failings of writers such as Hobhouse on this score are identical with the failings of John Rawls, since both left the final level of acceptable inequality to be worked out amid the exigencies of a real political community. There is little doubt, though, that both intended their principles to mandate a substantial assault on the economic inequalities that characterised the actual political communities they addressed.

3.5 Egalitarian strategies

This section concludes my discussion of this episode of egalitarian thought by providing an overview of the Left's debates about 'the strategy of equality'.[123] In spite of the fertility of the phrase, there was nothing as straightforward as *the* 'strategy of equality'. Instead, egalitarians proposed a variety of policies designed to ameliorate or eliminate economic inequality, some commanding wider support than others, and certain of their proposals standing in tension with one another.

The minimum and the maximum

As we have seen, it was widely agreed that the first order of business was setting a floor constraint on the distribution of income and establishing certain minimum workplace standards. In this context, a legally enforceable minimum wage was clearly one important tool, although it remained controversial whether to achieve this through a national minimum wage law or by using trade boards to set separate minimums in individual industries.[124] Egalitarians (and allied social reformers) also hoped to reduce the length of the working day: an eight-hour day was thought to be a realistic short-term objective.[125] However, these state-led interventions in the labour market raised difficult questions about the role of trade unions in the pursuit of equality. Enhanced trade union rights and legislation constraining the bargaining power of private industry were certainly important components of the Left's strategy to achieve a civic minimum. Nonetheless, the unions could perceive certain legislative interventions in the labour market or some state subsidies to working-class incomes as usurping their legitimate role in bargaining for the highest possible wage for working-class families.[126] Deeply ingrained assumptions about differentials due to skilled workers could also conflict with the more egalitarian ideas about pay equity held by progressive intellectuals or the political idealists in the labour movement. Leading intellectuals were aware that trade unionists might veto egalitarian policies on the grounds that they interfered with the unions' right to bargain collectively, and even worried that the unions might fail to appreciate broader public interests at stake in distributive conflicts.[127]

In addition to lifting up the wage rates of the lowest paid through labour market interventions and strong trade unions, welfare provision targeted at periods of particular need in the life cycle also followed from the commitment to provide a civic minimum. Various schemes were proposed (and sometimes enacted) along these lines, most notably unemployment insurance, state pensions, social housing and of course family allowances to assist with the costs of raising children. As discussed earlier, proposals for a universal income grant or 'social dividend' were also canvassed in this period, although they were never seriously entertained by left-wing policy-makers. Further provision for needs was to be furnished through social services free at the point of use, as for instance in the case of healthcare and education.[128] Of course, the introduction of such measures could be used as the occasion for horizontal rather than vertical redistribution. Indeed, the Liberal government's introduction of contributory social insurance caused divisions within the Labour Party precisely over the distributive unfairness of forcing the working class to pay for their own welfare benefits through a 'poll tax' rather than funding it from general taxation. 'The poverty of the workers can never be cured by taxing their poverty', ran the slogan in the *Labour Leader*.[129] From an egalitarian perspective, the source of the funding of these measures was crucial. Vertical redistribution was clearly preferable, but an important tension existed between this consideration and the allure of the contributory principle as a means of establishing entitlement to welfare benefits, and of underlining the productive contribution made by the working class.

Progressive taxation was therefore seen as an important tool to reduce the largest incomes derived from work, capital and land, and to provide resources for public services and income transfers. Much of this was pioneered by Lloyd George in his 1909 budget, the strategic vision of which set the agenda for every subsequent Liberal and Labour manifesto aimed at ameliorating class inequality. Although the motivations and objectives of Lloyd George and the Liberal government were not necessarily egalitarian, they nonetheless opened the way for future attempts to use progressive taxation to lessen economic inequality.[130] Of particular importance to the Left was the taxation of inherited wealth, a classically 'functionless' species of income. Various policies were proposed, most notably the Rignano plan, which sought to tax only the wealth that bequeathers had inherited from previous generations and not wealth that they had earned or saved by themselves.[131] In the immediate aftermath of the War, there was also considerable support on the Left for a capital levy, a one-off, steeply graduated tax on personal wealth, as a means of reducing war debts and putting wartime capital gains to socially beneficial use.[132]

Ambiguities

While these policy tools offered a clear way forward in pursuit of an egalitarian society, important issues remained either underdeveloped or unresolved in this period. One issue, already mentioned, was the extent to which trade unions should be granted autonomy in wage-bargaining. A second was the role of public ownership. Here at last was a significant difference between left liberals and socialists. Although the most advanced liberals, notably Hobson and Hobhouse, enthusiastically supported a limited amount of public ownership, socialists remained committed to a more extensive programme of socialisation as the ultimate solution to class inequality. Of course, socialists also supported the introduction of a national minimum or individual welfare measures, but they often viewed them as merely preparatory for a deeper attack on capitalism. As Hardie put it, such 'humanitarian' measures were 'important' but 'not socialism': 'they are but a clearing of the decks for action, a caring for the sick and wounded, before entering upon the battle royal'.[133] According to this analysis, broadly shared by leading Labour politicians and socialist intellectuals, modern industrial production was so complex, and grand in scale, that equitably sharing the fruits of productive property could only be achieved through collective rather than individual ownership, and probably through some form of centrally co-ordinated or planned production in order to avoid slumps and unemployment. In contrast, taxation was 'tortuous and necessarily imperfect' as a device for achieving equality.[134] The desire to alter 'the basis of the economic structure of society' in order to secure 'production for use and not for profit' and 'the economic enfranchisement of the worker' differentiated the socialist from the mere social reformer.[135] In spite of these rousing sentiments, it was by no means clear that socialists necessarily favoured an across-the-board socialisation strategy or the kind of state planning later associated with the Soviet Union. They stressed instead that their style would be experimental and gradual rather than prescriptive.[136] The practicalities of this agenda remained sketchy, though, and the character of a socialist economy was never satisfactorily disclosed in this period, partly because the advocates of socialisation failed to engage in any detailed analysis of the economics of public ownership. In contrast to this socialist position, left liberals argued that some public ownership coupled with an egalitarian fiscal strategy could simultaneously yield a wider diffusion of private property between individuals and preserve certain forms of economic liberty fostered by market mechanisms.[137] Arranged somewhere in between these two positions were more pluralist socialists like Cole and Tawney, who regarded a large amount of socialisation as important, but were conscious of the potentially illiberal consequences of a straightforwardly collectivist socialism, and were accordingly supportive of mutualist forms of public ownership and sympathetic to other attempts to diffuse individual property ownership.

A related disagreement arose with respect to unemployment policy: progressives agreed that the state should play a role in maintaining full employment, but differed over precisely what that role should be. Labour exchanges and unemployment insurance were favoured by the Liberal government; more radical ideas about using the state as the employer of last resort were initially favoured by Labour, although this radicalism quickly evaporated when Labour entered government in the 1920s. As with the broader questions about the character of state intervention in the economy, an unresolved tension throughout this period was whether socialism constituted the only route to full employment or, as suggested for example by Hobson, redistribution of income aimed at the poor could succeed in reflating a broadly capitalist economy.[138]

These differences were certainly not resolved in this period, and even within the Labour Party there was considerable disagreement over the relative merits of socialisation and fiscal policy as vehicles of egalitarian progress.[139] The role of public ownership in the promotion of equality therefore remained a significant source of division on the British Left, and I will return to debates about its role in egalitarian strategy in later chapters.

A third area of ambiguity was education policy. Although wider access to education was clearly central to the egalitarian society envisaged by left liberals and socialists, it is interesting to note the extent to which they were tolerant of educational reforms regarded as inadequate by later egalitarians. The immediate priority of progressives in the early twentieth century was ensuring that every child was able to attend secondary school free of charge for a decent length of time (preferably up to the age of sixteen). In order to achieve this objective, egalitarians argued not only for the abolition of tuition fees, but also for the state provision of (means-tested) maintenance grants for school pupils. This latter measure was intended to make a later leaving age financially possible for working-class families who relied on their children's earnings to bolster the household income.[140] Preoccupied by these immediate objectives, egalitarians did not criticise the use of academic selection within the state school system, and did not consider the extent to which a formal equality of educational access could itself still mask a grave inequality in life chances.[141] Similarly, while the role of private schools in perpetuating class inequality was subjected to savage critique, no attempt was made to develop policies that might seriously address this problem.[142] In this period, therefore, the ground was prepared for the Left's initial enthusiasm for the system of academic selection introduced in the 1944 Education Act.

Succeeding generations of egalitarians were to grapple with all three of these issues. Nonetheless, the egalitarians of this earlier period provided an indispensable ideological core that was transmitted to their successors: they established a clear philosophical framework for subsequent debate, and they anchored the Left's political identity in a staunch commitment to economic equality.

Notes

1 Cole, 'Diffusion of ownership', 753.
2 'Equality of income', *Nation*, 10.5.1913, 223.

3 See for instance Mallock's specious insistence on treating Shaw as a representative socialist figure in his *The Limits of Pure Democracy* (London, 1918), 189.

4 S. Webb and B. Webb, 'What is socialism? XII – the approach to equality', *NS*, 28.6.1913, 364.

5 Dalton, *Inequality of Incomes*, 21. For similar points, see Laski, *Grammar*, 152–4; Tawney, *Equality*, 46–50.

6 H. Dalton, 'Shaw as economist and politician', in C. Joad (ed.), *Shaw and Society* (London, 1953), 252, 256, 262; E. Bentley, *Bernard Shaw* (London, 1967), 16.

7 G. B. Shaw, *Everybody's Political What's What* (London, 1944), 54–7. For further discussion of the communist view of social justice, see section 4.3.

8 G. B. Shaw, 'The simple truth about socialism' [1910], in his *The Road to Equality* (Boston, 1971), 193. For this interpretation of Shaw's motives, see McBriar, *Fabian Socialism*, 57–8; G. Griffiths, *Socialism and Superior Brains: The Political Thought of Bernard Shaw* (London, 1993), 108–10. However, note that Shaw also explained to Beatrice Webb that his intention was to propose 'primitive socialism' so that less ambitious proposals for social reform would appear moderate and sensible in comparison. 'Nonetheless', he added, 'I believe quite seriously in the soundness of equality of income'. G. B. Shaw to B. Webb, 26.6.1909, Passfield Papers 2/4/D/40, 2.

9 S. K. Ratcliffe, 'Mr Shaw's dogma', *NS*, 9.6.1928, 292. Shaw had a different perception of his influence. He later implausibly claimed that after he 'gave the [Fabian] Society a shock' by endorsing strict equality, 'the Webbs, momentarily taken aback, at once agreed with me, and from that time equalisation became an article of faith in the Fabian programme and, bowdlerised as equality of opportunity, in all the programmes'. G. B. Shaw, 'Correspondence: equalisation of income', *NS*, 29.1.1949, 104. In fact, disagreements with Shaw's egalitarianism may have led the Fabians to refuse to publish Shaw's 1913 lecture on equality: see A. Chappelow, *Shaw: 'The Chucker-out': A Biographical Exposition and Critique* (London, 1969), 280. Shaw's egalitarianism did attract academic interest: see the influential attempt to apply it to economic theory by H. D. Dickinson, 'The economic basis of socialism', *PQ*, 1 (1930), 561–72.

10 Shaw, *Intelligent Woman's Guide*, 6; his 'Socialism: principles and outlook', *FT No. 233* (London, 1930), 3.

11 Shaw, *Intelligent Woman's Guide*, 97–8.

12 This was approximately the rejoinder to Shaw presented in 'Equality of income', *Nation*, 10.5.1913, 223–4; 'Correspondence: equality of income', *Nation*, 17.5.1913, 269–70.

13 Shaw, *Case for Equality*, 28–9; Hobson's criticism of Shaw is at 18–21. For an account of this debate, see Chappelow, *Shaw*, 257–71.

14 Shaw, *Intelligent Woman's Guide*, 17–18, quote at 18. See also Laski's similar remarks in his *Grammar*, 199–200.

15 Shaw, *Intelligent Woman's Guide*, 21–2, 27–9; Shaw, 'Simple truth', 156–60.

16 B. Wootton, 'Shavian socialism', *EJ*, 39 (1929), 74.

17 E.g. 'Equality of income', *Nation*, 10.5.1913, 223; B. Crick, 'Shaw as political thinker', in his *Crossing Borders: Political Essays* (London, 2001), 199.

18 An objection like the 'Wilt Chamberlain' argument famously articulated by Robert Nozick could also be raised against Shaw, namely that maintaining strict equality would require considerable state restrictions on wealth transfers between citizens: R. Nozick, *Anarchy, State and Utopia* (Oxford, 1974), 160–2. A similar point was indeed made at the time by Mallock, *Limits*, 198–9. I set this aside because I want to focus on the objections to Shaw made by fellow progressives.

19 Shaw, *Intelligent Woman's Guide*, 340, 341.

20 Wootton, 'Shavian socialism', 76.

21 Shaw, *Intelligent Woman's Guide*, 78.

22 Dickinson, 'Economic basis', 566–9. Shaw himself was not completely consistent in his advocacy of strict equality, since he concluded his book by arguing that artistic or creative talent was entitled to command unequal rewards, but managerial ability was not, since only differentials in remuneration for authority roles in the workplace would create an unacceptable class hierarchy: *Intelligent Woman's Guide*, 332–7; see also his 'Socialism and superior brains', 20.

23 Laski, *Grammar*, 190.

24 Rowntree, *Poverty*, 133–8; see e.g. E. Rathbone, *The Disinherited Family: A Plea for the Endowment of the Family* (London, 1924), 40–2; Brailsford *et al.*, *Living Wage*, 20.

25 Shaw, *Intelligent Woman's Guide*, 88. For further discussion of the principle of needs, see section 3 of this chapter.

26 G. D. H. Cole, *Self-Government in Industry* (London, 1917), 110–11; G. D. H. Cole and W. Mellor, *The Meaning of Industrial Freedom* (London, 1918), 1–8. See Wright, *Cole*, 51–65; Stears, *Progressives*, 88–123. The future Labour Prime Minister Clement Attlee was one of many socialists impressed by this guild socialist argument, approvingly noting its insight that socialism 'was not merely a revolt against the unequal distribution of wealth', but also 'a protest against the enslavement of man by machine': C. R. Attlee, 'Guild socialism v. municipal socialism: a reply', *SR*, 116 (1923), 214.

27 G. D. H. Cole, *Social Theory* (London, 1920), 156.

28 G. D. H. Cole, 'Guild socialism', *FT No. 192* (London, 1920), 15; his *Guild Socialism Restated*, 72–3. In his journalism, Cole was less supportive of strict equality: see his 'The basis of wages', *NS*, 17.4.1920, 35.

29 Cole, *Guild Socialism Restated*, 73. Cole also made this point in his otherwise much less radical *Next Ten Years*, 198–200. Compare with Marx, *Critique*, 614–15.

30 Cole, *Payment of Wages*, 113; see also Cole's evidence to the War Cabinet Committee on Women in Industry, 30.10.1918, Cole Papers F5/1/1, 42; his *Next Ten Years*, 199–200.

31 G. D. H. Cole, *Principles of Economic Planning* (London, 1935), 234–7, quote on 235. Cole apparently picked up this idea from Milner's state bonus scheme: *Social Theory*, 85. See also Chapter 2, note 49.

32 P. Van Parijs, 'Competing justifications of basic income', in his (ed.), *Arguing for Basic Income* (London, 1992), 33, 34–5; Van Trier, 'Everyone a king', 387–95; J. Cunliffe and G. Erreygers, 'Introduction', in their edited collection, *The Origins of Universal Grants* (Basingstoke, 2004), xxiv–xxv.

33 Cole, *Principles*, 252.

34 Cole, *Principles*, 263, 264. These pages are not included in the excerpt from this book reprinted in Cunliffe and Erreygers, *Origins*, 152–60.

35 This was one of the four core principles of socialism Cole identified in his *The Simple Case for Socialism* (London, 1935), 7. For the idea of a 'participation income', see A. B. Atkinson, 'The case for a participation income', *PQ*, 67 (1996), 67–70. The original 'state bonus' proposal made by Milner could in any case be misunderstood as entailing just such a norm of economic reciprocity. While Milner and his allies were clear that the bonus would be paid unconditionally, some readers focused on the fact that individuals would be expected to contribute a share of their income in taxes (Milner suggested a fifth) in return for receiving an equal bonus payment from the state. It was sometimes assumed that the scheme therefore required some form of productive contribution from recipients, a form of conditionality that exponents of the state bonus in fact ruled out: compare J. R. MacDonald, 'Book reviews', *SR*, 16 (1919), 394–5 with B. Pickard, *A Reasonable Revolution* (London, 1919), 36–7, 44–5.

36 Cole, *Guild Socialism Restated*, 71–2; see also Russell, *Roads to Freedom*, 194–5.

37 J. A. Hobson, 'Our social heritage', *Nation* (New York), 21.9.1921, 322; see also his *Incentives*, 147–53. Hobson is here reporting, and endorsing, the view of Graham Wallas.

38 S. Webb and B. Webb, *The Consumers' Co-operative Movement* (London, 1921), 465; see also B. Glasier, 'Arm-chair industrial emancipation', *SR*, 12 (1914), 292.

39 I. Kramnick and B. Sheerman, *Harold Laski: A Life on the Left* (London, 1993), 227–31; M. Newman, *Harold Laski: A Political Biography* (London, 1993), 74–7; P. Lamb, 'Laski's ideological metamorphosis', *Journal of Political Ideologies*, 4 (1999), 239–44.

40 Cole, *Next Ten Years*, 183–5 and *passim*. For discussion of this point, see M. Stears, 'Needs, welfare and the limits of associationalism', *Economy and Society*, 28 (1999), 570–89.

41 Marx, *Critique*, 615. Marx himself adopted this slogan from the French socialist Louis Blanc. For its use by British egalitarians, see e.g. Laski, *Communism*, 177–8; Hobson, *Wealth and Life*, 220–2; Clarke, *Liberals and Social Democrats*, 50.

42 On the conceptual architecture, see Miller, *Principles*, 206–13; for a comparative historical account of the development of ideas of need in this period, see Freeden, 'Coming of the welfare state', 16–19.

43 Daunton, *Trusting Leviathan*, 142–7.

44 Freeden, *New Liberalism*, 12–15; Collini, *Liberalism and Sociology*, 43–6; den Otter, 'Thinking in communities', 73–5; Bevir, 'Sidney Webb', 223–5. For criticisms of Benthamite utilitarianism along these lines, see *R. H. Tawney's Commonplace Book*, 62–7, entry dated 29.7.1913; Hobhouse, *Liberalism*, 31–6; Burns, *Industry and Civilisation*, 113. Ruskin was one source of these criticisms of the Benthamite tradition, particularly when it appeared in the guise of neo-classical economics: see J. A. Hobson, *John Ruskin* (London, 1898), 85–6, 92–100, 309.

45 Collini, *Liberalism and Sociology*, 117.

46 Professional economists from this earlier period also employed more or less utilitarian arguments: e.g. Dalton, *Inequality of Incomes*, 9–11. See section 5.3 for discussion of the influence of welfare economics on later debates about equality.

47 D. Weinstein, 'The new liberalism of L. T. Hobhouse and the re-envisioning of nineteenth-century utilitarianism', *Journal of the History of Ideas*, 57 (1996), 487–507; his 'The new liberalism and the rejection of utilitarianism', in Simhony and Weinstein, *The New Liberalism*, 159–83.

48 'Equality of income', *Nation*, 10.5.1913, 224.

49 Author's reply, 'Letters to the editor: equality of income', *Nation*, 17.5.1913, 269–70.

50 Hobson, *Wealth and Life*, 230; also Hobson, *Work and Wealth*, 164–6. Note that at times Hobson's views could veer in a purely aggregative direction: see his comments in Shaw, *Case for Equality*, 19–20.

51 Hobhouse, *Elements*, 109.

52 Laski, *Grammar*, 194; also Laski, *Communism*, 178.

53 Hobson, *Wealth and Life*, 231–2, quote at 232.

54 Hobson, 'Towards social equality', 25.

55 Laski, *Grammar*, 160.

56 S. Webb, 'National finance and a levy on capital: what Labour intends', *FT No. 188* (London, 1919), 19; also Hobhouse, *Elements*, 109. This point was frequently made at this time: see e.g. Shaw, 'Simple truth', 166–7; 'Labour in conference', *NS*, 2.3.1918, 512; 'Seven Members . . .', *Labour Party's Aim*, 52; Laski, 'Socialism and freedom', 9.

57 Cole, *Next Ten Years*, 200.

58 J. W. S. Davidson, 'The standard of comfort', *SR*, 11 (1913), 72.

59 Rowntree, 'Industrial unrest', 97. See B. S. Rowntree, *The Human Needs of Labour* (London, 1918), 121–9; Briggs, *Social Thought*, 37–40, 150–6.

60 J. H. Veit-Wilson, 'Paradigms of poverty: a rehabilitation of B. S. Rowntree', *Journal of Social Policy*, 15 (1986), 69–99.

61 E.g. Hobhouse, 'Regulation of wages', 168–72; Cole's evidence to the War Cabinet Committee on Women in Industry, 30.10.1918, Cole Papers F5/1/1, 40.

62 Snowden, *Living Wage*, 66; see also 133.

63 Webb and Webb, *Prevention of Destitution*, 1. According to the Webbs, therefore, while 'destitution' was an absolute condition, 'poverty' was not.

64 Hobhouse, *Labour Movement*, 28; also Hobhouse, *Elements*, 133–4. See also Tawney's scepticism about 'subsistence' as a workable criterion for setting a minimum in his 'The minimum wage in Great Britain', *New Republic*, 28.6.1922, 126–7.

65 L. T. Hobhouse, 'The right to a living wage', in W. Temple (ed.), *The Industrial Unrest and the Living Wage* (London, 1913), 70; also Laski, *Grammar*, 195.

66 Labour Party, *Labour and the New Social Order* (London, 1918), 5. See also A. Henderson, 'The character and policy of the British Labour Party', *IJE*, 32 (1921–2), 121–2; Harris, 'Political thought and the welfare state', 133.

67 M. Freeden, 'The concept of poverty and progressive liberalism', in his *Liberal Languages*, 71–3.

68 Snowden, *Socialism Made Plain*, 3; see also A. F. Brockway, 'The purpose of socialism: a full human life for all', *LL*, 1.5.1913, 11; M. Freeden, 'Rights, needs and community: the emergence of British welfare thought', in A. Ware and R. Goodin (eds), *Needs and Welfare* (London, 1990), 65–8.

69 See G. Searle, *The Quest for National Efficiency* (Oxford, 1971).

70 J. Winter, *Socialism and the Challenge of War* (London, 1974), 234–69.

71 Webb and Webb, *Industrial Democracy*, 766–84, 817, 820–1; their *A Constitution for the Socialist Commonwealth of Great Britain* (London, 1920), 320–3; their *Decay*, 15. The Webbs' initial recommendation was for the minimum to be set at a subsistence level, but they were ambitious about increasing it in the medium to long term.

72 Webb and Webb, *Constitution*, 101; also National Committee for the Prevention of Destitution, *Case for the National Minimum*, 18. For more general revisionist thoughts about the Webbs along these lines, see Bevir, 'Sidney Webb'; Morgan, *Webbs and Soviet Communism*.

73 See E. Rathbone, 'The remuneration of women's services', *EJ*, 27 (1917), 55–68; Webb, *Wages of Men and Women*, 15–20 and *passim*. This was a debate that in some sense continued at least until the 1945 Labour government: Francis, *Ideas and Policies*, 206–8.

74 Published as Webb, *Wages of Men and Women*, see especially 28–9. For its reception, see 'Women in industry', *NS*, 17.5.1919, 157; C. M. Lloyd, 'Incomes for children', *NS*, 10.3.1923, 651. Here I differ from Susan Pedersen's more downbeat assessment of Beatrice's report in her *Eleanor Rathbone and the Politics of Conscience* (New Haven, 2004), 153.

75 Hobhouse, 'Regulation of wages', 168–71.

76 Hobhouse, *Elements*, 146–7, fn. 1; also Hobhouse, 'Right to a living wage', 71–3. The average family size was from Rowntree, *Human Needs*, 15–48, 121–44.

77 G. D. H. Cole, evidence to War Cabinet Committee on Women in Industry, 30.10.1918, Cole Papers F5/1/1, 40; see also his 'The minimum wage', *SR*, 23 (1924), 62.

78 G. D. H. Cole, '"Equal pay" for teachers', *NS*, 9.4.1921, 8; see also his 'Summary of points' [to War Cabinet Committee], 30.10.1918, Cole Papers F5/1/2, 9; Webb, *Wages of Men and Women*, 42–4.

79 Brailsford, *Families and Incomes*, 5. Brailsford's figures came from Eleanor Rathbone's *Disinherited Family*, see especially 14–38. See also Webb, *Wages of Men and Women*, 68–9.

80 Rathbone, *Disinherited Family*; her *The Ethics and Economics of Family Endowment* (London, 1927); Pedersen, *Eleanor Rathbone*, 151–3, 201–18, 359–68. On the history of family allowances more generally, see J. MacNicol, *The Movement for Family Allowances 1918–45: A Study in Social Policy Development* (London, 1980); S. Pedersen, *Family, Dependence and the Origins of the Welfare State* (Cambridge, 1993).

81 Rathbone, *Disinherited Family*, 64–161; Pedersen, *Eleanor Rathbone*, 107–11, 151–2, 211–12.

82 For a full discussion see D. Howell, *MacDonald's Party: Labour Identities and Crisis, 1922–31* (Oxford, 2002), 356–69, quote at 356; also Pedersen, *Dependence*, 195–6; Pedersen, *Eleanor Rathbone*, 211–17.

83 Brailsford, *Families and Incomes*, 10–13.

84 E.g. E. Burns, 'Wages and wealth redistribution', *SR*, 14 (1917), 52–6; Webb, *Wages of Men and Women*, 69–70; Brailsford, 'Socialism in our generation: the living wage as lever', *NL*, 1.1.1926, 9; H. Dalton, 'To each according to his need: grants for children', *NL*, 15.1.1926, 9; Brailsford *et al.*, *Living Wage*, 20–6; Cole, *Next Ten Years*, 185–7; Brailsford, 'The children or the debt? The wage and the family', *NL*, 23.9.1927, 9; E. D. Simon, *How to Abolish the Slums* (London, 1929), 94–5. On the 1926 'living wage' proposals, and the hostility of some trade unionists and Labour politicians to them, see F. M. Leventhal, *The Last Dissenter: H. N. Brailsford and His World* (Oxford, 1985), 188–95; Pedersen, *Dependence*, 189–219; Howell, *MacDonald's Party*, 264–87.

85 Although it should be noted that Hobhouse was sceptical of a 'family endowment' precisely because he was worried by its assertion of collective responsibility over the family: 'Right to a living wage', 71–2, fn.

86 E.g. P. Snowden, *HCD*, 161, 20.3.1923, cols 2474–6.

87 J. A. Hobson, *The Economics of Unemployment* (London, 1922); Clarke, *Liberals and Social Democrats*, 46–54, 124–6, 226–34; Allett, *New Liberalism*, 96–130. See section 5.2 on this argument's affinities with Keynesian economics.

88 See e.g. Snowden, *Living Wage*, 148; J. W. S. Davidson, 'Interests and profits', *SR*, 11 (1913), 533–4; H. N. Brailsford, 'Poverty and unemployment: ironing out the trade cycle', *NL*, 29.8.1924, 9; Brailsford *et al.*, *Living Wage*, 8–12; J. Wheatley, 'A new socialist policy I: why capitalism is failing', *NL*, 26.12.1926, 9; Freeden, *New Liberalism*, 130–1, 208.

89 See Stears, *Progressives*, 177–8.

90 Cronin, *Labour and Society*, 57–61. For criticism of employers' attitudes, see e.g. 'The problem of output', *NS*, 27.11.1920, 222; Tawney, *Acquisitive*, 131; also Hobson's critique of scientific management: *Work and Wealth*, 202–27.

91 J. M. Keynes, *The Economic Consequences of the Peace* [1919], *JMK* 2, 11–12. For similar views see Cole, *Guild Socialism Restated*, 20–3; Dalton, *Inequality of Incomes*, 6–8; MacDonald, *Socialism: Critical and Constructive*, 9–11; Hobson, *Wealth and Life*, 170.

92 'Seven Members . . .', *Labour Party's Aim*, 53; also C. D. Burns, 'Productivity and reconstruction', *IJE*, 28 (1917–18), 393–401; Cole, *Chaos and Order*, 16–17; Simon, *Inheritance*, 12.

93 Hobson, *Work and Wealth*, 303; also Tawney, *Acquisitive Society*, 40–1, 146–8.

94 Hobhouse, *Elements*, 141–2; Hobson, *Incentives*, 91–3.

95 Snowden, *Individual Under Socialism*, 9; J. R. MacDonald, 'The outlook for trade unionism VI: what should be its spirit?', *SR*, February 1923, 81–4; Glasier, *Socialism*, 95; Hardie, *Serfdom to Socialism*, 95.

96 C. Gore, 'The quality of justice', in R. Hogue (ed.), *British Labour Speaks* (New York, 1924), 146–7; also Cole, *Guild Socialism Restated*, 61; Laski, 'Socialism and freedom', 10.

97 Attlee, 'Guild v. municipal socialism', 216.

98 It also depended on a view of the workplace as necessarily a site of self-realisation, an assumption that other progressives resisted: Wright, *Cole*, 62; Stears, *Progressives*, 173–5.

99 Hobson, *Wealth and Life*, 253–4; also Hobhouse, *Labour Movement*, 34; his *Elements*, 142; H. Reynard, 'The guild socialists', *EJ*, 30 (1920), 328–30; D. H. Robertson, 'Mr Cole's social theories', *EJ*, 30 (1920), 540–1; G. Wallas, 'Acquisitive society', *Nation*, 11.6.1921, 401.

100 Hobson, *Incentives*, 142–4.

101 Webb and Webb, 'What is socialism? Part XII', 365.

102 Laski, *Grammar*, 197–8; also Laski, 'State in the new social order', 14; Tawney, *Equality*, 152–64.

103 G. D. H. Cole, *Incentives Under Socialism* (Girard, KS, 1931), 8–9; his *Next Ten Years*, 16–19, 160–2; his *Guide Through World Chaos*, 498–500. Glasier took a similar view: *Socialism*, 64.

104 J. A. Hobson, *Poverty in Plenty: The Ethics of Income* (London, 1931), 89.

105 E.g. MacDonald, *Socialist Movement*, 175–6; Hobhouse, *Labour Movement*, 116; Webb and Webb, 'What is socialism? Part XII', 365; Hobhouse, *Elements*, 141–2; B. Russell, 'Motives in industry', *NL*, 13.10.1922, 11–12; Brailsford, *Socialism*, 132–8; Burns, *Industry and Civilisation*, 52–5, 84–5; Hobson, *Wealth and Life*, 224–5.

106 Hobson, *Incentives*, 38.

107 Hobson, *Taxation*, 98. See Clarke, *Liberals and Social Democrats*, 110–11.

108 Hobson, *Wealth and Life*, 435.

109 McBriar, *Fabian Socialism*, 37–41; Harrison, *Life and Times*, 27–33; Bevir, 'Sidney Webb', 229–31.

110 On the apparent vagueness of such theories, see Collini, *Liberalism and Sociology*, 130–7; Collini, 'Moral mind: R. H. Tawney', 186; Ellison, *Egalitarian Thought*, 2, 21–7; Foote, *Labour Party's Political Thought*, 79–80. On the problematic lack of criteria to justify inequalities, see F. A. Hayek, *The Road to Serfdom* (London, 1944), 82–4; Gutmann, *Liberal Equality*, 78, 80, 85, 90; J. Kloppenburg, *Uncertain Victory: Social Democracy and Progressivism in European and American Thought 1870–1920* (Oxford, 1986), 282–5.

111 Laski, *Grammar*, 157; also Laski, *Liberty in the Modern State* (London, 1930), 18; compare with J. Rawls, *A Theory of Justice* (Oxford, 1999 [1971]), 53. On the affinities between the difference principle and Laski's view, see Freeden, *Liberalism Divided*, 306–7; Kramnick and Sheerman, *Harold Laski*, 229. Tawney used similar language to Laski in *Equality*, 152–8. See also White, *Civic Minimum*, 13.

112 H. Laski, 'The individual and the common good', *Nation*, 13.5.1922, 227. See also M. de Wolfe Howe (ed.), *The Holmes–Laski Letters: The Correspondence of Mr Justice Holmes and Harold Laski, 1916–35* (London, 1953), 388, 391.

113 Hobhouse, *Liberalism*, 63.

114 Hobhouse, *Elements*, 107–20, 144–6, 148–9; Weinstein, 'Rejection of utilitarianism', in Simhony and Weinstein (eds), *The New Liberalism*, 175–80.

115 Rawls, *Theory of Justice*, 72.

116 Hobhouse, *Labour Movement*, 35; Hobson, *Problems of a New World*, 181; his *Wealth and Life*, 442–3; Burns, *Industry and Civilisation*.

117 My understanding of this point is indebted to Stears and White, 'New liberalism revisited', 43–6. For an analytical discussion of this idea of an 'egalitarian social ethos', see G. A. Cohen, *If You're an Egalitarian, How Come You're so Rich?* (Cambridge, MA, 2001), 117–47. As Cohen points out, this concern with an egalitarian social ethos is absent from Rawls's account of social justice.

118 Hobson, *Work and Wealth*, 304.

119 Hobson, *Wealth and Life*, 234; see also his *Poverty in Plenty*, 89–90.

120 Webb and Webb, *Constitution*, 351; also their *Decay*, 173.

121 Lansbury, *Your Part in Poverty*, 111.

122 Hobhouse, *Labour Movement*, 18. See also Glasier's characterisation of the ideological and institutional growth of 'the principle of mutual help and collective effort' as a trend inherent in complex industrialised societies: his *Socialism*, 133–83.

123 The phrase is Tawney's (*Equality*, 165), but was subsequently made famous by J. Le Grand, *The Strategy of Equality* (London, 1982).

124 For discussion of both options, see Cole, 'The minimum wage', 58–63. See also Tanner, 'Development', 59–60 on MacDonald's distinctive approach to this question.

125 Hardie, *Serfdom to Socialism*, 100–1; J. K. Hardie, 'The battlefield of Labour', *LL*, 11.2.1910, 89; Glasier, *Socialism*, 94; Hobson, 'New industrial revolution', 639, 642–3; P. Snowden, *Labour and the New World* (London, 1921), 209–220; Morgan, *Webbs and Soviet Communism*, 97–100.

126 See section 3 of this chapter. On the complexities of the broader relationship between the 'political' and the 'industrial' elements of the labour movement at this time, see Howell, *MacDonald's Party*, 93–8, 194–221, 404–7.

127 Webb and Webb, *Industrial Democracy*, 282–323, 796–806, 809–26, 831–3, 842–4; J. R. MacDonald, 'The outlook for trade unionism II: wages and leadership', *SR*, August 1922, 68–75. It should be noted in this context that some intellectuals were certainly willing to grant the unions autonomy over the determination of working-class wage rates. See Beatrice Webb's interesting criticism of certain elements of the ILP's 'living wage' proposals on the grounds that they conflicted with the trade union commitment to differentials: B. Webb to H. N. Brailsford, 17.4.1926, Passfield Papers 4/19/34.

128 For an influential synthesis of all of these welfare proposals, see Tawney, *Equality*, 172–210.

129 K. O. Morgan, *Keir Hardie: Radical and Socialist* (London, 1997 [1975]), 238–9; Daunton, *Trusting Leviathan*, 366; J. Shepherd, *George Lansbury: At the Heart of Old Labour* (Oxford, 2002), 99–103. Quote from *LL*, 15.12.1911, in Morgan, *Keir Hardie*, 239. The majority of the parliamentary Labour Party supported the Liberal Bill, although for tactical rather than ideological reasons.

130 On the 1909 budget and its political and ideological context, see B. Murray, *The People's Budget 1909–10* (Oxford, 1980); Daunton, *Trusting Leviathan*, 360–6. Labour's fiscal policy at this time was similar: see *LPACR* 1909, 102–12.

131 E.g. Dalton, *Inequality*, 316–27; H. D. Henderson, 'Inheritance and inequality: a practical proposal', *'The New Way' Series XV* (London, 1926), 17–19; Cole, *Next Ten Years*, 375–9. See also M. Daunton, *Just Taxes: The Politics of Taxation in Britain, 1914–79* (Cambridge, 2002), 147–9; see also Chapter 2, note 33.

132 Webb, 'National finance and a levy on capital', 15–18; Snowden, *Labour and National Finance*, 68–81; F. W. Pethick-Lawrence, 'The capital levy and its critics', *SR*, November 1922, 225–31; H. Dalton, *The Capital Levy Explained* (London, 1923); Freeden, *Liberalism Divided*, 151–4; R. Whiting, *The Labour Party and Taxation* (Cambridge, 2000), 23–34; Daunton, *Just Taxes*, 49–50, 66–74.

133 J. K. Hardie, 'The compliments of the season', *LL*, 1.1.1909, 9.

134 Webb and Webb, 'What is socialism? Part XII', 364.

135 Snowden, *Twenty Objections*, 9; Snowden, *Labour and the New World*, 38; Hardie, 'Compliments', 9.

136 E.g. MacDonald, *Socialism and Society*, 177–9; P. Snowden, *HCD*, 161, 20.3.1923, cols 2482–4.

137 For helpful juxtaposition, see N. Thompson, 'Hobson and the Fabians: two roads to socialism in the 1920s', *History of Political Economy*, 26 (1994), 203–20.

138 On these debates about unemployment policy, see Harris, *Unemployment and Politics*; R. Skidelsky, *Politicians and the Slump* (London, 1967); R. McKibbin, 'The economic policy of the second Labour government, 1929–31', in his *Ideologies of Class*, 197–227.

139 Daunton, *Trusting Leviathan*, 353–7.

140 Lansbury, *Your Part in Poverty*, 121–2; R. H. Tawney (ed.), *Secondary Education For All: A Policy for Labour* (London, n.d. [1922]), 60–72, 83–92; C. P. Trevelyan, 'How to give education a chance: the obstacle of poverty', *NL*, 7.1.1927, 11.

141 E.g. G. Wallas, *Our Social Heritage* (London, 1921), 97; Tawney, *Secondary Education*, 7, 78; Cole, *Next Ten Years*, 349–51. See also R. Barker, *Education and Politics 1900–51: A Study of the Labour Party* (Oxford, 1972), 26–45.

142 See e.g. Tawney, *Equality*, 94–8; his 'The problem of the public schools' [1943], in R. H. Tawney, *The Radical Tradition* (London, 1964), 55–73; Barker, *Education*, 34, 99–107; A. Arblaster, 'Tawney in retrospect', *Bulletin of the Society for the Study of Labour History*, 54 (1989), 97–8.

Part II
1931–45: Economics

4

Marxists and social democrats

4.1 Introduction: the Marxist turn

Throughout the early twentieth century, the Left's egalitarian ideals had been grounded on a hidden and largely uncontroversial premise. Progressives assumed that arguments about political values were central to legitimating policy proposals and political strategies, and consequently believed that a fairer society could be advanced through reasoned democratic debate about the ethical virtues of an egalitarian distribution. However, these beliefs only appeared uncontroversial in an ideological climate that emphasised the importance of ethical discourse to politics and the conviction that rational debates about values could produce significant moral and political progress. Both of these characteristics of British political debate were to be sorely tested by the upheavals of the 1930s and 40s. Consequently, the Left's ideological vocabulary gravitated towards two bodies of theory that sought to downplay the importance of normative arguments about distributive justice: Marxism and economic theory. As David Howell has suggested, 'the fight for Labour's soul in the early thirties' can schematically be described 'as a contest between Marx and Keynes'.[1]

The next chapter will examine the ideological impact of Keynes and other economists, but this part of the book begins by focusing on the dissemination of Marxist theory into progressive thought during the 1930s and its application to theorising about equality. As a first step, the remainder of this section indicates why Marxism achieved such unprecedented prestige in the political debates of this period. The second and third sections of this chapter examine in more detail the materialist critique of social democratic egalitarianism developed by Marxist writers, and the principles of justice they ultimately defended. The final section discusses the partial retreat from this materialist position precipitated by the arrival of the Second World War.

The crisis
As we have seen, progressives of the early twentieth century had been optimistic about the possibilities for social reform within the existing British political system,

and saw the elaboration of egalitarian ideals and policies as providing relevant guidance for this task. In 1929, the prospects for a further instalment of social reform looked bright, as Labour made further gains in the general election of that year under the leadership of MacDonald and Snowden, and entered office for a second time as a minority government. Two disastrous events were to undermine this optimism, and to challenge the assumptions that underpinned the egalitarian theories examined in previous chapters.

First, the infamous self-destruction of the Labour government in 1931 over cuts in unemployment benefit was attributed particular historical significance by one section of the Left.[2] To certain writers and activists, it revealed the bankruptcy of the gradualist road to equality: the political and financial establishment simply would not permit a socialist government to enact substantial changes to British capitalism. MacDonald and Snowden's capitulation to the Treasury View demonstrated the true distribution of power concealed by the formally democratic procedures of the British state. The parliamentary road to socialism was ineffective, such critics suggested, because British democracy was essentially managed for the economic benefit of the ruling class. Exponents of the interests of the working class could gain no traction over such a biased set of institutions and processes. The lesson of 1931 was simply that 'socialistic measures' were 'not obtainable by constitutional means. Whenever a party in office seeks by legislative action to alter seriously the distribution of wealth, finance-capital will not accept the rule of parliamentary government.'[3]

A second factor combined with this analysis to set a section of the Left on a radical path. The persistence of economic depression during the 1930s, and in particular its impact on working-class life, was seen as definitive proof that capitalism had irretrievably collapsed and that the human costs of this failure were intolerable.[4] Suddenly, in this climate of intense economic and political crisis, the writings of Karl Marx acquired a resonance they had previously lacked in British politics. So ended what John Strachey called 'one of the most remarkable intellectual boycotts in the history of human thought', namely the studied disinterest in Marxist theory that British socialists had elevated to the status of a virtue over previous decades.[5] In Britain in the early twentieth century, Marxist theory had been the province of working-class autodidacts or the occasional upper-class dilettante; it had made only a minimal impact on cultural and political life. In contrast, one of the distinguishing characteristics of British intellectual life in the 1930s was the emergence of the first generation of university-educated Marxists. They brought to their writings a depth and rigour that reflected their academic backgrounds, and they tended to be dismissive of the purportedly amateurish genre of Marxist philosophising that had previously captured the imagination of the most radical section of the working class. The works of Marx and Engels, along with those of Lenin and Stalin, were now widely read and discussed by intellectual and political elites. Marxism had become a mainstream intellectual phenomenon.[6]

Indeed, during the 1930s it sometimes appeared as if the Left's leading intellectuals were converting to Marxism en masse. Famously, a number of prominent cultural and scientific figures publicly declared themselves Marxists in this period, many of them rallying behind the increasingly dynamic Communist Party of Great Britain (CPGB).[7] Amongst political writers, a significant indication of the new climate was the conversion of Harold Laski and the sometime Labour MP John Strachey to a broadly Marxist outlook, as well as the Webbs' infamous enthusiasm for Soviet communism. Laski and Strachey had spent the 1920s proclaiming fidelity to orthodox social democratic politics, but by the early 1930s both were disillusioned by the failure of the Labour Party in government, and they began to view the future of 'capitalist democracy' in increasingly apocalyptic terms.[8] While the political outlook of the Webbs was less clear than that of Laski and Strachey, they nonetheless expressed an admiration for Stalin's regime that reveals as much about the political context of the 1930s as it does about the shortcomings of the Webbs themselves.[9] This chapter draws on the writings of Laski, Strachey and the Webbs, along with other influential texts of the period: the publications of the startlingly successful Left Book Club (run by Victor Gollancz along with Strachey and Laski); Kingsley Martin's New Statesman, which see-sawed throughout the 1930s between radical Marxist politics and a nascent Keynesian social democracy; and the orthodox communist analysis produced by the leaders of the CPGB, notably R. Palme Dutt, Emile Burns and Harry Pollitt.

A similar political perspective emerges from all of these sources: Marx had been proved correct by events. The state was the executive committee of the ruling class. After all, the Labour Party had been removed from power the moment it resisted the agenda of capitalist financiers, while the examples of Germany, Italy and Spain all showed that the bourgeoisie was prepared to annul democracy and collaborate with fascists if its economic interests were threatened. It also seemed increasingly plausible to think that capitalism would face a series of inescapable economic crises, and that these might well mark the beginning of a new historical epoch. Even liberals like J. A. Hobson acknowledged the force of these claims: 'That a collapse of capitalism in accordance with the Marxian prediction is taking place, there can be no doubt.'[10] While capitalist regimes were powerless in the face of economic disaster, Soviet central planning appeared much more successful: it had purportedly staved off mass unemployment and fostered rapid industrialisation, thus demonstrating the folly of persisting with the market.[11] Given these assumptions, it was easy to believe that Marxism was 'the great political-intellectual movement of the time', and 'an international culture just reaching its phase of full maturity'.[12]

4.2 Materialism and egalitarian strategy

In the 1930s, and particularly during the early part of that decade, the appeal of Marxism primarily rested on its claim to offer the only coherent alternative to the obvious strategic bankruptcy of egalitarian social democracy. Marxist critics could plausibly argue that fascism, depression and the poor record of social democratic governments had discredited the egalitarian strategies proposed by progressives in the early twentieth century. Former social democrats now joined with orthodox communists in arguing that those who advocated social reform essentially belonged to the same camp as the straightforward defenders of laissez-faire. As Palme Dutt put it, Britain now confronted 'the great "Either-Or"': either a radical, qualitative change in the organisation of society, or capitalism, continuing on its way to crisis, misery and ultimately fascism.[13] The ideology of social democracy could not address this fundamental issue, Marxists argued, because it was irretrievably compromised by its moralism and gradualism. Why did they think these features of social democratic thought were fatal for the egalitarian strategies examined at the end of the previous chapter?

The impotence of ideals

To take the charge of 'moralism' first, Marxists maintained that elaborating ethical principles to guide material distribution was both politically impotent and theoretically misguided. Theorising about social justice was politically impotent because it relied on weak moral sentiments rather than a concrete struggle for power by the working class, and theoretically misguided because advocates of 'equality' misunderstood the status of moral propositions, believing them to be independent of economic conditions when historical materialism had demonstrated that the reverse was true. Strachey's verdict was characteristic of the genre:

> Some idealistic philosophers, it is true, claim to be able to change the world by means of their moral exhortation. Indeed, as they believe that 'the idea' is the basis of 'the thing'; and not the thing of the idea, moral exhortation leading to a 'change of heart' on the part of all men, is the only dynamic method open to them. All that we need say as to this claim is that experience has shown, after a trial of some three thousand years, that it is unjustified.[14]

Harold Laski offered an arresting example of this critique of earlier egalitarian strategies in a review of the Left Book Club edition of Tawney's *The Acquisitive Society*. This book had significantly influenced Laski's political thought in the 1920s.[15] However, in the feverish climate of the 1930s, Laski's feelings were now more ambivalent. He acknowledged that *The Acquisitive Society* had 'caught, as no other English book of its time, the mood of that liberalism which was sick to the heart at the inequities of a business civilisation and sought so to define them that no man could mistake their meaning'.[16] The classification of Tawney as a liberal rather than a socialist gave an indication of the ideological agenda. As a liberal, continued Laski, Tawney placed considerable emphasis on ideals: 'his book remains a contrast between two societies with no hint of how the bridge is built between them. Does this mean that, for him, the reasonableness of his ideal is, as it were, self-sufficient, that he believes its own inherent claims give it the assurance of triumph?'[17] This was an awkward matter. If Tawney believed in the self-sufficiency of ideals, then from a Marxist perspective this would indeed be a grave defect in his political outlook. Laski brushed over the issue, expressing confidence that Tawney did not believe that the answer to fascism was 'simply the persistent reformulation of the claims of the ideal'. Instead, Laski suggested an interpretation of the book as 'a magnificent *cri de coeur* rather than a programme for action', and accordingly recommended 'the classic literature of Marxism' as 'the necessary supplement to Mr Tawney's book'.[18] Tawneyite idealism in isolation from Marxist theory was indeed considered impotent. Consequently, when Laski dismissed the ethical socialism of Philip Snowden as embodying 'more an emotional distaste for inequality than a positive or coherent doctrine', this criticism actually had a wider application than the relatively easy target of Snowden.[19]

According to this Marxist analysis, a serious strategic weakness of British ethical socialism was that it failed to come to terms with the decisive importance of economic interests to political outcomes and, in particular, had nothing to say about class conflict. The British Left usually restricted its appeal to 'Liberal-Christian nonsense', and relied on 'the power of an abstract reason of the community to accept the abstract justice of their cause', when in reality 'wages under capitalism are not fixed by "ethical principles," but by economic forces and relative class strength'.[20] This led reformists to overestimate the latitude for redistribution within a political system that granted formal democratic rights to the working class. In fact, a materialist perspective revealed that, far from being neutral between classes, the capitalist state was dominated by a property-owning minority. Any elected government would be dependent on the co-operation of key interests that would be opposed to extensive redistribution; sabotage 'from the banks or the civil service, or both, would make impossible the existence of any "socialist" government *not already equipped with a backing of sufficient revolutionary force to crush both forms of resistance*'.[21] While private ownership of productive assets existed, real democracy and communal solidarity were utopian ambitions. The stratification of the citizenry into an owning and a working class meant that 'it is impossible to speak of such a society as a "community," since there is a direct antagonism of interests between those two classes'.[22] Social democrats were therefore misguided to think that the invocation of principles of justice or solidaristic sentiments could in itself effect significant political change.

This is not to say that Marxists necessarily thought that the concept of justice was insignificant. Marxist or Marx-influenced writings of the 1930s frequently referred to the importance of social justice, and to the need for a concerted attack on economic inequality as an important step towards securing a just society. Communists, argued the Marxist poet Stephen Spender, regarded 'the abolition of private property and the establishment of a classless society' as 'claims of justice',[23] while the newly radicalised Labour MP Stafford Cripps emphasised that behind the proposed 'fundamental change of the whole economic system' should be 'the spirit of the movement, the intense desire for social justice', grounded on a recognition of 'the essential ethical, moral and religious rightness of the cause'.[24]

Of course, Cripps was not by inclination much of a theorist, and his recourse to moral principle and religious inspiration sat uneasily with the materialism that was such a dominant note in Marxist discourse. More systematic thinkers relied on a deeper claim: the content of justice was not determined by reasoned argument, but by material circumstances. Different social classes, argued Laski, had radically different views of what constitutes justice, since their perception of justice was determined by their position within the capitalist system of production. Classes were bound together by a similarity in economic interest, which was then given ideological expression in 'a similar notion of what constitutes justice'.[25] If a subordinated class found that its perception of justice was not being satisfied, then it would attempt to seize control of the state, and by doing so it would aim 'to make its view of justice prevail'.[26] There was little possibility of the gap between the classes being bridged by sympathy or rational dialogue. Given their elevated social positions, argued Spender, liberals simply could not appreciate that 'liberal justice' was based 'on the institution of property and the interests of a certain class'.[27] The radical differences between the economic positions of social classes prevented the emergence of genuine social solidarity and a normative consensus about distributive fairness.[28] The assumption was that an egalitarian form of justice would ultimately win out in the class struggle, since the more or less explicit political sociology informing this view was that the working class were the largest (and ultimately most powerful) social group and, as a result of their distinctive social experiences, the bearers of egalitarian values.

It was precisely this materialist understanding of justice that led Marxists to vent their frustration with George Orwell's famous book, *The Road to Wigan Pier*. Although published by the Left Book Club in 1937, it had been released in the face of objections from the CPGB, and misgivings on the part of Gollancz.[29] While Marxists recognised the important achievement of the first part of the book, a shocking account of working-class life, they took exception to the second part, which contained a broad brush attack on the state of British socialism. The latter included 'some resounding thwacks at Anglo-Communism',[30] and offered an unashamedly idealist account of socialism as the embodiment of traditional liberal values: 'We have got to fight for justice and liberty, and socialism does mean justice and liberty when the nonsense is stripped off it.'[31] The critique of Orwell's definition of socialism became a minor industry. Gollancz contributed a cautionary foreword to the book, pointing out that in fact Orwell did not explain 'what he understands by the words "liberty" and "justice"', a point echoed by Laski, who diagnosed Orwell's error as the assumption 'that we all mean the same things by liberty and justice'. In fact, continued Laski, differences over the content of those ends 'very closely reflects our class position in society. Broadly speaking, those who today own the instruments of production believe that our system is both just and free.' Orwell's socialism was too reliant on moral exhortation, ignoring 'the urgent reality of class antagonisms', and resting on 'an emotional plea' when 'men live too differently to think similarly by being asked to embrace abstractions'.[32] While it was fair to say that Orwell had not provided a clear definition of what he meant by the ideals of liberty and justice, the recourse to a purely materialist interpretation of ethical values was a more contentious line of criticism, since it appeared to rule out any kind of ethical socialism as a viable political option.[33]

Orwell himself courted further controversy with his next book, *Homage to Catalonia*, which contained such a brisk critique of Soviet intervention in the Spanish Republic that Gollancz refused to publish it.[34] But this work also disclosed further details about the character of Orwell's socialism, revealing that he adhered to a familiar kind of egalitarian political morality. Famously, Orwell provided an evocative account of the egalitarian ethos that prevailed in Barcelona during the Spanish Civil War. Economic equality was the order of the day: 'the wealthy classes had practically ceased to exist'. 'There were no "well-dressed" people at all' since 'practically everyone wore rough working-class clothes', and 'there was no unemployment' and 'very few conspicuously destitute people'. Social relationships were also characterised by equality: workers 'looked you in the face and treated you as an equal. Servile and even ceremonial forms of speech had temporarily disappeared.' Most of all, there was a spirit of optimism abroad, 'a belief in the revolution and the future, a feeling of having suddenly emerged into an era of equality and freedom'.[35] In Barcelona, Orwell 'had breathed the air of equality':

> I am well aware that it is now the fashion to deny that socialism has anything to do with equality. In every country in the world a huge tribe of party-hacks and sleek little professors are busy 'proving' that socialism means no more than a planned state-capitalism with the grab motive left intact. But fortunately there also exists a vision of socialism quite different from this. The thing that attracts ordinary men to socialism and makes them willing to risk their skins for it, the 'mystique' of socialism, is the idea of equality; to the vast majority of people socialism means a classless society or it means nothing at all.[36]

Orwell's vision of socialism was entirely in keeping with the egalitarian outlook explored elsewhere in this book. Inevitably, though, his emphasis on moral ideals meant that he was at odds with the iron historical certainty of his Marxist contemporaries. The mere fact that Orwell's writings aroused such opposition reveals much about political debate in the 1930s, and illustrates the distance that writers like Laski and Strachey had travelled from a social democratic form of egalitarianism.

The implausibility of gradualness

In addition to its moralism, the second charge against social democratic egalitarian strategy was its reliance on gradual rather than revolutionary change. Cripps summarised the lesson of recent events: 'Gradualness has been proved to be anything but inevitable.'[37] The difficulty with the famous Fabian slogan was that it implausibly maintained that capitalists would permit an incremental accumulation of social reforms leading to the eventual abolition of their wealth. 'A Fabian tactic of change assumes the co-operation in the task of attack of the very men to whom the system stands not merely as the protective armament of their own interests but, not less important, as the guarantee of national well-being.'[38] Gradualism was problematic in two ways. First, the Fabian strategy presumed that, against their own material interests, capitalists would consent to redistribution and voluntarily relinquish their possession of power. Viewed from a Marxist perspective, this seemed implausible, and in fact a fascist counter-reaction was considered to be a more likely outcome.[39]

Second, the Marxist argument was also that the rich were in a sense right to fear that such reforms would inhibit the efficiency of the capitalist system. Marxists argued that the parameters of a capitalist economy would only permit a very limited amount of redistribution, particularly during a period of economic depression. This view had a curious similarity to the claims of the Right. Like many conservatives, radicals like Cripps also worried that excessive taxation might undermine the incentive to produce on the part of the capitalist class: 'Just as a worker will strike if his conditions of labour are made too hard and too rigorous, so the profit-earner will "strike" if he thinks he is not getting the profit to which he is entitled.'[40] Marxists also argued that substantial tax and transfer programmes or higher wages would eventually cause a shortage of investment, and therefore prevent the necessary capital accumulation for optimal economic efficiency under capitalism.[41] A further worry was that increased social control over the economy through piecemeal socialisation or other forms of state intervention would simply open the way to a sinister and more explicit merger of capital with the state, paving the way for 'state capitalism' and ultimately fascism. The communist writer and activist Ralph Fox, for example, saw reformism as fundamentally of a piece with fascist corporatism, since 'no amount of "planning" of the Roosevelt-Hitler-MacDonald type can alter certain fundamental features of capitalism'.[42] The equation of the New Deal with the economic policies of the British National Government and Nazi Germany was a characteristic communist claim in the early 1930s.[43]

Marxists acknowledged that meaningful concessions could be won for the working class at an early stage in capitalism's historical trajectory, as it expanded and generated strong economic growth. Some of the surplus could then be directed into social insurance schemes or public services in order to retain the allegiance of the working class to the system. In this phase of economic development, it was possible for social democracy to serve as 'the licensed purveyor of the crumbs of reforms to the workers'.[44] But by the time capitalism had matured and reached its late phase of crisis and depression, as appeared to be the case in the 1930s, this strategy became altogether less plausible. Social services and welfare benefits could not be maintained during a time of economic retrenchment and were indeed the first items to be cut when public spending had to be restrained. Social democratic parties could even obtain power during this late phase of capitalism, argued Strachey, as in the case of Labour in 1929. However, economic circumstances prevented 'a programme of even liberal social reform'. Capitalism would hoist 'the social democrats into office only to impose on them the repulsive task of taking back from the workers those concessions which had been won under liberalism'.[45]

British Marxists were therefore initially sceptical of Keynesian economics and, as we have seen, regarded the New Deal as reactionary.[46] Similar doubts were also expressed by CPGB theorists in response to Hobson's theories of underconsumption and the ILP's 'living wage' campaign from the late 1920s onwards. The 'farrago of nonsense' offered by the ILP erroneously assumed that the distribution of material resources could be dealt with in isolation from the organisation of production.[47] From the Marxist perspective, the only coherent solution to the injustices of the capitalist system was to pursue its outright abolition as a mode of production. Marxist writers uncompromisingly called for 'the revolutionary expropriation of the capitalist class', and 'the abolition of private ownership, which can only be achieved by the conquest of power by the working class'.[48] The attainment of an egalitarian society was not only seen as dependent on the socialisation of production (after all, many reformists would have agreed), but also on the rapidity and ruthlessness of the transition from capitalism to socialism.

The polemical impact of this model of egalitarian strategy was undoubtedly reduced after 1935 by the Comintern's adoption of the Popular Front as the communist movement's new strategy to defeat fascism. One consequence of this decision to cultivate alliances between communist and bourgeois parties was that leading communists began to stress short-term objectives that were significantly closer to the goals of their potential social democratic partners. Although communists and communist-sympathisers remained critical of social democratic ideology at a theoretical level, their popular political appeals were more emollient in tone and organised around a defence of 'bourgeois liberties', along with demands for limited measures of socialisation, greater taxation of the rich, and higher wages and social benefits.[49] Indeed, as I will discuss in the final section of this chapter, this shift in communist tactics eventually had the unintended consequence of leading some Marxists to publicly disavow their earlier uncompromising critique of social democracy.

4.3 From rewarding merit to satisfying needs: the Marxist theory of justice

Although Marxist critics of social democracy were sceptical of the political utility of ethical claims about justice and inequality, it would be a mistake to suppose that they simply refused to engage in any philosophical discussion of these ethical ideals. It was inevitable that Marxists would have to describe the distributive mechanisms that would operate under a communist regime, and the normative principles that ought to guide them. Despite their professed distaste for the whole enterprise, the vocabulary of a normative conception of social justice was in fact present in the work of Marxist theorists and activists during the 1930s. This section examines the content of this Marxist view of social justice and argues that it differed in some respects from the principles of justice espoused by social democrats.[50]

Back in the USSR

The Marxist view of justice was influenced both by empirical accounts of distributive institutions in the Soviet Union, and by the ideological support provided for these practices in the writings of Marx, Engels, Lenin and Stalin. The most influential reference work on the Soviet Union in this period was the Webbs' monumental *Soviet Communism*, and it hardly needs saying that many of its claims now make for disturbing reading.[51] Nonetheless, the Webbs were not alone in their sympathy for Stalin's regime. Their book was merely the most systematic and expansive statement of a set of perceptions widely held on the Left (both reformist and revolutionary) and even by some on the Right.[52] In any case, the accounts of Soviet policy offered by the Webbs and other commentators provide a useful starting point for the analysis of the Marxist view of justice, since they reveal the impressions of Soviet practice that influenced more theoretical works.

One significant point noted by the Webbs was that the Soviet Union did not restrict itself purely to material incentives to secure higher productivity, but rather drew on a whole range of motives that mixed both egoistic and altruistic elements. The list was extensive, including the use of so-called 'socialist competition'; a system of public honours and shaming; the encouragement of self-criticism as a stimulus to improvement; and even the pure motive of rendering social service itself.[53] While some commentators regarded the Webbs' account of these new forms of incentive as carrying positive lessons about the viability of a socialist economy, other writers who had witnessed their implementation at first hand were sceptical of the extent to which such incentives were genuinely unconnected to material advantages, and noted their illiberal consequences.[54]

Indeed, it was generally agreed that, in spite of the USSR's apparent development of non-material incentives, recent Soviet policy had moved away from the egalitarian imperatives that had animated the early stages of the Bolshevik regime. At an ideological level, Stalin himself had explicitly disavowed wage equality as a socialist goal, while in policy terms it was known that the Soviets had started to make greater use of material incentives in order to enhance productivity. It could even be argued that, in the words of one (critical) commentator, 'the common denominator' of this greater emphasis on material rewards 'was the abandonment of "equality" – in income, living standards, social privileges, etc – as a socialist objective'.[55] Accounts of Soviet policy emphasised the growth in material inequality as a result of these new policies,[56] leaving communist sympathisers in Britain with the task of explaining the socialist purpose behind these developments. As the Labour politician John Parker wrote to Beatrice Webb, 'the most serious criticism made about the USSR among younger socialists is the growth of inequality in recent years', with the result that 'many socialists' had come to think that the Soviet Union 'has moved a long way away from socialist ideals in the sphere of incomes'.[57] How did the Webbs and other Soviet supporters account for this growth in inequality within the terms of socialist theory?

Inequality in Marxist theory
In defence of Soviet policy, the Webbs argued that the objective of wage equality had in fact never had any currency amongst Marxists, and made the familiar point that the ideal of distribution according to need was itself 'diametrically opposite to an equality among individuals, in the sense of identity either in rewards or in sacrifices'. The authoritative pronouncements of Lenin and Stalin on this matter were also given due consideration, in particular Stalin's 1934 address to the Seventeenth Congress of the Soviet Communist Party, where he denounced those who claimed that socialism entailed strict material equality as 'leftist blockheads'. In practice, both Stalin and Lenin agreed, inequality of remuneration was required to provide the necessary incentives for production.[58] For this purpose, reported the journalist Eugene Lyons, Stalin 'made the word *uravnilovka* – the

equalising of economic returns – a term of contempt and one of the major Soviet sins'.[59] However, it was claimed that economic inequality in the USSR did not result in the emergence of distinct social classes, as it did in Britain or the USA, because payments were always for services rendered, rather than simply for ownership. Variation in such payments, the Webbs suggested, need not impair the 'general condition of social equality' that was 'fundamental' to socialism and communism, since the mere fact that all income was derived from labour was sufficient to guarantee an egalitarian society.[60] As Fox put it, by introducing collective ownership of the means of production, the Soviet Union had successfully abolished 'wage slavery, by which one man is compelled to sell his labour power to another', and this was the decisive blow against class-based injustice.[61]

The writings of John Strachey illustrated the characteristic theoretical route taken from the evidence provided by the Webbs and other students of the Soviet experiment.[62] Strachey was quite explicit in his view that inequality of income was not, in itself, the most objectionable feature of capitalism.[63] Instead, Strachey argued, socialists sought to correct for the existence of exploitation; the most pressing injustice of the capitalist system was a parasitic owning class that accrued income by living on the labour of others. This meant that Strachey was relaxed about the possibility of even quite large income inequalities developing, so long as they represented a reward for more skilled or arduous work. It was important to remember that it was the 'identity in the source from which all incomes are derived, rather than any precise similarity in their amounts, which characterises a communist society'.[64]

Marxists therefore advocated the idea of proletarian self-ownership that had been criticised by earlier social democrats, and accordingly dispensed with the social democratic view of economic value as created by the co-operative interaction of the whole community (including the owners of capital). Instead, workers were portrayed as rightfully entitled to a reward proportionate to the value of their product, as measured by the quantity or quality of labour input that they contributed. This contrasted with capitalist distributive arrangements, where the worker 'produces goods greater in value than his own wages', and 'the capitalist receives a quantity of unpaid labour' forced from the workers by monopoly control over the means of production.[65] This sort of thinking led Strachey to a surprisingly moderate conclusion: 'A socialist community abolishes exploitation wholly and absolutely, even though it may decide to pay its most skilled workers twice or even ten times as much as its least skilled. For it still pays for work and for nothing else.' Or, more bluntly: 'If you are a better workman than I; if you turn out goods worth double what I turn out, you do not exploit me if you are paid double what I am paid. In the present state of economic and social development, I have no complaint against you.'[66]

The key phrase was of course the final sentence about 'the present state of economic and social development'. As we have seen, Marxists emphasised that principles of justice were relative to particular material conditions, so they did not advocate the distribution of reward in proportion to labour as a transcendent normative goal. Rather, they based their distributive objectives on Marx's *Critique of the Gotha Programme*, and employed Marx's distinction between what Lenin called a 'socialist' and a 'communist' phase to the post-revolutionary society. Famously, Marx argued that in the initial stages of the new society, socialists should still expect to confront a community that is 'in every respect, economically, morally, and intellectually, still stamped with the birth marks of the old society from whose womb it emerges'.[67] This meant that for some time material distribution would be related to the amount of labour performed by each individual, since conditions of scarcity would still exist, and the perception of fairness held by the citizenry would be conditioned by the experience of the previous economic system. However, since collective ownership would eliminate exploitation, distribution according to labour input should be seen as a significant advance from capitalism, ensuring that a 'fair' exchange of equal value takes place. Nonetheless, as Marx acknowledged, this was ultimately an unsatisfactory principle, since it allowed natural inequalities in productive capacity to influence material distribution, and ignored the differing needs of individuals. Accordingly, Marx envisaged a later stage in post-capitalist society, emerging after collective ownership has fully exploited the productive potential of modern industry, and perceptions of fairness have evolved from capitalist norms. 'Only then', wrote Marx, 'can the narrow horizon of bourgeois right be crossed in its entirety and society inscribe on its banners: from each according to his ability, to each according to his needs!'[68]

Strachey's defence of reward as proportionate to labour was therefore taken directly from Marx's dictum that 'right can never be higher than the economic structure of society'.[69] Strachey maintained that, for capitalist production to succeed, it had been necessary to motivate workers with the hope of individual enrichment. As a consequence, it was widely believed that increased individual reward was both appropriate and necessary to stimulate increased work. Accordingly, if the revolution occurred tomorrow, workers would still be accustomed to working for an individual reward, and if 'we attempted to give equal pay for unequal work, we should flout one of our most strongly held conceptions of justice'.[70] Pervasive ideological support for this conception of justice was given by the bourgeois moral ideal that workers were both entitled to earn what they produced, and deserved to do so as a measure of their productive contribution to society. Indeed, Strachey's diagnosis was that reward according to contribution was not only just in present economic conditions, but that it was also a necessary incentive to greater production. Considerations of efficiency and equity overlapped, since he saw the ideology of merit as ultimately a functional device to stimulate higher productivity. All of this led Strachey to conclude that 'enormously as man's powers of production have developed, they have not yet developed to the point at which we can dispense with varying rewards to those who make varying contributions to society'.[71] Cripps, influenced by these Marxist arguments, made the same point, suggesting that initially socialist distribution would 'give each person, in return for his contribution to the community of labour by hand or brain, a share which accords with the individual and social value of the work he performs'.[72]

In popular political argument, this analysis could become unequivocally merito-cratic. Soviet sympathisers sometimes made a virtue out of necessity by robustly defending an essentially bourgeois ideal of equal opportunity. The unequal distri-bution of income in the USSR, they argued, was fair precisely because the Soviet system offered a more satisfactory realisation of the ideal of equality of opportunity than was possible under capitalism.[73] 'Is it not clear', asked one commentator, 'that when everyone has equal opportunity, differential pay is a reward of higher industry or talent in the popular service, not of chance good fortune, and when it takes this character no one grudges its giving and everyone is proud to receive it?'[74]

In spite of this distortion of Marx's case, more sophisticated Marxists acknow-ledged the limitations of proportioning reward to labour, and ultimately hoped to realise the superior distributive ideal of distribution according to need. The Webbs saw the long-term objective of Soviet policy as:

> The establishment of a community in which every able-bodied person, without exception, would be expected to repay to the community the cost of his upbringing, as well as to contribute to the common well-being, in whatever way his faculties permitted; whilst being secured in his own share in the common product, in a form and to an amount appropriate to his particular needs.[75]

With such an ideal in mind, Strachey argued that strict egalitarianism was in any case undesirable, since an equal distribution of income would indeed take no account of differing individual needs. Strict equality, he wrote, 'is probably the vaguely defined ideal of those who feel intensely the monstrous injustices of capitalist society but have not devoted much attention to the question of what form of distribution would be "just"'.[76] As Strachey pointed out, a consequence of strict material egalitarianism was that considerable disparities would develop between nominal economic equals, because individuals have radically different needs and tastes. 'One man's health forces him to live a long way from his work; one family must have, because it contains several young children, much more house room than another; one woman is, and another is not, naturally ascetic, and so on and so on.'[77] Strachey therefore returned to the question that earlier progressives had faced when attempting to interpret the principle of needs, namely how expansive a conception of individual needs should be accommodated within a theory of justice? Should the principle be seen as an attempt to satisfy the idiosyncratic requirements of each individual? While earlier progressives had considered this objective to be impractical, Marxists were prepared to bite the bullet and aim at satisfying the most expansive understanding of needs. In their view, it was more important to focus on the creation of individual well-being than to fall into the trap of making a fetish of an equal or a minimum share of material resources.

Did distribution according to need then mean 'that everybody is to be allowed to have as much of everything as he likes, and, more extraordinary proposal still, that nobody is to be compelled to do more work than he wants to?' Strachey's answer was unequivocal: 'Yes, that is just what is meant.'[78] In contrast to the understanding of needs defended by social democratic thinkers, which concentrated on the provision of a basic set of goods required by the average individual, Strachey advocated the most elaborate version of need satisfaction as equalising individuals' capacities to realise their idiosyncratic life plans. Strachey felt that this was more than a utopian aspiration; a communist society was entirely feasible once certain technical and psychological prerequisites were accomplished. Once it was technically possible to secure material abundance, and human psychology had adjusted to the elimination of scarcity, distribution according to need would be a relatively straightforward matter. Although these prerequisites seem, to put it mildly, formidable, Strachey argued that while 'we should waste and spoil the social store of wealth if we had free access to it', it should not be assumed that 'our descendants will be as churlish or as childish as we are'.[79] While communists strove to be realistic about human nature, in the sense that they accepted in the short term the necessity of meritocratic social justice, they also argued that 'human nature' in this context should not be reified, as an eternal, immutable category that could not be altered throughout history. 'The nature of human beings is, on the contrary, invariably modified by any major change in the social system under which they live', and this included our perceptions of justice and the grounds of individual motivation.[80] Critics of this egalitarian vision, noted Emile Burns, might see it as 'a far-off, utopian ideal', and regard current Soviet practice as 'full of injustices, weaknesses and changes'. But in fact this was 'only because such critics are still encumbered with the ideas of primitive utopian socialism, before Marx made socialism into a science'.[81]

These points invite two important observations about the Marxist position on social justice. First, despite their protestations to the contrary, normative arguments about the nature of the just society were simply unavoidable in their political discourse. Marxists certainly argued that principles of justice were ultimately conditioned by economic circumstances, and consequently that there was a limit to the power of moral and political argument to alter public perceptions of social fairness. Nonetheless, their claims, for example Strachey's criticism of strict egalitarianism, did rely on transcendental principles of justice, even though they appeared unaware of this feature of their discourse. When Strachey defended the principle of needs he implied that this was in fact the most ethically desirable principle to guide material distribution; he ranked distribution according to need as a fairer principle than an equal distribution of income.[82]

Second, the Marxists' short-term preoccupation with exploitation left them with some incongruous conclusions about immediate reforms to a capitalist distribution. By concentrating particularly on the source and not the relative size of incomes, Marxists could find themselves, at least for the foreseeable future, in the unlikely position of defending large income differentials on broadly meritocratic grounds, while simultaneously demanding that all capital incomes, no matter how small, be eliminated.[83] In this respect, Laski's position in the 1930s makes an interesting contrast with other Marx-influenced writers of the same period, since the focus of his critique of capitalism was always the inequality it fostered rather than its tendency to rob the workers of the fruits of their labours. Laski preserved some of his social democratic instincts by maintaining a staunchly egalitarian attitude to income differentials, retaining some of the arguments about permissible inequalities discussed in the previous chapter.[84] The idiosyncrasy of the pure Marxist case was that in the short run writers such as Strachey were committed to a view of social justice that was potentially less egalitarian than the position of supposedly discredited writers of the old school such as Hobhouse and Tawney. Meanwhile, in the longer term, the extreme psychological and technological optimism that informed Strachey's defence of the principle of needs seemed to render this aspiration utopian, in the pejorative, Marxist sense of the term.[85]

However, these observations do not indicate that an unbridgeable gulf separated the Marxists of the 1930s from their social democratic counterparts. Stated in more general terms, their distributive objectives were similar: a more equal distribution of productive obligations; the satisfaction of individual needs; and, under present social conditions, income inequalities in so far as they promoted the common good. Differences between the two camps were over the interpretation of these broad principles and, to a lesser extent, over the Soviet Union's attempt to put these objectives into practice. In this sense, there was more philosophical common ground between Marxists and social democrats than the partisans of either faction were willing to concede.

4.4 A faith to fight for

While the materialist egalitarianism advocated by Marxist writers offered a powerful rebuttal of the idealism and rationalism of British social democracy, this insight was purchased at a high price. Although it was certainly arguable that social democrats were overly optimistic about the capacity of ethical discourse to alter political outcomes,[86] the Marxist analysis of the 1930s embodied the opposite weakness, namely a neglect of political values that led to a crude and indeed cynical treatment of crucial moral principles. The flexibility of the normative vocabulary used by Marxists, the disavowal of 'eternal, ethically universal truth', was trumpeted by its advocates as a virtue, and the rapid shifts in Soviet policy reported as vindication of this method: 'There is scarcely any ethical question that has not undergone modification, even the superficial appearance of reversal, during the headlong progress of the workers' state.'[87] As the 1930s progressed, however, this approach to ethical questions became less and less convincing. By the late 1930s, a growing number of Marxists and social democrats was questioning its illiberal implications. The ruthless consequentialism of the Communist Party in this period began to provoke considerable criticism, not only among social democrats affiliated to rival parties, but also among literary and cultural figures sympathetic to the humanism of Marxism but increasingly vociferous in their rejection of its impoverished view of morality. Books such as Orwell's *Homage to Catalonia* and Arthur Koestler's *Darkness at Noon* drew attention to the violation of individual rights that communist ethics presented as a necessary means to a much greater end; a point given further emphasis by the publication of increasingly critical accounts of the purges in the Soviet Union and the communist takeover of the

Spanish Republic.[88] As Britain moved towards war with fascism, the defence of individual liberty and parliamentary democracy became an overriding imperative for the Left, trumping earlier Marxist rhetoric that equated 'capitalist democracy' with fascism. In keeping with this new mood, the CPGB's Popular Front strategy explicitly tried to distance British communism from the 'vulgarisation' of Marxism that saw 'not a ha'porth to choose between fascism and bourgeois democracy'. On the contrary, argued Pollitt, the preservation of democracy was crucial because it granted the labour movement the freedom to pursue 'class struggle'.[89] But despite this important modification of communist discourse, the much-trumpeted flexibility of Marxist theory was made to look preposterous by the subsequent tactical somersaults of the CPGB, as it was forced to follow the Moscow line on the Molotov–Ribbentrop pact in 1939 and, in spite of the Party's previous endorsement of an armed struggle with Germany, to oppose the War as an imperialist conflict.[90] These events served as a catalyst for a more general debate about the relationship between Marxist theory and ethics.

The priority of liberty
The ground for this discussion had already been prepared. From the mid-1930s onwards, leading social democrats such as Clement Attlee, Hugh Dalton, Evan Durbin, and Douglas Jay responded to the Marxist turn with robust statements of their own political philosophy. As the young Labour politician Richard Crossman put it, the resurgence of Marxist theory had forced mainstream Labour 'to think out its own positive philosophy and to argue not with the card vote but with its head'.[91] The main burden of these writings was that Marxists came dangerously close to claiming that individual freedom and democratic procedures could legitimately be sacrificed in order to obtain a more egalitarian society. While it was certainly common ground between the two camps that inequality 'makes a mockery of freedom', since 'we have no freedom to spend money we have not got',[92] Marxist theory could be taken to imply not merely that economic coercion was as morally troubling as legal coercion, but that in fact economic coercion was a more serious violation of individual liberty than legal regulations forbidding freedom of speech or association. Some Marxist rhetoric simply dismissed the classic British 'bourgeois freedoms' as irrelevant to the workers or saw them as rights that would have to be temporarily suspended in order to obtain and stabilise proletarian rule. If this view was accepted, then it might well seem acceptable to trade-off a loss in terms of legal freedoms in order to gain greater equality and hence economic freedom. Something like this argument was indeed used by British Marxists in order to defend Bolshevik political strategy and the Soviet regime from liberal critics.[93] In reply, social democrats maintained that a respect for individual rights and democratic procedures could not be sacrificed for these purposes, for to do so would simply create a fresh set of inequalities and injustices.

The most sustained argument along these lines was given by the socialist economist and Labour politician Evan Durbin in his celebrated book *The Politics of Democratic Socialism*. He saw the objective of socialists as 'social justice', which he defined as the greatest feasible combination of liberty and equality, with the protection of a set of basic liberties taking priority over attempts to enforce greater equality. 'The minimum content of the idea of social justice', he wrote, 'is the combination in one society of political liberty . . . with economic equality'.[94] While it was 'perfectly possible for persons to prefer equality in the distribution of wealth to political liberty', and to 'advocate a political terror in order to make the distribution of income less unequal', this attitude did not in any way 'touch the problem of constructing a just society'.

> Economic equality can be fully achieved, and social justice remain as far away as ever, because one kind of injustice has replaced another – because one kind of privilege (political) has been substituted for another (economic). The problem of a just society is not the single problem of economic equality, but the much more difficult problem of achieving simultaneously in one society both liberty and equality.[95]

Social democrats therefore offered a strict defence of 'bourgeois' liberties and stipulated that democratic procedures took priority over any substantive outcomes, even greater economic equality, for while 'social justice is the spire and the crown of the human habitation', democracy was the only possible 'foundation and corner-stone of the temple'.[96]

Marxists and social democrats

Some on the radical Left were hostile to these defences of civil liberties and democratic procedures, and Durbin was singled out for particular censure for reverting to MacDonaldism and 'red baiting'.[97] However, other Marxists became increasingly sympathetic to the social democratic position. The intellectual climate perceptibly shifted in the late 1930s; the arrival of war and the Nazi–Soviet pact led a number of prominent converts to Marxism to echo some of the social democratic concerns about Marxist ideology. This was particularly noticeable in the Left Book Club, which began to distinguish itself from the CPGB.[98] Gollancz himself had become increasingly uncomfortable with the intellectual censorship practised by the Communist Party,[99] and he coupled this with the ideological concern that Marxist theory unduly neglected the moral ideals at the base of socialism: '*Why* in heaven's name are we on the progressive side of politics? It is because we want men to be free: it is because we want every man to be able to realise the potentialities of which humanity is capable.'[100] Elements of the social democratic critique of Marxism could be discerned in his remarks, and indeed Gollancz now accepted that attention should be devoted to the normative dimension of socialist thought: 'We proclaim that it is good for men to be free and equal and brothers and *that* is why we desire to establish socialism.'[101]

Gollancz's interventions created opposition from more orthodox Marxists,[102] and generated broadly supportive comments from a number of activists and writers, including Orwell, Laski and Strachey.[103] Gollancz subsequently edited a book devoted to attacking the communist line on the War, *The Betrayal of the Left*, which collected various essays originally published in *Left News* on this topic. Gollancz contributed a new epilogue on political morality, which criticised Marx himself for 'appearing to banish from his examination of capitalism any moral considerations whatsoever', and consequently leading his followers to focus on capitalism's inefficiency or inevitable historical demise rather than the basic fact 'that it is wicked'.[104] Indeed, one contributor to the debate in *Left News* pointed out that this substitution of historical inevitability for moral principle committed orthodox Marxists to a quite peculiar characterisation of 'right or wrong'. For Marxists, 'the "right" thing to do was to understand how society was actually changing, namely, toward a victory of the proletariat over the capitalists, and to work for that victory'. In short, 'what was right was to spot which way the cat was going to jump and to give it as hard a kick as possible in that direction'.[105]

Similar points were also made, sketchily, by Laski and, at greater length, by Strachey. Laski's wartime writings contained the same mixture of liberal and Marxist ideas evident in his pre-war work, but he did return to certain of his earlier, associationalist themes, once again becoming engaged by normative debates, particularly the difficulties for individual freedom posed by economic planning.[106] Strachey was quite explicit about his disenchantment with Marxism. In the course of his enthusiastic support for the Popular Front, Strachey had already begun to attenuate the polarised understanding of the differences between Marxists and social democrats that had dominated his earlier writings.[107] This had in turn led him to become interested in Keynesian economic theory, and the possibilities it opened up for gradualist social reform.[108] While formerly he had 'put with disturbing precision the "either-or" which the strict Marxist loves', he now argued that there was in fact 'another method; his "either-or" was a mistake'.[109] The behaviour of the CPGB at the beginning of the War finally shattered Strachey's faith in the Soviet Union and, in a similar fashion to Gollancz, he reconsidered his earlier dismissal of ethical ideals.[110] As Strachey made clear in his book *A Faith to Fight For*, he was still convinced that Marxism had uncovered certain fundamental truths about the course of history, and so remained in this sense an advocate of scientific socialism.[111] Nonetheless, he now appreciated that normative principles were also essential to specify more precisely the objectives that socialists were aiming for, and consequently to motivate and move the mass of the population in a leftwards direction. In particular, Strachey thought it vital that the War was waged in the name of certain strong moral ideals, to be counter-posed to the immorality of the Nazi regime. This was the 'faith to fight for' referred to in the title of the book.[112] While previously Strachey had suggested a straightforward causal line from economics to ideology, he now saw a mutual interpenetration of material circumstances and political beliefs, with both sides influencing each other. Ideas were in fact 'an integral part of the rest of reality, growing naturally and powerfully out of human development itself'. They were therefore both a part of, and an indispensable agent for carrying forward, that development. This theoretical adjustment opened the way for his new emphasis on morality, but also enabled him to retain certain materialist convictions, which arguably remained with him even in his later social democratic writings.[113] Like Laski, Strachey had become both a Marxist and a social democrat.

In spite of their earlier criticisms of Orwell for passing off a thin ethical idealism as socialism, many prominent Marxists, particularly those who had converted from social democracy in the first place, began the 1940s by shifting towards a more moralised political discourse. An obvious conclusion, then, is that the 1940s witnessed the chastening of radical Marxism and the return of ideological momentum to social democracy. There is certainly some truth in this, but in the study of this period above all others it is important not to be lured into unreflective social democratic triumphalism. It should also be noted that Marxism persisted as an important ideological resource for the British Left, in large measure due to the pioneering efforts of the Marxists of the 1930s. As I will discuss in later chapters, elements of the post-war Labour Left and the self-styled 'New Left' were to draw moral and theoretical inspiration from the Left Book Club and its insurgent challenge to orthodox social democracy. It appeared to these later movements that writers such as Laski and Strachey had raised an important issue for egalitarian strategy that had not been adequately addressed by social democrats, namely the possibility that there were clear structural limits to the gradual pursuit of equality in a broadly capitalist society. The next chapter will pick up this theme and explain why social democrats in this period remained unmoved by this objection.

Notes

1 D. Howell, *British Social Democracy: A Study in Development and Decay* (London, second edition, 1980), 60.

2 The authoritative study of the 1931 crisis is P. Williamson, *National Crisis and National Government* (Cambridge, 1992). On its impact on the radical Left, see B. Pimlott, *Labour and the Left in the 1930s* (Cambridge, 1977), 9–20, 41–67; Howell, *British Social Democracy*, 38–41, 54–6; MacIntyre, *Proletarian Science*, 184–8; N. Riddell, *Labour in Crisis: The Second Labour Government, 1929–31* (Manchester, 1999), 199–220.

3 H. Laski, 'Some implications of the crisis', *PQ*, 2 (1931), 467.

4 On the depression and its impact, see A. Thorpe, *Britain in the 1930s* (Oxford, 1992), 60–126; J. Stevenson and C. Cook, *Britain in the Depression* (London, 1994), 40–109; McKibbin, *Classes and Cultures*, 111–14, 151–60.

5 J. Strachey, *The Theory and Practice of Socialism* (London, 1936), 459.

6 On the journey of British Marxism to this high water mark, see MacIntyre, *Proletarian Science*, 93–105 and *passim*; J. Ree, *Proletarian Philosophers: Problems in Socialist Culture in Britain 1900–40* (Oxford, 1984), 23–78 and *passim*; E. A. Roberts, *The Anglo-Marxists: A Study in Ideology and Culture* (Lanham, MD, 1997), 55–102. For the social context, see R. McKibbin, 'Why was there no Marxism in Great Britain?', in his *Ideologies of Class*, 1–41.

7 N. Wood, *Communism and British Intellectuals* (London, 1959); G. Wersky, *The Visible College* (London, 1978); M. Heinemann, 'The People's Front and the intellectuals', in J. Fryth (ed.), *British Fascism and the Popular Front* (London, 1985), 157–86.

8 M. Newman, *John Strachey* (Manchester, 1989), 1–25, 48–55; N. Thompson, *John Strachey: An Intellectual Biography* (London, 1993), 10–73; Kramnick and Sheerman, *Harold Laski*, 210–19, 226–35, 259–62, 309–11, 359–63.

9 S. Webb and B. Webb, *Soviet Communism: A New Civilisation* (London, second edition, 1941 [1935]). The Left Book Club apparently sold ten thousand copies of this 1,200-page book (G. B. Neavill, 'Victor Gollancz and the Left Book Club', *Library Quarterly*,

41 (1971), 206). Laski was in fact one of the few who publicly criticised the Webbs' benign view of Stalinism: see his review in *PQ*, 9 (1938), 130–3. For an excellent discussion of this episode in the career of the Webbs, see Morgan, *Webbs and Soviet Communism*.

10 J. A. Hobson, 'The economics for a People's Front', *LM*, January 1937, 20.

11 E.g. J. Strachey, *The Coming Struggle for Power* (London, 1932), 138.

12 E. Wilson, 'Marxist history', *NS Autumn Books Supplement*, 15.10.1932, v–vi.

13 R. Palme Dutt, 'Notes of the month: the great turning point', *LM*, October 1931, 597.

14 Strachey, *Coming Struggle*, 174.

15 See section 2.3. Indeed, the influence of *The Acquisitive Society* can be seen even in Laski's Marxist phase. See his *Democracy in Crisis* (London, 1933), 19, 61–5, 179–82; *The State in Theory and in Practice* (London, 1935), 309; *Parliamentary Government in England* (London, 1950 [1938]), 38–41; *Faith, Reason and Civilisation* (London, 1944), 192–3.

16 H. Laski, 'Review of *The Acquisitive Society*', *LN*, September 1937, 514.

17 Laski, 'Review of *The Acquisitive Society*', 515.

18 Laski, 'Review of *The Acquisitive Society*', 515. Strachey was more dismissive of Tawney, criticising *The Acquisitive Society* for lacking any 'comprehension of historical forces': *What Are We to Do?* (London, 1938), 119, fn. 1.

19 H. Laski, 'Philip Snowden', *NS*, 8.9.1934, 300.

20 R. Palme Dutt, 'Notes of the month: the ILP and revolution', *LM*, September 1932, 535; H. Laski, 'Review of *Post-War History of the British Working Class*', *LN*, June 1937, 407; R. Palme Dutt, *Socialism and the Living Wage* (London, 1927), 26, see also 66.

21 T. A. Jackson, *Dialectics: The Logic of Marxism and Its Critics* (London, 1936), 445, Jackson's emphasis.

22 J. F. Horrabin, 'The class struggle', in L. Anderson Fenn *et al.*, *Problems of Socialist Transition* (London, 1934), 173–4.

23 S. Spender, *Forward From Liberalism* (London, 1937), 83.

24 S. Cripps, 'The future of the Labour Party', *NS*, 3.9.1932, 256; on Cripps's political journey, see P. Clarke, *The Cripps Version* (London, 2002), 52–67.

25 Laski, *State in Theory*, 164; also his *Parliamentary Government*, 194.

26 Laski, *State in Theory*, 168.

27 Spender, *Forward*, 83.

28 Laski, *Democracy in Crisis*, 158–9. This was also Strachey's view: see his *Theory and Practice*, 90–2; and his *Why You Should Be a Socialist* (London, 1938), 40–1.

29 P. Stansky and W. Abrahams, *Orwell: The Transformation* (London, 1994 [1979]), 176–83; R. Dudley Edwards, *Victor Gollancz: A Biography* (London, 1987), 246–8; B. Crick, *George Orwell: A Life* (Harmondsworth, 1992), 309–11; Kramnick and Sheerman, *Harold Laski*, 367–8.

30 H. Miles, 'Coal and caste', *NS*, 1.5.1937, 724.

31 G. Orwell, *The Road to Wigan Pier* [1937], *GO 5*, 205.

32 V. Gollancz, 'Foreword', in *The Road to Wigan Pier*, *GO 5*, 216–25, quote at 224; H. Laski, 'Review of *The Road to Wigan Pier*', *LN*, March 1937, 275–6. See also H. Pollitt, 'Mr Orwell will have to try again', *Daily Worker*, 17.3.1937, 7; J. Lewis, 'The groups month by month', *LN*, May 1937, 352; 'Ex-public school, ex-university', 'Forward from Wigan Pier', *LN*, May 1937, 379–80.

33 Stansky and Abrahams judge that Gollancz's criticism of Orwell was fair, but they do not consider the materialist understanding of moral values that animated this Marxist critique: see their *Orwell*, 181.

34 Dudley Edwards, *Victor Gollancz*, 244–6.

35 G. Orwell, *Homage to Catalonia* [1938], *GO 6*, 2–4.

36 Orwell, *Homage*, *GO 6*, 83–4.

37 Cripps, 'Future', 256.

38 Laski, *State in Theory*, 279.

39 K. Martin, 'A gentlemanly revolution', *NS*, 25.2.1933, 225–6; K. Martin, 'Fascism and Mr Shaw', *NS*, 24.2.1934, 256–7; H. Laski, 'Review of *The Labour Party in Perspective*', *LN*, August 1937, 465; H. Laski, 'Marxism dissected', *NS*, 26.4.1941, 442.

40 S. Cripps, *Why This Socialism?* (London, 1934), 97; also E. Burns, *The Only Way Out* (London, 1932), 38–40.

41 J. Strachey, *The Nature of Capitalist Crisis* (London, 1935), 248–53.

42 R. Fox, *Communism and a Changing Civilisation* (London, 1935), 38, also 14–16. See also Jackson, *Dialectics*, 334–5; E. Roll, 'The decline of liberal economics', *Modern Quarterly*, 1 (1938), 87–90.

43 E.g. R. Palme Dutt, 'Notes of the month: the world economic conference and war', *LM*, August 1933, 477–80. Some Labour socialists had similar reservations about the New Deal: H. Pelling, *America and the British Left* (London, 1956), 139–44.

44 R. Palme Dutt, 'Notes of the month: the fight for socialism and the daily struggle', *LM*, February 1933, 76.

45 Strachey, *Coming Struggle*, 306; also Laski, *State in Theory*, 271; his *Parliamentary Government*, 44–5.

46 Burns, *Only Way Out*, 40–50, 59–61, 73–84; Strachey, *Nature of Capitalist Crisis*, 40–55.

47 Palme Dutt, 'The ILP and revolution', 544; Palme Dutt, *Socialism*, 127–35 and *passim*; MacIntyre, *Proletarian Science*, 162–4.

48 H. Rathbone, 'Left-wing socialism and communism: money and the ILP', *LM*, November 1931, 700; R. Palme Dutt, 'Notes of the month', *LM*, January 1931, 8.

49 See e.g. H. Pollitt, 'Raise the standard of united advance', 28, 32; 'Political report to the Fifteenth Congress of the Communist Party', 82–5; 'Will it be war?', 140; all in his *Selected Articles and Speeches, Volume 2: 1936–9* (London, 1954).

50 My account in this section is indebted to the important philosophical discussion of these questions in N. Geras, 'The controversy about Marx and justice', *NLR*, No. 150, 1985, 47–85; S. Lukes, *Marxism and Morality* (Oxford, 1985), 48–61; G. A. Cohen, *Self-ownership, Freedom and Equality* (Cambridge, 1995).

51 In stressing the importance of the Webbs' book, I differ from Roberts, *Anglo-Marxists*, 73, who suggests that *Soviet Communism* was 'out of step' with communist orthodoxy and thus 'useless' for the purpose of 'spreading party views'. Roberts underestimates the propaganda value of prestigious figures such as the Webbs writing sympathetically about the Soviet Union: see e.g. R. Palme Dutt's enthusiastic 'Notes of the month: a landmark of the British labour movement', *LM*, January 1936, 3–26.

52 See the effusive reviews by the following luminaries: W. Beveridge, 'Soviet Communism', *PQ*, 7 (1936), 346–67; A. C. Pigou, 'The Webbs on Soviet Communism', *EJ*, 46 (1936), 88–97; G. B. Shaw, 'The Webbs' masterpiece', *LN*, August 1937, 467. For useful discussion of attitudes towards the Soviet Union at this time, see J. Callaghan, *Rajani Palme Dutt: A Study in British Stalinism* (London, 1993), 169–72.

53 Webb and Webb, *Soviet Communism*, 734–85.

54 Enthusiasts included Spender, *Forward*, 265–9; and A. C. Pigou, *Socialism Versus Capitalism* (London, 1937), 99–101. More critical were B. Wootton, *Plan or No Plan* (London, 1934), 333–7; and E. Lyons, *Assignment in Utopia* (London, 1938), 208–10.

55 Lyons, *Assignment*, 419.

56 E.g. E. Burns, *Capitalism, Communism and the Transition* (London, 1933), 236–44; Wootton, *Plan or No Plan*, 261–4; Lyons, *Assignment*, 419–23; W. Miller, *How the Russians Live* (London, 1942), 20–7.

57 J. Parker to B. Webb, 29.7.1941, Passfield Papers 2/4/M/31, 2.

58 Webb and Webb, *Soviet Communism*, 701–2, quote at 702.

59 Lyons, *Assignment*, 421.

60 Webb and Webb, *Soviet Communism*, 702–3, quote at 703.

61 Fox, *Communism*, 97.

62 Despite later attempts to distance himself from the Webbs, Strachey relied heavily on their picture of life in the Soviet Union: see his *Theory and Practice*, 49; H. Thomas, *John Strachey* (London, 1973), 157–8; Thompson, *John Strachey*, 233–5.

63 Strachey, *Theory and Practice*, 93–4.

64 Strachey, *Coming Struggle*, 344; his *Why You Should Be a Socialist*, 72.

65 Fox, *Communism*, 1.

66 Strachey, *Why You Should Be a Socialist*, 72. For a similar defence of material inequality, see Webb and Webb, *Soviet Communism*, 1206–11.

67 Marx, *Critique*, 614. Engels's critique of egalitarianism was also influential in this period: see his *Anti-Dühring* [1894], in *The Collected Works of Karl Marx and Frederick Engels Volume 25* (London, 1987), 95–9.

68 Marx, *Critique*, 615.

69 Marx, *Critique*, 615.

70 Strachey, *Theory and Practice*, 108.

71 Strachey, *Theory and Practice*, 109; see also his *Coming Struggle*, 342.

72 Cripps, *Why This Socialism?*, 17. For other examples of this use of *Critique of the Gotha Programme*, see e.g. Jackson, *Dialectics*, 386; H. Pollitt, 'Salute to the Soviet Union' [1937], in his *Selected Articles and Speeches Volume 2*, 47–8; P. Sloan, 'The new Soviet constitution', *LM*, January 1937, 50; E. Burns, *Introduction to Marxism* (London, 1952 [1939]), 43–4.

73 This was also a widespread ideological strategy within communist countries themselves: see G. Marshall *et al.*, *Against the Odds? Social Class and Social Justice in Industrial Countries* (Oxford, 1997), 222–8.

74 I. Montagu, 'The USSR month by month: riches', *LN*, September 1936, 96. Meritocratic themes were also emphasised by many of the scientists who converted to Marxism in this period, some of whom believed that genetically-based inequalities justified hierarchical social organisation: J. B. S. Haldane, 'The inequality of man', in his *The Inequality of Man and Other Essays* (Harmondsworth, 1937 [1932]), 22–35; Wersky, *Visible College*, 196–7, 205–11; Ree, *Proletarian Philosophers*, 85–6.

75 Webb and Webb, *Soviet Communism*, 604.

76 Strachey, *Theory and Practice*, 109.

77 Strachey, *Theory and Practice*, 110.

78 Strachey, *Theory and Practice*, 112; also his *Coming Struggle*, 341–2; P. Sloan, *Soviet Democracy* (London, 1937), 280–2.

79 Strachey, *Theory and Practice*, 115.

80 Strachey, *Theory and Practice*, 107, 116; also Webb and Webb, *Soviet Communism*, 1019–21; Burns, *Introduction to Marxism*, 45–6.

81 Burns, *Capitalism*, 242.

82 This point has been made about Marx's own distributive maxims: see Geras, 'Controversy', 58–61.

83 A criticism put by D. Jay, *The Socialist Case* (London, 1938), 130–1.

84 Laski, *State in Theory*, 35–6, 74–6, 297; his *Parliamentary Government*, 47–8; Ellison, *Egalitarian Thought*, 6–7.

85 It should be acknowledged that Marxists of this period adhered to a particularly impractical interpretation of the second phase of communist society, and that other construals of Marx's position are certainly possible: see J. Elster, *Making Sense of Marx* (Cambridge, 1985), 229–33.

86 See e.g. the robust (but non-Marxist) argument along these lines in J. Goldthorpe, *Social Mobility and Class Structure in Britain* (Oxford, 1987), 28; and in his 'A response', in J. Clark *et al.* (eds), *John H. Goldthorpe: Consensus and Controversy* (London, 1990), 402–3.

87 Montagu, 'The USSR month by month: riches', 96.

88 See Lukes, *Marxism and Morality*, 117–38. Strachey later sympathetically assessed this anti-Stalinist 'literature of reaction' in his *The Strangled Cry and Other Unparliamentary Papers* (London, 1962), 11–77.

89 Pollitt, 'Political report', in his *Selected Articles and Speeches Volume 2: 1936–9*, 82–5, quotes at 83.

90 K. Morgan, *Against Fascism and War: Ruptures and Continuities in British Communist Politics, 1935–41* (Manchester, 1989), 85–253; A. Thorpe, *The British Communist Party and Moscow 1920–43* (Manchester, 2000), 256–76.

91 R. H. S. Crossman, 'The faith of British socialism', *NS*, 6.4.1940, 466.

92 H. Dalton, *Practical Socialism for Britain* (London, 1935), 320; see also C. R. Attlee, *The Labour Party in Perspective* (London, 1937), 141–2.

93 E.g. Palme Dutt, 'Landmark', 18–20; Jackson, *Dialectics*, 507–9, 512–14; Sloan, *Soviet*, 256–73.

94 E. Durbin, *The Politics of Democratic Socialism* (London, 1940), 215.

95 Durbin, *Politics*, 270; also E. Durbin, 'Why I'm not a Marxist', *Daily Herald*, 16.2.1937, 8; a reply to J. Strachey, 'Why I am a Marxist', in the same issue.

96 Durbin, *Politics*, 273. Durbin was influenced by Reginald Bassett's *Essentials of Parliamentary Democracy* (London, 1935), which strongly criticised Laski's analysis of democracy: see 97–118, 182–215. See also Durbin's 'Democracy and socialism in Great Britain' [1935], in E. Durbin, *Problems of Economic Planning* (London, 1949), 30–4. For similar defences of democracy, see R. H. Tawney, 'Christianity and the social revolution', *NS*, 9.11.1935, 684; Attlee, *Labour Party*, 148–52; Jay, *Socialist Case*, 356; H. Morrison, 'Social change – peaceful or violent?', *PQ*, 10 (1939), 4–9; G. Orwell, *The Lion and the Unicorn: Socialism and the English Genius* [1941], *GO 12*, 410; E. Bevin, *The Job to Be Done* (London, 1942), 117. As with some other aspects of the egalitarian thought discussed in this book, a parallel can be made here between the points made by Durbin and Rawls's theory of justice: compare with Rawls, *Theory*, 54–5, 214–20, 474–80.

97 F. Horrabin, 'MacDonald's ghost returns', *Tribune*, 19.4.1940, 18–19; A. Hutt, 'Philistine gospel', *LM*, April 1940, 251.

98 Morgan, *Against Fascism*, 254–72.

99 V. Gollancz to H. Pollitt, 16.1.1939, Gollancz Papers MSS.157/3/DOC/1/1.

100 V. Gollancz, 'Slow down', *LN*, January 1940, 1416–17, Gollancz's emphasis.

101 V. Gollancz, 'Recapture the spirit of socialism', *LN*, June 1941, 1743–6, quote at 1746, Gollancz's emphasis.

102 E.g. the reply of one anonymous writer, who maintained that morality was ultimately determined by class position and that socialist 'oughts' 'will be determined by the interests of the proletariat'. 'A Marxist', 'Socialism and ethics (III)', *LN*, April 1941, 1696–701, quote at 1698.

103 H. Laski, 'The climate of intellectual freedom', March 1940, 1450–2; J. Strachey, 'The struggle for power', December 1940, 1575–80; G. Orwell, 'Our opportunity', January 1941, 1608–12; J. Strachey, 'Acland v. Strachey: (ii) John Strachey writes', February 1941, 1635–6 (all in *LN*). See also E. Muir, 'Communications', June 1940, 1507–8; R. Acland, 'Moral motives decide', February 1941, 1633–5; A. Tustin, 'Socialism and ethics (I)', March 1941, 1656–61; O. Stapledon, 'Socialism and ethics (II)', March 1941, 1661–5; 'Socialism and ethics (IV): correspondence', April 1941, 1701–6; J. MacMurray, 'Socialism and ethics (V)', May 1941, 1725–31 (all in *LN*).

104 V. Gollancz, 'Epilogue on political morality', in V. Gollancz (ed.), *The Betrayal of the Left* (London, 1941), 273; see also his *More For Timothy* (London, 1953), 27–8.

105 Stapledon, 'Socialism and ethics (II)', 1661.

106 H. Laski, *Reflections on the Revolution of Our Time* (London, 1943), 305–67; his *Will Planning Restrict Our Freedom?* (Cheam, 1945); Brooke, *Labour's War*, 283–6.

107 J. Strachey, 'We are all "reformists" now', *NFRB Quarterly*, summer 1938, 14–19.

108 See J. Strachey, *A Programme for Progress* (London, 1940), which also expressed sympathy for the New Deal. Compare with his withering remarks on Keynes in *Coming Struggle*, 114–30, 200–5. On the influence of Keynes on Strachey and others, see section 5.2.

109 K. Martin, 'A social democrat', *NS*, 30.3.1940, 436.

110 Thomas, *John Strachey*, 182–221; Thompson, *John Strachey*, 148–83.

111 J. Strachey, *A Faith to Fight For* (London, 1941), 38–46.

112 Strachey, *Faith*, 154.

113 J. Strachey, 'Socialism and ethics (VII)', *LN*, June 1941, 1751; J. Strachey, *Contemporary Capitalism* (London, 1956), 12–13; see also Newman, *John Strachey*, 159. I return to Strachey's vestigial Marxism in section 6.3.

5

Social justice and economic efficiency

5.1 Introduction: enter the economists

Surveying the ideology of the British Left in 1933, a young economist called Hugh Gaitskell identified an important philosophical and strategic cleavage between two different types of socialist. For Marxists, he wrote, 'the transition to socialism' was 'not something which can be effected by the mere appeal to reason', being instead 'an inevitable process of historical development'. In contrast, for the 'mild tempered evolutionary idealists' of 'the British labour movement', it was assumed 'that man is a rational being, free to choose his own future. He is asked to select this programme, this line of development rather than any other.'[1]

As the previous chapter demonstrated, these divergent views had in fact led radicals of the 1930s to mount an important challenge to social democratic egalitarian strategy. This chapter shifts the focus back from the Marxist tradition to the 'mild tempered evolutionary idealists' and considers the arguments social democrats of the 1930s used to promote egalitarian objectives. As Gaitskell observed, such social democrats adhered to a voluntaristic rationalism that set them apart from the more deterministic Marxists, and in this respect social democratic political thought of the 1930s and 40s was similar to earlier egalitarian discourse. The principles of social justice and proposals for social reform developed by the new liberals and early socialists remained crucial to reformists of this period. Familiar arguments grounded on principles of equal opportunity, function, need and incentive therefore remained important ideological resources after 1931.[2] A detailed discussion of this continuity in social democratic political theory would inevitably involve the repetition of many points already made in earlier chapters, so for the purposes of this chapter I will concentrate instead on the innovations in the social democratic egalitarianism of the 1930s and 40s. In particular, this chapter shows that an important theme was now given greater prominence and theoretical sophistication in the Left's egalitarian thought: the claim that equality could be reconciled with, and indeed enhance, economic efficiency.

It would be an overstatement to say that efficiency-based arguments for equality were absent from earlier progressive thought. As we have seen, some egalitarians, most notably Hobson, had indeed argued that redistribution would enhance economic growth or promote 'national efficiency'. However, Hobson's arguments lacked authoritative support from the economics profession and progressives themselves generally saw efficiency arguments as secondary to the ethical attractions of a community of equals. In contrast, social democrats of the 1930s and 40s were able to draw more easily on the intellectual prestige of academic economics, and gave greater attention to arguing that a more equal distribution of wealth would have beneficial consequences for both maximising economic output and achieving a more efficient use of material resources.

This shift in social democratic thought was prompted by two developments. First, the political circumstances made philosophical discussion seem less important than technically sophisticated proposals for social and economic policy. Stung by the disastrous showing of Labour in government during the 1920s, advocates of the gradualist road to equality drew a different lesson from the Marxist catastrophists. Rather than seeing the failure of Labour in power as a definitive lesson about the inability of gradual reform to secure any meaningful concessions from capital, social democrats regarded it as an indication that the Left had failed to examine seriously the complex, detailed practicalities involved in implementing their normative ideals.[3] The demise of capitalism, observed the socialist economist, and future politician, Douglas Jay, was best engineered 'not by fanaticism and pseudo-metaphysical jargon', but by those who had 'a clear, balanced and rational understanding of the economic forces that confront them. Otherwise injustice will merely be followed by chaos.'[4] In this spirit, Evan Durbin responded to the writings of the Marxist theoreticians by commenting: 'Intellectual socialists would serve the cause they profess to love more truly if they gave their minds to the concrete detail of good government instead of to the advocacy of extremism and violence.' He added that democratic socialists required 'a religious conversion to, and a rising passion for, detail'. One encouraging sign of such a conversion in the ranks of the British Labour Party, argued Durbin, was that party publications were 'increasingly complex and technical – and increasingly dull to the general reader for that reason'.[5]

However, this shift in emphasis was itself influenced by a second factor: a greater recognition by progressives that sheer moral argument was insufficient to legitimate egalitarian policies in the eyes of hostile bureaucratic and political elites. While the Marxist response to this predicament had been to downplay the importance of rational discussion altogether, social democrats argued that one of the key ideological weapons in the hands of their opponents, the language of neo-classical economic theory, was actually ripe for appropriation for egalitarian ends. Economic theory was transformed during the 1930s by a remarkable series of theoretical innovations, many of which had quite direct implications for public policy. This latter category included Keynes's *General Theory*; the reformulation of the principles of welfare economics; and the debate about allocative calculations under socialism.[6] Overall, the economic theory of this decade was characterised by such astonishing intellectual fertility that it is said to have generated 'the most profound, multi-faceted change in the very nature of economic thought since the marginal revolution in the 1870s'.[7] These startling changes in the academic economics of this period were matched by a growing conviction among political and intellectual elites that economists should play a more important role in the formation of public policy, and the government itself first employed professional economists on a systematic basis during the 1940s.[8] The impact of redistribution on economic prosperity was increasingly open to assessment by a body of external experts who purportedly owed no allegiance to political faction and who could analyse economic phenomena using a distinct set of techniques that were inaccessible to non-specialists. The support of economists and the particular theoretical discourse under their control was therefore an important way of diffusing objections to redistributive policy proposals and of signalling the plausibility of the socialist cause more generally.

The importance of economics to political debate was confirmed by the intellectual trajectory of a new generation of social democratic theorists and politicians. Just as the 1930s saw the emergence of the first university-trained generation of Marxists, an equally notable transition was occurring within the ranks of reformists. The most influential of the younger exponents of gradualist socialism were no longer political theorists or interdisciplinary chameleons who migrated between philosophy, economics and sociology. Instead, the new generation were first and foremost professional economists who adhered to many of the norms and practices of that discipline. These left-wing economists aimed to introduce what they saw as much needed economic rigour to the motley collection of reform schemes, economic heterodoxy and idealistic rhetoric that had previously provided ideological fuel for the Left. The most famous and politically powerful of these economists were the future Labour politicians Evan Durbin, Hugh Gaitskell and Douglas Jay, but others, such as the academics James Meade, Joan Robinson and Barbara Wootton, also deserve recognition. The dominant influence of economics in this period was such that even G. D. H. Cole found himself reinvented as an unlikely academic economist, and he played a considerable role in the organisation and programme of the New Fabian Research Bureau (NFRB), the engine of much of the detailed work on economic policy undertaken by the Left in this period.[9]

In essence, the egalitarian social democrats of this period tried to combine the traditional ethical idealism of writers such as Tawney with the economic theory of Marshall and Keynes. This chapter examines this ideological hybrid in three main stages. The first section discusses the influence of Keynes on egalitarian thought, and the use that could be made of his theories to justify redistribution as a policy compatible with productive efficiency. The second section considers the impact of welfare economics on social democrats, as demonstrated by their adoption of utilitarian arguments for equality. The third section examines the Left's treatment of economic incentives in this period and argues that earlier progressive beliefs about the development of motives of social service became less important to certain egalitarians in the 1930s. The chapter concludes by discussing the extent to which the experience of the Second World War both popularised the aspirations of egalitarians, and led them to misperceive the strength of their position.

5.2 Was Keynes an egalitarian?

It would be misleading to label the progressive economists active in political debate in this period as straightforward 'Keynesians'. Some, for instance Durbin, were sceptical of Keynes's theories, and saw themselves as distinctively socialist in their prescriptions for economic policy.[10] Nonetheless, it is fair to say that Keynes did set the agenda for theoretical discussion among left-wing economists, even if some of them ultimately disagreed with his conclusions. It is therefore worth investigating Keynes's own views about social justice, and considering the extent to which 'Keynesian' economics offered a vehicle for advancing egalitarian ends, particularly when contrasted with the traditional socialist analysis offered by economists such as Durbin.

The political affiliations of Keynes have of course been the subject of considerable debate, and there are two rival interpretations of his thinking about social justice. Peter Clarke has argued that Keynes was a new liberal, in that he rejected both laissez-faire economics and socialism, and instead advocated limited state intervention to advance social justice and economic efficiency. Clarke has described Keynes as fundamentally left of centre, in favour of 'the experimental use of the state to achieve the ends of social justice', and convinced that even when capitalism 'functioned well, it was unfair'.[11] In contrast, Robert Skidelsky and Michael Freeden have suggested that Keynes should be seen as inhabiting the political centre, since he was more of an individualist than the organicist new liberals, and showed little interest in the redistribution of wealth. According to this view, Keynes 'did not object (or object strongly) to the existing social order on the ground that it unfairly or unjustly distributed life-chances'; he only worried 'that *laissez-faire* did not protect existing economic and social "norms"'.[12] This verdict accords with the perceptions of earlier commentators, for example Keynes's friend Kingsley Martin, who claimed that Keynes 'disliked the whole idea of equality and had no ethical quarrel with capitalism', and Anthony Crosland, who likewise maintained that Keynes 'never had any belief in equality'.[13] Crosland's claim seems to me to be substantially correct, but should be subject to two caveats: first, Keynes's views on inequality were not entirely static. In his later works, especially *The General Theory*, he was arguably less tolerant of economic inequality than in his earlier writings. Second, although it would still be going too far to claim that Keynes explicitly advocated economic equality, his immediate disciples certainly did, and this had a decisive influence on the interpretation of his thought that was most widely disseminated into British political culture.

Keynes and social justice

The major difficulty with Clarke's interpretation of Keynes is that he does not discuss in detail the meaning of the term 'social justice'. As this book has emphasised, there are sharply diverging views about what might constitute social justice, and it is at least in part differences over the meaning of this ideal that demarcate leftist from centrist liberals. Clarke assumes that *any* attempt to promote social justice is definitive of a progressive liberal or social democratic outlook.[14]

Clearly, though, an extreme meritocrat could coherently reconcile great inequality with a commitment to social justice, so to shed further light on this issue it is necessary to look directly at how Keynes himself actually used the term.

Keynes frequently mentioned social justice as a desirable political goal in his writings during the 1920s and 30s, but he was elusive about a more precise definition of this objective. In this sense, he exemplified a more general drift away from the detailed discussion of political philosophy in this period, as technical social scientific concerns began to displace debates about normative theory.[15] However, while a normative commitment to equality remained discernible in the writings of Durbin and Jay, and even in the work of Keynes's disciples such as James Meade and Joan Robinson, Keynes himself held no such firm belief. Certainly, he thought that liberals like himself were 'inclined to sympathise with Labour about what is just', but his description of the political implications of this abstract commitment did not indicate a passionate sense of the intolerable injustice of economic inequality. Rather, his worry was that Labour's 'ignorant blind striving after justice' would 'destroy what is at least as important and is a necessary condition of any social progress at all – namely, efficiency'.[16] In contrast to the Left's pressing concern for greater social justice, Keynes appeared to be committed to a view that was almost a distorted version of Marx's *Critique of the Gotha Programme*: distributive justice was only to be systematically addressed in a later era, after the problems of production had been solved and sufficient wealth generated to redistribute.[17] Furthermore, Keynes's diagnosis of the extent to which liberals should care about justice revealed the distance between his position and left liberalism. The 'political problem of mankind' was to combine 'economic efficiency, social justice, and individual liberty', but Keynes argued that the attainment of social justice was not of crucial import for liberals, since it was 'the best possession of the great party of the proletariat', while efficiency and freedom stood out as the key liberal concerns.[18]

These remarks suggest that Keynes conceded that justice would demand redistribution, but thought that the immediate pursuit of this goal would result in a severe loss of individual liberty or economic efficiency (a price he was unwilling to pay). However, a second theme also emerges from Keynes's writings on this question. When Keynes invoked principles of justice to criticise or to recommend a certain course of action, his main concern was in fact procedural equity, especially the satisfaction of legitimate expectations, and only secondarily substantive economic or social inequalities.[19] Keynes was most struck by the unfairness of economic events or government policies that made distributive outcomes arbitrary and unpredictable. The only social injustice mentioned in his *A Treatise on Money* was the arbitrary distribution of earnings caused by commodity inflation, while his objection to the 1931 budget and Economy Bill on the grounds that they violated 'social justice' was mainly because the pay of schoolteachers and other public sector employees had been singled out for drastic cuts simply because it was easier for the government to cut their wages than those of other professions.[20] The procedural impropriety of targeting one group of people for arbitrary reasons excited his concern and not the distributive outcome itself.

Keynes's main priority was therefore macreconomic stability as a means of protecting individuals' expectations and property claims from unfair disruption. As a secondary concern, he also endorsed a certain amount of material redistribution, usually presenting this as a necessary concession to the working class or as a possible (but not necessary) mechanism for promoting economic stability.[21] These admissions were usually coupled with a strong defence of the need to maintain some economic inequality as an incentive for, and recognition of, increased effort and risk.[22] However, there is some evidence that Keynes became slightly friendlier to egalitarianism in his later work. As he tried to win over the labour movement to his proposals to fight unemployment and finance the Second World War,[23] he made some more explicit remarks about the need to at least narrow economic inequality. 'The outstanding faults of the economic society in which we live', Keynes said, 'are its failure to provide for full employment and its arbitrary and inequitable distribution of wealth and incomes'.[24] He now called for 'a liberal socialism' that would 'promote social and economic justice' while 'respecting and protecting the individual'.[25]

In the concluding chapter of *The General Theory*, Keynes explored the relationship between the argument of the book and traditional defences of inequality. In particular, he argued that the proposition that 'the growth of capital depends upon the strength of the motive towards individual saving', and hence on the savings of the rich, was refuted by his demonstration that without full employment the growth of capital 'depends not at all on a low propensity to consume, but is, on the contrary, held back by it'. Redistributive measures 'likely to raise the propensity to consume' may in fact 'prove positively favourable to the growth of capital'. Keynes therefore claimed to have removed 'one of the chief social justifications of great inequality of wealth'.[26] Tantalisingly, he even looked forward to the gradual 'euthanasia of the *rentier*, of the functionless investor'.[27]

However, Keynes stressed that ruling out this argument did not negate other possible defences of inequality, such as the need to provide incentives for risktaking. He saw 'social and psychological justification for significant inequalities of incomes and wealth, but not for such large disparities as exist today'. This led Keynes to make some speculative remarks about the importance of money-making as a safety valve for 'dangerous human proclivities' that otherwise would 'find their outlet in cruelty, the reckless pursuit of power and authority, and other forms of self-aggrandisement. It is better that a man should tyrannise over his bank balance than over his fellow citizens.' Nonetheless, he concluded, it was unnecessary that 'the game should be played for such high stakes as at present', since 'much lower stakes will serve the purpose equally well'.[28] Although these thoughts were reasonably close to arguments for incentives made by social democrats, the Left was suspicious of this diagnosis of the social benefits of acquisitive behaviour and, it must be said, of Keynes's flippant tone. Durbin complained to Keynes that this passage neglected 'the petty tyranny of the employer-employee relationship'. In Durbin's view, Keynes was effectively endorsing industrial autocracy: 'As Tawney says the religion of inequality seems to make it possible for even men of generous good will to forget that workmen are also men.'[29]

Overall, however, Keynes's disengaged treatment of egalitarian ideals was less significant to the Left than his acknowledgement that there was no straightforward trade-off between efficiency and equality, particularly during economic depression. Brutally summarised for political purposes, *The General Theory* could be characterised as arguing that economic recovery would require the state to redirect savings held by the rich to more economically productive purposes and, in particular, to expand working-class consumption. In this respect, Keynes could be seen as paralleling Hobson's theory of under-consumption.[30] Once again, Keynes himself was rather elusive about this apparent implication of his theory. In particular, Keynes explicitly differed from Hobson over the relationship between saving and investment. Hobson saw the two as synonymous. In his view, over-saving (and therefore over-investment) was the primary cause of capitalist instability, and he specifically argued that redistributing purchasing power to the poor to increase consumption would in turn rekindle economic growth. In contrast, Keynes had a more complex understanding of the way in which saving translated into investment, and ultimately thought that depression would be triggered by under-investment in an economy characterised by over-saving. This had an important implication for social policy. According to Keynes, the state's most effective strategy against depression would be to convert savings into investment, bringing savings into productive use by expanding credit and reducing interest rates, rather than via the material redistribution favoured by Hobson.[31]

From Keynes to Keynesianism

Keynes therefore offered some hints about the possibilities for redistribution latent within his political economy, but his principal interest was in securing economic stability rather than embarking on a grander assault on economic inequality. As his disciple Roy Harrod observed, Keynes's work opened the prospect 'of keeping the existing system running without any drastic upheaval', thus affording the community 'a breathing space' in which to consider other social reforms. 'His proposals are hardly likely to resolve the fundamental conflict of interests between rich and poor', but, contrary to the Marxist analysis, they would at least enable that conflict to be resolved peacefully.[32] Indeed, even this centrist Keynesian vision of steady economic growth and full employment promised a significant improvement in the position of the working class, since it would strengthen their bargaining power in wage negotiations and substantially reduce economic insecurity.[33]

Nonetheless, as John Strachey pointed out, there remained an important ambiguity in the politics of *The General Theory*. While Keynes prioritised the organisation of investment so as to mobilise all of the factors of production, at the same time he gestured towards a criticism of the distributive consequences of capitalism itself, even with all of the factors of production fully employed. As Strachey further observed, an attempt to resolve this ambiguity had been made by 'those younger economists who have been deeply affected by Mr Keynes's work', since they explicitly stressed redistribution as a key political implication of *The General Theory*.[34] Strachey had in mind the work of Roy Harrod,[35] Douglas Jay,

James Meade and Joan Robinson, the first generation of 'Left Keynesians', who made explicit the egalitarian implications of Keynes's theory by combining it with their own strong moral commitment to a more equal society. Their version of Keynesian reflation involved measures such as the progressive taxation of income and wealth; higher welfare benefits; and increased public sector investment. Jay was the most direct advocate of this point, explicitly arguing that Keynes 'overrates the importance of investment in comparison with consumption', when in fact the direct stimulation of consumption was 'the logical conclusion of his argument'.[36] Meade and Robinson were more cautious, but in their influential textbook versions of *The General Theory* they both suggested that the Keynesian policy-maker should supplement the regulation of investment with material redistribution, even floating a version of the 'social dividend' scheme proposed by Dennis Milner in the 1920s.[37] A similar combination of policies that promoted both redistribution and the manipulation of investment was later endorsed by William Beveridge in his 1944 report on full employment (presumably as a result of the work of Keynesian economists like Robinson and Nicholas Kaldor on the report).[38] Less sophisticated writers frankly presented Keynesian theory as 'the complete vindication' of certain of the labour movement's traditional distributive prescriptions: wages should not be cut during a depression; working-class consumption represented the key to industrial recovery; and in general economic inequality should be reduced.[39] 'It is nice to say: "I told you so"', as Wootton observed.[40]

For these Left Keynesians, an important lesson of Keynes's thought was that it was now possible to show with all the rigour at the disposal of economic theory that equality was compatible with productive efficiency. Keynes, they argued, 'has robbed the orthodox apologists for the capitalist system of their most important weapons', and *The General Theory* provided 'magnificent material' for 'progressive propaganda'.[41] From this point of view, Keynes's key contribution was that he undermined the assumption, shared by advocates of laissez-faire, Marxists and democratic socialist planners alike, that there was a basic incompatibility between economic redistribution and capitalism. Even moderate socialists like Durbin believed that substantial redistribution would simply retard economic efficiency because the greater burden of taxation on the wealthy would reduce saving and therefore the growth of capital. Durbin's ultimate solution was widespread socialisation and economic planning.[42] The significance of Keynes's remarks in *The General Theory* quickly becomes apparent in this context, since he claimed to have disproved a key economic premise that underpinned the positions of both the anti-egalitarian Right and the socialist Left.[43] In the view of Left Keynesians such as Meade and Robinson, Keynes's achievement was therefore not restricted to showing that an economic system based on private property and markets could, with a limited amount of state intervention, ensure prosperity and protect individual freedom. In a review of Strachey's *The Nature of Capitalist Crisis*, Meade had argued that 'the socialist must reject the Marxist analysis. Capitalism can certainly be made to work and is not made to work simply for lack of understanding.' However, this still left a crucial issue unresolved: 'can a greater measure of equality be attained on these lines without a further extension of state planning or of state ownership of capital?'[44] Keynes had opened the way to a positive answer to Meade's question.

Strachey, newly enthused by the implications of Keynes's work, engaged Durbin in debate on precisely this point, writing to him after the publication of his *The Politics of Democratic Socialism* to contest Durbin's view that Britain was characterised by a shortage of savings.[45] Strachey offered a Keynesian response, asking 'how can the level of savings be said to be inadequate as long as general unemployment exists?' Unemployment, argued Strachey, was in fact simply the existence of a margin of productive resources not being used for consumption. But this theoretical concern had important political implications, since 'is this not what makes you so extraordinarily hostile to further increases in the social services?' Strachey was 'frankly staggered' by Durbin's assertion that increasing consumption would reduce savings and thus the rate at which the productivity of labour could be raised. This was 'disastrously misleading for a country such as ours, the essential defect of which is under-employment and a general tendency to stagnation'. 'As you see', wrote Strachey, 'I have in this respect been convinced by Keynes's argument'. Bizarrely, the sometime Marxist's position 'leads to the view that there are many more evolutionary possibilities than yours does'.[46]

The form in which this efficiency argument for redistribution made its way into popular political discourse was significant. For instance, Labour's manifesto in 1945 proclaimed: 'Over-production is not the cause of depression and unemployment; it is under-consumption that is responsible.' To ward off such under-consumption, 'a high and constant purchasing power' should be promoted 'through good wages, social services and insurance, and taxation which bears less heavily on the lower income groups'.[47] When Attlee addressed the House of Commons during the second reading of the 1946 National Insurance Act, he explicitly defended social insurance in these terms. Allowing unemployment or sickness to reduce consumption was 'an economic loss to the country', and Labour's welfare measures would ensure 'a proper distribution of purchasing power among the masses'.[48] It is hard to resist the conclusion that it was Keynes who finally persuaded Labour's leadership to adopt Hobson's theory of under-consumption.

This is not to underplay the important point that most of Labour's leadership remained fundamentally convinced throughout the 1930s and 40s that the definitive route to equality was the socialisation of the economy coupled with economic planning.[49] As I will discuss in the next chapter, this assumption was only thoroughly scrutinised in later debates about egalitarian strategy, and in this period even Gaitskell continued to see public ownership as the 'only adequate method' of reducing inequality.[50] However, Keynesian theory undoubtedly prepared the ground for the more far-reaching revisionism of the 1950s by demonstrating that (at least in the short run) the reduction of inequality could be used as a means of enhancing the efficiency of a broadly capitalist economy. Although Keynes himself had professed little interest in equality, his economic theory was certainly open to an egalitarian interpretation. Keynes was not an egalitarian, but the important point was that his most influential disciples were.

5.3 The return of utilitarianism

While Keynesian analysis offered one source of fresh inspiration for egalitarians, the branch of economic theory directly concerned with distributional issues, welfare economics, also played a role in reshaping egalitarian thought. As we have seen, Keynesian theory could be used to legitimate redistributive policies on the grounds that they would actually help to reflate the economy or, at a minimum, would not undermine productive efficiency. Arguments derived from welfare economics complemented this finding, since the principal distributive claim of left-leaning welfare economists was that an egalitarian distribution would achieve a more efficient allocation of resources than would be the case under the unequal distribution inevitably generated by a laissez-faire regime. By employing both arguments, social democrats could claim that greater equality was compatible with productive *and* allocative efficiency. This section examines the character of this latter argument for redistribution.

Welfare economics and the Left

Important studies of Edwardian fiscal policy have stressed the role of economists like Alfred Marshall in providing influential support for a more progressive tax system.[51] Marshall's interventions are a significant example of the political use of the early findings of welfare economics, and in particular of the principle of diminishing marginal utility. However, Marshall himself was not an egalitarian and, as we have seen, the argument from marginal utility was by no means central to the Left's case for redistribution in the Edwardian era. Indeed, socialists of the early twentieth century conspicuously failed to engage with the work of Marshall and A. C. Pigou, the most influential welfare economists in this period, in spite of the fact that these economists reached conclusions about redistribution and market failure that overlapped with those reached by ethical socialists such as Tawney. It has even been suggested that the ideology of Labour socialism at this time was structurally inhospitable to the thinking of the early welfare economists, due to the generic suspicion of the market among socialists of this period and, in particular, their profound ethical objection to acquisitive consumer behaviour.[52] As a result, 'Pigouvian' welfare economics made little impact on socialist thought before the 1930s.

As trained economists, later socialists like Durbin and Jay were more receptive to the analytical framework developed in the texts of Marshall and Pigou. Unlike earlier socialists, they did not view academic economics as necessarily committed to laissez-faire, or as rationalising immoral, acquisitive behaviour, but rather as offering a powerful set of analytical tools that could be used to serve a variety of ideological ends.[53] In particular, and this is the main burden of this section, the utilitarian case for egalitarian redistribution played an important role in their political thought. The criteria for social choices about efficient resource allocation developed by writers such as Marshall and Pigou were frankly utilitarian and consequently, through application of the principle of diminishing marginal utility, susceptible to an egalitarian interpretation.[54] Just as Hobhouse had appropriated and radicalised the idealism of T. H. Green, economists like Durbin, Jay and Meade adopted and then made explicit the egalitarianism latent in the neo-classical economics of the Cambridge school.

This adoption of the criteria of welfare economists was an important change in emphasis for egalitarians. Writers such as Tawney or Hobhouse had offered arguments for redistribution that were mainly concerned with the justice of particular distributions between individuals or groups, and the impoverished social relationships fostered by a community stratified into social classes. In contrast, egalitarians of the 1930s also advocated redistribution on the grounds that it would result in greater overall economic welfare. Earlier egalitarians had of course used welfare arguments for equality, but they tended to espouse a 'social utilitarian' position. This argument regarded the collective welfare of the community as a separate consideration from the sum of its component parts, and maintained that 'social welfare' could only be raised to an optimal level by promoting the flourishing of each individual. In the 1930s, progressive arguments in this vein differed from their counterparts earlier in the century in that they made use of the straightforward Benthamite goal of aggregate utility rather than the organicist notion of 'social utility' popularised by the new liberals.[55] Significantly, the communitarian presuppositions of earlier decades were downplayed in favour of a framework that took the individual as the unit of analysis and defined welfare as simply the sum of each individual's well-being.

Economics and ethics

How can we account for this installation of the greatest possible aggregate welfare as a core justificatory strategy for egalitarians? Sen has speculated that utilitarianism came to be regarded as egalitarian 'through a peculiar dialectical process whereby such adherents of utilitarianism as Marshall and Pigou were attacked by Robbins and others for their supposedly egalitarian use of the utilitarian framework. This gave utilitarianism a ready-made reputation for being equality-conscious.' This analysis rightly identifies that the egalitarian implications of utilitarian thought were implicit in the earliest writings on welfare economics, although as Sen notes, economists such as Marshall were 'in no particular hurry to draw any radical distributive policy prescription out of this'.[56] However, the difficulty with this diagnosis is that it suggests that the utilitarian case for equality was accidental. It implies that the writers who made this argument unreflectively adopted their position as a knee-jerk reaction to the anti-egalitarian claims of Robbins and others. This neglects the fact that the growth in utilitarian egalitarianism was governed by considerations quite distinct from the greater egalitarian credibility that Robbins gave to Marshall and Pigou.

It is therefore worth broadening Sen's account to stress the wider political and philosophical influences that were shaping egalitarian thought in the 1930s. In addition to the sociological or dialectical processes that led to this interest in utilitarianism, a further important question is: why was the intellectual content of the utilitarian argument particularly persuasive to egalitarians at this time? One possible answer might be that its theoretical appeal stemmed from its claim to offer a 'scientific' argument for equality, in the sense that it purported to eschew normative judgements about a just distribution in favour of a statement about the most efficient use of resources. From this perspective, the value of advancing a utilitarian criterion was that it demonstrated that inequality was a wasteful deployment of the community's wealth. This proposition had the inestimable virtue of tailoring the case for equality to the methodological assumptions of the dominant intellectual elites of the period. The positivist spirit infused the writings of social scientists, especially economists, in the 1930s, while philosophical treatments of ethics, whether intuitionist or emotivist, stressed the apparently irresolvable plurality of moral beliefs.[57] This led to a philosophical nervousness about the rationality of ethical discourse, and a pessimistic analysis of the seemingly intractable controversy created by the invocation of ethical principles in political argument. As a result, an apparently value-neutral 'scientific' argument seemed to carry greater weight in political debate than one that depended on such subjective notions as 'justice'. Hugh Dalton, a former student of Pigou's, had made this point in the 1920s:

> While the canons of economic justice are highly disputable, the canons of economic welfare are, by comparison, matters of general agreement. There is comparatively little ground for dispute in the propositions that economic welfare will be increased, other things in each case being equal, by a more equal distribution of income, by an increase in production per head, by an increase, and by a more equal distribution, of leisure. It is probable that all these propositions would be accepted by a large majority among reflective and reasonable people. There is certainly no such majority unconditionally in favour of any one of the rival canons of economic justice.[58]

Allied to these doubts about the plausibility and political utility of discourse about justice was the conviction of certain writers on economics that it was in fact not part of their brief to render normative judgements about the possible principles or forms of social organisation that might regulate the distribution of income. Such economists were adamant that Hobson's model of a fundamental enquiry into the relationship between economics and human well-being broadly construed lacked intellectual rigour, and they advocated a sharper distinction between positive and normative discourse in social enquiry. As Meade put it: 'Whether certain types of people "deserve" more [income] than others is not a question on which the economist can pass any significant judgement.' However, argued Meade, it was certainly legitimate for the economist to point out that the diminishing marginal utility of income ensured that an equal division of income would secure the greatest overall satisfaction. 'This argument is not ethical; it does not assert that it is just or fair to divide the income equally . . . but only that it is *economic* to do so, since the greatest amount of satisfaction can be derived in this way.'[59]

Seen in this light, it could be argued that the utilitarian argument was valuable as a criterion that apparently demonstrated that egalitarian redistribution was mandated by science rather than by ethics. Could we then say that the significance of this change in egalitarian political thought was that it marked the transition from an ethical socialism saturated with moralising rhetoric to a technocratic socialism that premised its appeal on the efficient allocation and production of resources? Stated in these terms, this conclusion is too strong. The account given so far attributes the adoption of the utilitarian criterion to a loss of faith in the power of moral argument amongst socialist intellectuals, along with the more specialised division of intellectual labour that evacuated the discussion of ethical ideals from academic economics. However, this explanation over-simplifies the relationship between equity and efficiency arguments, as the most persuasive aspect of the utilitarian argument for equality was precisely that it blurred the distinction between allocative efficiency and distribution to the worst-off on the basis of need. After all, the reason why greater welfare would be produced through the direction of resources to the poor was because those resources would be meeting basic needs of fundamental importance to human flourishing, and it was the satisfaction of such needs that had been the overriding concern of social reformers throughout the early twentieth century. The distinctive contribution of the utilitarian argument for equality was that it merged the maxim of distribution according to need with the achievement of the greatest aggregate welfare, expressing both ethical and efficiency concerns. As William Beveridge pithily summarised this argument in one of his frequent radio addresses in 1935: 'I am one of those people who thinks that 1s in a poor man's pocket usually buys more welfare than 1s in a richer man's pocket; it meets more urgent needs.'[60] In effect, then, the real change of intellectual focus was not a simple-minded rush to the authority of science to mandate equality, but a growing realisation that arguments about ethics, though fundamental to the Left's cause, could be usefully supplemented, and to some extent expressed, by the technical vocabulary of the welfare economist.[61]

The greater attention given to this type of egalitarian argument relative to more traditional moral concerns should therefore be seen as a matter of intellectual and political strategy rather than a fundamental shift away from egalitarian values. Given that British political debate in the 1930s and 40s was dominated by the apparently intractable inefficiency of unregulated capitalism, this seemed to be a prudent step for egalitarians to take. As Meade observed in a later, more explicitly political work, this new line of argument made the point that inequality 'is not only inequitable', but that it 'is also extremely inefficient'. By inefficient Meade meant: 'If the rich are able to buy up milk to feed to their cats while the poor are unable to afford enough milk to feed to their babies, there is a real waste of milk . . . more real human satisfaction could have been obtained if the babies had drunk more milk.'[62] It would therefore be misleading to say that writers of this generation, under pressure from wider philosophical trends and political constraints, simply lost the ethical convictions expressed by earlier progressives and became unbridled technocrats. Rather, they adopted the terminology of the economist as a rough-and-ready proxy for the more complex ethical propositions that had been advocated by earlier egalitarians. The diminishing marginal utility of income offered a robust case for the reduction of inequality that was, at least in the short to medium term, able to do some important ideological work for the Left in an elegant, parsimonious fashion. As Durbin suggested:

The ethical case for equality has been stated by the economist in his own technical language. The argument in this form consists in the analysis of 'the diminishing marginal utility of income' – i.e. that the larger the income the less valuable a further addition to it must become. This is simply another way of emphasising the general probability that a sixpence spent by a poor man will satisfy a more urgent need, or a need which a just man would consider to be more urgent, than the same sixpence spent by a rich man.[63]

Similarly, Cole signalled his approval of this conjunction of equity and efficiency, noting that 'the standard laid down by the economists – the standard of maximum utility – sets up a strong presumption in favour of equality of incomes', and therefore offered a useful argument about why it was desirable to push for greater equality in distribution.[64] In this way, the moral case was 'cast into an economic mould' and 'the argument from social justice can be given an economic shape'.[65] The aggregative nature of the utilitarian calculus in fact resonated with Cole's socialism, since it suggested a collective attempt to secure the goods necessary for the greatest possible amount of happiness for all individuals, not just a privileged minority.[66] Jay also attributed ethical import to the utilitarian criterion. In his memoirs, he summarised the central argument of *The Socialist Case* as follows: 'The case for greater social justice rested on Alfred Marshall's "broad proposition" that "aggregate satisfaction can *prima facie* be increased by re-distribution of wealth . . . of some of the property of the rich among the poor".'[67]

Aiming at a collective sum of happiness appeared egalitarian in the sense that everyone's happiness counted: no social class or category of person was excluded from the calculus. Once every citizen was included, the more urgent welfare requirements of the poor suddenly assumed great economic significance. The egalitarianism of utility maximisation was therefore premised on an important empirical assumption: the principal victims of social injustice, the working class, constituted the majority of the community. To count everyone's happiness equally was to prioritise the interests of the majority who were disadvantaged relative to a wealthy minority. It seemed that the socialist economist Abba Lerner therefore expressed an important insight when he argued that upon the equalisation of every citizen's marginal capacity to enjoy income, 'we will have achieved a fulfilment of the principle: to each according to his needs'.[68]

In the context of a period dominated by debate about the apparent inefficiency of capitalism, and characterised by uncertainty about the logical status and political force of ethical language, utilitarian egalitarianism, supported by the solid technical achievements of neo-classical economics, found a peculiarly receptive audience. It was not the case that egalitarians simply leapt on the utilitarian bandwagon because its critique by anti-egalitarians lent the principle an egalitarian reputation, but rather that the political appeal of the principle of maximising utility offered an exceptionally persuasive tool to advance egalitarian ends given the intellectual and political circumstances of the 1930s and 40s. The subtle blending of the language of need-satisfaction with the purportedly value-neutral distributive theorems of welfare economics offered an argument that could draw on the growing political status of the economist to trump the rhetoric about efficiency produced by opponents of further economic redistribution. The beguiling appeal of the utilitarian case was its demonstration that fairness and efficiency were compatible objectives: to satisfy the basic needs of the poor as the first charge on the community was to maximise economic welfare. In this vein, Jay approvingly quoted Pigou: 'the reason why widely unequal distribution of income is an evil is that it entails resources being wasted, in the sense that they are used to satisfy less urgent needs while more urgent needs are neglected'.[69]

However, it was precisely the conjunction of efficiency and equity in the utilitarian argument that offered an open flank to economists less sympathetic to egalitarian concerns. As Sen observed in his remark quoted earlier, economists like Lionel Robbins and Friedrich Hayek mounted a serious critique of the scientific pretensions of the utilitarian argument, robustly exposing the normative claims that were hidden within this purportedly value-neutral theory. They argued that comparing the intensity of different individuals' needs was not as straightforward as egalitarians seemed to think, since it depended on controversial judgements of value rather than scientific observations. In response, egalitarians conceded that the argument from diminishing marginal utility was above all a moral claim about the importance of satisfying the needs of the poor relative to the more elaborate desires of the rich. As Cole put it, 'it is impossible to form any clear notion of either maximum production or maximum satisfaction without invoking ethical standards – for there is no purely economic answer to the question whose needs and wants are to be preferred'. While this concession reduced the scientific authority of marginalist arguments, it did not invalidate them: 'All economic thinking that is to have a practical conclusion involves an ethical standard; and such a standard is none the less valid because it cannot be expressed in purely quantitative terms or measured in accordance with a calculus of utilities and desires.'[70] As the next chapter will show, however, this clarification, when coupled with subsequent changes in the political and economic context, ensured that after the 1930s the utilitarian argument for equality would once again fade from the foreground of egalitarian thought.

5.4 Incentives in the new industrial order

While the utilitarian calculus bolstered the theoretical case for egalitarianism, it was recognised that in practice a trade-off would have to be made between economic equality and differential payments for incentive purposes, since it was likely that a uniform equality would reduce the level of production to an extent that would nullify the increase in satisfaction created by an equal distribution. As Durbin acknowledged, 'if the attainment of distributive equality involved the cessation of economic progress or a severe reduction in the general standard of living, it would be immoral to advocate it, because the loss of good things . . . would be greater than the gain'.[71] This concession also stemmed from a greater concern with the allocative function of wages than had been present in earlier discussions of incentives in left-wing circles. In particular, while the normative grounds of earlier theories about equality were not directly disputed, it was suggested that they had paid inadequate attention to the dual function of economic rewards. As Barbara Wootton put it, this was the distinction between payments as the reward for something done and as 'a means of causing that thing to be done or to be permitted'.[72] This was the same point that Wootton had earlier made in response to Shaw's egalitarianism: income inequalities legitimately raised questions that bore on both the justice of a particular distributive pattern and the distribution of labour between different occupations.[73] As Henry Dickinson observed, a decisive disadvantage of strict equality was that, coupled with a 'free choice of job, it will lead to great scarcity of labour in some occupations and to a redundance in others, as compared with the social need for such labour'.[74] Incentive payments were therefore important both as a means of evoking productive effort and as a means of ensuring that the right people were matched to the right jobs. This latter point was true in spite of the avowed 'clumsiness with which the mechanism operates in the actual world, where it is enormously obstructed by unequal distribution of opportunities, social prejudices and so forth'. Even once the deficiencies of this procedure had been accepted, it remained the case that 'it is the *only* force that even attempts to guide the distribution of labour on an intelligible system'.[75]

A major attraction of using unequal rewards to regulate the distribution of labour was that it helped to maintain freedom of occupational choice. Given the priority accorded to individual freedom by social democrats, this was thought to be a decisive advantage of a differentiated pay structure, although there were significant differences of opinion on the Left about whether market pricing (coupled with trade union collective bargaining) should determine wage rates or whether a socialist government should actually guide differentials through a wages policy.[76]

Earned and unearned incomes

From the well-worked perspective of encouraging productivity, the extent of justifiable material incentives remained an important issue. As we have seen, the Left's distinction between 'earned' and 'unearned' income prior to the 1930s cut across the conventional boundary between income derived from work and income derived from ownership or inheritance, since progressives argued that income derived from work could itself be unearned if it was the result of inequalities in ability that were natural monopolies, or if net incomes did not recognise the social contribution made to the individual's capacity to command such a salary. Conversely, certain forms of income from property ownership could qualify as earned. By the 1930s and 40s, however, social democrats were increasingly preoccupied by the specific problem of inequality in the ownership of property. Empirical evidence demonstrated 'inequality of distribution so grotesque as to be almost unbelievable', since 'only about 20 per cent even of persons over twenty-five have property worth more than £100', and 'about 6 per cent of the population hold 80 per cent of the property'.[77] Inequality in the distribution of property was therefore presented as a more significant source of economic injustice than inequalities in work incomes.[78] Given this reasoning, when Durbin turned to describe the 'egalitarian measures' that formed one component of his strategy for democratic socialism, he noted that it was not necessary to say much about their nature since it was 'largely agreed among socialists now' that inheritance tax was 'the most expeditious and most equitable policy' to pursue.[79] Interestingly, Durbin did not rank educational reform as of equal importance to wealth taxation in his model of egalitarian strategy; he saw the expansion of education as 'ameliorative' rather than egalitarian, since it tackled the 'consequences of inequality' rather than its causes.[80]

Did this emphasis on inequality of wealth rather than income represent a decisive shift from the arguments of earlier decades and signal the acceptance of a more meritocratic view of social justice? Ellison has suggested that, in particular, Jay's egalitarianism 'looked towards a form of equality of opportunity where the head-start afforded to some by inherited fortune had been eliminated in favour of a meritocracy based upon income'. In this sense, argued Ellison, Jay should be seen as forging a path for the revisionists of the 1950s, when this view of social justice 'would be widely endorsed'.[81] In the next chapter, I will in fact argue that categorising the revisionists as meritocrats misunderstands their view of social justice. For now, it is important to note that it is a mistake to trace this allegedly meritocratic view to Jay's earlier work, since Jay himself argued against a meritocratic defence of income inequality. Instead, drawing on the language developed by an earlier generation of progressive writers, he offered a functional justification for certain income inequalities. 'A wage is not a "reward" in the same sense as the marks which a schoolboy receives for good behaviour. It is paid to induce someone to perform a certain function.'[82] This analysis of the principles that ought to govern material distribution owed a great deal to Tawney, suggesting that 'nobody shall be paid anything who performs no genuine service at all . . . that over and above this all remuneration shall be adjusted to the value (determined by a reformed price system) of a man's services', and finally 'that all unearned income shall be diverted to provide for the needs of those – and their dependants – whose earnings are insufficient'.[83] Jay was clearer than Tawney in recommending the use of market pricing to determine the value of individuals' services, but his conceptual framework was similar to that of *The Acquisitive Society*, and indeed with the model of social justice defended by left liberals like Hobson and Hobhouse. Jay therefore argued that the danger of strict equality was not that it would leave merit unrewarded, but that it would determine the work/leisure trade-off decisively in favour of the latter. Those abilities that could command high salaries 'are of great value to the community, and it is probable that their possessors would not use them to the full if they were not rewarded more highly than those of lesser ability'. No doubt, thought Jay, 'the level of rewards is conventional', and the talented would be content so long as they received the same amount as others of similar abilities. Nonetheless, this still meant that 'some inequality of earned incomes is inevitable in a world where men do not predominantly act from altruistic motives'.[84] Similarly, Durbin thought it 'quite consistent to interpret "equality" to mean the removal of all *unnecessary* sources of inequality – thus leaving room for the maintenance of differences in earned income that promote hard work and the use of all the talents'.[85]

Conversely, the purported role of unearned income as an incentive appeared implausible:

> It has never been argued that the distribution of large sums of money through the chance good fortune of lotteries or horse-racing was necessary to the preservation of industry and vigour in the working population. Why then should it be argued that the distribution of even larger sums of money through the grand lottery of birth and inheritance is necessary to the same end?[86]

As economists, both Durbin and Jay regarded the payment of interest, rent and profits as economically functional, as necessary payments to induce individuals to wait or to take risks. However, as socialists, they also believed that the ownership of capital could be transferred to the state, and thus that the service of waiting would ideally be performed socially.[87] Risk-bearing was a more difficult issue, and here Jay departed from socialist orthodoxy. Although he conceded that it was an attractive idea for the state to 'take over the risk-bearing function' and 'by pooling . . . risk thereby destroy it as effectively as an insurance company destroys insurable risk', Jay argued that 'averaging out the profits and losses of speculative ventures' in this way would not be as effective in the case of new economic undertakings. In this respect, Jay echoed the very similar argument made by Hobson in his writings of the 1920s, concluding that 'the imagination and initiative required to start a new venture are essentially the qualities which private enterprise is best fitted to show'.[88] Indeed, this aspect of Jay's book won warm praise from Hobson himself, who applauded the fact that Jay had discarded 'the indiscriminate attack on profits, rent, and interest which Marxism put into the socialist theory'.[89]

Incentives and the egalitarian ethos

In comparison to earlier egalitarian thought, what was missing from this analysis was the aspiration to create a new social ethos. Earlier egalitarians had hoped to constrain the reward claims of the talented by altering the social conventions and individual preferences that influenced economic behaviour. While they had conceded that economic incentives would have to be retained to some extent, they also believed that a transformation in individual attitudes would in due course be one important outcome of social reform. Earned income inequalities were therefore not to be left completely at the mercy of the acquisitive urges of the most talented citizens, but would be compressed through the gradual emergence and cultivation of the virtues of fellowship and co-operation, at the expense of the competitiveness and selfishness created by capitalism.

This strand of thinking was absent from the writings of Dalton, Durbin, Gaitskell and Jay in the 1930s. They were more sceptical of the connections drawn between the ideals of equality and the common good by earlier progressive thinkers, a scepticism that was at least partly the product of the intellectual resources at their disposal. The substitution of economic theory for idealist philosophy or evolutionary imagery precipitated a shift from an organicist understanding of the social unit to a more individualist analysis. Michael Oakeshott made an interesting point when he observed that Durbin 'writes as if his philosophical education had been confined to a superficial study of Bentham and J. S. Mill', with the result that he adhered to 'a philosophy of crude and uncritical individualism' that was 'inconsistent with social democracy'.[90] Oakeshott overstated his case, but it would nonetheless be fair to say that Durbin and other socialist economists discussed the nature of productive motivation purely in the rational self-interested terms set by economic theory. In the draft notes for his projected volume on the economics of democratic socialism, Durbin examined the various socialist criticisms of capitalism, acknowledging one as 'the spiritual evil of concentrating on material ends, maximising wealth and income etc, instead of working for service'. Durbin was sceptical of its importance: 'This criticism was probably confined to a relatively few idealists, and needs to be applied with care.'[91] 'It is not', he argued elsewhere, 'necessary to appeal to new unselfish impulses to replace the ordinary connection between effort and income'. Though Durbin did not rule out such impulses developing at some point, their cultivation was not part of his case for egalitarianism. 'The fact remains that use can, and will, be made of normal economic motives within the socialised sector and in the new society based upon a planned economy and social equality.'[92]

It is possible that this shift in egalitarian thought was not only a product of the intellectual resources at the economists' disposal, but also reflected a wider suspicion of an overly prescriptive organicism nurtured during the First World War. As Gaistkell later recollected, his generation 'had been subjected to much war-time propaganda and experienced in an unusually intense fashion the pressures of the community on the individual', pressures that 'were both cruder' and 'less generally accepted' than during the Second World War. The result, reported Gaitskell, was that at university in the 1920s 'we were, therefore, suspicious of general ideas, especially when these involved some mystical, collective, common good'. Consequently, their utilitarian philosophy focused on 'the happiness of the individual as the only acceptable social aim',[93] and, it might be extrapolated, was wary of positing a wider collective good, or even of certain traditional socialist injunctions to cultivate 'fellowship'. It is difficult to adjudicate on the plausibility of this causal story; the more important point for our purposes is Gaitskell's own perception that his generation were cautious about employing the sort of organicist sentiment that had been widely canvassed by earlier egalitarians.

Nonetheless, the idea of fostering an egalitarian social ethos and gradually altering individuals' productive motivation remained important to other leading progressives in this period. Labour politicians schooled in the ILP's ethical socialism remained committed to these Ruskinian ideals.[94] Among theorists, Cole remained convinced that an egalitarian society would involve a fundamental moral transformation, and defended this view with a familiar set of arguments about the need to 'replace the monetary incentives on which capitalism relies' with an appeal to motives of social service.[95] This was obviously a long-term project, and in the transitional period, Cole proposed to introduce a substantial equal income payment, a 'social dividend', for all workers. By far the majority of material rewards would be distributed through this dividend, with only modest differentials being offered for incentive purposes.[96] Cole's conviction was that the shared interest in increasing the size of the social dividend would make it 'the common interest of all' to improve the productivity of the economy. The result would be 'an overwhelmingly strong public sentiment in favour of decent economic behaviour', and 'a fair day's work would come to be recognised as a social obligation binding upon all healthy and normal persons'.[97]

Egalitarians of the 1930s and 40s were therefore not only split between Marxists and social democrats. They also disagreed over the extent to which the promotion of equality involved not only the redistribution of material goods between social classes, but also an effort to foster a qualitative shift in the character of social relations and individual productive motivation. Egalitarian economists such as Durbin and Gaitskell were sceptical of this latter ambition; other egalitarians, such as Cole, remained true to the more ambitious egalitarianism that had united the Left earlier in the century. The importance of this disagreement was not immediately apparent in this period, but, as the following chapters show, it was to become increasingly salient after the Second World War. Significantly, the political relevance of wartime experiences was itself a contentious issue in this later debate; the next section concludes this chapter by discussing the impact of the War on egalitarian thought.

5.5 The egalitarian consequences of the War

'Out of the vortex of this terrible struggle', said Ernest Bevin in 1941, 'may not there be a great renaissance resulting in a new Britain, freed from the snobbery at one end and the poverty at the other'. Bevin hoped that 'the birth of a higher and nobler civilisation may be a compensation for the horrible struggle, the nightmare and the bitterness and loss of life that Hitler has imposed upon us'.[98] As Bevin's remarks suggested, the Second World War created a social climate that seemed to the Left to be more conducive to the popularisation of egalitarianism than any previous period covered by this book. This apparent political consequence of wartime experiences has in fact aroused a great deal of controversy among historians. Revisionist studies have argued that the War did not necessarily have the radicalising impact that earlier historians ascribed to it, and indeed that it is overly simplistic to see the War as straightforwardly advancing greater equality.[99] However, the important point for the purposes of this book is not that the War necessarily promoted more egalitarian attitudes among the masses, but that important political and intellectual elites strongly believed that it had done so. In particular, many on the Left believed that the popularisation of egalitarian policies had finally been accomplished as a result of the exigencies of total war, which had given, as Jose Harris has put it, 'an existential reality to the organic conception of society in a way that had never been achieved by abstract analysis'.[100] Two aspects of this perception are worth considering in more detail.

First, the Left believed that the War had fostered a stronger sense of solidarity between otherwise separate social groups and had popularised an egalitarian solution to the problem of a fair distribution of sacrifice and reward. 'War brings it home to the individual', said Orwell, 'that he is *not* altogether an individual'. This wartime solidarity was clearly linked to a shared national identity, but patriotism was itself now open to use as 'a tremendous lever' in the hands of socialists seeking to alter the distribution of wealth.[101] In contrast to the equivalent sentiments of national patriotism aroused by the First World War, the solidarity of 1939–45 was thought to be far more congenial to progressive politics, since it was premised on the defence of popular sovereignty; the failure of traditional ruling elites between the wars; and the need to secure the enthusiastic backing of the working class for Britain to emerge victorious. It was widely agreed that, as Beveridge put it, one consequence of the War was 'to make common people more important'.[102] The other side of this coin was that the upper classes, the Conservative Party and profit-maximising capitalists became the most plausible targets of social disapproval.

As a result, wartime media were saturated with a stridently egalitarian populism.[103] 'The supreme question stirring in men's minds in the midst of war is that of inequality', claimed the sociologist Richard Titmuss in one of his earliest political interventions.[104] There was lengthy discussion of what sort of behaviour offended 'people's sense of social fair-play', with the implicit conclusion that most profit-seeking or income-maximising activity was unjust, and the explicit demand 'that the necessary burdens and sacrifices of the War shall be so distributed that each shall contribute according to his means and his ability'.[105] In this climate, sober Labour moderates forthrightly condemned the 'selfishness among the rich' that made 'any enlightened man feel physically sick',[106] while even *The Times* wrote of the need for 'political equality' not to be 'nullified by social and economic privilege', and for 'equitable distribution' to complement the aim of maximising production.[107] The new social spirit, thought Orwell, demanded 'that such monstrosities as butlers and "private incomes" should disappear forthwith', since the workers would only fight if they have 'proof that a better life is ahead for themselves and their children. The one sure earnest of that is that when they are taxed and overworked they shall see that the rich are being hit even harder.'[108]

The bluntness of this populism was complemented by a more generous note that invoked classical progressive organicism. Wartime solidarity was taken as proof that the welfare of the community should take priority over private interests. One of the key exponents of this new mood, the writer J. B. Priestley, argued in his enormously popular radio broadcasts that it was wrong to see 'a country as a thing, and a collection of things on that thing, all owned by certain people and constituting property'. Instead, he argued, it was better to think of a country as 'the home of a living society', and 'the welfare of that society, the community itself' should be seen 'as the first test'.[109] Seen in this light, economic liberties formerly perceived as inviolable rights of the individual were now viewed with greater scepticism. Beveridge, for example, said he 'did not regard private ownership of the means of production and the power to employ other people on the means of production as an essential British liberty'; any decision between private or public ownership, he said, was a purely practical matter.[110] The pervasive organicist discourse also suggested that the War had brought to the fore motives of social service previously suppressed by capitalism. According to some egalitarians, the war effort demonstrated that, as Ruskin and Morris had claimed, service to the common good was in fact a more efficient and morally superior means of evoking productive effort than using the corrupt motives of greed and fear.[111] The new social order emerging from the War, it was argued, should take on board all of these wartime lessons, recognising that 'we must help each other if we are to sustain together a common life – from each according to his powers, to each according to his need!'[112]

In addition to this perceived growth of social solidarity, the Left saw the second political consequence of the War as a new-found readiness among both the public and governing elites to entertain policies that had previously been stigmatised as dangerously radical and financially unrealistic. Long-standing plans for social reform now coursed through a more porous political system. One of the most important examples of this apparent readiness to entertain novel social experiments was the rapturous reception that greeted the Beveridge Report on its release in December 1942.[113] Egalitarians quickly supported Beveridge's proposals on the basis that they were important steps towards equality, a fact that subsequent commentators have seen as surprising, since in their view this model of the welfare state was not specifically intended to promote greater economic equality.[114] Why was the Beveridge Report perceived as compatible with egalitarian aspirations?

Beveridge himself was not fond of explicitly egalitarian language,[115] although in his *Full Employment in a Free Society* he did point out that in attacking the famous giants of Want, Disease, Ignorance and Squalor 'we shall reduce also the evil of Inequality, at the points where it is most harmful'.[116] Notwithstanding Beveridge's own views, it in any case proved possible for the Left to appropriate Beveridge's proposals, and to claim that they advanced the ideal of equality. In particular, three aspects of Beveridge's report were seen as consonant with the egalitarianism discussed in this book. First, the report was seen as advocating a floor constraint on income levels, and it offered the prospect of family allowances, a policy that had long been seen as mandated by the principle of distribution according to need. Beveridge himself freely described his report as aiming to abolish want and thus establish a 'national minimum', although the level of the minimum was to be set at a subsistence level, rather than the more generous 'civic minimum' ultimately envisaged by the Left. Nonetheless, Beveridge was regarded as providing the first step towards equality that the Left had long favoured: the introduction of a national minimum aimed at abolishing extreme poverty and economic insecurity.[117] Left-wingers claimed that it would be possible to build on this in the interests of greater equality at a later date.[118]

Second, Beveridge's report was egalitarian in a more subtle sense, since the idea of the collective sharing of risk through social insurance invoked principles of civic equality and social solidarity. Every citizen would participate in, and be treated equally by, the scheme; no section of the community would be singled out as the recipients of charity. Every citizen would 'stand in on the same terms; none should claim to pay less because he is healthier or has more regular employment', so that individuals would 'stand together with their fellows', pooling their risks.[119] Social insurance offered every citizen equal status as contributors to, and beneficiaries of, the insurance fund, entrenching a shared social citizenship that transcended class boundaries.[120] It also levelled the playing field somewhat between the less and the more fortunate, allowing those most at risk from unemployment or illness to share the same coverage as the luckier members of the community.

Finally, the use of compulsory contributive insurance for unemployment benefit embodied a familiar principle of economic reciprocity. Through their productive labour, citizens would contribute to the fund for benefits, which would then pay out at times of income disruption or to meet special needs. Citizens would therefore qualify for redistributive transfers through their contribution to the productive labour of the community. The Beveridge Report itself made this connection explicit. In particular, the language of productive responsibility developed by earlier progressives was invoked by Beveridge on the question of unemployment: 'The correlative of the state's undertaking to ensure adequate benefit for unavoidable interruption of earnings, however long, is enforcement of the citizen's obligation to seek and accept all reasonable opportunities of work.'[121] This principle had been advocated on the Left immediately before Beveridge wrote his report, with the Fabian Society, for example, arguing in their evidence to the Beveridge Committee that there was a 'reciprocal obligation upon the citizen to co-operate fully in the restoration of his earning power'.[122] In words reminiscent of the Webbs, Beveridge summarised his position as: 'First things first: bread for all on condition of service before cake for anybody.'[123] Interestingly, however, Beveridge and his supporters on the Left were just as adamant that, when it came to the design of state policy, no explicit time-limit or coercive work requirement should in fact be applied to the receipt of benefits; in some sense they believed that the wartime contribution of the working class had already established the entitlement of the workers to social security.[124]

It was of course recognised that aspects of the Beveridge scheme were certainly not ideal from an egalitarian perspective. For instance, flat rate insurance contributions were less progressive in their impact on income distribution than funding the scheme from general income taxation.[125] But as studies of this period have made clear, an egalitarian critique was prevented from gathering support by a myriad of factors, such as the apparently overwhelming public support for Beveridge; the symbolic importance of the insurance metaphor; and all-important perceptions of affordability.[126] Proposals that recommended the integration of taxation and benefits into a universal income conditional on labour market participation, along the lines of the social dividend earlier proposed by Cole, gained little attention, although Cole himself saw the introduction of family allowances as potentially the social dividend in an embryonic form.[127] The ideological ecumenicalism of the Beveridge Report was its greatest short-term strength, in that it prescribed measures that could be supported on the basis of varying conceptions of social justice, and accordingly commanded widespread political enthusiasm. Progressive conservatives, liberals and socialists could all agree on the urgency of meeting the subsistence needs of all. However, this ecumenicalism was also the source of a significant long-term weakness, as it gradually became apparent after the War that Beveridge's scheme could not fully deliver on the egalitarian goals desired by his more radical supporters.

The Left, inspired by what it took to be the popular mood, glossed over some important political problems during the War. One was the distributive impact of the welfare state. A second was the extent to which wartime social solidarity could resolve the tension within progressive thought over the relationship between an egalitarian distribution of material goods and older ambitions to create more co-operative and fraternal social attitudes. By 1945, many on the Left believed that this question had been solved by the experiences of the War. A new and durable commitment to social justice and collective solidarity was now thought to have encompassed and transcended the working class. The ethos of British society at last seemed close to that spirit of mutual service that had been commended in the idealistic writings of Ruskin and Morris. Since leading progressives articulated and supported this mood, giving it theoretical and political substance, it was not immediately apparent that progressive ideology had in fact been slowly evolving away from the organicism of earlier generations, towards a more economistic emphasis on a fair or even an efficient distribution of material goods. Although the result of the 1945 general election apparently confirmed a decisive ideological victory for the Left, it became increasingly clear in succeeding decades that this was an overly sanguine perception of political sociology, and that progressive ideology was riven by significant tensions. In the meantime, it was only imperfectly understood by the Left that they were the beneficiaries of historical contingencies that could not last, and that ultimately careful rethinking of the politics of equality would be required if they desired an enduring and stable instalment of social justice.

Notes

1 H. Gaitskell, 'Socialism and wage policy', typescript, n.d. [1933], Cole Papers D1/55/3, 1–2. Date from P. Williams, *Hugh Gaitskell* (London, 1979), 41.

2 E.g. Dalton's remarks, drawn from Tawney's *Equality*, in his *Practical Socialism*, 319–21; Attlee, *Labour Party*, 139–48.

3 Contrast G. D. H. Cole's sobriety in 'Labour's opportunity', *NS*, 8.4.1933, 437–8, with Laski's apocalyptic 'Labour and the constitution', *NS*, 10.9.1932, 276–8.

4 D. Jay, 'The economic strength and weakness of Marxism', in G. Catlin (ed.), *New Trends in Socialism* (London, 1935), 122.

5 Durbin, *Politics*, 318, 319.

6 D. Winch, *Economics and Policy: A Historical Study* (London, 1969); Clarke, *Keynesian*; D. Lavoie, *Rivalry and Central Planning: The Socialist Calculation Debate Reconsidered* (Cambridge, 1985); D. Ritschel, *The Politics of Planning: The Debate on Economic Planning in Britain in the 1930s* (Oxford, 1997). On welfare economics, see section 3 of this chapter.

7 M. Blaug, 'The formalist revolution or what happened to orthodox economics after World War Two?', in R. Backhouse and J. Creedy (eds), *From Classical Economics to the Theory of the Firm* (Cheltenham, 1999), 260; also R. Backhouse, *A History of Modern Economic Analysis* (New York, 1985), 275–6.

8 Winch, *Economics*, 329–30; S. Howson and D. Winch, *The Economic Advisory Council 1930–39* (Cambridge, 1977), 5–29.

9 On the left-wing economists of the 1930s, and their role in shaping the policy of the Labour Party, see Durbin, *New Jerusalems*, 93–115, 79–81, 116–132; Brooke, *Labour's War*, 231–68; Thompson, *Political Economy*, 87–133; R. Toye, *The Labour Party and the Planned Economy 1931–51* (Woodbridge, 2003), 34–86. On Cole's difficult relationship with economics, see M. Cole, *The Life of G. D. H. Cole* (London, 1971), 206–9; Wright, *Cole*, 176–207.

10 Durbin, *New Jerusalems*, 142–6, 152–9; Thompson, *Political Economy*, 93–4, 111–14; S. Brooke, 'Problems of "socialist planning": Evan Durbin and the Labour government of 1945', *Historical Journal*, 34 (1991), 694–5, 699; Ritschel, *Politics*, 5–7.

11 Clarke, *Keynesian*, 79–83, quotes at 79, 80; also A. Fitzgibbons, *Keynes's Vision* (Oxford, 1988), 181–5; R. M. O'Donnell, *Keynes: Philosophy, Economics and Politics* (Basingstoke, 1989), 316–21.

12 R. Skidelsky, *Keynes* (Oxford, 1996), 43–8, quote at 44; also R. Skidelsky, *John Maynard Keynes: The Economist as Saviour 1920–37* (London, 1994 [1992]), 222–4; Freeden, *Liberalism Divided*, 154–73; Winch, *Economics*, 339–50; M. Cranston, 'Keynes: his political ideas and their influence', in A. Thirlwall (ed.), *Keynes and Laissez-Faire* (London, 1978), 110–15; E. Johnson, 'Keynes the man: scientist or politician?', in E. Johnson and H. Johnson, *The Shadow of Keynes: Understanding Keynes, Cambridge and Keynesian Economics* (Oxford, 1978), 28–9.

13 K. Martin, 'J. M. Keynes', *NS*, 3.2.1951, 133; C. A. R. Crosland, 'The greatness of Keynes', *Tribune*, 23.2.1951, 16.

14 Clarke, *Keynesian*, 79–80.

15 R. Tuck, 'The contribution of history', in R. Goodin and P. Pettit (eds), *A Companion to Contemporary Political Philosophy* (Oxford, 1993), 72–3; Harris, 'Political thought and the state', 20–2.

16 J. M. Keynes, 'Liberalism and industry' [1927], *JMK 19*, 639.

17 See O'Donnell, *Keynes*, 319–20; Skidelsky, *Economist*, 232.

18 J. M. Keynes, 'Liberalism and Labour' [1926], *JMK 9*, 311.

19 See Skidelsky, *Economist*, 223.

20 J. M. Keynes, *A Treatise on Money* [1930], *JMK 5*, 265; 'The Economy Bill' [1931], *JMK 9*, 146–7; 'Notes for a speech to Members of Parliament', 6.9.1931, *JMK 20*, 608; Keynes to J. R. MacDonald, 5.8.1931, *JMK 20*, 590–1; see also 'Am I a liberal?' [1926], *JMK 9*, 306.

21 J. M. Keynes, 'The question of high wages' [1930], *JMK 20*, 13; Skidelsky, *Economist*, 223.

22 E.g. J. M. Keynes, *How to Pay for the War* [1940], *JMK 9*, 377.

23 On the complexities of the Keynes–Labour relationship, see Skidelsky, *Economist*, 232–4, 437–8; his *John Maynard Keynes: Fighting For Britain 1937–46* (London, 2000), 58–64; Toye, *Labour Party*, 91–113.

24 J. M. Keynes, *The General Theory of Employment, Interest and Money* [1936], *JMK 7*, 372.

25 J. M. Keynes, interviewed by K. Martin, 'Democracy and efficiency', *NS*, 28.1.1939, 123.

26 Keynes, *General Theory*, *JMK 7*, 372–3.

27 Keynes, *General Theory*, *JMK 7*, 374–7, quote at 376.

28 Keynes, *General Theory*, *JMK 7*, 374.

29 E. Durbin to Keynes, 29.4.1936, *JMK 29*, 234; also E. Durbin, 'Professor Durbin quarrels with Professor Keynes', *Labour*, April 1936, 188.

30 A point made by Keynes himself: *General Theory*, *JMK 7*, 364–71; also Hobson–Keynes letters: *JMK 19*, 208–11.

31 Clarke, *Liberals*, 226–34; his 'Hobson and Keynes as economic heretics', in M. Freeden (ed.), *Reappraising J. A. Hobson* (London, 1990), 100–15; Freeden, *Liberalism Divided*, 168–9. This point was well made at the time by G. D. H. Cole, *The Means to Full Employment* (London, 1943), 48–63; also Keynes to G. D. H. Cole, 27.6.1940, Cole Papers C/4/8/1.

32 R. Harrod, 'Review of *The General Theory of Employment, Interest and Money*', *PQ*, 7 (1936), 297–8.

33 This is one reason why socialists worried that even centrist Keynesianism would be *politically* unsustainable in a capitalist society: see M. Kalecki, 'Political aspects of full employment', *PQ*, 14 (1943), 326–31.

34 Strachey, *Programme*, 311–13, 325.

35 Although Harrod's politics subsequently moved rightwards, in the 1930s he was sympathetic to the Left and contributed to the work of the NFRB: Durbin, *New Jerusalems*, 98, 105–6, 162–3; Clarke, *Keynesian*, 286, 321, fn. 26.

36 D. Jay, 'Mr Keynes on money', *The Banker*, April 1936, 14; Jay, *Socialist Case*, 192; D. E. H. Bryan, 'The development of revisionist thought among British Labour intellectuals and politicians, 1931–64' (DPhil thesis, Oxford University, 1984), 93. Cole made a similar point: Ritschel, *Politics*, 301.

37 J. Meade, *An Introduction to Economic Analysis and Policy* (Oxford, 1936), 12–60; J. Robinson, *Introduction to the Theory of Employment* (London, 1937), 91–2, 123; J. Robinson, 'Planning full employment' [1943], in her *Collected Economic Papers Volume 1* (Oxford, 1951), 81–3; Van Trier, 'Everyone a king', 349–65, 383–7. To Meade's book, recalled Jay, his own *Socialist Case* 'owed more than to any other printed work'. D. Jay, *Change and Fortune: A Political Record* (London, 1980), 63.

38 W. Beveridge, *Full Employment in a Free Society* (London, 1944), 180–7; J. Harris, *William Beveridge* (Oxford, second edition, 1997), 434–43.

39 A. L. Rowse, *Mr Keynes and the Labour Movement* (London, 1936), 13–15, 18–21, 41–2, 45–54, quote at 66. See also Toye, *Labour Party*, 93.

40 B. Wootton, 'Review of *Mr Keynes and the Labour Movement*', *EJ*, 47 (1937), 153. For an instructive contrast with this Left Keynesian vision, see John Hicks's criticism of Strachey for overemphasising the expansion of purchasing power. Hicks thought that Strachey neglected the lesson of the New Deal, namely that unemployment had remained disappointingly high in the USA because Roosevelt had been overly preoccupied with 'the direct maintenance of consumers' purchasing power' at the expense of investment: J. Hicks, 'Communism with a difference', *MG*, 2.4.1940, 3. Jay proposed an alternative explanation of the shortcomings of the New Deal, claiming that Roosevelt's mistake had been to expand consumption by coercively raising wages (consequently altering the ratio between profits and costs), rather than using alternative methods such as tax relief for low earners: *Socialist Case*, 219–20.

41 J. Robinson, 'Review of *A Programme for Progress*', *PQ*, 11 (1940), 282.

42 E. Durbin, 'The importance of planning', in G. Catlin (ed.), *New Trends in Socialism*, 151–2; his 'Socialist credit policy', *New Fabian Research Series No. 15* (London, 1934), 5; his *Politics*, 293–4, 298–300; J. A. Hobson and E. Durbin, 'Under-consumption: an exposition and a reply', *Economica*, 42 (1933), 402–27, especially Durbin at 424–5; Brooke, 'Evan Durbin', 46–50. For similar thoughts, see Cole, *Principles*, 403–4. Cole subsequently expressed enthusiasm for Keynes's *General Theory* ('Mr Keynes beats the band', *NS*, 15.2.1936, 220–2; *Means*, 48–63), although he still believed that a comprehensive remedy for class inequality required socialism: Wright, *Cole*, 196; Thompson, *Political Economy*, 119–20.

43 See Jay, *Socialist Case*, 248–51; Strachey, *Programme*, 72–5; J. Robinson, *An Essay on Marxian Economics* (London, 1942), 76–80; J. Robinson, 'Some reflections on Marxist economics', in her *Essays in the Theory of Employment* (Oxford, 1947), 187–8; Meade's review of Durbin's *Problems of Economic Planning*. *EJ*, 60 (1950), 119–20.

44 J. Meade, 'The Marxian theory of class', *University Forward*, 1 (1935), 25, copy in Meade Papers 18/2; J. Meade, 'The state and liberty', *Spectator*, 11.1.1935, 55.

45 See Durbin, *Politics*, 102–6, 137–8; also Durbin, 'Professor Durbin', 188; and Keynes–Durbin correspondence, *JMK 29*, 231–5.

46 J. Strachey to E. Durbin, 23.2.1940, Durbin Papers 7/6. Contrast with Strachey's earlier critique of Cole's under-consumptionism, on the grounds that this form of state intervention was a precursor of fascism: *Nature of Capitalist Crisis*, 333–51.

47 Labour Party, *Let us Face the Future* [1945], 54; also Labour Party, *Let us Win Through Together* [1950], 65; both reprinted in *Labour Party General Election Manifestos, 1900–97*, ed. I. Dale (London, 2000). See also Jay's pamphlet, published by the Labour Party, *The Nation's Wealth at the Nation's Service* (London, 1938), 2–5, 10–11.

48 C. R. Attlee, speech, House of Commons, 7.2.1946, in his *Purpose and Policy: Selected Speeches* (London, 1947), 94–6, quote at 94.

49 Brooke, *Labour's War*, 251–2, 268; Francis, *Ideas*, 65–99; Toye, *Labour Party*, 75–8, 236–9.

50 H. Gaitskell, *Money and Everyday Life* (London, 1939), 9; also his 'Economics', in N. Mitchison (ed.), *An Outline for Boys and Girls and Their Parents* (London, 1932), 670; Williams, *Hugh Gaitskell*, 65–9.

51 E.g. Daunton, *Trusting Leviathan*, 142–7.

52 J. Tomlinson, 'The limits of Tawney's ethical socialism: a historical perspective on the Labour Party and the market', *Contemporary British History*, 16 (2002), 10–11.

53 On earlier socialist hostility to economic orthodoxy, see McBriar, *Fabian Socialism*, 49–57; Wright, *Cole*, 180–1, 189; Tomlinson, 'Limits', 9–12. On the contrast with later socialists, see Durbin, *New Jerusalems*, 98–115, 265–79.

54 See A. Marshall, *Principles of Economics* (London, eighth edition, 1920 [1890]), 92–101, 128–31; A. C. Pigou, *Wealth and Welfare* (London, 1912), 401–2; A. C. Pigou, *The Economics of Welfare* (London, second edition, 1924 [1920]), 76–84; Winch, *Economics*, 28–46; R. Cooter and P. Rappoport, 'Were the ordinalists wrong about welfare economics?', *Journal of Economic Literature*, 22 (1984), 512–15. On equality and diminishing marginal utility, see section 3.3.

55 E.g. Cole, *Simple Case*, 16; Jay, *Socialist Case*, ix, 8–37.

56 A. Sen, *On Economic Inequality* (Oxford, 1973), 16.

57 The most celebrated English-language defence of logical positivism, A. J. Ayer's *Language, Truth and Logic* was not published until 1936, but the broader point is that most philosophical discussions of ethics in this period, whether logical positivist or not, were inhospitable to the notion that philosophical argument might be able to yield determinate ethical conclusions. See R. Plant, *Modern Political Thought* (Oxford, 1991), 4–22; J. Dancy, 'From intuitionism to emotivism', in T. Baldwin (ed.), *The Cambridge History of Philosophy 1870–1945* (Cambridge, 2003), 695–703.

58 Dalton, *Inequality*, 27; also H. Dalton, *Principles of Public Finance* (London, 1929 [1922]), 86–7. Dalton later noted that Pigou's book *Wealth and Welfare* 'helped me, more than any other, to formulate my own approach from ethics, through politics, to economics'. Dalton, *Call Back Yesterday: Memoirs 1887–1931* (London, 1953), 57–9, quote at 58.

59 Meade, *Introduction*, 206–7, Meade's emphasis. See also the use of diminishing marginal utility in Meade's 'The economics of utopia', unpublished section of his *Introduction*, *c.*1936, Meade Papers 2/12, 3.

60 W. Beveridge, 'Wages and skill', BBC radio broadcast, 26.3.1935, in his *Planning Under Socialism and Other Addresses* (London, 1936), 66.

61 As Ian Little subsequently pointed out, the concept of welfare had an ambiguous (but, I am suggesting, politically useful) status in these debates. Although purportedly value-neutral, it had clear ethical connotations: I. Little, *A Critique of Welfare Economics* (Oxford, 1960 [1957]), 75–83.

62 J. Meade, *Planning and the Price Mechanism: The Liberal Socialist Solution* (London, 1948), 35; also 38; his 'Economics of utopia', Meade Papers 2/12, 36; G. D. H. Cole, 'Fifty propositions about money and production', in his *Money: Its Present and Future* (London, third edition, 1947 [1936]), 360.

63 E. Durbin, 'The response of the economists to the ethical ideal of equality', in T. H. Marshall *et al.*, *The Ethical Factor in Economic Thought* (London, 1935), 20.

64 Cole, *Guide*, 125; Cole, 'Economics in the modern world', *PQ*, 4 (1933), 220.

65 Cole, *Means*, 48; Cole, *Money*, 148.

66 See Cole, *Guide*, 124; Cole, *Simple Case*, 15–18.

67 Jay, *Change and Fortune*, 62. The nested quote is from Marshall's *Principles of Economics* (London, seventh edition, 1916), 471.

68 A. Lerner, *The Economics of Control: Principles of Welfare Economics* (New York, 1946 [1944]), 28.

69 A. C. Pigou, quoted in D. Jay, 'Review of *Socialism Versus Capitalism*', *PQ*, 9 (1938), 147.

70 G. D. H. Cole, 'Socialism for radicals', *NS*, 20.11.1937, 846. For further discussion of the Left's response to Hayek and Robbins, see B. Jackson, 'The uses of utilitarianism: social justice, welfare economics and British socialism, 1931–48', *History of Political Thought*, 25 (2004), 523–35.

71 Durbin, 'Response of the economists', 21–2.

72 Wootton, *Plan or No Plan*, 20.

73 Wootton, 'Shavian socialism', 76.

74 H. D. Dickinson, *The Economics of Socialism* (London, 1939), 120–4, quote at 120.

75 Wootton, *Plan or No Plan*, 21, Wootton's emphasis.

76 This became an important political issue for the 1945 Labour government: Durbin, *New Jerusalems*, 268–71; Brooke, 'Problems', 690–702; J. Tomlinson, *Democratic Socialism and Economic Policy: The Attlee Years 1945–51* (Cambridge, 1997), 174–83, 299–301.

77 Jay, *Socialist Case*, 43–5, quote at 43. For influential empirical surveys, see Dalton, *Inequality*, 271–86; C. Clark, *National Income and Outlay* (London, 1937); Durbin, *Politics*, 363–76.

78 Durbin, 'Response of the economists', 13; his *What Have We to Defend? A Brief Critical Examination of the British Social Tradition* (London, 1942), 14–15; Meade, *Introduction*, 221.

79 Durbin, *Politics*, 297; see also Dalton, *Practical Socialism*, 334–43. As in earlier decades, the Rignano scheme was proposed as the most plausible wealth tax.

80 Durbin, *Politics*, 292–3.

81 Ellison, *Egalitarian Thought*, 19–20.

82 Jay, *Socialist Case*, 63.

83 Jay, *Socialist Case*, 314; see also his 'Economic strength and weakness', 115. For similar examples of the retention of functionalist theory, see Wootton, *Plan or No Plan*, 288;

Durbin, *Politics*, 135. Specifically on productive obligations, see Wootton, *Plan or No Plan*, 342; and her *Freedom Under Planning* (London, 1945), 88. Gaitskell also defended egalitarian objectives, citing Tawney as an inspiration: 'Socialism and wage policy', typescript, n.d. [1933], Cole Papers D1/55/3, 2–3.

84 Jay, *Socialist Case*, 127. See also Meade, *Introduction*, 252.

85 E. Durbin, 'The problems of the socialised sector' [1946], in his *Problems of Economic Planning*, 70, Durbin's emphasis; see also his 'Response of the economists', 23.

86 Durbin, *Politics*, 355–6. See also Wootton, *Plan or No Plan*, 288–9.

87 Jay, *Socialist Case*, 131; Durbin, *What Have We to Defend?*, 19, fn. 1.

88 Jay, *Socialist Case*, 237–8. Compare with e.g. Hobson, *Incentives*, 70–99.

89 J. A. Hobson, 'The socialist case', *MG*, 15.10.1937, 6.

90 M. Oakeshott, 'Democratic socialism', *Cambridge Review*, 19.4.1940, 348.

91 E. Durbin, 'The economics of democratic socialism', n.d. [1943–8], Durbin Papers 6/1/1, 1. Date from Brooke, 'Evan Durbin', 49.

92 Durbin, 'Problems of the socialised sector', 71; also Jay, *Socialist Case*, 253–60; Bryan, 'Development of revisionist thought', 66–7, 140–1.

93 H. Gaitskell, 'At Oxford in the twenties', in A. Briggs and J. Saville (eds), *Essays in Labour History* (London, 1960), 7. See Williams, *Hugh Gaitskell*, 12–13, 15–16; B. Brivati, *Hugh Gaitskell* (London, 1997), 19.

94 Attlee, *Labour Party*, 161–2, 277; H. Morrison, *Looking Ahead: Wartime Speeches* (London, 1943), 202–3, 236–7; S. Fielding, 'Labourism in the 1940s', *Twentieth Century British History*, 3 (1992), 147–51.

95 Cole, *Principles*, 326–7; see also his *Simple Case*, 47–56.

96 Cole, *Principles*, 236–7, 262–5.

97 Cole, *Simple Case*, 74.

98 Bevin, *Job to be Done*, 7.

99 Compare R. M. Titmuss, *Problems of Social Policy* (London, 1950), 506–8; A. Calder, *The People's War* (London, 1992 [1969]), 351–7, 396–400; P. Addison, *The Road to 1945: British Politics and the Second World War* (London, 1975), 115–63; R. Lowe, 'The Second World War, consensus and the foundation of the welfare state', *Twentieth Century British History*, 1 (1990), 175–8; J. Harris, 'War and social history: Britain and the home front during the Second World War', *Contemporary European History*, 1 (1992), 17–35; S. Fielding *et al.*, *'England Arise!' The Labour Party and Popular Politics in 1940s Britain* (Manchester, 1995), 19–45; McKibbin, *Classes and Cultures*, 531–6.

100 Harris, 'Political ideas', 236.

101 Orwell, *Lion and the Unicorn*, *GO 12*, 421, Orwell's emphasis. On the socialist patriotism at this time, see Brooke, *Labour's War*, 273–5. My discussion is greatly indebted to Brooke's interesting juxtaposition of the wartime writings of Orwell and Durbin.

102 W. Beveridge, 'Social security and social policy', speech, London, 3.3.1943, in his *The Pillars of Security* (London, 1943), 148.

103 Addison, *Road*, 129–54; Fielding, 'Labourism in the 1940s', 143–5; C. Waters, 'J. B. Priestley', in S. Pedersen and P. Mandler (eds), *After the Victorians* (London, 1994), 216–21.

104 R. M. Titmuss, 'The cost of living and dieing', *NS*, 5.4.1941, 357.

105 W. N. Warby, 'Labour's tasks in the second year of war', *LN*, November 1940, 1561.

106 Durbin, *What Have We to Defend?*, 44–5.

107 'The new Europe', *The Times*, 1.7.1940, 5; Addison, *Road to 1945*, 120–1.

108 Orwell, *Lion and the Unicorn*, *GO 12*, 415, 416. For similar views, see Strachey, *Faith*, 124–33; B. Wootton, *End Social Inequality: A Programme for Ordinary People* (London, 1941), 43–4; R. M. Titmuss, 'War and social policy', in his *Essays on the 'Welfare State'* (London, 1963 [1958]), 85.

109 J. B. Priestley, *Postscripts* (London, 1940), 37. See also W. Temple, *Christianity and Social Order* (London, 1976 [1942]), 69–77, 80–3, 93–4, 100.

110 W. Beveridge, 'Freedom from idleness', in G. D. H. Cole *et al.*, *Plan for Britain* (London, 1943), 98.

111 E.g. R. Acland, *The Forward March* (London, 1941), 63–110.

112 Durbin, *What Have We to Defend?*, 46; a slogan also invoked by Priestley, *Postscripts*, 90.

113 On the Beveridge Report and its reception, see Harris, *William Beveridge*, 365–423; J. Harris, 'Some aspects of social policy in Britain during the Second World War', in W. Mommsen (ed.), *The Emergence of the Welfare State in Britain and Germany* (London, 1981), 247–62; Harris, 'Political ideas', 246–54; Addison, *Road*, 211–28; Freeden, *Liberalism Divided*, 366–71; Brooke, *Labour's War*, 145–87.

114 See e.g. Tomlinson, *Democratic Socialism*, 265–7; R. Lowe, *The Welfare State in Britain Since 1945* (Basingstoke, third edition, 2005), 305.

115 W. Beveridge, *Social Insurance and Allied Services* (London, Cmd 6404, 1942), para. 294, 118. See also Beveridge's description of his ideal society, which would not 'abolish all individual inequalities of material fortune', because 'it knows that envy is not a master-passion of mankind'. Beveridge, 'My utopia', in his *Planning*, 142.

116 Beveridge, *Full Employment*, 31. The other 'giant' famously tackled by Beveridge, Idleness, was not mentioned in this context; presumably Beveridge thought that reducing unemployment would also reduce a very harmful form of inequality.

117 Beveridge, 'New Britain', speech, Oxford, 6.12.1942; his 'Social security', both in his *Pillars of Security*, 82, 84, 149; G. D. H. Cole, *Beveridge Explained* (London, 1942), 7, 20, 43; J. Griffiths, *HCD*, 386, 18.2.1943, cols 1965–6, 1968, 1975; 'Points for planners', *Fabian Quarterly*, January 1943, 1; *LPACR* 1943, 136–7, 140.

118 'Social security', *NS*, 5.12.1942, 367; H. Dalton, 'Our financial plan', in H. Morrison *et al.*, *Forward From Victory! Labour's Plan* (London, 1946), 49.

119 Beveridge, *Social Insurance*, para. 26, 13; see Freeden, *Liberalism Divided*, 369–70.

120 See W. Robson, 'The Beveridge report: an evaluation', *PQ*, 14 (1943), 154; J. Griffiths, *HCD*, 386, 18.2.1943, col. 1968; J. S. Clarke, 'Social insecurity', *PQ*, 16 (1945), 37–8.

121 Beveridge, *Social Insurance*, para. 130, 58; also para. 21, 11; para. 22, 12. See B. Wootton, 'Before and after Beveridge', *PQ*, 14 (1943), 361.

122 Fabian Society, *Social Security: Evidence Submitted to the Interdepartmental Committee on Social Insurance and Allied Services* (London, 1942), 5–6.

123 Beveridge 'Social security', in his *Pillars of Security*, 148. For the Left's earlier use of similar slogans, see Chapter 3, note 56.

124 Beveridge, *Social Insurance*, para. 130, 57. The wartime sacrifices made by the working class were frequently invoked in the parliamentary debate on Beveridge: see e.g. *HCD*, 386, 17.2.1943: J. McGovern, cols 1848–9; W. Oldfield, col. 1902; D. Adams, col. 1911; 18.2.1943: J. Griffiths, col. 1969.

125 See the following *NS* editorials: 'Social security', 5.12.1942, 367; 'Social security, wages and employment', 26.12.1942, 419; 'Can we afford it?', 27.2.1943, 135; also R. W. B. Clarke, 'The Beveridge Report and after', in W. Robson (ed.), *Social Security* (London, 1943), 275. A motion proposing to fund social security from graduated income tax was defeated at the Labour Party Conference, apparently on the grounds that the

unions supported contributory insurance: *LPACR* 1943, 140–1, 142. See also Beatrice Webb's scepticism of the Report; in the absence of a more full-blooded socialism, she thought that Beveridge's scheme would simply increase unemployment: N. MacKenzie and J. MacKenzie (eds), *The Diary of Beatrice Webb Volume 4, 1924–43: 'The Wheel of Life'* (London, 1985), 489–90, entry dated 6.12.1940.

126 Brooke, *Labour's War*, 146–7; J. Harris, 'Contract and citizenship', in D. Marquand and A. Seldon (eds), *The Ideas that Shaped Post-War Britain* (London, 1996), 129–32.

127 J. Rhys Williams, *Something to Look Forward To* (London, 1943); Cole, *Principles*, 252, 263–4; his *Money*, 147; his *Means*, 162. An unconditional basic income was advocated by H. S. Booker, 'Lady Rhys Williams' proposals for the amalgamation of direct taxation with social insurance', *EJ*, 56 (1946), 234–5; and by Meade, *Planning*, 43–5. See Harris, 'Some aspects of social policy', 257–8; Van Trier, 'Every one a king', 349–58, 403–6.

Part III

1945–64: Revisions

6
Means and ends

6.1 Introduction: high tide and after

The period 1940–51 saw the emergence of a British state that had unprecedented sympathy with working-class demands for equality. The egalitarian ethic of the War and the post-war government's policy of 'fair shares' produced a remarkable redistribution of income and social esteem to the working class. Although the extent of this redistribution was, and is, debateable, there had undoubtedly been a tangible shift towards a more egalitarian social order.[1] It was now possible for the Left to argue 'that Britain in recent years has come closer to being a just society than any other major country in recorded history'.[2] Conversely, voices from the Right such as Lionel Robbins could claim that the redistribution now embodied in public policy was 'quite indefensible save upon avowedly confiscatory theory', and constituted 'a discrimination against enterprise and ability such as has never before existed for any long time in any large scale civilized community'.[3] Unaccustomed to political success, the Left faced a unique strategic challenge: how to refresh its political programme to build on these successes and to take account of the growing elite perception that post-war Britain was undergoing substantial sociological change. That this change would prove to be uncongenial to socialist politics was apparently confirmed by the Labour Party's failure to win the general elections of 1951, 1955 and 1959. G. D. H. Cole provided a sombre diagnosis of this predicament: 'We have now to rethink the philosophical foundations of our socialism under highly unfavourable conditions, because we must square our philosophy with the conditions of the world of today and tomorrow, unless we are content to be merely the dying advocates of a lost cause.'[4]

An important feature of the ensuing debate about the nature of socialism was a renewed engagement with the ideal of equality. 'The subject of equality is very much in the air', noted one commentator, while another thought it could be a useful ideological glue for the increasingly fractious Labour Party: 'Equality, in fact, is a banner under which all socialists can unite.'[5] Under Hugh Gaitskell's leadership, the Party's National Executive Committee (NEC) convened a working group to discuss Labour's egalitarian philosophy, and to draft a policy document on the subject.[6] Reflecting on the reception of this document in his diary, Gaitskell observed that equality 'matters to socialists more than anything else. If you don't feel strongly about equality, then I think it is very hard to be a genuine socialist, and if we were to abandon this, then I think there would be very little left to distinguish us from the Tories.'[7]

This discussion of equality was regarded as novel because it marked a return to a more explicitly ethical socialism. As we have seen, moderate socialists of the 1930s and 40s had focused their attention on the compatibility of egalitarian objectives with economic efficiency, an ideological trend exemplified by their appropriation of both Keynesian arguments and the utilitarian egalitarianism of welfare economics. As Britain entered the 1950s, however, these considerations were losing their political salience. With full employment and steady economic growth, it could not be argued that a further redistribution of purchasing power was needed to reflate the economy.[8] Nor could it be said that egalitarian redistribution would unambiguously increase aggregate economic welfare, since the post-war distribution of income was said to be so compressed as to yield an indeterminate result in terms of the marginal gains and losses suffered by different groups in society.[9] At a theoretical level, Ian Little's celebrated critique of welfare economics was instrumental in clarifying the need for value commitments to be distinguished from economic theory in egalitarian argument.[10]

The justification for a more equal distribution of wealth therefore had to be elaborated independently of these efficiency arguments: it was necessary for the Left to return to the more familiar territory of fairness and solidarity. The most influential egalitarian writer of this period, Anthony Crosland, thought the aim of socialists should be 'to maintain and intensify the pressure' on inequality, but to do so 'less today on the classic redistributional welfare grounds, than in order to create a more just and democratic society; especially in Britain, scarred as we are by unusually deep class divisions in other, non-monetary spheres'.[11] This reversion to moral principle was an ambitious ideological gambit. As Richard Crossman observed, 'it was difficult enough to persuade people to become socialists when we could tell them that capitalism is not only immoral but also unworkable'. Would it not, asked Crossman, be much more difficult 'to persuade the majority of our countrymen that a workable system must be changed, simply because it is immoral and unjust?'[12] These were sobering questions for egalitarians to ponder as they thought anew about their political principles and policy proposals.

Their deliberations are discussed in this and the next chapter. This chapter begins by examining the well-known debate in this period about the status of public ownership within socialist thought. I argue that this was primarily a debate about the mechanism that could best realise an egalitarian society rather than a disagreement over the meaning of 'equality' itself; there was in fact only minimal disagreement within the Left in this period about the meaning of such distributive principles. Further support for this contention will be given by a detailed discussion of the principles of social justice recommended by the so-called 'revisionists'. In contrast to some widespread perceptions of revisionist ideology, I conclude that they were committed to an egalitarian, non-meritocratic view of justice. The next chapter shows that while substantial philosophical differences did emerge on the Left in this period, they in fact centred on the extent to which egalitarians should aim to foster a new spirit of fellowship and social solidarity. The chapter concludes by reviewing the new ideas about egalitarian strategy that emerged in the 1950s, focusing on educational reform; the welfare state; and plans to create a 'property-owning democracy'.

6.2 Public ownership and its critics

The controversy within the post-war Left about what was fundamental and what was ancillary to socialism was most obviously concerned with the role of public ownership within socialist ideology. One answer to this question was placed at the heart of the debate by the group of moderate politicians, activists and academics now known as the 'revisionists'.[13] The economist Arthur Lewis was the first to formulate their defining political slogan. In his widely read 1949 study for the Fabian Society, *Principles of Economic Planning*, Lewis contested what he saw as a widespread conflation of socialism with nationalisation and instead gave voice to the definition that would shortly be touted as the revisionist creed: 'Socialism is about equality. A passion for equality is the one thing that links all socialists; on all others they are divided.' Certainly, this egalitarian commitment required considerable attention to the distribution of property, but 'subject to the over-riding claims of equality, socialism is not committed to any one way of dealing with property, and property can be handled in many ways that are not inconsistent with socialism'.[14] Although one commentator was moved to remark of Lewis's definition that it seemed 'instructive that so unoriginal a remark should be so frequently quoted by his fellow socialists',[15] there was something innovative about the extent to which Lewis wished to hone socialism down to the pursuit of one particular, quantitative objective. In this respect, Lewis's succinct phrasing of socialist ambitions proved to be extremely influential, not least because he pushed the Left to clarify the relationship between public ownership and the distribution of material resources and social positions.

As we have seen, the Left had long been divided on this issue. The traditional socialist view, espoused by both gradualists and Marxists, was that equality (along with many other important social objectives such as full employment or economic stability) was ultimately unattainable under the private ownership of productive assets. Although limited palliative redistribution was thought to be possible in such circumstances, the scope for anything more ambitious would be heavily circumscribed by the need for substantial material inequalities to generate savings and capital. The logic of capitalist profit-making, it was said, simply could not permit a grander assault on social injustice. It was therefore vital to initiate widespread socialisation of the economy, so that the community could avoid the profit-seeking imperatives of capitalism by directly controlling production. Although this view split left-wing opinion in the first third of the twentieth century, it gained in popularity during the course of the 1930s. Even in the 1930s, though, there was a nascent split between socialists who adhered to this traditional perception of the logic of capitalism and those who, under the influence of Keynes and the Hobsonian strand of the new liberalism, began to downplay the importance of public ownership for economic equality. These latter egalitarians thought that the limits to redistribution in a profit-making economy were exaggerated, and they stressed the profound difficulties entailed by widespread public ownership, both in terms of securing economic efficiency and promoting individual freedom. Instead of solely advocating the collective ownership of productive resources, they also recommended a more even diffusion of property between individuals, a 'property-owning democracy' in the suggestive phrase first popularised in the 1950s.[16] Advocates of this strand of egalitarian strategy had been on the defensive during the 1930s and 40s, but in the 1950s this liberal socialist perspective now re-emerged in a new guise as the public philosophy of the right-wing of the Labour Party.

Equality and nationalisation

In the late 1940s, the tenor of debate on the Left began to change, as supporters of the Labour Party reflected on the impact of the economic policies pursued by the 1945 government. In retrospect, a widely discussed aspect of that government's nationalisation programme has been its apparent lack of connection to any of the major justifications for public ownership furnished by socialist ideology, and its legitimation in the Labour Party's public rhetoric as a measure to promote greater economic efficiency in the industries concerned.[17] These features of Labour's programme in government led revisionists to question the relevance of public ownership to egalitarian objectives. At the same time, the revisionists increasingly saw economic planning understood as widespread intervention in the price mechanism as politically unpopular, economically inefficient, and illiberal.[18] Significant indicators of this shift were the interventions of two economists broadly sympathetic to the aims of Labour in government, Arthur Lewis and James Meade. In two important works of political economy, they questioned the tacit assumption of many socialists that the only solution to economic inequality was to take a large proportion of the economy into public ownership and to further enhance state planning powers at the expense of the market. Meade's *Planning and the Price Mechanism* and Lewis's *Principles of Economic Planning*, although cloaked in the rhetorical authority granted by the word 'planning', were in fact powerful critiques of the model of planning and public ownership that informed much socialist thought. As Lewis put it, only 'totalitarians' could 'believe in 100 per cent public ownership'.[19] These books demonstrated that the Left possessed a nascent policy agenda that sought to combine liberal and egalitarian aspirations, but the intellectual vigour of these proposals could not disguise how politically contro-versial it would be to shift the Labour Party from one set of strategic assumptions to another. As an internal Labour discussion paper pointed out: 'Sooner or later there must be a decision between a further extension of state ownership and a wider distribution of property among individuals. It may be a valid criticism of Labour policy proposals that they do not make clear which of these is our ultimate goal.'[20]

The resulting struggle over this shift in socialist thinking is well known and has been recounted a number of times elsewhere.[21] Nonetheless, it is worth dwelling on certain aspects of this famous story. The revisionists were arguing against what they took to be the central assumption of Marxian socialism: that the abolition of private property rights in the means of production would be a sufficient condition for the existence of a classless society. Socialism, revisionists said, had been seen 'too exclusively in terms of nationalisation, as though this in itself would suffice to usher in the millennium'.[22] They took as their principal targets the writings of Laski and Strachey, and the hybrid liberal–Marxist ideology that emerged from the Left Book Club in the 1930s. By this time, Strachey had publicly retracted his more apocalyptic Marxism and had become a mainstream Labour MP and government minister, while Laski was a much weakened political figure between famously losing his high-profile libel case in 1946 and his death in 1950.[23] The revisionists argued that in spite of losing the support of its most celebrated exponents, the Marxist case still exerted a considerable persuasive force over left-wing opinion in Britain, persisting in much socialist discourse as an unargued assertion about the fundamental incompatibility of private ownership and an egalitarian distribution.[24]

The revisionists' objection to this assertion was partly based on the disappointing results of actually existing nationalisation. Since the Labour government had financially compensated the shareholders of industries taken into public ownership, the distributive impact of nationalisation in Britain had been negligible. As Gaitskell observed, financial compensation (which he supported) meant 'there was no longer any question of the transfer involving the disappearance of income from property: all that happened was the exchange of a larger uncertain income in the form of dividends for a smaller fixed income in the form of interest'.[25] Similarly, the example of the Soviet Union indicated that even a system characterised by wholesale collective ownership could retain a ruling class, and that incomes could 'be more unequally distributed in a collectivist than in a privately-owned economy', depending on a range of variables purportedly unrelated to ownership structures, such as taxation policy or the share of wages in the national income.[26]

The managerial revolution

Behind these specific empirical observations, though, lay a more general sociological theory that exercised a profound imaginative grip over socialist thought in this period. This was the theory of the 'managerial revolution', most famously expounded by the sometime American Trotskyist, James Burnham. Burnham's *The Managerial Revolution* was widely read on the British Left in the 1940s and 50s, and self-respecting socialist intellectuals of this period were obliged to situate their work in relation to it. The most influential part of Burnham's book was his claim that the trend towards larger productive units, from the joint stock company to the giant public corporation, entailed a split between ownership and management at the heart of capitalist enterprises. This argument, first voiced by Berle and Means in their seminal 1932 text, *The Modern Corporation and Private Property*, implied that ownership of an enterprise or industry no longer automatically conferred control over its operation.[27] Ownership was now dispersed among a number of shareholders, resting operational responsibility with a separate managerial class. Burnham's own treatment of this theme was much more radical than that of Berle and Means. Although he accepted many of their empirical findings, he regarded the idea of a 'separation' of ownership and control as incoherent: 'Ownership *means* control; if there is no control, then there is no ownership.'[28] Burnham proposed an alternative theoretical framework in which to understand the findings of Berle and Means. He distinguished between two different aspects of the control of private property: first, the ability 'to prevent access by others to the object controlled (owned); and, second, a preferential treatment in the distribution of the products of the objects controlled (owned)'.[29] The true significance of the managerial revolution, argued Burnham, was that these two aspects of control had been severed from one another: those who received the preferential distributive share no longer exercised control over access to the property in question.[30] He predicted that the managerial class would consolidate their control over access by increasing state incursions into private property rights, so that eventually they would be able to secure preferential distributive shares by controlling the state itself.

There are striking affinities between Burnham's claims about the consequences of greater state control of the economy and other well-known texts from this period, notably Hayek's similar treatment of these themes in *The Road to Serfdom* a few years later, and George Orwell's *1984*, which was directly influenced by Orwell's reading of *The Managerial Revolution*. All three were alert to the enormous power that a full-scale state collectivism would place in the hands of a small number of bureaucrats, while both Hayek and Burnham predicted that a socialist programme that employed state ownership and central planning as the principal means to secure greater economic equality would simply entrench new and dangerous forms of inequality and privilege.[31]

Burnham's ideas often surfaced in the socialist discourse of the 1950s. Crosland wrote an entire chapter on Burnham in his initial draft of *The Future of Socialism*, although it was cut from the published version.[32] As Samuel Beer observed, 'a principal theme' of virtually every contribution to the 1952 volume of *New Fabian Essays* was 'the danger of the managerial revolution in industry and government administration'.[33] For example, Crossman's introduction to the volume claimed that today's 'enemy of human freedom is the managerial society and the central coercive power which goes with it'. Crossman, however, did not share Burnham's pessimism about the future: 'Just as capitalism *could* be civilised into the Welfare State, so the managerial society *can* be civilised into democratic socialism.'[34] Burnham's rhetoric was co-opted into the vocabulary of British socialism, but with the traditional moral voluntarism of the British Left substituted for Burnham's gloomy diagnosis of inevitable social trends. In particular, the claim that ownership and control were inextricably linked proved to be a bridge too far for the revisionists, and their appropriation of Burnham was in fact characterised by an ideological sleight of hand. Instead of accepting his entire thesis, they settled on what Crosland took to be his core insight, the 'brilliant (though often exaggerated) analysis of the transfer of power within industry from the owning to the managing class', and combined it with a hefty dose of social democratic triumphalism.[35] The revisionist claim became that 'ownership itself has changed its nature'. Owners no longer possessed 'exclusive rights' over their property, a change that was the result of the new power of the state and trade unions to constrain the activities of property owners, and of the transfer of operational industrial control to managers 'who may own nothing at all', leaving 'the technical "owner"' as 'a functionless cipher. Ownership might change hands, but industries have still to be run by efficient managers; that explains why there is so little difference between the ethos of publicly-owned and privately-owned industry.'[36]

Put in these terms, the 'managerial revolution' meant that it was apparently not that important whether the state or private individuals were the formal owners of a company, since in practice state ownership conferred little additional control over the conduct of the enterprise. Indeed, since the powerful managerial class accrued rewards determined by a salary structure, it was argued that they had no personal financial interest in the maximisation of company profits, or at least the distribution of large dividends, and that it was therefore entirely possible for managers in private industry to incorporate some notion of the public interest into their managerial decisions.[37] State ownership had little impact on the distribution of wealth, ran this argument, so equality could be pursued more effectively through other means.

This was a rather convenient reinterpretation of Burnham's case, and it was arguable that the revisionists' optimistic conclusion was incompatible with the central sociological insight they had appropriated from him. After all, Burnham's arguments were a variation on the Weberian thesis that oligarchical tendencies are inherent within modern organisations, a claim about the necessary connection between elitism and the large scale and complexity of all contemporary organisations, whether formally socialist or capitalist. In effect, the revisionists argued that it was correct to see scale and complexity as the cause of inequality, but that this could be remedied through the activity of the state, under the control of a Labour government. Crosland's fundamental criticism of Burnham was his failure to grasp that 'the state machine is, in the democracies, a neutral agent, subject to the decisions of the parliamentary majority', and accordingly subject to the political will of a Labour government. State bureaucrats 'reflect the interests and purposes of the political authority', and could not have 'a common social purpose' with the managerial class.[38] But it could certainly be countered that this underestimated the nature of the problem, since it was the state that was precisely the foremost example of the oligarchical institutions that Burnham had identified. The revisionists assumed too readily that the actions of the state under the control of the Labour Party could be an agent of the public good without any taint of the elitism that characterised other organisations.

6.3 In defence of public ownership

The Labour Left noticed that the revisionists offered only one particular gloss on the relationship between ownership and control, but they did so from within a conventional socialist frame of reference that did not engage with the more difficult questions raised by Burnham, and that was remarkably light on specific policy proposals. As we have seen, the main burden of Burnham's argument about the transfer of power to a managerial class was precisely the opposite of the moral drawn by the revisionists, since he confidently expected the connection between the receipt of a preferential distributive share and control over access to be reasserted through state ownership. It could therefore be argued with equal plausibility that an egalitarian response to the rise of the manager should be an attack on two fronts: public ownership *and* industrial democracy. As the socialist economist Thomas Balogh put it, the revisionist claim confused 'the sufficient and necessary conditions of social progress'. Although public ownership itself did not bring about a socialist society, it was nonetheless true that 'without nationalising a large sector of the economy' there could be no progress towards socialist ideals.[39] On this account, private ownership of productive assets should still be abolished (or significantly reduced), but to counteract the tendencies towards oligarchy identified by Burnham the new regime should then introduce greater democratic control over production and distribution, which would prevent the emergence of another ruling class.[40]

This emphasis on a pluralistic model of public ownership was the home territory of G. D. H. Cole, and he repeatedly stressed the virtues of a decentralised social-ism in his frequent interventions in these debates. Against the revisionists, Cole denied that he was guilty of making a fetish of public ownership by construing it as synonymous with socialism. He claimed never to have defined socialism in these terms, and doubted whether this tendency was as widespread as many revisionists believed: 'Surely we always regarded public ownership as a necessary means to an end, and socialism as including the end as well as the means.'[41] Indeed, Cole found it hard to imagine how the laudable egalitarian objectives cited by the revisionists could be realised within a society that continued to allow a large role for profit-making private industry. The idea that taxes and controls would be able to 'restrict the rewards accruing to owners of means of production' to any degree that was democratically agreed, and indeed that it would be possible to convert 'the managers to a code of professional conduct consistent with socialist objectives', was described by Cole as 'entirely unrealistic'.[42] Cole favoured a society characterised by a variety of socialised ownership structures, including a mixture of nationalised and co-operative enterprises, and some small private enterprises. In keeping with his guild socialist roots, he maintained that democratic control and participation should be the hallmark of socialised production, thus hoping to evade the illiberal consequences of complete state ownership predicted by Burnham and Hayek (and indeed, in an earlier period, by Cole himself).[43] How-ever, this was not to be brought about through a further programme of national-isation of the kind undertaken by the Attlee government, but rather by the state gradually absorbing inherited wealth and property, along with some company profits, so that it became the 'part proprietor of a host of productive businesses', and gradually moved towards ending private ownership of joint stock enterprises altogether. The state would then be free to sell or lease some of them to the co-operative movement and for others to continue under state control.[44] As I will discuss in the next chapter, elements of this programme were actually not as far from revisionism as they might seem.

The Bevanites and public ownership

Crucial political support for the egalitarian salience of public ownership came from the front-rank politicians of the Bevanite Left, but they were not as clear as Cole about the policies that followed from their ideological commitments. In so far as there was a distinctive Labour Left position on this issue it was that while equality, understood in a quantitative, distributive sense, was an important goal for socialists, it should not be seen as exhaustive of socialism. As Strachey put it, 'social equality will be one of the effects of socialism: it is not the thing itself'.[45] Politicians on the Labour Left such as Aneurin Bevan, Richard Crossman, Barbara Castle and even Harold Wilson all voiced this argument. Although the tensions between Bevanites and Gaitskellites seem in retrospect more to do with clashes between exotic personalities and differences of political culture than clashing political principles, when there was a specifically ideological disagreement between them it tended to be over the importance of public ownership. Consequently, Harold Wilson introduced the party conference debate on the policy document *Towards Equality* by putting equality in its place:

> I want to make this clear right away: we do not say as an executive that equality is the be-all and end-all of socialist policy; far from it. There cannot be socialism in this country or any other country unless we control the levers of economic power and there cannot be anything approaching equality either.[46]

The Bevanite faction composed fewer theoretical works than the revisionists, and when they did venture onto this terrain, it was noted that they had 'really very little to say about social equality'.[47] But this disinclination to discuss egalitarian ideals did not simply reflect a lack of theoretical interest on the part of the Bevanites, it followed from the Marxian premises that grounded their socialism. Bevan and his followers shared certain assumptions in common with the Left Book Club Marxism of the 1930s, albeit in a much less apocalyptic form. In particular, Bevanites stressed that abstract ethical language should not distract socialists from understanding the fundamental conflicts of economic interest that characterised capitalism. The Bevanites were suspicious of revisionist attempts to rest the entire weight of socialism on the single value of equality, particularly when this apparently abstract moral commitment came at the expense of a clear perception of the constraints that the market set to the Left's emancipatory objectives. They were convinced that, under a system of private ownership, attempts to redistribute wealth would rapidly meet resistance from property owners, so that, as Barbara Castle put it, 'the capitalists may refuse to run capitalism if they are denied its rewards'.[48] Incentives would be undermined and capital flight would take place. In short, the revisionists would 'simply starve the goose which is laying the golden eggs', as Crossman argued to Crosland.[49] So any serious attempt to reduce inequality would naturally have to entail public ownership of production, economic controls, and the exercise of power by the state, rather than relying on the grand moral sentiments purportedly commended by the revisionists.

Bevan himself provided a more reflective justification for public ownership. There was, he argued, a deep inconsistency in attempting to preserve a broadly individualist society characterised by private ownership while simultaneously seeking to alter the pattern of resource distribution through taxation for public spending. Individuals in such a society were inevitably conditioned to believe that the income that accrued to them was theirs by right, so that in 'a society where the bulk of property is privately owned, public spending is always an invasion of private rights'.[50] As a result, Bevan continued, spending on collective goods or transfer programmes becomes perceived as an appropriation by the state of money which the individual feels he or she is entitled to keep, and the electorate becomes increasingly tax resistant. A flourishing consumer society was likely to make this problem even more intractable: 'As modern industry produces new and attractive forms of private consumption, the individual citizen is made all the more reluctant to see his income taken away from him for remote purposes.'[51] In Bevan's view, there was 'a definite limit to taxation as a means of redistributing wealth'.[52] From a post-Thatcher vantage point, these remarks have a prophetic ring. Of course, for Bevan they did not indicate the end of redistribution as a viable goal; rather, they showed that public ownership remained a tool of decisive importance for the attainment of the Left's distributive objectives. As he put it, 'one of the central principles of socialism is the substitution of public for private ownership. There is no way around this.'[53]

It remained unclear whether this belief in harnessing the power of the state for socialist ends could or should recommend a pluralistic socialism of the sort advocated by Cole. Given the Bevanite emphasis on the importance of economic planning and state control of production, effecting a reconciliation between these themes and Cole's ideas would have been difficult. In a number of works, Crossman explored the importance of greater decentralisation and democratic participation as bulwarks against the managerial despotism envisaged by writers such as Burnham, but he never clarified how this agenda could accommodate fundamentalist claims about public ownership.[54]

Public ownership and self-ownership

Although the bulk of the debate about public ownership focused on the most plausible mechanism for achieving equality, the writings of John Strachey contested both revisionist political economy and the character of their distributive goals. As has been shown elsewhere, attempts to assimilate Strachey to Croslandite revisionism are problematic for various reasons.[55] Most importantly, his reaction to Crosland's *The Future of Socialism* showed that he was unconvinced by the revisionist attempt to separate distribution from production, and regarded Crosland's 'sincere equalitarianism' as 'quite inconsistent with his economic analysis', since outside of the depression conditions of the 1930s Strachey believed that substantial changes to the distribution of wealth could only be made through direct intervention into the structure of ownership.[56]

As we have seen, Strachey's view of distributive justice in the 1930s had been distinctively Marxist in that he focused on exploitation rather than inequality as the fundamental distributive ill produced by capitalism. Strachey continued to argue in this vein in the 1950s. In his 1956 book *Contemporary Capitalism*, he noted that for Marxists 'it is the *source*, not the size, of incomes that matters'. In other words, they were 'perfectly prepared to tolerate large *inequalities* of income if they are all received from work'.[57] Reviewing the book, Douglas Jay thought this a 'calamitous economic fallacy'. For social democrats, the most significant fact about a distributive pattern was the size of the relative shares and not whether a particular share was proportionate to productive contribution: 'There is nothing wrong in a working man drawing £15 a year in interest from the Post Office on his own savings. But there is something very wrong in a company chairman drawing £44,000 a year, mostly tax free, from one company!' Once 'the Marxist fallacy that certain types of income are always evil, and certain other types always good' had been abandoned, Jay concluded, then it would be seen that progressive taxation 'is the fundamental part of socialism, and public ownership a useful ally and partner'.[58]

In response to Jay's criticism, Strachey declared his fidelity to the characteristic Marxist objection to capitalism. 'Capitalism is still capitalism. So long as the decisive parts of the means of production are owned by private persons and operated, in the last resort, for their profit, the system will be recognisably itself and the basic socialist criticism of it will stand.' Against revisionism, Strachey persisted in drawing a connection between the Left's distributive objectives and public ownership: 'I for one shall never be satisfied until the decisive parts of the means of production have passed into some form of social ownership.' This was the only way of eliminating 'large unearned, property-derived, incomes', and ensuring that 'every man and woman is paid, as near as may be, the value of their work'.[59]

Interestingly, then, Strachey not only maintained that widespread socialisation was a necessary pre-condition for the attainment of the Left's distributive goals, but he also defended public ownership on the basis of a slightly different understanding of what those goals should be. Commentators have conventionally taken the view that Strachey had little to say about the ethical principles that were widely discussed by socialists in the 1950s, since he has been interpreted as advocating a rough-and-ready egalitarianism of more or less the same type as the revisionists.[60] While it is true that Strachey made little direct comment on the distributive pattern he considered fairest at an abstract level, it is clear from his remarks on public ownership that he still advocated the labour theory of value as a normative principle, just as he had in the 1930s. On Strachey's view of socialism, the aim was 'to redistribute the national income not only more equally, but above all more justly, so that every man and woman able to work receives what he or she earns and no able bodied man or woman receives what he or she has not earned'. 'The just society', thought Strachey, was one 'in which the labourer is rewarded in proportion to the work of his hand or his brain'.[61] By emphasising the normative importance of exploitation, Strachey played on the language of entitlement that was such a vital rhetorical move for popular Marxism, and he proclaimed that only under public ownership could 'the vital moral principle that what a man has made should belong to him, to enjoy or to exchange, be reasserted amidst the thunder of the forges, the looms and the conveyor belts of our contemporary world'.[62]

While Strachey's use of the idea of self-ownership differed from the revisionists, however, he shared their optimism about the capacity of the state and British democratic institutions to deliver on social reform. Although he acknowledged that oligarchical tendencies were inherent in a capitalist economy, Strachey assumed that this was a phenomenon that could be analysed within Marxian categories; the dominant elites were the capitalists, seeking to maximise their accumulation. Inspired by the exhilarating success of the 1945 government, Strachey maintained that the power of the capitalists could be constrained and eventually effaced by the concerted counter-pressure of the working-class majority through the ballot box.[63] In Strachey's view, the state was just 'an apparatus' that could 'be used oppressively by this or that interest, or group, or class of persons', but which had no 'independent existence of its own apart from the men, or categories of men, who wielded its power'. It seemed to Strachey that the fashionable discussion of the managerial society (the 'new despotism') was ideological in the Marxist sense; it was simply an expression of middle-class fear of the workers' new found willingness to employ the state to advance their interests.[64] But this post-1945 faith in the ideological neutrality of the democratic state was even more vulnerable than revisionist thought to the challenge of writers such as Burnham or Hayek. By regarding state ownership of productive property as the fundamental mechanism of economic redistribution, Strachey and the Bevanites were overly sanguine about the power that they would place in the hands of the elites who controlled the state. In the absence of a more decentralised, participative polity, there could be little democratic control over the productive process. Although at times they might have signalled their support for a democratic agenda of this kind, there was no systematic attempt to work out how this might be combined with their desire for central control and direction over the economy.[65]

Having reviewed the basic positions in the debate over public ownership, is it fair to say that the revisionists were simply proposing a different (and, they said, more effective) means to the same ultimate objective that had historically animated socialist thought? One cause for doubting this claim would be the subtle but important difference between the distributive goal cited by Strachey as the central ambition of socialism and the rival objective defended by his contemporaries such as Jay or Crosland. However, it should be clear from previous chapters that Strachey occupied a minority position on the British Left. The view of social justice expressed by Jay in reply to Strachey was in fact much closer to the egalitarianism of earlier British socialists.

A more important difference between the revisionists and socialists like Strachey was that they saw inequality as the product of a variety of social and economic factors and not simply as the result of one particular system of economic ownership. It followed that a modern egalitarian strategy would have to pay attention to these myriad causes of social stratification, and to the various social institutions that distributed life chances; it could not remain wedded to the traditional socialist intuition that a change in the structure of ownership would put an end to inequality. Whether this shift in emphasis involved a change in the means or the ends of socialism is a difficult question. To develop a full answer, I will first clarify the nature of the revisionists' egalitarianism, and then consider whether their focus on greater distributive equality involved not only a change of socialist policy but also an adjustment to the structure of socialist ideals. The remainder of this chapter and much of the next will offer an assessment of each of these issues, before returning in conclusion to the implications of these debates for egalitarian policy-making.

6.4 Sociologists and the rise of the meritocracy

Commentators on the revisionists generally agree that the characteristic feature of their political thought was a stress on equality as the pre-eminent goal of socialism, but disagree over the more difficult question of precisely what the revisionists understood by the term 'equality'. One influential interpretation has been that the revisionists, and in particular Crosland, were meritocrats in the straightforward sense that they believed that individuals with similar talents deserved the same chance to develop and be rewarded for their skills.[66] However, other writers on this question have found rather different views of social justice at the heart of the revisionist project. Raymond Plant has drawn attention to the similarities between Crosland's egalitarianism and John Rawls's notion of 'democratic equality'.[67] Present-day debates about social democratic ideology have even cultivated the impression that the revisionists desired a strict equality of outcome,[68] while other commentators have suggested that Crosland was fundamentally concerned with the distribution of social status, not with wealth, and explicitly changed the objective of socialist theory from economic to social equality.[69] Matters are further complicated by conflicting claims about the extent to which there was a unified revisionist position on equality at all. Some historians have argued that the leading revisionists were in fact sharply divided over their distributive objectives, and have distinguished between egalitarian and meritocratic strands of revisionist thought. Unfortunately, there is no agreement about exactly who was in each camp. Ellison has argued that a contrast can be drawn between the more egalitarian position advocated by Crosland and the meritocratic outlook of other leading revisionists such as Gaitskell, Jenkins and Jay, suggesting 'a "majority" and "minority" perspective within Gaitskellism' on this question.[70] Other writers have shuffled the same names into slightly different ideological constellations. For instance, Bryan has also detected an internal split within revisionist thought, but differs from Ellison in characterising both Crosland and Jenkins as egalitarians, setting them apart from Jay and Gaitskell 'who did think merit or desert could justify rewards'.[71]

In the face of these contradictory interpretations, it is tempting to conclude that some of this confusion must stem from the revisionists themselves, and that they were either internally inconsistent or straightforwardly in disagreement with each other about the kind of equality they favoured. While tempting, this conclusion would be too quick. To get a fuller understanding of what the revisionists meant by 'equality', it is necessary to look more systematically at the specific historical context of the revisionist debate. While it might seem that these historical circumstances have been discussed at exhaustive length, in practice one important aspect of the context of revisionism has been passed over in silence by the existing secondary literature. As has been widely discussed, the revisionist turn in socialist thought emerged from a particular set of political circumstances: the astonishing legislative success of the 1945 government; the subsequent electoral failures of the Labour Party; the bitter divide between Gaitskellites and Bevanites over the leadership and strategy of the Party; and the perceived emergence of a so-called 'affluent society'. While these features of the social and political context of revisionism have been well documented,[72] the *intellectual* context of revisionist ideas has yet to be investigated in comparable detail. This can be done both synchronically and diachronically: by investigating the ideological opponents and allies that the revisionists engaged in debate with, and by identifying the political ancestors whose ideas they absorbed. What can we learn about revisionist egalitarianism if we use these techniques to examine its intellectual context?

Investigating social mobility

Although it might seem that an obvious avenue to pursue would be the revisionists' clear anti-Bevanite agenda, and their engagement with aspects of Marxist theory, the previous section has shown that although this debate was of some consequence for the revisionist conception of social justice, its principal contribution was a negative one. As the discussion between Jay and Strachey illustrated, the ideological contest with Marxism certainly revealed, as far as the revisionists were concerned, the shortcomings of the labour theory of value as a principle of distributive justice. However, the debate with the Bevanites was not structured around a contest over competing distributive ideals; it was rather focused on the different question of how to deliver a more egalitarian distribution of wealth and opportunity, given varying theoretical and empirical assumptions about the nature of economic power.

It is therefore important to shift the focus from the overrated Bevanite/ Gaitskellite debate, and to consider instead a novel body of academic research that was very influential on political thought in post-war Britain, and that directly shaped the egalitarianism of revisionist writers and politicians. This body of research, which appeared immensely promising to some of the most creative minds in the Labour Party at this time, was sociology, a discipline that was starting to gain widespread academic recognition in Britain in the 1950s and that was tackling a research agenda that appeared directly relevant to the difficult political questions preoccupying the revisionists.[73] The sociological genre that initially attracted most attention was the study of social stratification, an area of research that acquired much greater quantitative and theoretical sophistication in the post-war era. The emergence of this style of sociology provided an important new ideological resource for egalitarians, analogous to the role that economics played in the 1930s. Just as the cutting-edge treatises on Keynesian economics had provided the Left with a powerful new argument for the redistribution of economic resources, mobility surveys that catalogued the grave inequality of life chances between individuals born into different classes gave fresh impetus to the Left's case for the radical reform of the social institutions that structured those inequalities. The inspiration for much of this work came from the United States, where a number of studies had been completed into rates of class mobility and the mechanisms by which individuals were grouped into social classes,[74] although there was also an obvious overlap between this type of inquiry and the British tradition of detailed empirical investigations into poverty and inequality. Influenced by the American research, British sociologists began to tackle similar questions in a number of pioneering studies produced in the 1950s and 60s, most importantly in the research undertaken by David Glass and his colleagues at the London School of Economics, and the related work undertaken by A. H. Halsey and Jean Floud on the relationship between social class and educational attainment.[75] The sociologists made three points of particular importance for socialist revisionism.

First, they stressed the heightened salience of merit (measured by educational qualifications) as a distributive principle in post-war Britain. Since the 1944 Education Act was thought to have created a meritocratic school system based on academic selection rather than ability to pay, it did not take much sociological insight to notice that there was a growing link between formal educational qualifications and occupational status. Nonetheless, professional sociologists were unusually authoritative disseminators of this observation. T. H. Marshall's famous book *Citizenship and Social Class*, for example, drew attention to this change in social selection mechanisms and pointed out that a meritocratic distributive principle would in turn produce a fresh set of inequalities. 'The more confident the claim of education to be able to sift human material during the early years of life, the more is mobility concentrated within those years, and consequently limited thereafter.' In a pithy phrase that was subsequently much quoted in socialist circles, Marshall drew the moral that 'the ticket obtained on leaving school or college is for a life journey'. Marshall himself was sanguine about the inegalitarian effects of stratification on the basis of educational ability, believing that the advantages of this system 'in particular the elimination of inherited privilege, far outweigh its incidental defects'.[76] As Jean Floud put it, education had therefore become 'the primary agency of occupational and social selection'. Since the framework of the British education system had recently been altered in the interests of encouraging greater equality of opportunity, Floud speculated that the consequences of such reform, although unclear, might be 'considerable changes both in the social hierarchy of occupations and in the degree of mobility within and between occupations'.[77]

Second, the sociologists undermined the empirical basis of the belief that British society had historically offered a route to the top for the talented regardless of their social class and, in spite of Floud's initial optimism about the social fluidity that would be fostered by the 1944 Act, they also cast doubt on the widespread conviction that the post-1944 system of academic selection had settled the issue of equality of opportunity once and for all. The work on social mobility conducted by David Glass and his colleagues provided an effective and widely read summary of the substantial inequalities in opportunity that characterised Britain before the 1944 Act was passed. Their research demonstrated that there was a strong correlation between the social status of fathers and sons at the top of the class hierarchy, and that over successive generations there had been no change in the intensity of this correlation.[78] In spite of some mobility elsewhere within the class structure, the most prestigious professions were largely closed shops; they recruited from within, excluding talented members of the working class. Implicit within this study was also a pessimistic view of the likely impact of the 1944 reforms. The evidence on the effect of education on social mobility suggested that while working-class children who were selected to attend grammar schools were more likely to move up the class structure than those who went to other types of school, the overall pattern of association between fathers and sons still displayed the same basic characteristic, in that the children of fathers from lower status occupations still had a poorer chance of entering the higher status occupations than their grammar school colleagues from more privileged backgrounds. In short, 'education as such appears to modify, but not to destroy, the characteristic association between the social status of fathers and sons'.[79]

Indeed, the early research into the effects of the 1944 Act, notably studies conducted by Halsey and his colleagues, drew attention to a disturbing fact: there remained a strong class bias in the allocation of children between grammar and secondary modern schools. The basic finding of this early fieldwork was that the class distribution of pupils at grammar schools was heavily skewed towards the middle class and what was known as the 'upper working class'.[80] Floud, Halsey and Martin argued that this could largely be attributed to the unequal distribution of measured intelligence between social classes.[81] Additionally, the performance of working-class children once they reached grammar schools was worse than that of their middle-class contemporaries, and working-class pupils were more likely to drop out before reaching the sixth form.[82] Floud et al. concluded the first phase of their research into schools in Hertfordshire and Middlesbrough on an equivocal note: 'If by "ability" we mean "measured intelligence" and by "opportunity" access to grammar schools, then opportunity may be said to stand in close relationship with ability in both these areas today.' Accordingly, they characterised their central finding as 'the chances of children at a given level of ability entering grammar schools are no longer dependent on their social origins'.[83] However, their work explicitly questioned the premise that equality of opportunity could be construed in these narrow terms, and expressed grave doubts about the equity of distribution according to measured intelligence, given that it seemed likely that access to measured intelligence was itself dependent on a range of environmental rather than genetic variables.[84]

Third, these empirical findings led sociologists to comment on the normative plausibility of the ideal of equality of opportunity currently embodied in Britain's social institutions. As the sociologist Peter Willmott pointed out, it was not obvious that the growing link between educational qualifications and occupational status had a straightforward relationship with social mobility. The greater emphasis on formal education might not mean, as many suggested, that there was greater social mobility than before; nor did it mean that there was less, as some radicals argued. Rather, 'the evidence suggests that there has been little change in the *extent* of mobility in both countries [Britain and the USA]; the difference is almost certainly in the *means* of achieving mobility, which was formerly via the shop floor and is now characteristically through the 11-plus, grammar school and university'. One consequence of this, thought Willmott, was 'that society is becoming inflexible in new and dangerous ways'. In short, 'mobility has become institutionalised'.[85]

This worry about the 'institutionalisation' of mobility led a number of sociologists to point out that such a system might endow unjust social inequalities with greater legitimacy than previous social selection mechanisms, and create new hierarchies of social status with damaging effects on the self-respect and life chances of those at the bottom. One of the most influential social scientists of this period, Richard Titmuss, offered a particularly evocative description of this development:

> This is perhaps one of the outstanding social characteristics of the twentieth century; the fact that more and more people consciously experience at one or more stages in their lives the process of selection and rejection; for education, for work, for vocational training, for professional status, for promotion, for opportunities of access to pension schemes, for collective social benefits, for symbols of prestige and success, and in undergoing tests of mental and physical fitness, personality, skill and functional performance. In some senses at least, the arbiters of opportunity and of dependency have become, in their effects, more directly personal, more culturally demanding, more psychologically threatening.[86]

This warning was echoed by virtually all of the professional sociologists working in this area. For example, Glass had introduced his study with a cautionary message about the ambiguities of the particular understanding of equality of opportunity embodied in the 1944 Education Act. He was concerned about the potential for academic selection at an early age 'to reinforce the prestige of occupations already high in social status and to divide the population into streams which many may come to regard – indeed, already regard – as distinct as sheep and goats'.[87] The most celebrated expression of these worries came in Michael Young's 1958 work, *The Rise of the Meritocracy*. The specific concerns expressed by Young and others are explored later in this chapter. For the moment, the important point to note is that debates about the justice of a meritocratic distribution gained greater political salience and empirical specificity as a result of this burgeoning sociological literature.

Tawneyite social democracy
In addition to the influence of academic sociology, a second aspect of the intellectual context of revisionism should be noted: the revisionists perceived

themselves as located within an ideological lineage, a tradition of gradualist liberal socialism that had deep roots in British political history and culture.[88] As well as the synchronic influences just examined, then, there is also a diachronic question: who were the intellectual ancestors whose work helped to form the revisionists' thoughts on equality? In one sense, the previous chapters of this book can be read as an extended answer to this question, but to focus the discussion it is worth singling out one particular text: R. H. Tawney's *Equality*. The way in which Tawney was appropriated and sanctified by the Labour Party as an in-house philosophical guru is a complicated story, and has rightly been subjected to some sceptical treatment by succeeding generations of scholars.[89] Nonetheless, giving due regard to these health warnings, Tawney's work on equality did exert a substantial influence on revisionist thought, both directly and through its dissemination into the Labour Party's conventional wisdom. As should be clear from earlier chapters, Tawney's egalitarianism was representative of the British Left's thinking in the first third of the twentieth century, so this claim about his influence serves as a proxy for the continuing vitality of this broader social democratic discourse about equality.

The fourth edition of Tawney's *Equality* was published in 1952, with a new epilogue that detailed his favourable assessment of the 1945 government and exhorted further progress along the road to an egalitarian society.[90] A further edition was released in 1964, with an introduction by Richard Titmuss. Tawney's egalitarianism was continually cited and praised by each of the political and ideological factions on the Left,[91] and the Tawneyite critique of equality of opportunity was strongly in evidence throughout the revisionist writings of this period. Tawney's text had exposed the fragile coherence and limited plausibility of the traditional ideology of equality of opportunity on two counts. First, he argued that it was impossible to obtain an equal chance for individuals of like ability to develop and exercise their abilities in the presence of the kind of material inequalities that were generated by unregulated capitalism. Second, he further demonstrated that a single-minded focus on facilitating greater social mobility would be unjust, since it would accord prestige, financial reward and greater personal fulfilment to those who were fortunate enough to possess marketable skills. Opportunities to rise up the occupational hierarchy, argued Tawney, must be complemented by greater equality of condition in order to ensure that the majority, and not just the exceptional few, have the opportunity to live fulfilling lives.[92]

In summary, both the findings of the sociologists and the tradition of socialist theory the revisionists located themselves within pointed in the same direction: towards a distributive theory that not only acknowledged a meritocratic distribution as an important improvement on existing inequalities, but also emphasised that this objective was not exhaustive as far as social justice was concerned. Clearly, though, setting out the intellectual environment surrounding the revisionists is only the first stage in understanding their ideas, since it is then necessary to examine how these environmental influences shaped the arguments made by the revisionists themselves. The next section aims to do just that.

6.5 Egalitarians or meritocrats?

There are a number of well-known connections between the revisionists and both the sociological debates and social democratic tradition examined in the previous section. Crosland was an assiduous reader of sociological research, and his writings are replete with references to the sociological literature summarised above.[93] Indeed, when Crosland served as Secretary of State for Education from 1965–7, Halsey served as his special advisor.[94] Michael Young was a friend and intellectual sparring partner of Crosland's. As Head of the Labour Party's Research Department until 1950 he had access to the inner circles of the Party, and after he left he was a regular fixture at the numerous conferences and seminars convened throughout the 1950s to rethink socialism. Young's new career as a professional sociologist meant that he was a vital link between the work of academic sociologists and the revisionist politicians who were setting the intellectual agenda within the Labour Party. As well as joining Socialist Union (and serving on the editorial committee of their journal *Socialist Commentary*), he regularly exchanged views about politics and sociology with Crosland.[95] Many sociologists frequently wrote for directly political audiences in journals such as the *New Statesman* and *Socialist Commentary*, and a few, for example Peter Willmott and the Oxford industrial relations scholar Alan Fox, actively contributed to the work of groups such as Socialist Union. Through these links, the findings of social stratification research became widely discussed on the Left. Similar connections existed between the revisionist camp and Tawney: Gaitskell was eventually to provide a generous tribute to Tawney at his funeral, and Rita Hinden edited a book of Tawney's essays, *The Radical Tradition*.[96] The writings of Socialist Union were more or less explicitly based on Tawneyite principles, and Tawney himself corresponded with Hinden about drafts of Socialist Union publications.[97]

Were the revisionists meritocrats?

More importantly, it is possible to show not just the mechanisms by which egalitarian ideas were transmitted, but also the adoption of these ideas by the revisionists in their political thought.

As with previous debates on the Left about equality, revisionists began by allaying any fears that they might advocate a Shavian position. Gaitskell emphasised that this omnipresent anti-egalitarian allegation was untrue: 'Let us have no more nonsense about us being in favour of an exact and precise equality of income with no differentials at all.'[98] Socialists did, however, 'start from a presumption in favour of equality', asking: 'What are the various factors justifying differentials?'[99] An immediate challenge to the revisionist position was to offer a more precise characterisation of how such differentials could be justified: did they entail an acceptance of the justice of social inequalities so long as they were grounded on individual merit, or were they simply a concession to the necessity of incentives for efficiency purposes? In short, were the revisionists meritocrats?

The latter position was certainly the interpretation of revisionist socialism that their opponents on the Left sought to promote, and some other commentators agreed with this assessment. For example, A. J. Ayer classified Crosland's egalitarianism in the following terms:

> [Crosland] is not, indeed, an out and out egalitarian. He sees that power and authority cannot be equally distributed, and he allows that those who have greater responsibilities, and those who have the talents to render greater services, in one way or another, should be more greatly rewarded. What he is chiefly concerned with is equality of opportunity. This is partly defensible on grounds of national interest ... But mainly, for Mr Crosland, it is a matter of justice. Not everybody can enjoy the bigger plums; there are not and never can be enough to go round, but it is right that everybody should be given a fair chance to pick them.[100]

Norman Birnbaum, one of the editors of the influential 'New Left' journal *Universities and Left Review*, took a more critical view. The sociologist Daniel Bell had in fact reported to Crosland after meeting the editors of this journal that 'you will be amused to know that they consider the chief enemy to be "Croslandism"'.[101] This was borne out as Birnbaum took Crosland to task for his anaemic conception of equality:

> Mr Crosland would like Britain to become more egalitarian – but his conception of equality is one of equal right to enter this unequal contest. He proposes, for instance, to broaden educational opportunity so that the possibility of easy ascent into the elite will diminish resentment at the existence of an elite. But he does not suggest eliminating the elite or seriously diminishing its advantages.[102]

Other writers aligned with the emerging 'New Left' also criticised the 'mediocre meritocracy' and the 'competitive ethos' allegedly envisaged by the revisionists as their social ideal, an objective that they argued simply 'disarmed the labour movement', robbing it of its basic critique of capitalism.[103] Birnbaum suggested elsewhere that Labour had restricted itself to attacking 'the Conservatives for denying equality of opportunity', when in fact what was required was 'a new conception of opportunity for another sort of society'.[104]

This perception of *The Future of Socialism*, and of revisionism more generally, was mistaken. The revisionists had far more substantial ideas about such 'a new conception of opportunity' than the New Left gave them credit for. Crosland himself responded to Birnbaum's criticism with the rejoinder: 'This shows, what I have long suspected, that one should not waste one's time writing books; for no one reads them.'[105] As Crosland then pointed out, he *was* keen to diminish the favoured position of the elite and was not simply interested in creating a more meritocratic society. This defence can be extended to other revisionists. When Socialist Union observed that equality of opportunity could be 'taken to mean no more than that everyone should have an equal start in life', they stressed that this 'liberal conception of equality' was 'part of what socialists want too, but only part'.[106] The idea of granting every citizen an equal chance to compete within a given hierarchical order of positions and rewards was, in Crosland's phrase, 'not, from a socialist point of view, sufficient', and therefore could not satisfy the revisionists.[107] In short, they advocated a far more expansive and pluralistic conception of equality of opportunity than that embodied by the conventional understanding of that term. Virtually all of the major revisionists of this period made the same point, including Gaitskell, Jay, Jenkins, Young and the members of Socialist Union. Despite differences of emphasis, the most important feature of their political outlook was precisely a critique of the conventional view that construed equality of opportunity as demanding access to social positions and material rewards on the basis of the attainment of certain educational qualifications. The revisionists joined with sociologists such as Glass, Halsey and Titmuss in expressing anxiety about the fairness and desirability of a society structured along such reductively meritocratic lines.

For and against meritocracy

It is true that the revisionists saw meritocratic equality of opportunity as one dimension of social justice. This is probably where critics from the New Left managed to glean some textual justification for their categorisation of the revisionist position as meritocratic, since the revisionists stressed that the allocation of social positions on grounds of ability was of great importance, and that there was some way to go before Britain would even approach this standard. Partly, they saw this objective as important for reasons of economic efficiency, to ensure that 'talents and capabilities, instead of being wasted, will be utilised to their utmost'.[108] However, it was also felt to be a significant injustice that class background influenced the extent to which individuals could develop and exercise their abilities. As Jay noted, 'it is a sheer denial of basic human rights to deprive anybody of the chance to use and cultivate the capacities with which they are born', an injustice that was particularly profound given that one section of society was denied 'opportunities of development which are in fact offered to others at a price'.[109] But while this was certainly an important theme in revisionist writings, it should be recognised that it did not exhaust their view of social justice. The critics of revisionism who focused only on the rhetoric about encouraging greater social mobility and a fair start in life offered only a partial account of their conception of socialist ends.

   This can be substantiated by noting two more egalitarian principles of social justice defended by the revisionists. First, while they recognised that efficiency and fairness suggested that jobs should be allocated according to ability, the egalitarians of this period were convinced that the distribution of 'merit' was a product of environmental influences rather than genetic inequalities. Although sociologists had demonstrated that there was an unequal distribution of measured intelligence between social classes, the revisionists agreed with progressive sociologists such as Halsey that this could largely be accounted for by the unequal environmental conditions to which individuals from different social classes were exposed. Accordingly, it was argued that the distribution of ability could itself be equalised through the use of education and social policy.[110] This commitment picked up on the argument classically expounded by Tawney: a genuine attempt to facilitate social mobility would itself demand substantive equality of economic condition. This principle required radical reforms to the distribution of resources and opportunities in society, especially the organisation of the education system, and I will give it detailed consideration in the next chapter, which discusses more directly the relationship between egalitarian ideals and education policy.[111]

Second, it was clear that even once class biases in the distribution of measured intelligence had been corrected, there would still be wide variations in the capacities of individuals. While the 'monopoly' element in the higher salaries commanded by the talented would be eliminated, a society that continued to proportion rewards to productive capacities would still be characterised by significant inequalities of wealth and social status. The revisionist thinkers who wrote at the greatest length about this question anticipated this implication, and concluded that there did not seem to be any obvious moral reason to distribute material resources, or social status, on the basis of productive ability.

Indeed, although there are always hazards associated with retrospectively attributing causal influence to one individual within a group of thinkers, there is a strong case that the contribution of Michael Young to this aspect of revisionist thinking has been underestimated. While the egalitarianism of revisionist politicians, and in particular Crosland, has received considerable attention, the role of Young in transmitting both Tawneyite ideals and sociological evidence to the more famous and politically powerful revisionist thinkers has not been sufficiently emphasised. Young's major work on this theme, *The Rise of the Meritocracy*, did not appear until 1958, after the revisionist debate was well under way. However, it is clear from archival and textual evidence that Young had in fact been elaborating his arguments about 'meritocracy' amongst progressive elites from the late 1940s onwards.

Famously, Young has been credited with introducing the word 'meritocracy' into the English language. Although Young intended the word to have a negative connotation, in subsequent political debate it increasingly came to be used to indicate a highly desirable social objective. As a prescient reviewer observed at the time, Young had 'supplied a shibboleth to test the tongue of every aspirant to power in contemporary Britain'.[112] Intriguingly, there is at least one earlier published instance of the word being used: in a 1956 article by Alan Fox in *Socialist Commentary*, where Fox made the point that a society stratified through equality of opportunity would be a ' "meritocracy"; the society in which the gifted, the smart, the energetic, the ambitious and the ruthless are carefully sifted out and helped towards their destined positions of dominance, where they proceed not only to enjoy the fulfilment of exercising their natural endowments but also to receive a fat bonus thrown in for good measure'.[113] It is unclear whether Fox coined this term himself or whether he first heard it from Young at first hand. It is likely to be the latter, since Young's first draft of the text that later became *The Rise of the Meritocracy* was produced in the early 1950s as a possible contribution to the *New Fabian Essays*,[114] and Young had elaborated his nascent critique of meritocracy in other early works, notably a private research paper he wrote for the Labour Party NEC at the end of his tenure as Head of Research in 1951, entitled *For Richer, For Poorer*, and his PhD thesis, supervised by Richard Titmuss and awarded by the London School of Economics in 1955.[115]

In any case, Young played a crucial role in disseminating the insight that a meritocratic society would be extremely unfair and unattractive, since if taken to its logical conclusion it would concentrate material resources and social status on the section of the community who were fortunate enough to possess one particular kind of ability, namely marketable talents. The result, speculated Young, would be the creation of a fresh class hierarchy, just as pernicious as the class divisions that characterised Britain in the 1950s, but without the consoling message that those in the lower classes were trapped in their subordinate position by the unfairness of the system. On the contrary, in terms of the dominant social morality, they would know that their inferior status was entirely their own fault. The narrator of Young's book conveyed the unjustified sense of superiority that would characterise the upper echelons of such a society, and their condescension and inhumanity towards the 'meritless': 'the eminent know that success is just reward for their own capacity, for their own efforts, and for their own undeniable achievement. They deserve to belong to a superior class.' Those at the bottom 'know they have had every chance' and, if they have failed to make the grade, 'are they not bound to recognise that they have an inferior status – not as in the past because they were denied opportunity; but because they *are* inferior?'[116]

A central theme of the book was the way in which socialists and other progressives had unwittingly prepared the way for the meritocracy by campaigning for equality of opportunity and undermining the moral legitimacy of inherited wealth and other mechanisms that transmitted intergenerational advantage. The socialists had instilled self-respect and ambition in the working class, and had offered such persuasive arguments against parental partiality that it was no longer conceivable for the wealthy to argue openly for inherited wealth or nepotistic appointments. In the end, 'the wealthy could not fight because their morale was sapped by socialist teaching'.[117] The ironic praise for these great achievements of the labour movement was both Young's subtle expression of disquiet about the future direction of Labour policy after the triumphs of the 1945 government, and a philosophical meditation on the kind of equality that socialists ought to aim at. Although he was not particularly prescriptive in *The Rise of the Meritocracy*, the warning he offered about impoverished thinking about 'equality of opportunity' was clear. As the narrator observed, the introduction of merit as a social selection mechanism 'made nonsense' of 'loose talk of the equality of man':

> Men, after all, are notable not for the equality, but for the inequality, of their endowment. Once all the geniuses are amongst the elite, and all the morons amongst the workers, what meaning can equality have? . . . What is the purpose of abolishing inequalities in nurture except to reveal and make more pronounced the inescapable inequalities of nature?[118]

Young's book was widely read, reviewed and discussed after its publication in 1958.[119] As we have seen, the central arguments of the book were in any case accessible to a number of important socialist intellectuals before 1958, thanks to Young's personal connections to, and indefatigable participation in, the many debates about socialist ideology during the 1950s. There is direct evidence of Young's influence in the case of Crosland's *The Future of Socialism*.

Contrary to the interpretation of the New Left and other reviewers, Crosland did state that the meritocratic ideal was unjust: 'Admittedly, from the point of view of social justice, an aristocracy of talent is an obvious improvement on a hereditary aristocracy, since no one is in fact denied an equal chance. Yet I do not believe, as a personal value judgement, that it can be described as a "just" society.'[120] Crosland's reason for this was twofold. One was that it seemed unfair to reward individuals for having greater intelligence than others, given 'that superior intelligence is largely due to parental status, through a combination of heredity and beneficial upbringing: and that no one deserves either so generous a reward or so severe a penalty for a quality implanted from outside, for which he himself can claim only a limited responsibility.' More fundamentally, however, Crosland argued that no matter whether a particular individual trait was 'inbred or not':

> Why should this one trait, or even a group of traits, alone determine success or failure, riches or poverty, a high or low prestige? Why should no marks be given for saintliness, generosity, compassion, humour, beauty, assiduity, continence, or artistic ability? ... It is the injustice of isolating, as a basis for extreme inequality, certain selected ones out of the multiple strands that go to make up the human personality, which constitutes the fundamental ethical case against any elite or aristocracy.[121]

Obviously, Crosland conceded that there were practical reasons for continuing to offer higher rewards to those with greater ability, but 'if this requires such large differential privileges as to create a distinct elite, differently educated and socially select, it must be regarded as an unpleasant concession to economic efficiency, and not as being intrinsically just'.[122] All of which offered an analysis that was broadly in line with Young's, and indeed Crosland acknowledged in a footnote to these passages: 'My views on this point owe much to discussions with Mr Michael Young.' Young's comments on the draft of *The Future of Socialism* support this claim.[123]

The injustice of a formal equality of opportunity was also seen by Socialist Union. Rather than 'an equal start with the race left to the swiftest', Socialist Union argued, 'what socialists want is an equal chance for everyone, taking their lives as a whole. They are concerned with the whole bundle of opportunities which society distributes throughout a lifetime.'[124] While socialists had previously concentrated on the importance of tackling class distinctions, and the role of class background in preventing working-class individuals from developing their talents, this did not exhaust the socialist concern about inequality:

> Even if all class distinctions were wiped out, the inequalities inherent in man would remain. Society would still face the task of honouring the claim of every man to an equal chance in life. There would still be the weak and the strong, the bright and the backward, the lucky and the unlucky. These inequalities can never be eliminated but they can be prevented from becoming a source of social discrimination.[125]

As Arthur Lewis approvingly remarked, this was socialism as 'a philosophy for underdogs, championing their rights against those of the top dogs', whether the latter were 'born in the purples, or have made their way up by brains, work or local authority awards'.[126] There are numerous other examples of this criticism of meritocracy in revisionist or other mainstream Labour Party writings of this period.[127]

Since the revisionists rejected both a strict equality of income and a meritocracy, it was necessary to formulate an alternative criterion that could specify the range of permissible inequalities. In line with earlier egalitarians, the revisionists aimed to reduce inequality to the minimum level necessary to stimulate productive contributions. Lewis argued that socialists 'believe that wide differences of income and property are bad, and we desire to limit differences of income to the minimum required to stimulate and reward initiative, effort and responsibility'.[128] It should be stressed that not all of the pronouncements of the revisionists on this question achieved a level of consistency that would satisfy the rigorous scrutiny of a political philosopher. In particular, there was an occasional tendency for writers to blur together meritocratic and incentive-based arguments for inequalities of material reward. Gaitskell himself was prone to do this:

> While we do not say that all should receive the same income, we hold that the differences should be related to generally accepted criteria of merit – such as the nature of the work – more being paid for dirty, harder, more skilled, better performed, more responsible jobs. We say too that these differences should not be greater than are necessary to provide adequate incentives in the interest of economic progress.[129]

In a similar vein, Jay argued: 'The skilful or diligent or responsible worker is felt to deserve more; but this perfectly valid moral judgement does not tell us how much more. The only rational answer to the question "how much more?" is, therefore, this: that amount more which will ensure that their talents are exercised and that society benefits from them.'[130] It was uncertain whether these occasional gestures towards the idea that more skilled work deserved a greater reward signalled an endorsement of differential rewards on this basis, perhaps as a concession to popular opinion about the justice of desert, or whether these remarks were intended as an incentive-based justification for inequality, or even one grounded on the idea of compensatory equalisation.

Since absolute logical precision and consistency was not a priority for the kind of political argument the revisionists were constructing, it would be unrealistic to expect an exhaustive treatment of these intricate conceptual distinctions. However, if we take into account the contextual and textual evidence discussed earlier, especially the scepticism about the use of merit as a distributive ideal, there are strong grounds for taking incentives to be the basis for the revisionist justification of differentials. As Labour's study group on equality argued, 'socialists recognise the validity of income differences, not as a recognition of differences in merit, but for the practical purpose of providing incentives to persons performing the more skilled and responsible, or the heavier and less congenial work of society'.[131] It was necessary, thought Crosland, to ground inequalities on the idea of rent of ability, understood as necessary incentive payments to secure the performance of important economic functions; 'that is, the additional reward which exceptional ability can in practice command from the community'.[132] The revisionist aim is therefore best understood as 'the minimum practicable inequality', this commitment carrying with it the clear implication 'that inequality is not justified beyond the point necessary to ensure that the productive abilities of the community are reasonably fully used'.[133] This position was consonant with that adopted by earlier egalitarians and, as both Crosland and Young later noted, was similar to the 'democratic equality' advocated by John Rawls in his *A Theory of Justice*.[134] All of this provided some justification for the revisionist claim to be merely revising the means rather than the ends of socialism.[135]

Although the revisionist view of social justice therefore allowed some material inequality, it did so on the same basis as earlier egalitarians, and there is little evidence that the ideological rivals of the revisionists from the Left endorsed distributive principles that were somehow more egalitarian. The major ideological disagreement in this period was in fact focused on a more complex issue: the relationship between these egalitarian ideals and the Left's other traditional aim of cultivating a more co-operative society. It is this debate that will be discussed in the next chapter.

Notes

1 For an assessment of the distributional impact of the 1945–51 government, see Tomlinson, *Democratic Socialism*, 265–83. The idea of a 'redistribution of esteem' during this period is taken from McKibbin, *Ideologies of Class*, 290–2.

2 D. MacRae, 'The ideological situation in the labour movement', *PQ*, 24 (1953), 78.

3 L. Robbins, 'Notes on public finances', *Lloyds Bank Review*, No. 38, October 1955, 8.

4 G. D. H. Cole, 'Notes on "British socialist way of life"', paper for Fabian Conference on Problems Ahead, Oxford, March 1950, Cole Papers D1/19/3, 5.

5 'This month's *Encounter*: all about equality', *Encounter*, July 1956, 2; 'A Labour policy-maker', 'The future of Labour: "thoughtful socialists"', *MG*, 11.1.1955, 6.

6 The members of this 'study group on equality' were Gaitskell, J. Cooper, J. Griffiths, A. Skeffington, J. H. Wilson, C. A. R. Crosland and R. Jenkins. See 'Membership of study groups and the local government subcommittee', LPRD, R547/November 1955; 'A synopsis for a research project on equality', LPRD, RE5/November 1955. Their deliberations were published by the Labour Party as *Towards Equality: Labour's Policy for Social Justice* (London, 1956), alongside a similar document on liberty: *Personal Freedom: Labour's Policy for the Individual and Society* (London, 1956). Both were subsequently debated at Party Conference: *LPACR* 1956, 82–9, 117–32.

7 P. Williams (ed.), *The Diary of Hugh Gaitskell 1945–56* (London, 1983), 542; entry dictated 14.7.1956.

8 R. Jenkins, *Fair Shares for the Rich* (London, 1951), 3; C. A. R. Crosland, *The Future of Socialism* (London, 1956), 191, fn. 2.

9 C. A. R. Crosland, *Future*, 190–1. The welfare argument did not disappear; indeed, Crosland's discussion of it was partly a rebuttal of the utilitarian egalitarianism of R. Jenkins, 'Equality', in R. H. S. Crossman (ed.), *New Fabian Essays* (London, 1952), 71.

10 Little, *Critique*, 274–9; [N. Davenport], 'Cat among the pigeons', *TLS*, 22.9.1950, 599 (attribution of author from N. Davenport, *Memoirs of a City Radical* (London, 1974), 74); C. A. R. Crosland, 'Review of *A Critique of Welfare Economics*', *Universities Quarterly*, 5 (1951), 180–3; I. Little, 'Critique of welfare economics' and D. MacCrae, 'Sociology and welfare economics', papers for First Buscot Park Conference, 23–5.5.1952, Gaitskell Papers A137/2; D. Reisman, *Anthony Crosland: The Mixed Economy* (Basingstoke, 1997), 9; D. Reisman, *Crosland's Future: Opportunity and Outcome* (Basingstoke, 1997), 127.

11 Crosland, 'Inequalities of wealth', in his *The Conservative Enemy* (London, 1962), 40. Nonetheless, Crosland did use certain efficiency arguments for greater equality, for example the familiar claim that an egalitarian society would widen opportunity and thus make a more efficient use of the available pool of talent: *Future*, 214–15.

12 R. H. S. Crossman, 'Planning for freedom' [1956], in his *Planning for Freedom* (London, 1965), 61.

13 On revisionism, see S. Haseler, *The Gaitskellites: Revisionism in the British Labour Party* (London, 1969); D. Howell, 'The restatement of socialism in the Labour Party, 1947–61' (PhD thesis, Manchester University, 1971); Bryan, 'Development of revisionist thought'; C. Torrie, 'Ideas, policy and ideology: the British Labour Party in opposition, 1951–9' (DPhil thesis, University of Oxford, 1997). I take the most important generators of revisionist thought to be the politicians Hugh Gaitskell, Anthony Crosland, Douglas Jay, Roy Jenkins and Hugh Dalton; and the academics or writers Michael Young, Rita Hinden, Arthur Lewis and James Meade. I also include the intellectuals and activists affiliated to the Socialist Union group, and their periodical *Socialist Commentary* (edited by Hinden). This list is relatively uncontroversial, although I exclude, for reasons explained later, John Strachey, who is sometimes classified as a revisionist.

14 W. A. Lewis, *Principles of Economic Planning* (London, 1969 [1949]), 10–11. Crosland referred approvingly to Lewis's definition in his 'The transition from capitalism', in Crossman, *New Fabian Essays*, 61, as did Jenkins, *Fair Shares*, 3; Socialist Union, *Twentieth Century Socialism* (Harmondsworth, 1956), 23. The slogan is often attributed to Crosland or Gaitskell: e.g. J. Vaizey, 'Whatever happened to equality? 3: equality and fairness', *Listener*, 16.5.1974, 629; Drucker, *Doctrine and Ethos*, 46; Reisman, *Crosland's Future*, 57.

15 T. Wilson, 'Changing tendencies in socialist thought', *Lloyds Bank Review*, July 1956, 4.

16 See B. Jackson, 'Revisionism reconsidered: "property-owning democracy" and egalitarian strategy in post-war Britain', *Twentieth Century British History*, 16 (2005), 419–25; see also section 7.5.

17 Francis, *Ideas and Policies*, 65–99; Tomlinson, *Democratic Socialism*, 94–123.

18 I. Zweiniger-Bargielowska, *Austerity in Britain* (Oxford, 2000), 214–55; Toye, *Labour Party*, 185–242.

19 W. A. Lewis, 'The distribution of property', *SC*, December 1955, 366. See Meade, *Planning and the Price Mechanism*, 6–7; Lewis, *Principles*, 7–29; Meade on Lewis, *EJ*, 60 (1950), 117–22.

20 'A synopsis for a research project on equality', LPRD, RE5/November 1955, 1.

21 E.g. Haseler, *Gaitskellites*; Howell, *British Social Democracy*, 181–241; A. Warde, *Consensus and Beyond* (Manchester, 1982), 49–93; Thompson, *Political Economy*, 149–68; A. Thorpe, *A History of the British Labour Party* (Basingstoke, 2001), 125–44.

22 Socialist Union, *Socialism: A New Statement of Principles* (London, 1952), 21.

23 Thompson, *John Strachey*, 148–265; Kramnick and Sheerman, *Harold Laski*, 421–579.

24 As Martin Francis has suggested, another factor motivating this engagement with Marxism, never explicitly stated by the revisionists, was probably the influence of the Cold War, and the need to distinguish British democratic socialism from Soviet communism: 'Mr Gaitskell's Ganymede: reassessing Crosland's *Future of Socialism*', *Contemporary British History*, 11 (1997), 54.

25 Gaitskell, *Recent Developments*, 25–6.

26 Crosland, *Future*, 71–3, quote at 72. See also Socialist Union, *Socialism*, 19–20; R. Hinden, 'The public ownership debate', *SC*, March 1960, 4; Jay, *Socialism in the New Society* (London, 1962), 16–17.

27 A. Berle and G. Means, *The Modern Corporation and Private Property* (New York, 1932). On its reception by socialists, see S. Brooke, 'Atlantic crossing? American views of capitalism and British socialist thought 1932–62', *Twentieth Century British History*, 2 (1991), 111–18; D. Sassoon, *One Hundred Years of Socialism* (London, 1997), 246–7.

28 J. Burnham, *The Managerial Revolution* (London, 1942), 87, Burnham's emphasis.

29 Burnham, *Managerial Revolution*, 56.

30 Burnham, *Managerial Revolution*, 89–90.

31 See G. Orwell, 'Second thoughts on James Burnham' [1946], *GO 18*, 268–84; his 'Burnham's view of the contemporary world struggle' [1947], *GO 19*, 96–105.

32 Crosland, 'Chapter 6: Burnham and the managerial revolution', typescript, *c.*1956, Crosland Papers 13/7.

33 S. H. Beer, 'Fabianism revisited', *Review of Economics and Statistics*, 35 (1953), 204.

34 R. H. S. Crossman, 'Towards a philosophy of socialism', in Crossman, *New Fabian Essays*, 12, Crossman's emphasis. See also Austen Albu's essay in the same volume, 'The organisation of industry', 132–42.

35 Crosland, 'Transition from capitalism', 49; also Crosland, 'Insiders and controllers', in his *Conservative Enemy*, 68.

36 Hinden, 'Public ownership debate', 5; also Crosland, *Future*, 68–76; Socialist Union, *Twentieth Century Socialism*, 127–30.

37 Crosland, *Future*, 33–8; Labour Party, *Industry and Society* (London, 1958), 16–18.

38 Crosland, 'Chapter 6: Burnham and the managerial revolution', typescript, *c.*1956, Crosland Papers 13/7, 23, 14.

39 T. Balogh, 'Simpletons and confidence tricksters', *Tribune*, 25.7.1952, 8. See also W. Camp's famously vituperative review of Crosland: 'Socialism? How dare he use the word', *Tribune*, 5.10.1956, 5.

40 P. Shore, 'In the room at the top', in N. MacKenzie (ed.), *Conviction* (London, 1958), 52–3.

41 Cole, 'Notes on "British socialist way of life"', paper for Fabian Conference on Problems Ahead, Oxford, March 1950, Cole Papers D1/19/3, 1.

42 G. D. H. Cole, 'Twentieth century socialism?', *NS*, 7.7.1956, 8.

43 G. D. H. Cole, *Socialist Economics* (London, 1950), 53–4; his *The British Co-operative Movement in a Socialist Society* (London, 1951), 70–3, 134–43; his 'Shall socialism fail? Part I: the democrat's dilemma', *NS*, 5.5.1951, 496–7; his 'Shall socialism fail? Part II: lost chances and future needs', *NS*, 12.5.1951, 524–5; his 'Socialism and the welfare state', *NS*, 23.7.1955, 88–9.

44 G. D. H. Cole, *Is this Socialism?* (London, 1954), 19–20, 28–9, quote at 20.

45 J. Strachey, 'Socialist traditions', letter to *The Times*, 1.7.1952, 7. Strachey was not a Bevanite in any straightforward sense; nonetheless, his firm adherence to an explicitly socialist egalitarian strategy meant that his political thought was similar to that of Bevan and his allies.

46 H. Wilson, speech, 3.10.1956, in *LPACR 1956*, 117.

47 B. Wootton, 'Return to equality?', *PQ*, 23 (1952), 263.

48 B. Castle, 'It's not just about equality but power', *Forward*, 31.8.1956, 10; Ellison, *Egalitarian Thought*, 58.

49 R. H. S. Crossman to C. A. R. Crosland, 23.10.1956, Crosland Papers 13/10/2. See also B. Castle, 'An open letter to Tony Crosland', *NS*, 24.9.1960, 414–16; R. H. S. Crossman, 'The taxolators', *NS*, 23.2.1962, 254–6; Ellison, *Egalitarian Thought*, 44–72.

50 A. Bevan, *In Place of Fear* (London, 1952), 106.

51 Bevan, *Place of Fear*, 107.

52 Bevan, *Place of Fear*, 108.

53 A. Bevan, 'The fatuity of coalition', *Tribune*, 13.6.1952, 2.

54 R. H. S. Crossman, 'Socialism and the new despotism', *FT No. 298* (London, 1956); his 'Labour in the affluent society', *FT No. 325* (London, 1960).

55 Bryan, 'Development of revisionist thought', 215–19; Thompson, *John Strachey*, 186–225. For an influential attempt to incorporate Strachey into revisionism, see Haseler, *Gaitskellites*, 81–2.

56 J. Strachey, 'The new revisionist', *NS*, 6.10.1956, 397.

57 Strachey, *Contemporary Capitalism*, 86, Strachey's emphasis. See also section 4.3.

58 D. Jay, 'What is socialism? Marx's basic blunder', *Forward*, 28.7.1956, 2. See also the less polemical version of these points in Jay, *Socialism*, 43–6.

59 J. Strachey, 'Of course capitalism has changed – but it is just as deadly', *Forward*, 7.9.1956, 5.

60 Haseler, *Gaitskellites*, 87–90; Bryan, 'Development of revisionist thought', 237.

61 J. Strachey, 'The object of further socialisation', *PQ*, 24 (1953), 69; J. Strachey, *The Just Society: A Reaffirmation of Faith in Socialism* (London, 1951), 4–6, quote at 6.

62 Strachey, 'Object of further socialisation', 75.

63 Strachey, *Contemporary Capitalism*, 254–84. Compare with Crosland, 'Chapter 6: Burnham and the managerial revolution', typescript, c.1956, Crosland Papers 13/7, 7, 14.

64 J. Strachey, 'Correspondence: the new despotism', *NS*, 11.9.1954, 294.

65 Strachey offered a few remarks in favour of decentralisation in his *Just Society*, 13–15.

66 B. Barry, *Political Argument* (London, 1990 [1965]), 104; F. Parkin, *Class Inequality and Political Order* (London, 1972), 122–3; S. Lukes, 'Socialism and equality', in L. Kołakowski and S. Hampshire (eds), *The Socialist Idea* (London, 1977), 82–3; Howell, *British Social Democracy*, 193; Stedman Jones, 'Why is the Labour Party in a mess?', in his *Languages of Class*, 240–1; S. Fielding, *The Labour Party: Continuity and Change in the Making of 'New' Labour* (Basingstoke, 2003), 70.

67 Plant, 'Democratic socialism and equality', 135–55; his 'Social democracy', in D. Marquand and A. Seldon (eds), *The Ideas That Shaped Post-War Britain* (London, 1996), 165–94; his 'Crosland, equality and New Labour', in D. Leonard (ed.), *Crosland and New Labour* (Basingstoke, 1999), 19–34.

68 See B. Jackson and P. Segal, 'Why inequality matters', *Catalyst Working Paper* (London, 2004), 7–11, 21–38.

69 Francis, 'Mr Gaitskell's Ganymede', 58.

70 Ellison, *Egalitarian Thought*, 84–98, quote at 85.

71 Bryan, 'Development of revisionist thought', 231–5, quote at 232.

72 See e.g. L. Black, *The Political Culture of the Left in Affluent Britain, 1951–64: Old Labour, New Britain?* (Basingstoke, 2003), 124–54.

73 See G. Hawthorn, *Enlightenment and Despair: A History of Social Theory* (Cambridge, 1987), 245–52, and the contrasting verdicts of P. Anderson, *English Questions* (London, 1992), 51–60, 205–7; and A. H. Halsey, *A History of Sociology in Britain* (Oxford, 2004), 70–112.

74 See D. MacRae, 'Social stratification: a trend report', *Current Sociology*, 2 (1953–4), 21–7; S. M. Lipset and R. Bendix, *Social Mobility in Industrial Society* (Berkeley and Los Angeles, CA, 1959); R. Bendix and S. M. Lipset (eds), *Class, Status and Power: Social Stratification in Comparative Perspective* (London, 1967).

75 On the origins of British social stratification research, see R. A. Kent, *A History of British Empirical Sociology* (Aldershot, 1981), 124–86; Goldthorpe, *Social Mobility*, 1–36.

76 T. H. Marshall, *Citizenship and Social Class* (Cambridge, 1950), 62–8, quotes at 65, 67; also his 'Social selection in the welfare state', in Bendix and Lipset, *Class, Status and Power*, 640–8. See the citation of Marshall's phrase about 'the ticket obtained on leaving school' in Socialist Union, *Twentieth Century Socialism*, 36; P. Willmott, 'The status seekers', *NLR*, No. 3, 1960, 71. Crosland also used a similar phrase, though he did not attribute it to Marshall: 'Comprehensive education' [1966], in his *Socialism Now and Other Essays* (London, 1974), 195.

77 J. Floud, 'The educational experience of the adult population of England and Wales as at July 1949', in D. V. Glass (ed.), *Social Mobility in Britain* (London, 1954), 122–3; also A. H. Halsey, 'Inequalities in education', *New Reasoner*, Spring 1958, 102.

78 D. V. Glass and J. R. Hall, 'Social mobility in Great Britain: a study of inter-generation changes in status', in Glass, *Social Mobility*, 177–217, especially 216–17; also MacRae, 'Social stratification', 19–20.

79 J. R. Hall and D. V. Glass, 'Education and social mobility', in Glass, *Social Mobility*, 307.

80 A. H. Halsey and L. Gardner, 'Social mobility and achievement in four grammar schools', *British Journal of Sociology*, 4 (1953), 60–75; discussed by Crosland, *Future*, 259. See also B. Jackson and D. Marsden, *Education and the Working Class* (London, 1962), 51–3, 152–3.

81 J. Floud *et al.*, *Social Class and Educational Opportunity* (London, 1956), 44–58.

82 Central Advisory Council for Education, *Early Leaving* (London, 1954), 16–21, 34–48, 56–63; Jackson and Marsden, *Education*, 10–13.

83 Floud *et al.*, *Social Class*, 139.

84 A. H. Halsey, 'Genetics, social structure and intelligence', *British Journal of Sociology*, 9 (1958), 15–28; MacRae, 'Social stratification', 29–30; Jackson and Marsden, *Education*, 211–12.

85 Willmott, 'The status seekers', 71; his 'Opportunities for all?', *SC*, April 1960, 32, Willmott's emphasis.

86 R. M. Titmuss, 'The social division of welfare: some reflections on the search for equity' [1956], in his *Essays on the 'Welfare State'*, 43–4.

87 D. V. Glass, 'Introduction', in Glass, *Social Mobility*, 25–8, quote on 25–6; also MacRae, 'Social stratification', 30; Floud *et al.*, *Social Class*, xviii–xix.

88 See e.g. Gaitskell's foreword to the 1954 edition of Durbin's *Politics of Democratic Socialism*, 7–14.

89 E.g. Arblaster, 'Tawney in retrospect', 95–102; Collini, 'Moral mind: R. H. Tawney', 177–94.

90 Tawney, *Equality* (London, 1952 edition), 239–68.

91 R. Miliband, 'Equality to date', *NS*, 17.5.1952, 589–90; Wootton, 'Return to equality?'; Gaitskell, *Recent Developments*, 18–19; R. Williams, *Culture and Society, 1780–1950* (London, 1958), 220–6; R. M. Titmuss, 'Introduction', in R. H. Tawney, *Equality* (London, 1964 edition), 9–11. Tawney also influenced the sociologists: see A. H. Halsey and N. Dennis, *English Ethical Socialism: Thomas More to R. H. Tawney* (Oxford, 1988), vii–xiv, 149–238.

92 Tawney, *Equality* (1952 edition), 108–13; his 'British socialism today', *SC*, June 1952, 129–30. See also Cole's warning about the 'new class structure' created by the 11-plus: *Is this Socialism?*, 16.

93 Crosland, *Future*, 231–2; S. Crosland, *Tony Crosland* (London, 1983), 54, 66; Torrie, 'Ideas, policy and ideology', 245–6; K. Jeffreys, *Anthony Crosland* (London, 1999), 57.

94 See A. H. Halsey, *No Discouragement: An Autobiography* (Basingstoke, 1996), 121–37; and his 'Education and ethical socialism', in G. Dench *et al.* (eds), *Young at Eighty* (Manchester, 1995), 129–34.

95 Crosland, *Tony Crosland*, 46; A. Briggs, *Michael Young: Social Entrepreneur* (London, 2001), 66–109, 221–3. For Young's membership of Socialist Union, see 'Foundation meeting of Socialist Union, 31 March 1951', typescript, Socialist Union Papers MSS.173/12, 1; and Young's membership form, MSS.173/15. On the links between Socialist Union and senior Labour Party figures, see L. Black, 'Social democracy as a way of life: fellowship and the Socialist Union, 1951–9', *Twentieth Century British History*, 10 (1999), 499–539.

96 R. Hinden, 'Editor's preface' and H. Gaitskell, 'Postscript – an appreciation', both in Tawney, *Radical Tradition*, 7–9, 220–3. On Tawney's influence on Gaitskell, see Williams, *Hugh Gaitskell*, 21, 42, 71–2; Brivati, *Hugh Gaitskell*, 16, 291.

97 E.g. R. H. Tawney to R. Hinden, 9.3.1952, Socialist Union Papers MSS.173/11.

98 H. Gaitskell, speech, 3.10.1956, in *LPACR* 1956, 130.

99 'Synopsis for a research project on equality', LPRD, RE5/November 1955, 3.

100 A. J. Ayer, 'Forward from the welfare state', *Encounter*, December 1956, 77; see also B. Crick, 'Socialist literature in the 1950s', *PQ*, 31 (1960), 368.

101 D. Bell to C. A. R. Crosland, n.d. [*c.*1957–60], Crosland Papers 10/1/2a. On the New Left's preoccupation with Crosland, see also Kenny, *First New Left*, 65, 126–9.

102 N. Birnbaum, 'Ideals or reality?', *SC*, September 1959, 6.

103 S. Hall, 'The supply of demand', in E. P. Thompson (ed.), *Out of Apathy* (London, 1960), 96; E. P. Thompson, 'A psessay in ephology', *New Reasoner*, Autumn 1959, 6.

104 N. Birnbaum, 'Foreword', in Thompson, *Out of Apathy*, x.

105 C. A. R. Crosland, 'A reply', *SC*, September 1959, 9.

106 Socialist Union, *Twentieth Century Socialism*, 25; see also Jenkins, 'Equality', 87.

107 Crosland, *Future*, 237. See also M. Young, interviewed by P. Hennessy, 'The 1945 general election and the post-war period remembered', *Contemporary Record*, 9 (1995), 96.

108 'Preliminary memorandum on equality', LPRD, RE36/March 1956, 2; also Crosland, *Future*, 214–15.

109 Jay, *Socialism*, 243.

110 E.g. Lewis, *Principles*, 36–7; R. Marris, 'How unfair are incomes?', *Twentieth Century*, May 1955, 411, 413.

111 See section 7.4.

112 C. Curran, 'The fable of 2034 AD', *Encounter*, February 1959, 68.

113 A. Fox, 'Class and equality', *SC*, May 1956, 13. Fox later reviewed *Rise of the Meritocracy*: 'Top people', *SC*, December 1958, 20–2. Interestingly, although *The Future of Socialism* was also published in 1956, and was the subject of private discussion between Young and Crosland, it does not use the word 'meritocracy', although Crosland analysed the shortcomings of the idea in all but name, referring to the dangers of 'an aristocracy of talent': *Future*, 235–7, quote at 235.

114 Young, interviewed by Hennessy, '1945 general election', 96.

115 See Briggs, *Michael Young*, 155–7.

116 M. Young, *The Rise of the Meritocracy: An Essay on Education and Equality* (London, 1961 [1958]), 106–8, Young's emphasis.

117 Young, *Rise*, 129–31, quote at 130.

118 Young, *Rise*, 115.

119 E.g. R. Williams, 'Democracy or meritocracy?', *MG*, 30.10.1958, 10; R. Hoggart, 'IQ plus effort = merit', *Observer*, 2.11.1958, 21; P. Shore, 'More than opportunity', *NS*, 29.11.1958, 766. See P. Barker, 'The ups and downs of the meritocracy', in Dench *et al.*, *Young at Eighty*, 153–62; Briggs, *Michael Young*, 160–82.

120 Crosland, *Future*, 235.

121 Crosland, *Future*, 236.

122 Crosland, *Future*, 236.

123 Crosland, *Future*, 235, fn. 1; M. Young to C. A. R. Crosland, 30.1.1956, Crosland Papers 13/8/5–6.

124 Socialist Union, *Twentieth Century Socialism*, 25.

125 Socialist Union, *Twentieth Century Socialism*, 26. See also P. Willmott, 'Attitudes towards class', typescript, March 1956, Socialist Union Papers MSS.173/13.

126 W. A. Lewis, 'Underdog-ism', *Observer*, 22.7.1956, 8. This reference to 'underdogs' was reminiscent of Cole's famous definition of the ILP's socialism as 'a broad human movement on behalf of the bottom dog': G. D. H. Cole, *A Short History of the British Working Class Movement Volume 3* (London, 1937), 22.

127 E.g. Jenkins, 'Equality', 85; Fabian Society Local Societies Committee, *About Equality* (London, December 1954), 2, copy in Fabian Society Papers, F47/4, Item 1; 'Preliminary memorandum on equality', LPRD, RE36/March 1956, 2–3 (compare with Young, *Rise*, 169); R. Marris, 'An economist's challenge', *Twentieth Century*, February 1955, 166; Jay, *Socialism*, 15–17; B. Magee, *The New Radicalism* (London, 1962), 61–3.

128 W. A. Lewis, 'A socialist economic policy', *SC*, June 1955, 171.

129 H. Gaitskell, 'Socialism and nationalisation', *FT No. 300* (London, 1956), 3.

130 Jay, *Socialism*, 8–9. See also the similar ambiguity in Labour Party, *Towards Equality*, 14.

131 'Preliminary memorandum on equality', LPRD, RE36/March 1956, 4. Socialist Union indicated that inequalities freely chosen by individuals were also acceptable in their *Twentieth Century Socialism*, 28.

132 Crosland, *Future*, 212.

133 Jay, *Socialism*, 8.

134 In the 1970s Crosland and Young explicitly aligned their view of social justice with Rawls's: M. Young, 'Is equality a dream?', First Rita Hinden Memorial Lecture, supplement to *SC*, January 1973, 4; Crosland, *Socialism Now*, 15–16; M. Young, 'Introduction', in *Rise of the Meritocracy* (New Brunswick, NJ, 1994 edition [1958]), quoted in R. Dore, 'Man of merit', in Dench *et al.*, *Young at Eighty*, 173. See also S. Hampshire, 'A new philosophy of the just society', *New York Review of Books*, 24.2.1972, 36–7. Rawls himself referred to Tawney's *Equality*, Young's *The Rise of the Meritocracy* and James Meade's *Efficiency, Equality and the Distribution of Property*: Rawls, *Theory*, 63, fn. 11; 91, fn. 21; 241–2, fn. 12, fn. 13; 245, fn. 15.

135 One outstanding issue, addressed in the next chapter, is the extent to which the revisionists advocated the functional theory of productive burdens proposed by earlier egalitarians: see section 7.5.

7

Let us face the future

7.1 Introduction: equality and fellowship

In the previous chapter, I argued that the ideal of social justice defended by the revisionists was robustly egalitarian and involved a powerful critique of the idea of a 'meritocracy'. Attempts to portray the revisionists as meritocrats have therefore misunderstood the revisionist case, and have distorted accounts of the public philosophy of the Labour Party in this period. However, it would be misleading to conclude my analysis at this point. While putative critics of revisionism might be prepared to concede that both the contextual and textual evidence supports the claims of the previous chapter, they might nonetheless reformulate their criticism as follows. It is certainly correct, such a critic might concede, that the revisionists adhered to a radical ideal of social justice. In keeping with Arthur Lewis's celebrated definition, they believed that the essence of socialism was the redistribution of wealth and opportunities according to a loosely egalitarian pattern, and they were rightly critical of the shortcomings of a society that distributed resources and status according to a narrow definition of merit. But these distributive aspirations have historically only been one element of the socialist critique of capitalism; by exclusively focusing on them, the critic might continue, the revisionists did in fact deviate from traditional socialist ends. In particular, it could be said that the revisionists neglected the importance of community and therefore 'attacked socialist ideology at its heart – the doctrine of fellowship'.[1] How plausible is this argument? In this chapter, I argue that this reformulated criticism does indeed provide a useful diagnosis of the basic ideological difference between certain revisionists and other socialists in this period. However, I also suggest that it is misleading to pose this theoretical contrast as one between 'revisionist' and 'traditional' socialism *tout court.*

It will be helpful to begin by reviewing the argument of the book so far. As we have seen, early British progressives had both an egalitarian and a communitarian agenda, in that they aimed to promote not only a more equal distribution of goods and life chances between social classes, but also to foster a society charac- terised by co-operation rather than competition. As part of this latter aspiration, progressives hoped that individuals would come to be motivated not only by their own (or their family's) material interests, but also by their identification with the interests of a broader community and hence a desire to serve, and solidarise with, their fellow citizens. These egalitarian and co-operative objectives were seen as complementary and mutually reinforcing by socialists and left liberals in the early part of the twentieth century. They thought that the redistribution of material goods would begin to change the character of social relations and individual attitudes, which would in turn persuade citizens to support further reductions in material inequality. This way of thinking about the relationship between equality and community remained influential on the Left in succeeding years. For example, leading figures in the 1945 Labour government, such as Attlee and Morrison, retained something of this basic ideological commitment.[2] However, as we have seen, some younger socialists, such as Gaitskell or Durbin, felt less enthusiasm for these communitarian ideals. In their political thought, the pursuit of an egalitarian distribution became separate from, and more important than, the promotion of a co-operative society.[3] The significance of this intellectual shift was initially obscured by the intense solidarity of the War, which appeared to have reduced the importance of this issue. But the spirit of the Blitz proved to be only a temporary solution, and it was precisely by engaging with the political legacy of the War that socialists of the 1950s reacquainted themselves with the difficult questions already raised in the 1930s. The remainder of this chapter will provide a detailed anatomy of the ensuing debate about the importance of community. It will then conclude by examining the influence of the egalitarian theories discussed in this and the previous chapter on the Left's plans for a more egalitarian education system and for the redistribution of income and wealth.

7.2 Classes and cultures in post-war Britain

It is clear that certain revisionist thinkers were keen to dispense with the socialist idea of community and to focus on purely distributive objectives instead. An instructive example can be found in *The Future of Socialism*, where Crosland addressed the traditional socialist 'ideal of fraternity and co-operation'. He rattled through his discussion with disarming speed, prefacing his handful of paragraphs with the remark that 'I propose to discuss the co-operative aspiration first, in order to get it out of the way'.[4] He concluded:

> While, therefore, I realise that as a matter of verbal precision the co-operative ideal is certainly embraced by the word 'socialism,' and while I accept that it would clearly be in some sense 'better' if there were a more general awareness of a common social purpose, I do not feel able, in what is intended to be a reasonably definite and practical statement of socialist aims, to include this as part of the goal. I shall no doubt be corrected by those with clearer views.[5]

Crosland was not disappointed, since it was on this issue that the New Left made their most telling criticisms of revisionism.

The New Left and Croslandism

Although they had missed the target with their attacks on the revisionist view of social justice, the New Left were more successful in articulating the further, and more fundamental, criticism that the revisionists had abandoned the characteristic socialist ideal of community. In a lengthy critique of what he termed the 'Crosland revolution' in Labour ideology, Stuart Hall argued that socialism fundamentally rested on 'the concept of a community of equals', 'the moral principle of sharing and co-operation', and 'the planned command of skills and resources so that they can be *made* to serve the full needs of the community'.[6] New Left writers such as Hall, Charles Taylor and E. P. Thompson consistently associated terms such as 'community' and 'society' with equality, returning to the overlap between resource distribution and social solidarity espoused by earlier egalitarians. In Hall's view, the Labour Party 'had ceased to be alive' to 'the human and revolutionary priorities which a proper understanding of the words "welfare" and "community" would have given'. In current Labour discourse, claimed Hall, these concepts had lost their connection to the 'central themes of socialism – a classless society, a just division of wealth, a society of equals'.[7] The ambition of the early New Left was to place the connection between these ideas back on the socialist agenda, and to return to the lofty ethical goals that had been set by earlier generations of socialists.

Although generally characterised as Marxists, the early exponents of the New Left differed from the generation of Marxist writers aligned with the Left Book Club in that they took as their inspiration the newly accessible writings of the young Marx, and rejected the historical determinism popularised by Laski and Strachey in the 1930s. This meant that, as one commentator observed, the New Left was obliged to undertake 'the dual task of outlining in detail the future society and, at the same time, attempting to justify it'. Rather than relying on the alchemy of history to deliver socialism, they were forced to engage in normative reflection, undertaking 'abstruse discussions of ethical philosophy' and defending the young Marx's 'humanistic ethic'.[8] In short, as a revisionist critic of the New Left put it, 'the Left has discovered and embraced the *moral* foundations of socialism'.[9] Aspects of the revisionist critique of Marxism were therefore broadly acceptable to leading figures in the early New Left, and their attempts to create a humanist Marxist ethic in fact sometimes drew on traditions of British radicalism that had also inspired earlier social democrats, notably the writings of William Morris.[10] Nonetheless, these neo-Marxists were clear that their moralised Marxism led to a more radical political outlook than the social democracy of writers such as Crosland. E. P. Thompson, for instance, was deeply suspicious of the apparent hedonism and materialism that informed the famous peroration of *The Future of Socialism*. Crosland's fervent wish for more open-air cafes and better-designed furniture struck Thompson as simply the desire to make everyone middle class, offering 'no sense of a socialist community', and instead concentrating on 'a list of things' that paid no attention to qualitative shifts in human attitudes and behaviour.[11]

The New Left's use of communitarian ideals also brought into question the revisionist assumption that public ownership was only one among various means to achieve socialist ends. New Left theorists not only offered an ethical judgement about the virtues of a more co-operative society, they also claimed that communitarian social relationships could only be realised within a certain institutional environment, that 'the "ends" are contained by the "means"'.[12] As Charles Taylor put it, socialism should in fact be seen as 'a relation between a set of institutions ("means") and the human relations they embody ("ends")', with the latter dependent upon the former: 'common ownership can be "just one of the means" to greater productivity, or equality of opportunity, or something like that, but it cannot be "just one means" to a socialist society'.[13] If this analysis was accepted, then the revisionist case was in fact grounded on the mistaken premise that public ownership was designed to advance equality in a quantitative, material sense. This may have been the underlying point that some of the 'Old Left' critics of revisionism, notably Cole, had been trying to express, since if the objectives of socialism were broadened to encompass the kind of communitarian aspirations that Crosland regretfully placed to one side, then the acceptance of the competitive ethos of the market could be seen as antithetical to a more co-operative society. However, as I will now discuss, other advocates of ideals of fellowship and co-operation did not see a necessary connection between their communitarian goals and public ownership.

Organicism and revisionism

While the contrast between the position of Crosland and that of the early New Left seems clear enough, it would be inaccurate to suggest that this distinction offers a straightforward ideological difference between revisionism broadly construed and neo-Marxism. In fact, some revisionists shared the worries expressed by Hall and Taylor about the role of 'fraternity' in Crosland's thought. Looking back on the debates of the 1950s, even Michael Young expressed reservations: 'Socialism for me is about fraternity. Tony Crosland said socialism is about equality. I think he got it wrong. It is about equality, but only secondary to being about fraternity.'[14] A more precise way of conceptualising the divergence within progressive thought in this period than 'revisionists versus fundamentalist socialists' is to see a politically influential subset of revisionists as primarily focused on distributive goals, while a variety of other groups, some of whom were affiliated to revisionism, defended the importance of creating a more co-operative society.[15] The most important exponents of this latter position were Socialist Union, the New Left, and the school of radical sociologists connected to Richard Titmuss.

Although different in terms of their institutional affiliations and intellectual origins, these groups were united by their defence of a form of moderate organicism. This mid-twentieth-century organicism was not as explicit as earlier versions in drawing a parallel between a human community and a biological organism. The prevailing intellectual trends of the 1950s were, after all, rather different from the set of scientific and political premises that shaped the organicism of the new liberals or the early Fabians in the late nineteenth century, and it would have seemed peculiar to draw directly on the biological analogy that was central to this earlier discourse. Nonetheless, the underlying thought that had first motivated the Left's interest in biological terminology remained crucial to their ideological successors: the belief that the fullest expression of individual flourishing can only be achieved in a flourishing social unit, where institutions and individual behaviour express the values of co-operation and mutual service rather than competition and personal advancement.

Socialist Union, and its influential journal *Socialist Commentary*, were both organicist and revisionist.[16] Their publications repeatedly stressed that 'fellowship' was a socialist value that was just as important as equality, and perhaps even more so. 'Society', they wrote, 'is a network of loyalties which bind people to each other and make each feel responsible for something more than his own advantage'. Such sentiments of solidarity were vital and required strengthening 'if the fabric of a socialist society is to be woven'.[17] Indeed, Socialist Union was prepared to make a stronger claim, that socialism required a sense of solidarity not only in order to gather political support for redistributive policies, but also in order to realise the maximum welfare of the individual. 'Man cannot find his fulfilment in selfish isolation', they wrote in an early publication; 'complete expression comes to man through his contribution to the lives of others'.[18] Such was the ideal of 'fellowship', which required 'not only giving every man his due; it means going out of one's way to help him. It starts with the courtesy and neighbourliness which can be infused into everyday life, and broadens out into the higher reaches of selfless community service.' Rather than resorting to a biological analogy to illustrate this notion of interdependence, the authors employed a more familiar parallel: 'It is a sense of kinship extending far beyond the limits of the family.'[19]

Writers affiliated to Socialist Union were explicit that this emphasis on fellowship marked a departure from the position of Crosland and certain other revisionists. Rita Hinden noted in her review of *The Future of Socialism* that 'Crosland is very confused on fraternity', and observed, in correspondence with Gaitskell, that she thought Gaitskell was 'not really in sympathy' with the Socialist Union formulation of socialist ends. Gaitskell accorded more importance to equality than fellowship and disliked Socialist Union's treatment of freedom as necessarily entailing creative self-expression in the workplace.[20] Hinden expanded on this theme when discussing Jay's *Socialism in the New Society*. Jay, like Crosland, expressed little interest in the ideal of fellowship. As Hinden observed, Jay's book 'is focused only – or almost only – on equality; he is dumb about the values which dominate our society and our thinking. Indeed, he identifies socialism with equality, and all his major argument flows from this premise.'[21] In Hinden's view, this was misconceived, for 'it ignores the whole, vital question of values, of everything that Tawney inveighed against and pleaded for in *The Acquisitive Society*. Equality is not our sole aim; socialists have always aspired also, and just as passionately, to a society where money and profits are not the sole determinants of industrial conduct.'[22] Socialism aimed not only to distribute material goods, but also to help individuals 'share in some finer, more co-operative way of living'.[23] Socialist Union's vision was publicly endorsed by Attlee, who saw it as the descendant of the ILP socialism that had first fired his own political imagination.

He praised Socialist Union for correctly recognising that socialism 'is not just built up by changing institutions' but also 'by changing human beings'.[24]

However, Socialist Union did accept the revisionist case discussed in the previous chapter: the importance of the distinction between ends and means, and of the sociological changes that made public ownership less significant for the advancement of these ends than socialists had previously assumed. This aspect of Socialist Union's thought caused bewilderment to more radical socialists. The group's belief that 'a mixed economy *is* socialism', and that there would consequently be 'a permanent continuance of profit-seeking capitalist enterprise', seemed to Cole inconsistent with their theoretical commitment to 'a deep transformation of human values and a new way of life based on human fellowship and social equality'.[25] While Cole may have been right to see this as an uneasy compromise, it is nonetheless clear that Socialist Union differed from revisionists like Crosland and Jay precisely on seeing fellowship and equality as related socialist objectives.

Organicism and sociology

The relationship between community and equality was not discussed solely in abstract conceptual terms. Indeed, the abstract moral justification of the ideal of community was given vastly more persuasive power by its association with two historical-sociological moments that had a deep resonance on the British Left. These two moments were the persisting memory of the solidaristic ethic of the War, and an image of a particular kind of mutualist, working-class community organised in opposition to the dominant ethical code of capitalism. It is difficult to find an appropriate category to capture their precise status in the political discourse of the Left: they were at one and the same time an inspiring abstract moral principle; actual historical or sociological reality; and a shared ethical experience that prefigured the socialist community to come. Undoubtedly, both memories hovered in the background of the writings of Socialist Union, but they were unmistakably thrust to the foreground in the work of many academic sociologists in this period, as well as in the writings of the various cultural critics affiliated to the New Left.

As we have seen, the experience of the Second World War had persuaded many on the Left that it was plausible to expect a qualitative transformation in social relationships and productive motivation. 'There had been', remembered Young, 'the most extraordinary object lesson in the power of fraternity in the War'.[26] This impression was partly drawn from the personal experiences of leading socialists. Richard Titmuss, for example, encountered the transformed social ethos of wartime Britain at first hand, supplementing his research with voluntary work as a firewatcher at St Paul's. As Reisman has stressed, intellectuals like Titmuss 'found in unpaid activities such as fire-watching the camaraderie, the equality of respect, the sense of belonging which for them was the essence of the One Nation ideal'.[27] Similarly, the sociologist and anti-poverty campaigner Peter Townsend situated his politics in relation to an evocative personal account of the role of the War in creating 'a readiness to share the good things in life and to see that others got the same privileges as oneself'. For members of his generation, claimed

Townsend, the experience of 'evacuation, sleeping in shelters, civil defence, farming and forestry camps during school holidays and finally service in the armed forces' had given them 'a sense of fair shares, of common effort, of mixing with people of different class and of planning for the future', a set of experiences, emotions and ethical values that 'could at times be intoxicating'.[28] The willingness to forgo material self-interest formed a central component of Townsend's egalitarian vision, just as it had purportedly done during wartime mobilisation on the home front. He saw individual attitudes and behaviour as crucial to cultivating an egalitarian society, since the pursuit of equality was not only about working to change social institutions, but also involved prefiguring an egalitarian ethic in individual conduct ('you cannot live like a Lord and preach as a socialist'). Egalitarians, added Young, should be concerned with undermining the legitimacy of capitalism 'where it matters most – in the minds of men'.[29]

While the recollection of wartime experiences made these views appealing to many on the Left, the powerful memory of the mutualism practised in traditional working-class communities was also influential.[30] Townsend illustrated his point by referring to the personal generosity of his grandmother, taking her unselfish behaviour under conditions of extreme poverty as an example of the ethic of mutual service he had in mind.[31] An important aspect of the sociologists' interest in working-class communities was their emphasis on the contribution of the family to social flourishing, and their use of kinship ties as a model of the kind of social relationships that should ideally obtain more widely in society. As we saw earlier, this was also an argument made by Socialist Union. It might even be said that the organicists of this generation discarded the analogy with a biological organism in favour of what might be called a 'kinship analogy'. The most powerful exponent of this view was Michael Young. Even before Young had left party politics to embark on his sociological investigations, he had signalled his commitment to a communitarian ideal that pictured the family as the germ of the egalitarian society. Although his 1948 Labour Party pamphlet, *Big Man, Small World*, was a discussion document necessarily couched in equivocal terms, it was premised on the attractions of a society 'built on the model of the family, which is not only more comradely but more efficient'.[32] Young was more explicit in his contribution to a Fabian conference in 1950, where he affirmed his conviction that the basic normative ideal underlying the Labour Party's programme should be 'brotherhood', arguing that his 'ideal for society was based on the model of the good family, in which the governing principle was that needs should be met by holding all resources available for use where they were needed most'.[33] However, as he conceded at the end of his talk, there was a need for much more sociological and psychological research into the mechanisms that would enable this spirit of community to develop.[34]

Young was convinced that a better understanding of these social processes would be of profound political significance, and it was with a view to undertaking a more detailed exploration of them that he founded the Institute of Community Studies.[35] Famously, along with Townsend and Willmott, Young produced influential research into the way of life of one particular working-class community, Bethnal

Green, in which they emphasised the importance of the family for sustaining the sense of social belonging that Young thought so important. At one level, these studies were presented as an argument against the type of progressive social planning that attempted to re-house the poor without any concern for the social relationships and kinship ties that bound them to their existing neighbourhoods. At a deeper level, the sociologists wrote with barely disguised admiration for the sense of community that characterised such traditional working-class areas. They perceived the ties that bound together the three-generation family as superior to the contractual relationships and hierarchical evaluations that marked capitalist society, offering a tangible example of the ethical advantages of *Gemeinschaft* over *Gesellschaft*. Family members were 'secure in the knowledge that they are valued because they are members of the family, not because they have this or that quality or achievement to their credit', with the result that they were prepared to perform duties that were 'not so much the nicely balanced correlative of rights as a more or less unlimited liability beyond the bounds of self-interest or rational calculation. The mother does not inquire whether she will be repaid before she does the washing for her sick daughter, the daughter whether she can afford the time to nurse her mother through a long illness.'[36]

This emphasis on the importance of the family was unusual. As Townsend observed: 'Traditionally socialists have ignored the family or they have openly tried to weaken it – alleging nepotism and the restrictions placed upon human fulfilment by family ties.'[37] Indeed, the narrator of Young's *The Rise of the Meritocracy* was fulsome in his praise for the important contribution made by socialists to undermining the family, since for meritocrats it had clearly been an illegitimate mechanism of intergenerational advantage.[38] Yet it was the inter-generational interdependence found in Bethnal Green that these sociologists saw as an embryonic instantiation of the normative principles necessary to guide a community of equals, and of the mutual dependence that was expressed on a grander scale by welfare services. 'The working man's ethic of solidarity and mutual aid' was a first approximation of a broader commitment to regard society 'as an organic whole'.[39]

Similar ideas about the normative importance of working-class communities were developed within the New Left by the influential literary critics Richard Hoggart and Raymond Williams. Although they were often bracketed together as representatives of the cultural turn in neo-Marxist thinking, Williams and Hoggart were actually pursuing rather different projects in their respective examinations of working-class culture.[40] Hoggart's work evoked the loss of an apolitical form of working-class solidarity, lamenting its replacement by rival values from mass culture that offered 'a view of the world in which progress is conceived as a seeking of material possessions, equality as a moral levelling and freedom as the ground for endless irresponsible pleasure'.[41] In contrast, Raymond Williams stressed the moral attractions of the politically assertive aspect of working-class culture: the creation of autonomous proletarian political institutions as sites of active resistance to the inequalities and individualism of capitalism. The proletarian way of life, 'with its emphases of neighbourhood, mutual obligation, and common betterment, as expressed in the great working class political and industrial institutions, is in fact the best basis for any future English society'.[42] Though located in a particular social formation, Williams thought these ideals were capable of transcending their class base and gaining a wider purchase on political debate. The decisive contribution of this 'working class idea' was to interpret 'development and advantage ... not individually but commonly'. Williams therefore joined other socialists of this period in rejecting a narrow form of equality of opportunity that prioritised social mobility for the most talented of the working class,[43] but he also criticised 'the visible moral decline of the labour movement', exemplified by its readiness to compromise with capitalism and abandon its basic principle of 'the substitution of co-operative equality for competition'.[44] In their willingness to adjust to the apparent success of consumer capitalism, the Labour Party establishment had neglected the need to disseminate a new consciousness, 'a real feeling of community – the true knowledge that we are working for ourselves and for each other'. But the fundamental obstacle to this realisation was 'the plain fact that most of us do not own or control the means and the product of our work'. If the claims of community and equality were to be adequately realised, public ownership would have to return to the top of the socialist agenda.[45]

This emphasis on the political significance of working-class social practices and wartime solidarity raised a number of difficult questions about the applicability of this organicist orientation to a post-war Britain that was arguably facing the dissolution of precisely those social practices that some egalitarians sought to ground their political recommendations on. Was this understanding of the relationship between community and equality simply an elaborate exercise in nostalgia? Indeed, could it not be said that this kind of organicism was premised on a rather controversial claim about the need for individual fulfilment to take place through participation in family life and communal activity?

7.3 Egalitarianism divided

The organicist stance shared by writers such as Titmuss, Hinden and Williams contrasted with the scepticism expressed by Crosland and other revisionist politicians about the viability of the political agenda that could be generated from this communitarian philosophy. In search of policy ideas for a Labour government, revisionist politicians could make little sense of an emphasis on moral transformation and the creation of an ethic of mutual service. Certainly, they agreed that the War had done much to lend greater legitimacy to Labour and the egalitarian principles that the Party hoped to advance, but they could derive from this no general lesson that would help with the business of constructing an electorally appealing party programme. However, it would be a mistake to see the response of Crosland and others as purely the reflex reaction of pragmatic party politicians to the ambitious theoretical speculations of the intellectual.[46] There were also important political differences between the two camps. As one commentator noted at the time, within the Labour Party 'there is a profound and logically unbridgeable gulf between the "plural society" envisaged by the Right, and the dimly imagined but passionately desired "organic" utopia of the Left'.[47]

For instance, the organicists placed a lot of weight on anecdotal and sociological evidence derived from two particular examples of social solidarity: working-class communities and the influence of the War on British society as a whole. But there were obvious weak points in this analysis, since the issue was not simply whether it was possible for individuals to feel moved by a sense of communal obligation in their everyday activities; the more difficult question was rather, what were the sociological conditions that might generate such sentiments outside of an extreme emergency or serious deprivation? As Crosland observed, the evidence from the nationalised industries illustrated that it was not sufficient 'to tell people that they are working for the public good, nor even that they should in fact be working for the public good'. Socialists with this more ambitious agenda of ethical reform had to devise an institutional framework that would enable workers to 'see it, and feel it, themselves'.[48] In this vein, the philosopher Richard Wollheim contributed a trenchant critique of the communitarian strand of socialist thinking in a Fabian Society pamphlet, 'Socialism and culture'. Wollheim could see that what he took to be widespread 'nostalgia about the old working-class life' was 'comparable to that strong desire, which many express, and many more, perhaps cherish, for a return to the comradeship and the warm easy intimacy of war-time life'. As Wollheim conceded, there was much that was attractive in that memory, but it would nonetheless be a mistake to generalise a political position from the unique conditions that had created these sentiments, since there was 'no good reason to think that this spontaneous fraternity and unity of sentiment can be recreated without the circumstances that were its occasion: and no-one in his sane mind would think the price worth it'.[49] Of course, as Williams pointed out, Wollheim's remarks were themselves premised on controversial sociological claims: 'Why always this complaint about looking backward, when working class life still exists?'[50]

Private lives versus public spirit

Aside from the charge that the organicists were sociologically naive, a further problem was that their belief in individual fulfilment through involvement in the community conflicted with the markedly more libertarian conception of individual flourishing defended by certain revisionists. Wollheim observed that Williams's attempt to overcome the tensions between the individual and the community 'recalls the dry, musty philosophising of T. H. Green', and prescribed a 'collective, unalienated folk society' that resembled 'the ideal of Ruskin and William Morris'. A sign of the philosophical times was that Wollheim saw all this as 'weak and unconvincing', and 'indifferent to the values of nonconformity with a small "n"'.[51] Crosland singled out Williams's emphasis on working-class culture for particular censure on this point, since Crosland felt that this kind of working-class life, 'for all its great historic virtues, is not wholly favourable to personal liberty ... The values of solidarity, community, and even traditional neighbourliness may well threaten the opposite (and equally "socialist"!) values of freedom, autonomy and critical revolt'. Crosland was clear that the latter were more important to socialism than the communitarianism invoked by Williams.[52] Although he did not discuss his favoured understanding of liberty in any detail, it is plain from Crosland's writings that he regarded the maximisation of individual choice, free from both legal restrictions and social censure, as an essential component of socialist morality. He was suspicious of, and indeed scathing about, the idealist conceptions of freedom that he detected in other socialists. In Crosland's view, the individual was the ultimate authority over those forms of behaviour and valued goals that impacted on the individual alone. For this reason he recommended that redistributive transfers should take the form of expanding individual purchasing power rather than services in kind; he repeatedly condemned legal restrictions on divorce, homosexuality, artistic expression and other aspects of individual behaviour; and he concluded *The Future of Socialism* with his famous remarks about the need for socialists to place greater emphasis on 'private life, on freedom and dissent, on culture, beauty, leisure, and even frivolity'.[53]

In this respect, Crosland's views were similar to other revisionist politicians such as Jay, Jenkins and Gaitskell. Although there was much that Gaitskell sympathised with in the writings of Socialist Union, he stressed that he disagreed with its communitarian ethic. Commenting on the draft of Socialist Union's *Twentieth Century Socialism*, he specifically criticised its assumption that individuals should manifest 'a sort of positive love of the community', questioning whether it was desirable for strong social bonds, modelled on kinship ties, to exist between all citizens. 'As you know, I get impatient with those who think that everybody must continually be taking an active part in politics or community affairs! The vast majority find their happiness in their family or personal relations, and why on earth shouldn't they!'[54]

Wollheim's Fabian pamphlet had made a powerful case against the organicists on just these grounds. The difficulty with the image of working-class community conjured up so brilliantly by Hoggart and others, wrote Wollheim, was that it was one-sided. While they rightly noted the dignified sense of unified resistance and mutual co-operation that characterised working-class life in the face of a brutal and unjust social system, they ignored the impact of this social unity on the liberty and self-development of the individual members of such communities. This was an inevitable result of the basis of these communitarian sentiments in 'an intensive and pervasive family-life which extends across the generations and which is bound to be an agent of conservatism on the one hand and conformism on the other'.[55] Hostility 'to innovation and deviation' was virtually a necessary condition of the existence of such communities in the first place.[56] Wollheim made the important point that this was not simply an objection to be made against the gurus of the New Left. It also applied to the work of the Institute of Community Studies, which proposed in a more concrete way than Hoggart or Williams to incorporate the traditional three-generation working-class family into public policy, more or less as an alternative to certain kinds of government welfare services. Wollheim argued that this proposal neglected both the exercise of power within the family, and the social conditions necessary to secure individual freedom. Those 'who feel a concern with liberty and innovation, who think that there may be some good cause advanced by the permanent rebellion of youth, should very seriously reflect upon the dangers involved in so firmly ensconcing family life in this extended sense into the structure of the society to be'.[57] Given the potential for the claims of community life to constrain individual choice, more libertarian egalitarians preferred a model of individual flourishing that emphasised a sceptical detachment from inherited traditions and that located the fullest expression of individual freedom within an individual's private rather than public life.[58] Such egalitarians therefore presented the pursuit of material equality as a way of endowing individuals with the equal capacity for free choice.

All of this contrasted with the organicists' implicit critique of a conception of liberty that neglected the close connections between individual and communal fulfilment. Although conscious of the importance of individual choice over a range of self-regarding behaviour, the organicists qualified this commitment by stressing the social interdependence of individuals and offering a moral judgement that it was only through exercising social responsibilities that the fullest expression of individual freedom could be achieved. 'While socialists share the liberal belief in liberty for the individual', thought Young, 'they recognise that the individual, as a social being, can be very lonely and isolated even when very free'. It followed that socialists desired 'a new society in which individuals will find their highest fulfilment and their greatest freedom through co-operation with others'.[59] Similarly, for the New Left, Crosland's objective of 'enlarging the area of free personal choice' was insufficient since he did not probe the assumption 'that men are genuinely free in our type of society', instead envisaging the good life as one lived in private, and in competition with others.[60]

In defence of consumption

A final difference between the two camps was that some revisionists thought that there was nothing necessarily unsocialist about equalising access to high levels of personal consumption. Crosland objected to the moralising tone of much socialist rhetoric about the social corrosion consequent on the growing affluence of the working class. While in the organicist writings there was, at a minimum, a worry that the working class's acquisition of consumer goods and a rising standard of living would simply generalise a pattern of inegalitarian and frankly selfish economic behaviour across the whole of society, Crosland robustly expressed the contrary view. Drawing on sociological research, he pointed out that in fact it was differing patterns of personal consumption that constituted an important determinant of social stratification along class lines.[61] His conclusion was simple: if socialists wished to eliminate class, they had to raise the consumption levels of the worst off. This would not, contrary to the fears of many socialists, result in a society that 'coarsened and debased' individual character and social relationships, but would rather dramatically improve the material conditions of the working class.[62] Crosland therefore condemned the Left's 'profound aversion to (other people's) high consumption'. On the contrary, he argued, the so-called 'affluent society' should be seen as 'the most beneficial social development in world history' since the possession of money 'is the essential condition – which the mass of people have utterly lacked until very recent times – of privacy, a dignified family life, and reasonable hope for the future'.[63] Jay expanded on this thought by explicitly arguing that personal freedom was dependent on the ownership of private property. For Jay, 'a fundamental condition both of equality and freedom' was that individuals should own 'some resources *of their own* which they can spend as, where, and when they please'. This would enhance equality because it aimed to provide all individuals and not just the fortunate minority with the security and liberty that flowed from property ownership.[64]

Although more libertarian revisionists objected to a political agenda rooted in an attachment to traditional working-class social practices, they nonetheless still regarded it as important to seek a society that effaced socially recognised distinctions in status. They thought it undesirable that citizens should be divided from one another 'in a series of almost water-tight social compartments', with little social mixing between classes.[65] Overcoming these divisions would partly be a matter of redistributing material resources, but could also be influenced through other policy instruments (for instance education). Although this indicated some enthusiasm for more fraternal social relations, it should be noted that arguments based on social justice were regarded as a more fundamental part of their egalitarian case.[66] The ideal of community commended was also more restrictive, confined to a thinner critique of the persistence of class consciousness rather than the thicker claims about the superiority of communal interaction made by organicists. This was a 'narrower' interpretation of 'fellowship', argued Gaitskell, regarded as 'an extension of the ideal of equality' and not a more controversial claim about the interconnection between individual and social fulfilment.[67] Indeed, rather than taking working-class culture as a model for social organisation, the revisionists planned to achieve social integration at least partly through equalising consumption in the market, with the aim of actually eliminating many of the lifestyles and social practices endorsed by other socialists.

In conclusion, although the political legacy of the War had been unambiguously beneficial for the Left, its sociological implications, or at least the progressive elite's perception of those implications, were more complex. While the apparent realisation of communitarian sentiments as a result of the war effort could be seen from one perspective as confirming socialist doctrine, the lessons that could be drawn from that singular set of circumstances were in fact contestable, and open to challenge from egalitarians who could tell a different, and increasingly plausible, story about the sociological trajectory of Britain. All of this meant that the most significant ideological innovation of certain revisionists was not to advocate an impoverished ideal of equality, but to accord the objective of creating a more co-operative society a subordinate role in their political thought.

Having discussed the philosophical issues raised by the egalitarian thought of this period, I will now consider the egalitarian strategies that emerged from these debates. As the traditional socialist vision of public ownership became increasingly controversial, the Left turned its attention to other mechanisms that might advance equality. Two aspects of egalitarian strategy absorbed particular attention: educational reform and a search for alternative methods of redistributing income and wealth.

7.4 Equality and the comprehensive school

Among the many injustices inflicted on the working class by capitalism, socialists had long considered the rationing of education and healthcare on the basis of regressive user fees to be the gravest infringement of their egalitarian ideals. The 1940–51 governments had made substantial advances towards rectifying these inequalities by introducing both education and healthcare free at the point of use. But while the introduction of the National Health Service was greeted with enthusiasm by left-wingers as a potent example of their commitment to decommodify basic human needs, the 1944 Education Act was replete with ideological ambiguity. Although Bevan could plausibly argue that a health service in which 'the rich and the poor are treated alike' was 'pure socialism', challenging 'the hedonism of capitalist society',[68] the purported egalitarianism of a hierarchically structured school system was open to obvious, and increasingly vociferous, objections.

It should be clear from the previous chapter that both the sociology and legislative regulation of education were the focus of considerable egalitarian attention during the 1950s. Socialist thinkers 'who are especially interested in creating a more equal society in the future', said Gaitskell, were 'inclined especially to favour education' as a policy area of central importance to this project.[69] As we have seen, earlier egalitarian thinking on this issue had been primarily concerned with securing universal state education free at the point of use. Egalitarians had little to say about private schools beyond a general critique of the inequality they produced, and they had been relaxed about the prospect of academic selection within the state system. In contrast, egalitarians of the 1950s became increasingly critical of the 1944 Act, and turned to the introduction of comprehensive schools as the best means of promoting educational equality.[70] Why did egalitarians of this period see comprehensive schools as preferable to academic selection and private schooling? It is sometimes suggested that the fundamentally egalitarian virtue of the comprehensive school is that it enables social mixing across class boundaries.[71] It might therefore be argued that the increased commitment to the comprehensive ideal among egalitarians in the 1950s stemmed directly from their deep dislike of status inequality and the consequent social segregation between classes discussed at the end of the last section. After all, the exceptionally segregated British education system offered an obvious site for political action designed to attenuate such social inequalities. In fact, this was one of two distinct lines of argument that were used by the advocates of comprehensive schools, since reformers also deployed a radical principle of equal opportunity. This section examines each argument in turn, starting with the latter.

Equality of opportunity

As Francis has observed, during the course of the 1945 government 'equality in education was identified in terms of providing children from *all* social backgrounds with the same opportunities in the competitive system which had previously been monopolised by the middle and upper classes'.[72] This view of educational equality was enshrined in the 1944 Act, and was in essence the agenda earlier laid out in Labour's 1922 policy document *Secondary Education For All*. The Act was subsequently defended in these terms by Ellen Wilkinson and George Tomlinson during their respective terms as Labour's Secretary of State for Education during the 1945–51 government.[73] Representing a substantial body of opinion within the labour movement, they regarded grammar schools with affection because of their role as vehicles for working-class self-advancement, and argued that some form of 'parity of esteem' could be achieved within a differentiated school system. However, it seemed increasingly obvious to egalitarians during the 1950s that the formal view of educational opportunity defended by the 1945 government was inadequate. In the view of one Labour MP, although it was sometimes assumed that since the 1944 Act 'the day of equal opportunity has dawned', in practice 'we are still as far from genuine equal opportunity as we were during my school days'.[74] If this was so, it was incumbent on educational reformers to say more specifically what 'genuine' equal opportunity might look like. There were obvious practical problems associated with realising equality of opportunity within the existing system, such as the arbitrary distribution of grammar school places between local authority areas, or the very unequal resource allocations between school types, and these were certainly cited in political argument.[75] But reformers also had at their disposal a more fundamental critique of the narrow definition of equal opportunity that was used by defenders of the status quo. They recognised that there was something distinctive about education as a social good, both in the sense that its distribution was decisive for the life chances of the individual, and in the sense that a formal equality of access unfairly ignored the various other social and material inequalities that shaped the individual's capacity to take advantage of this opportunity. Reformers aimed to shift the focus of debate from the straightforward issue of whether or not charges were made for tuition to the profound influence exercised on individual intelligence and academic performance by socio-economic factors that varied between social classes.

The nostalgia that many in the labour movement felt for grammar schools was slowly undermined by the dissemination of recent sociological and psychological research in the periodicals, pamphlets and books that were influential on Labour's policy-making. As we have seen, the pioneering surveys of access to educational opportunity showed that under the 1944 Act 'middle class children still enjoy vastly superior chances' of a superior education: 'The probability that a working class boy will get to grammar school is not strikingly different from what it was before 1945.'[76] While this was thought to be a consequence of the unequal distribution of measured intelligence between social classes, it was a basic empirical finding of educational research in this period that an individual's intelligence level was not fixed genetically but was rather the product of interaction between hereditary and environmental factors. This finding directly rebutted the contrary assumption that had underpinned the influential Hadow, Spens and Norwood Reports, and indeed eventually the 1944 Act itself, namely that intelligence was an inherited characteristic independent of cultural influences, and which could be accurately measured in children from a very early age.[77] As Crosland summarised, the new consensus was that intelligence was 'not something given in limited measure in the genetic make-up of the new-born child. What is given is a bundle of assorted potentials, and what happens to them is a matter of nurture, of stimulus and response.'[78]

In the light of this finding, it was argued that the class bias in the distribution of measured intelligence, and indeed academic performance more generally, could be traced to the disparate environmental influences experienced by children from different social classes. It could now be plausibly maintained that even with a formal equality of opportunity 'the competitive advantage would lie strongly with those whose family background was materially and culturally enriched', since the intellectual capacity of children was 'greatly affected by the family environment, family size, the education and attitudes to education of the parents and of course (though to a lesser extent nowadays) the grosser material handicaps such as poverty and bad housing. Environmental factors therefore still load the dice against the working class young.'[79] Once explained in these terms, the evidence of social science could be employed to confirm what had in essence always been the instinctive belief of the Left: 'Educational equality cannot at best run far ahead of the growth of social equality in other fields.'[80]

Given the evidence about the barriers to working-class access to education, and its obvious congruence with the traditional concerns of egalitarians, it was possible to reformulate a principle of equality of opportunity that demanded the neutralisation of environmental influences on educational attainment in order to create a level playing field for the working class. The most sophisticated argument along these lines was developed by Crosland. In *The Conservative Enemy*, he distinguished between a 'weak' and a 'strong' interpretation of educational equality of opportunity. 'Weak' equality of opportunity, argued Crosland, could be construed as ensuring 'that access to elite education is based not on birth or wealth, but solely on intelligence as measured by IQ tests'.[81] Even taking this goal as a metric of educational equality would have radical consequences for policy, he claimed, since it would involve a substantial assault on private education and the variations in social backgrounds that caused a disproportionate number of working-class children to drop out of grammar schools. Nonetheless, it would still be the case that the higher social classes would do better out of the regime of weak equal opportunity, since mean IQ levels at the ages of 11 and 18 varied with social class. But since these intelligence levels were a combination of hereditary and environmental factors, the class bias in the distribution of IQ was unlikely to be fully explained by the superior genetic stock of the middle and upper classes. Rather, it was at least partially caused by unequal social conditions.[82] According to this analysis, then, 'measured intelligence at age 11 or 18 is *not* a fixed quantity' but instead should be seen as 'partly the function of opportunities in earlier life'. This led Crosland to formulate a 'strong' version of equality of opportunity, namely the claim that 'every child should have the same opportunity for *acquiring* measured intelligence, so far as this can be controlled by social action'.[83]

This claim led to a set of policy proposals that were far from the minimalist ameliorative measures imagined by the critics of revisionism. First steps along the road to strong equality of opportunity would involve such radical objectives as the elimination of poverty and poor housing, along with the abolition of selective schooling. In this sense, the analytical contrast between 'equality' and 'equality of opportunity' was overdrawn, and Crosland urged the Left to reclaim the radical interpretation of the latter from the minimalist view espoused by the Right. To imagine equality of opportunity 'in terms of a narrow ladder up which only a few exceptional individuals, hauled out of their class by society's talent scouts, can ever climb' would be to 'concede the narrow, reactionary interpretation' favoured by the Left's opponents. Echoing the similar claims of Tawney, Crosland powerfully argued that 'strong' equality of opportunity would place less emphasis on social mobility and greater stress on 'an immensely high standard of *universal provision*'. This 'would carry us a distinctly long way towards equality and a socialist society' since 'a high degree of equality is a pre-condition of equal opportunity'.[84] Alan Fox had made a similar point, observing that the implication of recent educational research was 'that the cry for "equality of opportunity" is every bit as revolutionary as the cry for equality itself, and indeed amounts to much the same thing in the end'.[85]

Crosland's formulation of these two conceptions of equality of opportunity, and his stress on the strong version, provided powerful ammunition for the advocates of comprehensive education. It now seemed that a school system that segregated children from an early age was making a fundamental decision while the child's intelligence was still nascent, and did not allow time for 'the beneficial influence of education to compensate for the deficiencies of upbringing and early circumstance'.[86] Crosland assumed that regardless of the individual child's natural endowment or social circumstances, high-quality and lengthy education would improve his or her intellectual capacity and, in a comprehensive system, defer important life choices for the maximum amount of time. As he put it: 'the system must allow the individual to pick up, to make good, to try again. You do not feed a child less because it grows slowly or has some initial handicap to overcome.'[87]

There are difficult empirical issues concealed within this position. If, as the sociological evidence had begun to suggest, it was primarily the contrast between social classes in their levels of parental involvement, family size and social values that was driving the distribution of measured intelligence, then it was open to question how much difference altering the structure of the school system would actually make. Nonetheless, it could plausibly be argued that it would have some impact, particularly when the evidence suggested that the mere fact of segregating children into two streams of clearly unequal status had a significant influence on the expectations of pupils and teachers and, as a result, lowered the educational attainment of children at secondary moderns.[88] One way to buttress the position of 'strong' equality of opportunity in this respect might in fact be to propose higher educational spending on the poor relative to such spending on more advantaged groups. Although Crosland himself remained silent on this point, this proposal seems an obvious implication of his position. If the objective of education is actually to compensate the poor for their environmental disadvantages, then perhaps greater resources should be invested in the education of the poor compared to the share allocated to the better-off.[89] For instance, this was the implicit conclusion of Raymond Williams's similar treatment of the influence of hereditary and environmental factors on individual ability, drawing on much the same evidence as Crosland.[90] In any case, it should be noted that Crosland's case for comprehensive schools rested to a significant extent on this radical principle of equal opportunity. As he put it: 'the central and irresistible argument against the 11-plus lies in the denial of social justice and equal opportunity which it implies'.[91]

Citizenship and social unity

The egalitarian case for comprehensive education also drew attention to the undesirable social consequences of selective education. As a Fabian Society pamphlet commented, education was not just about the individual, it was also about 'helping to create the sort of society we want to see by moulding the attitudes of individuals in relation to each other. If, as socialists, we want to create a classless society, we must be sure where our educational system leads and that it does not produce an exclusive educational elite to take the place of the social one.'[92] The Left's fears about the emergence of a meritocratic elite, and the consequent stratification of society into distinct social classes lacking in mutual interest or imaginative sympathy, were therefore directly relevant to debates about education policy. While the argument from equal opportunity criticised the labour movement's affection for grammar schools as agents of working-class mobility, this second argument developed a parallel critique of the idea of 'parity of esteem', which had played a prominent role in the rhetoric supporting the 1944 Act. For Labour proponents of the Act, a virtue of the selective system was that it recognised the equality of status between the different kinds of ability that existed within the nation. A crucial feature of such a differentiated school system, it was argued, was that it delivered an education that was closely aligned with the individual's capacities and interests, but simultaneously ensured that there would be no straightforward status hierarchy attached to different school types. This was the view famously expounded by Ellen Wilkinson, who claimed that there would be no hierarchical relationship between grammar and secondary modern schools; their existence would, on the contrary, 'make for equality', since these separate but equal types of school undermined the idea 'that you are in a higher social class if you add up figures in a book than if you plough the fields and scatter the good seed on the land'.[93]

This argument appeared increasingly feeble as evidence accumulated of the palpably poorer facilities and resources allocated to secondary moderns, and the clear social and economic advantages associated with attendance at a grammar school (and indeed at a fee-paying school). More fundamentally, it begged an important question: if the aim was to create a community that possessed some form of equality of regard between citizens, then surely the obvious solution was to help create these egalitarian social relationships through a common, and socially mixed, educational experience for all? The majority of the Left in the 1950s and 60s answered this question in the affirmative.

In addition to arguing for educational reform to advance equality of opportunity, Crosland also objected to the social divisiveness of selective and fee-paying schools. The aim of comprehensive schools was 'not to abolish all competition and all envy, which might be a rather hopeless task', but rather 'to avoid the extreme social division caused by physical segregation into schools of widely divergent status'.[94] A shared educational experience would reduce social tension, and enable clearer communication between different classes. As Crosland observed, 'if the only time we can, as a society, achieve this common language is when we go to war, then we are at a much less advanced stage than many societies which the anthropologists describe as primitive'.[95]

One way of phrasing this argument about social unity was by connecting it to the ideal of democracy. A school system that enabled 'those who would otherwise have no social or cultural relationships to know each other' was seen as an important pre-condition of democratic government.[96] It was frequently argued that the hierarchical, explicitly elitist British education system was grounded on a pre-democratic model of leadership, which emphasised the need to train the ruling class, or perhaps the extremely able minority, but neglected both the educational needs of the rest of the community and the importance of the leadership caste sharing in the experiences or beliefs of the majority. This form of education, it was said, was not suitable for a democratic society, since 'a free democratic society depends for its survival, not on an elite, but on the existence of an educated democratic community'.[97] Indeed, citizenship in a democracy brought with it 'the right of every child to be educated to a standard consistent with membership of an educated democracy'.[98]

This emphasis on educating citizens for their role as participants in democratic decision-making was not, as might be assumed, the sole preserve of the New Left's radical democrats, since there was a significant strand of mainstream Labour thinking that stressed similar themes. While Labourists tended to be more conventional in terms of imagining the continuation of some sort of elite of political rulers, they were conscious of the potential dangers of this from an egalitarian perspective. The widespread worries about the emergence of a 'managerial society' implied the need for greater popular scrutiny of political decision-making, including the emergence of a more democratic education system that would empower the citizenry to render managerial power more accountable. On this point, the critique of the meritocracy merged with the desire to counterbalance the managerial revolution. As Margaret Cole argued in the *New Fabian Essays*, 'whether the managerial-technical society which we are now creating turns in this country into a Burnham or Orwell nightmare, a *Servile State*, or a socialist democracy' was largely dependent 'on how far education can create social consciousness', and would develop a 'sense of public service' and 'social as well as individual personality'.[99] Whether the ruling class was the aristocratic rich or the meritocratic elite, the moral was clear: segregating the rulers at an early age was disastrous for both the rulers and the ruled. 'In the type of society we want to bring about', argued one correspondent to the *New Statesman*, elite positions should be filled only by 'those who have knowledge of their fellows gained by working and living alongside them'.[100]

Apart from these concerns about democracy, there was a more general belief on the Left that the divisions of social status entrenched by the 1944 Act were undesirable in their own right, regardless of their effect on citizenship in a strict political sense. As Socialist Union put it, the 'main effect' of the British education system was 'to reinforce the exclusiveness of certain classes in society by isolating the children of these groups from the rest'.[101] In order to secure the parity of esteem between classes that Ellen Wilkinson desired, egalitarians argued, there had to be both an end to academic selection within the state system and, at a minimum, some attempt to dissipate the exclusivity of the private schools.[102] As long as the rich or the able were educated separately from other groups in society, then this elite would inevitably take on the characteristics outlined by Michael Young. Education would continue to exercise 'a deeply divisive influence on our whole system of social relations', helping to make Britain 'the most class conscious, snobbish and stratified country in the world'.[103] Conversely, 'the more a school can resemble a diversified community, embracing children of all kinds', then the greater chance that children will learn 'to get on with other people and to respect human personality in all its manifestations'.[104]

Praising the defenders of a formal view of educational equality, the narrator of *The Rise of the Meritocracy* noted the important role of the 'great political theorists of the past century' in changing 'the mental climate of their time by reinterpreting old values in terms of new situations – for instance, by hailing the post-1944 educational system in the name of equality'.[105] As the preceding discussion of equality and education policy has shown, leading figures on the British Left were keen to prevent the fulfilment of this prophecy. They offered incisive arguments that sought to detach the 1944 settlement from the values of equality and social justice and, in due course, they too contributed to changing both 'the mental climate of their times' and the structure of the British education system.

7.5 'Welfare state' and 'property-owning democracy'

It is sometimes suggested that revisionists exhibited little interest in the material inequalities deemed unacceptable by earlier egalitarians, with some commentators arguing that, for writers such as Crosland, 'the classic socialist objective of redistribution had lost its importance'.[106] This interpretation is difficult to sustain and excessively influenced by the New Left rendering of revisionist thought discussed in the previous chapter. All egalitarians active in political debate in this period, whether revisionist, New Left or Bevanite, believed that current income and wealth inequalities were unjust. The differences between them were much more complex than either professing or denying the abstract justice of economic equality, since they stemmed from the way in which their shared egalitarian commitments meshed with a range of assumptions about matters of fact, political strategy, the relative priority of other political ideals, and emotional political allegiances. Two important policy debates provide helpful illustrations of these complexities: discussions about the role of the welfare state in promoting equality; and revisionist proposals to equalise wealth holdings by diffusing private property ownership across social classes and initiating novel forms of collective capital ownership.

Equality and the welfare state

In the 1940s, egalitarian support for social insurance, and other measures that established a minimum level of material decency, had been premised on the belief that they represented only the first step in a systematic assault on inequality.[107] Given the palpable public enthusiasm for Beveridge's proposals, and the related growth in the political prestige of the Left, the deficiencies of his social insurance scheme from a more egalitarian perspective were ignored, or accorded little significance. Instead, egalitarians valued the Beveridgean welfare state as the first approximation of a new social commitment to constrain the inequities of the market in the name of the principle of needs. Critically, Beveridge's social insurance scheme also embodied an ideal of social equality, since every citizen participated in and was treated equally by the system. No group or class was singled out as the recipient of charity; the right to material resources from the state was premised on citizenship and not membership of a particular social class or the manifestation of particular patterns of social behaviour.

This interpretation of welfare institutions was given its most famous exposition in T. H. Marshall's *Citizenship and Social Class*, published in 1950, which extended this analysis from social insurance to include other social services, such as education or healthcare. In Marshall's view, the social reforms of the twentieth century marked the completion of an evolution in individual rights, from the introduction of civil and political rights in the eighteenth and nineteenth centuries to the establishment of 'social rights' in the twentieth, by which he meant rights to education, healthcare, housing and a minimum income.[108] The acquisition of such rights, argued Marshall, was essential to the exercise of civil and political citizenship, and more generally to attenuate the extreme economic inequalities created by the market.[109] Marshall further claimed that the creation of an 'equality of status' through the social services enabled a 'class fusion . . . expressed in the form of a new common experience', as all citizens received the same healthcare and education, and every citizen had to queue at the Post Office to collect family allowances or pensions.[110] Although Crosland was somewhat sceptical about this latter example, thinking it 'doubtful whether the fact that everyone now has an insurance card, and repairs to the local post office, really does much to foster social equality', he was typical of the revisionists and mainstream Labour opinion generally in agreeing with Marshall that high-quality state-provided healthcare and education would promote 'a greater equality in manners and the texture of social life'.[111] The fact that social services were provided universally 'as of right and not on sufferance' was also regarded by many on the Left as entrenching the equal status of all citizens, avoiding the invidious social stigma associated with means testing.[112]

This use of rights language raises an important question: did egalitarians of this period retain the strong notion of productive obligation maintained by their counterparts earlier in the twentieth century, coupling their commitment to welfare rights with an assertion of the reciprocal duty to contribute productively to society? Some commentators have seen the writings of Marshall and his contemporaries as conveniently marking the moment at which welfare discourse became organised around unconditional rights, dispensing with the connection between rights and duties earlier posited by the new liberals and ethical socialists.[113] As a matter of textual interpretation, this is inaccurate. Writers in the post-war period, including Beveridge, assumed that income should be related to some form of productive contribution, usually through participation in the labour market.[114] Although Marshall himself was somewhat elusive on this topic, he did stress that civic rights should be accompanied by civic duties, including within this category 'the duty to pay taxes and insurance contributions', and 'the duty to work' and expend productive effort.[115] As one Labour Party policy document baldly stated, 'rights mean duties. No one who benefits from the welfare state, from full employment or from better education can contract out of the social obligations which must support these reforms.'[116]

However, it is certainly fair to say that the idea of economic reciprocity began to fade from the foreground of egalitarian thought in this period, often becoming an implicit assumption rather than an explicit political argument. An important factor in this shift was that post-war social conditions made the question of whether the working class were 'doing their bit' significantly less controversial. Criticism of the idle rich remained a staple of egalitarian rhetoric, but the existence of more or less full employment meant that purported 'loafers' did not cause much public anxiety. Meanwhile, the powerful social memory of the huge collective effort made during the Second World War was seen as establishing beyond doubt the entitlement of the working class to a fair share of the social product. In these circumstances there seemed to be little need for policies, or political rhetoric, that took a firm line on the enforcement of work obligations as a condition of state support.

In addition to Marshall's discussion of social rights, another notable aspect of his essay was his assumption that, after the reforms of the 1945 government, an inevitable trend towards greater material equality and perhaps even socialism was underway. Although Marshall was ambivalent about these developments, and worried that this egalitarianism might be carried to excess, his verdict was nonetheless congenial to the intellectuals and politicians aligned to the Labour leadership. But for other, more radical groups, this characterisation of the legacy of 1945 was altogether too uncritical. The assumption that 'there are no just causes left' was open to question on a number of grounds.[117]

As we have seen, one radical response was to advocate the continued importance of public ownership to securing the underlying objectives of socialism, and to treat the welfare state as only a staging post along the way to an egalitarian society in which 'the distribution of income is got broadly right in the first instance, and does not need to be put right by complicated and wasteful methods of redistribution through taxation and private benevolence'.[118]

A second radical critique came from those sociologists who specialised in the study of the welfare state itself. The group of social policy experts loosely organised around Richard Titmuss was extremely influential on Labour's social policy in the 1950s and 60s, with Brian Abel-Smith and Peter Townsend playing a particularly important role. In certain respects, their concerns overlapped with those of the New Left, although they shied away from any direct engagement with the question of public ownership.[119] They focused instead on what they took to be the complacent assumptions that dominated mainstream Labour thinking about the achievements of the welfare state, and the misconceived understanding of the concept of poverty that had led Labour to its current impasse. While this so-called 'rediscovery of poverty' has conventionally been dated as taking place in the 1960s, and more precisely from 1965 when Townsend and Abel-Smith published *The Poor and the Poorest*,[120] 1965 is perhaps more accurately seen as the date from which this group obtained its maximum public exposure and marshalled its most rigorous empirical evidence. Prior to 1965, the basic ideas of Abel-Smith, Titmuss and Townsend had in fact made some headway in elite-level political debates, since they had been presented in a series of incisive journalistic articles and academic papers in the late 1950s. Indeed, it would not be too much of an exaggeration to say that the political structure of the position of Abel-Smith and Townsend was clearly expounded in their respective contributions to the 1958 *Conviction* anthology, edited by Norman MacKenzie. Their central claims were both empirical and normative, in that they sought on the one hand to argue that poverty was far more widespread than was popularly believed, while on the other they sought to ground their empirical research on a powerful normative claim about the proper meaning of the concept of poverty. In the words of Deacon and Bradshaw: 'Poverty was rediscovered only after it had been redefined.'[121]

While these sociologists acknowledged that the significance of the post-war settlement was that it entrenched the idea that 'rights were created by virtue simply of citizenship' and affirmed that 'people's needs were of like value',[122] they also argued that, in distributional terms, 'the middle classes get the lion's share of the public social services', and received substantial occupational welfare benefits (notably pensions) and generous tax allowances.[123] This was a direct response to the widespread assumption that Britain was now characterised by a radically egalitarian distribution of income,[124] and the Left's teleological belief that there was a natural tendency inherent within the mixed economy that led to the levelling of relative positions. Titmuss's *Income Distribution and Social Change* claimed that, in fact, massive economic inequality remained, sustained by novel and often quite subtle social mechanisms (such as the provision of benefits in kind by private employers).[125]

In addition, Abel-Smith and Townsend began working on the measurement of poverty, in order to confront the assumption that 1945 had rendered poverty a problem of the past. Rowntree's 1951 survey, *Poverty and the Welfare State*, claimed that poverty had been substantially reduced, indeed virtually abolished, by the implementation of the Beveridge Report and other related policies, and this study was brandished by many Labour figures as a vindication of the 1945 government's record.[126] In contrast, Abel-Smith and Townsend were very critical of Rowntree's study. This was not only because of its methodological deficiencies or the need to update the level of the subsistence standard that served as the poverty line,[127] but also because they disagreed with the theoretical basis of a subsistence definition of poverty. Townsend noted that this method of defining a minimum standard depended on expert opinion about the range and cost of the goods that were thought to be necessary for subsistence, and he suggested that it was precisely the role of the external, middle-class expert in these judgements that was untenable. He argued that the standard developed by Rowntree inevitably involved unpleasantly moralistic and class-biased judgements about the kind of expenditure that the poor were permitted to make if they were to receive financial support. Close scrutiny of what Rowntree was prepared to include as a 'necessary' good was thought to reveal some arbitrary distinctions:

> If clothing, money for travel to work and newspapers are considered to be 'necessaries' in the conventional sense, why not tea, handkerchiefs, laundry, contraceptives, cosmetics, hairdressing and shaving, and life insurance payments? Are we indeed so sure that a list of necessaries must exclude cigarettes, beer, toys for children, Christmas gifts and cinema entertainment?[128]

This worry led Abel-Smith and Townsend to conclude that, in the words of their ally Norman MacKenzie, 'a definition of poverty has to take account of the way people *actually* live and what sanctions their behaviour, not how social reformers think they *ought* to live'.[129]

More fundamentally, the subsistence minimum was criticised for inadequately taking account of the relative character of deprivation; of the fact that poverty was a measure of the share of resources that certain individuals had relative to the other members of their community. As Townsend put it, 'the central choice in social policy lies in fact between a national minimum and equality'.[130] The idea of a subsistence minimum was described by Abel-Smith as 'the legacy of mutton-eating Beatrice Webb and the Poor Law' and, in the context of rising living standards, as a recipe for 'ever increasing inequality and class distinction'.[131] The conflation of the Webbs (and indeed Rowntree) with the Poor Law was an interesting rhetorical manoeuvre, since it suggested that these two quite distinct approaches to welfare policy were similar, embodying a condescending Victorian morality that sought to impose a spartan and disciplined regime on the poor. This did an injustice to these earlier social reformers. As we have seen, the Webbs had distinguished between the relief of destitution (an absolute standard) and the relief of poverty (a relative one), and proposed a minimum standard only as a staging post on the road to equality in a society where the ideal of equality was very far from the political and social agenda.[132] Townsend's criticisms of Rowntree were likewise excessively polemical, since Rowntree's definition of poverty did take some account of shifting social perceptions of need, and aimed to set a minimum standard that enabled social participation.[133] The same has even been argued about Beveridge's subsistence definition of poverty.[134]

In spite of their protestations to the contrary, the social policy experts from the 1950s and 60s therefore offered an analysis that had many affinities with their counterparts from earlier in the century. Townsend argued that a human being 'is not a Robinson Crusoe' but 'a social animal entangled in a web of relationships' that influence 'his consumption of goods and services'. Any list of necessary goods ought to refer 'to the structure, organisation, physical environment and available resources of that society'.[135] The Rowntree definition, said MacKenzie, did not take account of 'the social obligations and psychological as well as physical needs which modern society lays on its citizens, and in which advertising, eating habits, entertainment, work and education play vital parts'.[136] Citizens, concluded Townsend, were simply 'rich or poor according to their share of the resources that are available to all'.[137] Earlier socialists and left liberals would have agreed.

How far did the revisionists share this egalitarian understanding of poverty and the purpose of welfare services? Some commentators have suggested that the revisionists 'talked up the disappearance of poverty', and were therefore reluctant to acknowledge the work of Townsend et al. 'Revisionism', it has been argued, 'marginalised evidence that contested its vista on the affluent society'.[138] In fact, Crosland was an enthusiastic supporter of much of the work of Titmuss and his colleagues. He agreed with Titmuss's evidence that the welfare state was not as redistributive as widely believed, and praised the essays by Abel-Smith and Townsend in Conviction for exposing complacency about the extent of poverty. He also agreed that 'the traditional Beveridge and 'national minimum' concepts' were 'irrelevant' to 'present day social problems'.[139] Indeed, in the second edition of The Future of Socialism, Crosland explicitly argued that poverty was not 'an absolute, but a social or cultural, concept'. Standards of poverty were constantly evolving, and 'we should not behave like medical officers of health, concerned only to provide sufficient food and clothing to ward off starvation and ill-health. We are surely concerned with happiness and social justice also.' This led Crosland to defend 'a relative, subjective view of poverty, since the unhappiness and injustice which it creates, even when ill-health and malnutrition are avoided, lies in the enforced deprivation not of luxuries indeed, but of small comforts which others have and are seen to have, and which in the light of prevailing cultural standards are really "conventional necessities"'.[140] Although not fully explicit about how this standard would work in practice, Crosland's understanding of poverty was undoubtedly influenced by the work of Abel-Smith, Titmuss and Townsend.

Crosland did separate the relief of poverty from the pursuit of equality as two distinct socialist objectives, and saw the main purpose of the social services not as the promotion of equality but as 'the relief of social distress and hardship, and the correction of social need'.[141] The social services were consequently to serve humanitarian ideals, while more egalitarian goals were to be the province of other policy areas. However, as Crosland conceded, the distinction between humanitarian and egalitarian objectives was not a hard and fast one, since in practice social policy would inevitably also serve egalitarian ideals. This was highlighted by the fact that the better-off were in a much less vulnerable position than the poor 'for those periods in life in which needs rise sharply relative to income'.[142] One of the most important roles of social policy was therefore to reduce this inequality by ensuring that the disadvantaged had access to resources that could prevent poverty and insecurity during vulnerable periods of the life cycle. The most widely discussed issue of this kind during the 1950s was the stark inequality between the conditions endured by old people reliant on the state pension and those who had access to an occupational pension scheme. The growth of 'two nations' in old-age, it was agreed, 'offends against social justice', since it created 'greater inequalities in living standards after work than in work', and raised the possibility of 'a dangerous social schism'.[143] On these grounds, the Labour Party eventually adopted a new policy for a graduated state pension that was heavily influenced by proposals first made by Abel-Smith and Townsend.[144]

Equality and property ownership

These pension proposals should be contextualised within a broader debate about the Left's understanding of egalitarian strategy. Since the revisionists had abandoned nationalisation as the principal vehicle of equality, the most creative egalitarian thinkers affiliated to this school formulated some alternative methods of equalising the distribution of wealth that they deemed more suitable to the political circumstances of the 1950s and 60s. Seen in this light, the revisionist interest in pension reform was one of a range of policy proposals they planned to deploy to redress wealth inequality, and the vulnerability of the poor, by equalising access to property and financial assets. In the view of the economic journalist Andrew Shonfield, if there was 'any philosophical significance' in the transition from Attlee to Gaitskell it was a shift in emphasis 'from minimum standards of welfare for the poorest to the achievement of the highest possible degree of equality for the community at large'. This meant that the central issue for Gaitskell was 'how to reduce the concentration of capital in the hands of a comparatively small number of owners'.[145]

The available statistics on the distribution of wealth indicated that there was, in the words of James Meade, 'a really fantastic inequality in the ownership of property': 75 per cent of personal property in 1960 was owned by the wealthiest 5 per cent of the population, with 92 per cent of income from property accruing to the top 5 per cent.[146] The revisionists argued that this gross disparity in the distribution of wealth was one of the two most important causes of social class inequality in Britain (the second being educational inequality). Their focus on property ownership as a fundamental cause of inequality enabled the revisionists to present themselves as differing from the New Left and the Titmuss school, both of which allegedly concentrated on the social injustices created by the benefits in kind that accrued to executive and professional positions.[147] However, in addition to this tactical consideration, an important point of political principle was also invoked by revisionists to justify focusing on property ownership, namely that the inequality between a property-owner and a wage-earner was not only a material one. Individuals with property were said to have 'great bargaining strength and a great sense of security, independence, and freedom', since they could rely on their own resources at times of need and would enjoy 'a wider range of economic choice both between occupations, and between work and leisure'.[148] An unequal distribution of property, it was argued, contributed to an unequal distribution of security, freedom and status. The libertarian aspirations of certain revisionists naturally led to an interest in policy measures that would promote both freedom and equality, and the redistribution of property was seen as a proposal that would advance both of these ideals. 'The ardent desire of young people in all classes to acquire some property', wrote Crosland, 'is due not to vulgar acquisitiveness, but to a natural longing for a measure of security, independence and freedom of manoeuvre'.[149]

The idea of a 'property-owning democracy' began to appear in the revisionist lexicon.[150] This term was widely used by Conservative politicians in the 1940s and 50s to characterise their distributive objectives as progressive but non-socialist, demonstrating that they favoured the expansion of the base of private property ownership but were against radical redistribution or further social ownership. The revisionists appropriated the phrase from Conservative ideology and radicalised it, envisaging a 'property-owning democracy' as a society with an egalitarian distribution of private property. As Lewis explained, it was arguable that 'a society in which each person owned an equal amount of property would come much nearer the socialist ideal than one in which the government owned all the property'.[151] This form of egalitarian strategy generated three important policy implications.

First, revisionists placed considerable emphasis on the use of taxation to redistribute wealth. Four measures were the subject of particular discussion: the long-standing egalitarian proposal for a capital levy; the introduction of a capital gains tax; greater taxation of inherited wealth, including the taxation of gifts *inter vivos*; and the introduction of an annual tax on large property holdings. Although plans for a capital levy never commanded a great deal of support amongst revisionist politicians, the other three capital taxes became central to the Labour Party's fiscal policy from the 1950s onwards, and indicated a serious interest in achieving a more egalitarian distribution of property.[152]

Clearly, though, if the revisionists' aim was to expand individual property ownership, then it would also be necessary for the state to take measures that not only reduced the size of the fortunes accumulated by the rich but also increased the size of the property-holdings at the disposal of the disadvantaged. The second strand of a 'property-owning democracy' strategy therefore aimed at not only 'providing basic public services generally through the state, but also at assisting the individual to build up a reasonable fund of his own savings'.[153] A number of measures were proposed to realise this objective, for example subsidies to ensure that the interest on small savings had a yield proportionate to that on larger savings, or even the exemption of income used for savings from income tax (up to a maximum amount).[154] Other proposals included assistance for low earners wanting to purchase a house.[155] As Jay observed, however, if the principal driver of wealth inequality was in fact capital gains, then there was an egalitarian case for enabling the majority of citizens to acquire a share of the benefits of equity investment.[156] To this end, revisionists sometimes expressed a tepid (but critical) interest in profit-sharing and employee share-ownership schemes.[157] More ambitiously, Jay himself advocated a similar proposal to one made earlier by the economist Paul Lamartine Yates: the establishment of a national unit trust scheme for small savers through the Post Office or Trustee Savings Bank. Jay added the bold rider that rather than waiting for Labour to enter government, the labour movement could itself easily start such a scheme under the auspices of the Co-operative Society and Bank and/or the trade unions.[158] All of these proposals outlined a variety of ways 'in which the capital gains inevitable in the full-employment economy can be spread out . . . not merely by state ownership, but by widely diffused personal ownership also'.[159]

Third, revisionists also proposed to supplement the expansion of individual property ownership by undertaking a novel form of public ownership: the state ownership of shares in private companies. It was intended that the wealth taxes mooted in this period would permit payment in kind rather than cash, and this raised the prospect of the state taking ownership of buildings, land and, crucially, shares. Leading revisionists argued that such a portfolio of state property could form the embryo of a radical intervention in capitalist property rights. Since the appreciation of share values was said to be a key driver of wealth inequality, an important equality-promoting measure would be for the state itself to hold shares in enterprises in order to reduce the capital gains accruing to the wealthy and to divert the dividends to egalitarian purposes. The state would be able to 'tap for the first time the pool of capital appreciation which has hitherto been reserved to private ownership'.[160] In this way, argued Gaitskell, 'we can envisage simultaneously the community becoming the owner, not of whole industries, but of many different shareholdings and other forms of property', and in doing so it would be 'replacing the passive shareholder, receiving dividends, and reaping the capital gains'.[161] Jay controversially added that some of this additional revenue could eventually be used to reduce the level of income taxation.[162] These proposals were generally given a hostile reception by the critics of revisionism. To radicals such as Bevan, state ownership of shares appeared to blur capitalism and socialism rather than making the much-needed decisive break for a new socialist settlement.[163] In spite of this criticism, a more moderate version of these proposals was included in Labour's 1958 *Industry and Society* policy document.[164]

The revisionists therefore proposed a far more radical set of policies with respect to the distribution of wealth than they have been given credit for. Their political thought did not simply endorse existing ownership structures or place an exaggerated emphasis on the role of income tax and the welfare state, and nor did they solely concentrate on eliminating inequalities of social status. As Crosland argued, his ideal society would be one 'in which ownership is thoroughly mixed up – a society with a diverse, diffused, pluralist, and heterogeneous pattern of ownership, with the state, the nationalised industries, the co-operatives, the unions, government financial institutions, pensions funds, foundations, and millions of private families all participating'.[165] By most measures, this was a radical, liberal and egalitarian vision, and given the themes of the preceding pages it forms an apt moment in the Left's intellectual history to conclude this book.

Notes

1 S. Beer, *Modern British Politics* (London, 1969 [1965]), 238.
2 See Fielding, 'Labourism in the 1940s', 145–53; Fielding *et al.*, *'England Arise!'*, 80–3, 91–3; Francis, *Ideas and Policies*, 49–57.

3 See section 5.4.

4 Crosland, *Future*, 103, 105.

5 Crosland, *Future*, 112.

6 S. Hall, 'Crosland territory', *NLR*, No. 2, 1960, 4, Hall's emphasis.

7 Hall, 'Supply of demand', 76; also C. Taylor, 'What's wrong with capitalism? 1', *NLR*, No. 2, 1960, 9; E. P. Thompson, 'Revolution again!', *NLR*, No. 6, 1960, 28.

8 S. Rothman, 'British Labor's "New Left"', *Political Science Quarterly*, 76 (1961), 399. See S. Hall, 'The "first" New Left: life and times', in R. Archer *et al.* (eds), *Out of Apathy: Voices of the New Left Thirty Years On* (London, 1989), 27–8; C. Taylor, 'Alienation and community', *Universities and Left Review*, No. 5, Autumn 1958, 11–18.

9 J. Blumler, 'A look at the Left', *SC*, February 1960, 4, Blumler's emphasis.

10 Although significant tensions existed within the New Left on this question: see Kenny, *First New Left*, 69–85. For the retrieval of Morris's socialism for the 1950s, see E. P. Thompson, *William Morris: Romantic to Revolutionary* (London, 1955), 738–61, 790–845.

11 E. P. Thompson, 'Socialist humanism: an epistle to the philistines', *New Reasoner*, Summer 1957, 142–3.

12 Hall, 'Crosland territory', 4.

13 C. Taylor, 'Changes of quality', *NLR*, No. 4, 1960, 4.

14 Michael Young, interviewed by Hennessy, 'The 1945 general election', 88, also 97.

15 For a similar distinction see Bryan, 'Development of revisionist thought', 351–4, although Bryan restricted himself to thinkers affiliated to the Labour Party, and did not discuss the role of the New Left or academic sociologists other than Michael Young.

16 For this point see also Ellison, *Egalitarian Thought*, 114–25. On the communitarianism of Socialist Union's organisational practice rather than its political thought, see Black, 'Social democracy as a way of life', 522–39.

17 Socialist Union, *Twentieth Century Socialism*, 53; also 'Principles and objects of the Socialist Union adopted at foundation meeting, 31 March 1951', typescript, Socialist Union Papers MSS.173/15, 2.

18 Socialist Union, *Socialism*, 35; also R. Hinden, 'The dying community', *SC*, March 1959, 10–12.

19 Socialist Union, *Twentieth Century Socialism*, 53; see also Socialist Union, *Socialism*, 36; and Socialist Union, *Reflections on the Social Services* (London, 1958), 9–10. Briggs wrongly claims that Young was distinctive in his appeal to the family as a model for social organisation and Socialist Union 'never mentioned the family once': Briggs, *Michael Young*, 105.

20 R. Hinden, 'A different animal?', *SC*, November 1956, 28; R. Hinden to H. Gaitskell, 16.10.1955, Gaitskell Papers A140.

21 R. Hinden, 'Socialism by half', *SC*, March 1962, 14.

22 Hinden, 'Socialism by half', 15–16. Like Jay and Gaitskell, Lewis also disagreed with Socialist Union's criticism of private profits and their 'puritanical glorification of work as a means of self-expression', in his 'Underdog-ism', 8; W. A. Lewis to R. Hinden, 11.10.1955, Lewis Papers, Correspondence Box 6.

23 'Equality with quality', *SC*, July 1955, 199; see also Socialist Union, *Twentieth Century Socialism*, 144.

24 C. R. Attlee, 'This is my socialist faith', *Forward*, 5.7.1952, 6.

25 G. D. H. Cole, 'Twentieth-century socialism?', *NS*, 7.7.1955, 8–9, Cole's emphasis. Contrast with Hinden's defence of a 'middle position' on public ownership: 'Public ownership debate', 6–7.

26 Young, interviewed by Hennessy, 'The 1945 general election', 88.

27 D. Reisman, *Richard Titmuss: Welfare and Society* (Basingstoke, second edition, 2001), 20.
28 P. Townsend, 'A society for people', in MacKenzie, *Conviction*, 93–5, quotes from 95.
29 Townsend, 'Society for people', 117–19; M. Young, *Big Man, Small World: A Discussion of Socialist Democracy* (London, 1948), 6.
30 For a similar point, see also J. Goldthorpe, 'Intellectuals and the working class in modern Britain', in D. Rose (ed.), *Social Stratification and Economic Change* (London, 1988), 39–56.
31 Townsend, 'Society for people', 118–19.
32 Young, *Big Man, Small World*, 3–4, 13–14, quote at 13. See also Young's 1949 memo to Labour's Policy Committee, reprinted as M. Young, 'What might have been', *New Society*, 2.11.1972, 262–4; and his 'A plea for restatement of socialism', LPRD, RD353/April 1950, 2.
33 M. Young, 'The British socialist way of life', Fabian Conference on Problems Ahead, Oxford, 31.3–2.4.1950, Fabian Society Papers G50/3, Item 2, 3.
34 Young, 'British socialist way of life', 12; Young, *Big Man, Small World*, 12–13; G. D. H. Cole, 'Summary of points', typescript notes from Fabian Conference on Problems Ahead, Oxford, April 1950, Fabian Society Papers, G50/3, Item 1.
35 See Briggs, *Michael Young*, 128–48; M. Young, 'Proposal for establishing a London Institute of Community Studies', typescript, July 1953, Titmuss Papers 2/136; M. Young and P. Willmott, 'Institute of Community Studies', *Sociological Review*, 10 (1961), 203–13.
36 M. Young and P. Willmott, *Family and Kinship in East London* (London, revised edition, 1962 [1957]), 193–4, quote on 194; also P. Townsend, *The Family Life of Old People: An Inquiry in East London* (London, 1957). See also Taylor, 'Alienation and community', 14–15; Jackson and Marsden, *Education and the Working Class*, 221–5.
37 Townsend, 'Society for people', 119.
38 Young, *Rise*, 129–31.
39 R. M. Titmuss, 'The limits of the welfare state', *NLR*, No. 27, 1964, 34; Titmuss, 'Social division of welfare', in his *Essays*, 39; Reisman, *Richard Titmuss*, 29–31; also Socialist Union, *Reflections*, 7–8. Famously, Titmuss later cited the British system of voluntary blood donation as an evocative indication of how welfare services could promote altruism and fellowship: *The Gift Relationship* (New York, 1997 [1970]), 278–9, 290–2, 311.
40 Kenny, *First New Left*, 94–7.
41 R. Hoggart, *The Uses of Literacy* (London, 1957), 68–72, 148–57, 277–8, quote at 277.
42 R. Williams, 'Culture is ordinary', in MacKenzie, *Conviction*, 80.
43 Williams, *Culture and Society*, 326, 331–2.
44 R. Williams, *The Long Revolution* (London, 1961), 301–5, quotes on 301, 302.
45 Williams, *Long Revolution*, 335.
46 As argued, for example, by Bryan, 'Development of revisionist thought', 353–4.
47 D. Marquand, 'Passion and politics', *Encounter*, December 1961, 5. The same point was also made by R. Wollheim, 'The English dream', *Spectator*, 10.3.1961, 334.
48 Crosland, *Future*, 107–10, quote on 108.
49 R. Wollheim, 'Socialism and culture', *FT No. 331* (London, 1961), 11–12.
50 R. Williams, 'Definitions of culture', *NS*, 9.6.1961, 882. For further criticism of the 'sustained mediocrity' of Wollheim's pamphlet, see E. P. Thompson, 'The long revolution II', *NLR*, No. 10, 1961, 36. The sociological question hinted at by Williams was later authoritatively surveyed by J. Goldthorpe, D. Lockwood, F. Bechhofer and J. Platt, *The Affluent Worker in the Class Structure* (Cambridge, 1969).

51 Wollheim, 'English dream', 334–5.

52 Crosland, 'The mass media', in his *Conservative Enemy*, 210.

53 See Crosland's contribution to the discussion of Young, 'The British socialist way of life', Fabian Conference on Problems Ahead, Oxford, 31.3–2.4.1950, Fabian Society Papers G50/3, 10–11; *Future*, 164–5, 521–4; 'Radical reform and the Left', in his *Conservative Enemy*, 131; Torrie, 'Ideas, policy and ideology', 96.

54 H. Gaitskell, comments on draft of Socialist Union, *Man is the Measure* [later renamed *Twentieth Century Socialism*], typescript, 14.10.1955, Gaitskell Papers A140, 11–12. Compare with the similar point in C. A. R. Crosland, 'A social democratic Britain' [1970], in his *Socialism Now*, 89. See also H. Gaitskell to R. Hinden, 5.10.1955, Socialist Union Papers MSS.173/13; H. Gaitskell, 'The economic aims of the Labour Party', *PQ*, 24 (1953), 15–16; R. Jenkins, *Pursuit of Progress* (London, 1953), 172–4; R. Jenkins, *The Labour Case* (Harmondsworth, 1959), 146; Jay, *Socialism*, 5–7, 352–5; Magee, *New Radicalism*, 94–5; Howell, 'Restatement', 281–98.

55 Wollheim, 'Socialism and culture', 12.

56 Wollheim, 'Socialism and culture', 13.

57 Wollheim, 'Socialism and culture', 13; see also J. Vaizey, 'We call it wallop', *SC*, March 1959, 16–17. Interestingly, Titmuss had made a similar point in his comments on the draft of *Family and Kinship in East London*. He also felt that its conclusions gave 'an impression that the authors have decided what is good for people. Should not the stress be laid, however, on allowing people *freedom* to decide themselves whether they want to live near "mum?"' R. M. Titmuss, 'Notes on MS', 30.8.1956, Titmuss Papers 2/136, 3, Titmuss's emphasis.

58 B. Magee, 'Conservatism with a small "c"', *SC*, January 1963, 20.

59 M. Young, 'A plea for restatement of socialism', LPRD, RD353/April 1950, 2.

60 N. Birnbaum, 'Politics and "abundance"', *Dissent*, Summer 1958, 242; S. Hall, 'A sense of classlessness', *Universities and Left Review*, No. 5, Autumn 1958, 29–30; Taylor, 'Alienation and community', 15.

61 Crosland, *Future*, 173–8.

62 Crosland, *Future*, 287–9, quote at 287.

63 Crosland, 'Radical reform and the Left', 129; see also Jenkins, *Labour Case*, 54–5; Magee, *New Radicalism*, 143–7.

64 Jay, *Socialism*, 290–1, Jay's emphasis; see also Crosland, 'Inequalities of wealth', 39.

65 Jenkins, *Fair Shares*, 3; see also Crosland, *Future*, 214–15.

66 Jay, *Socialism*, 5; Gaitskell, comments on Socialist Union draft, typescript, 14.10.1955, Gaitskell Papers A140, 3.

67 Gaitskell, comments on Socialist Union draft, 14.10.1955, Gaitskell Papers A140, 11–12.

68 Bevan, *In Place of Fear*, 77, 81. See also Francis, *Ideas and Policies*, 111–14.

69 Gaitskell, *Recent Developments*, 34. However, Gaitskell did express some tactical reservations about Labour pursuing the outright abolition of selective education: see Ellison, *Egalitarian Thought*, 92–4. Note that, unlike Ellison, I do not think that Gaitskell's tactical reservations about this single policy provide evidence that he was an outright meritocrat in his view of social justice.

70 For the relevant educational history, see D. Rubinstein and B. Simon, *The Evolution of the Comprehensive School, 1926–72* (London, second edition, 1972); McKibbin, *Classes and Cultures*, 206–71. On the tortuous evolution of Labour's education policy, see Barker, *Education and Politics*; C. Benn, 'Comprehensive school reform and the 1945 Labour government', *History Workshop*, 10 (1980), 197–204; Brooke, *Labour's War*, 111–33, 187–203; Francis, *Ideas and Policies*, 141–68; Torrie, 'Ideas, policy and ideology', 282–95.

71 A. Swift, *How Not to be a Hypocrite: School Choice for the Morally Perplexed Parent* (London, 2003), 36–8; R. McKibbin, 'Nothing more divisive', *London Review of Books*, 28.11.2002, 3.

72 Francis, *Ideas and Policies*, 154, Francis's emphasis.

73 Barker, *Education and Politics*, 84–5, 88–90; Francis, *Ideas and Policies*, 153–6; McKibbin, *Classes and Cultures*, 233.

74 W. Fienburgh, 'Equal opportunity', *NS*, 21.3.1953, 332.

75 E.g. P. Doyle, 'Equality of opportunity', *SC*, November 1951, 265–7.

76 A. Fox, 'Chances for children', *SC*, February 1957, 26. See also section 6.4.

77 Conveniently, Crosland cited the literature that he thought demonstrated the influence of environmental factors on IQ levels in his 'Comprehensive education', 196: Central Advisory Council for Education, *Early Leaving*; Floud *et al.*, *Social Class and Educational Opportunity*; P. E. Vernon (ed.), *Secondary School Selection* (London, 1957); J. Douglas, *The Home and the School* (London, 1964). See also B. Simon, *Intelligence Testing and the Comprehensive School* (London, 1953), 39–111; B. Simon, *The Common Secondary School* (London, 1955), 48–70; Rubinstein and Simon, *Evolution*, 60–6; G. Sutherland, *Ability, Merit and Measurement: Mental Testing and English Education 1880–1940* (Oxford, 1984), 128–90; McKibbin, *Classes and Cultures*, 228–31.

78 Crosland, 'Comprehensive education', 195.

79 'Draft policy statement', LPRD, RE78/June 1956, 5; Fox, 'Chances for children', 26.

80 G. D. H. Cole, 'Education in danger', *NS*, 17.11.1951, 556; see also his 'Historical foundations of ideas of equality', typescript, *c*.1955, Cole Papers E3/17/3/24–5.

81 Crosland, 'The public schools and English education', in his *Conservative Enemy*, 169.

82 Crosland, 'Public schools', 172; see also Labour Party, *Towards Equality*, 7–8.

83 Crosland, 'Public schools', 173, Crosland's emphasis.

84 Crosland, 'Public schools', 173–4, Crosland's emphasis. For a similar interpretation, see Ellison, *Egalitarian Thought*, 96–7.

85 Fox, 'Chances for children', 26; also Wollheim, 'Socialism and culture', 31–4; Titmuss, 'Introduction' to Tawney, *Equality* (1964 edition), 11–12.

86 Crosland, 'Comprehensive education', 199; see also W. S. Hill, 'Real equality of opportunity', *SC*, October 1961, 21–3; R. Pedley, *The Comprehensive School* (London, 1964), 16–20, 24–5.

87 Crosland, 'Comprehensive education', 198–9. See also Simon, *Common Secondary School*, 77.

88 Simon, *Intelligence Testing*, 92–3; McKibbin, *Classes and Cultures*, 234. Crosland himself apparently revised his views on this point, and, influenced by later sociological studies, came to regard education as of limited importance for equalising opportunity when compared to family background: J. Nuttall, 'Psychological socialism: Tony Crosland and the politics of the mind' (DPhil thesis, Oxford University, 2001), 278–87.

89 For one suggestion along these lines, taking Crosland's position as a starting point, see H. Glennerster, 'Education and inequality', in P. Townsend and N. Bosanquet (eds), *Labour and Inequality* (London, 1972), 83–107. See also J. Roemer, 'Egalitarian strategies', *Dissent*, Summer 1999, 69–70, 72–4.

90 Williams, *Long Revolution*, 145–7.

91 Crosland, 'Comprehensive education', 199. Crosland also recognised that his strong principle of equal opportunity 'begs the still more fundamental question of whether educational opportunity should be based on measured intelligence at all'. He indicated that both he and Michael Young had in other work indicated reasons to be sceptical of this aspiration: Crosland, 'Public schools', 173, fn. 1.

92 Fabian Society Local Societies Committee, *About Equality* (London, December 1954), 3, copy in Fabian Society Papers, F47/4, Item 1.

93 E. Wilkinson, speech, 13.6.1946, *LPACR* 1946, 189; and her subsequent speech, reported in *Education*, 21.6.1946, quoted in Rubinstein and Simon, *Evolution*, 38; also Barker, *Education and Politics*, 88–9.

94 Crosland, *Future*, 272; see also his 'Public schools', 174–5.

95 Crosland, 'Comprehensive education', 204.

96 McKibbin, 'Nothing more divisive', 3.

97 R. St John Reade, 'Correspondence: "killing a school"', *NS*, 24.3.1951, 343; see also Pedley, *Comprehensive School*, 11, 181–2.

98 R. Williams, 'An educated democracy', *SC*, October 1959, 9; see also Williams, 'Culture is ordinary', 87; Williams, *Long Revolution*, 149–50; the Editors, 'The learning revolution', *NLR*, No. 11, 1961, 43–4.

99 M. Cole, 'Education and social democracy', in Crossman, *New Fabian Essays*, 105; see also Shore, 'Room at the top', 35–8.

100 J. P. Morris, 'Correspondence', *NS*, 6.8.1949, 149; see also Council for the Victory of Socialism, *Equality in Education: A Policy for Labour* (London, n.d. [1958]), 7. This sentiment was not universally shared, since Morris's letter was a response to an article by Richard Crossman, which argued for a Platonic early selection and intensive training of putative rulers in order to educate a 'responsible elite': 'The public school system', *NS*, 16.7.1949, 59–60.

101 Socialist Union, *Education and Socialism* (London, 1958), 14; see also Labour Party, *Learning to Live* (London, 1958), 5, 32.

102 Crosland proposed that the state should offer the vast majority of places at private schools to the public free of charge, with places allocated on a non-meritocratic basis: see his 'Public schools', 180–2.

103 C. A. R. Crosland, *HCD*, 642, 16.6.1961, col. 831.

104 'Equality', *Observer*, 15.7.1956, 6; see also Pedley, *Comprehensive School*, 199–200.

105 Young, *Rise*, 96.

106 Thompson, *Political Economy*, 169.

107 See section 5.5.

108 Marshall, *Citizenship*, 10–11.

109 Marshall, *Citizenship*, 46–7.

110 Marshall, *Citizenship*, 56–7.

111 Crosland, *Future*, 143; C. A. R. Crosland, 'Aims of social policy', *Fabian Journal*, No. 19, July 1956, 22.

112 Socialist Union, *Reflections*, 11; Jay, *Socialism*, 225–6.

113 E.g. A. Vincent, 'The new liberalism and citizenship', in Simhony and Weinstein, *The New Liberalism*, 210–11.

114 Beveridge, *Social Insurance*, para. 130, 58; Cole, *Socialist Economics*, 59, 65; Crosland, *Future*, 208; Socialist Union, *Reflections*, 7, 15.

115 Marshall, *Citizenship*, 78–80, quote at 78; White, *Civic Minimum*, 139–40.

116 Labour Party, *Personal Freedom*, 14, also 6; and 'Distribution of income and wealth', LPRD, R49/June 1951, 8.

117 Townsend, 'Society for people', 100.

118 Cole, 'Socialism and the welfare state', 88. See section 6.3.

119 They were certainly sympathetic to the critique of the power of private industry: see e.g. Titmuss, 'The irresponsible society' [1959], in his *Essays on 'the Welfare State'* (London, 1963 edition), 215–43.

120 B. Abel-Smith and P. Townsend, *The Poor and the Poorest* (London, 1965); R. Lowe, 'The rediscovery of poverty and the creation of the Child Poverty Action Group, 1962–68', *Contemporary Record*, 9 (1995), 602–11.

121 A. Deacon and J. Bradshaw, *Reserved for the Poor: The Means Test in British Social Policy* (Oxford, 1983), 61, quoted in Lowe, *Welfare State in Britain*, 148.

122 P. Townsend, 'The truce on inequality', *NS*, 26.9.1959, 381.

123 B. Abel-Smith, 'Whose welfare state?', in MacKenzie, *Conviction*, 57–63, quote at 63.

124 See e.g. B. de Jouvenal, *The Ethics of Redistribution* (Cambridge, 1951), 1–2; Robbins, 'Notes on public finances', 8.

125 R. M. Titmuss, *Income Distribution and Social Change* (London, 1962), especially 187–99; see also Townsend, 'Society for people', 101–2. The provision of benefits in kind was a central theme of *The Rise of the Meritocracy*, since under the meritocratic regime wages were formally equal but differential benefits were paid to those performing more prestigious or important jobs on the grounds that they 'compensated' the talented for their work: Young, *Rise*, 155–61.

126 B. S. Rowntree and G. R. Lavers, *Poverty and the Welfare State* (London, 1951), 37–45 and *passim*. For use of this study by Labour supporters, see J. Strachey, 'Labour's task', *FT No. 290* (London, 1951), 8; Tawney, 'British socialism today', 126; D. Jay, 'Equality and the fiscal problem', 2–3, paper for Fabian Buscot Park Conference, 24–25.1.1953, Gaitskell Papers A137/2. Crosland referred to the Rowntree study in the first edition of *The Future of Socialism* but not the second (published in 1964): *Future*, 43. For this point I am indebted to D. Reisman, 'Crosland's *Future*: the first edition', *International Journal of Social Economics*, 23 (1996), 48–9.

127 Both of these were indeed part of their critique: see P. Townsend, 'The meaning of poverty', *British Journal of Sociology*, 18 (1962), 211–15.

128 P. Townsend, 'Measuring poverty', *British Journal of Sociology*, 5 (1954), 131.

129 N. MacKenzie, 'Poverty, security and socialism: some afterthoughts on the failure of Beveridge', *Fabian Journal*, No. 15, March 1955, 26, MacKenzie's emphasis; see also his 'Poverty and welfare I: the secret poor', *NS*, 24.4.1954, 519–20; his 'Poverty-line', *NS*, 1.5.1954, 553–4, and the *NS* editorial: 'Poverty and welfare', 26.6.1954, 820.

130 Townsend, 'Society for people', 113.

131 Abel-Smith, 'Whose welfare state?', 69.

132 Webb and Webb, *Prevention of Destitution*, 1; their 'What is socialism? Part XII', 364–6. Indeed, Margaret Cole complained to Abel-Smith that he had made 'a spiteful post-mortem insult to Beatrice Webb' for precisely this reason: M. Cole to B. Abel-Smith, 29.11.1958, 18.12.1958, 4.1.1959, Abel-Smith Papers 14/9. See section 3.3.

133 Veit-Wilson, 'Paradigms of poverty', 69–99.

134 Harris, *William Beveridge*, 382, 386–9; Beveridge, *Social Insurance*, para. 27, 14. For a more sceptical view, see Veit-Wilson, 'Paradigms of poverty', 96.

135 Townsend, 'Meaning of poverty', 219.

136 MacKenzie, 'Poverty, security and socialism', 26.

137 Townsend, 'Meaning of poverty', 225.

138 Black, *Political Culture of the Left*, 152.

139 C. A. R. Crosland, 'Conditions of welfare', *Encounter*, March 1958, 68–70; his 'Leftover left to kill', *Spectator*, 24.10.1958, 555; his 'Aims of social policy', 19–20.

140 Crosland, *The Future of Socialism* (London, revised second edition, 1964), 89 (all other references to this work are to the first edition); his 'Aims of social policy', 22–3; also Jay, *Socialism*, 203–4.

141 Crosland, *Future*, 112–14, 148, quote at 148; 'Aims of social policy', 22.

142 Crosland, *Future*, 158.
143 B. Abel-Smith and P. Townsend, 'New pensions for old', *Fabian Research Series No. 171* (London, 1955), 6–7; C. A. R. Crosland, 'National superannuation', *SC*, May 1956, 19; Titmuss, 'Pension systems and population change' [1955], in his *Essays on 'the Welfare State'*, 73–4; also Jay, *Socialism*, 237–42.
144 Abel-Smith and Townsend, 'New pensions', 21–7; Labour Party, *National Superannuation* (London, 1957); Ellison, *Egalitarian Thought*, 129–32, 256, fn. 80; Torrie, 'Ideas, policy and ideology', 295–300.
145 A. Shonfield, 'Labour and equality', *Listener*, 9.2.1956, 203.
146 J. Meade, *Efficiency, Equality and the Ownership of Property* [1964], in his *Liberty, Equality and Efficiency* (Basingstoke, 1993), 33–4; see also 'Social services and redistributive taxation', minutes of Buscot Conference on Problems Ahead, July 1949, Cole Papers D1/15/2/2–4; 'The distribution of income and wealth', LPRD, R49/June 1951, 9–10; Jenkins, *Fair Shares*, 5–6.
147 Titmuss, 'Irresponsible society', 229–31; Titmuss, *Income Distribution*, 169–86; Shore, 'Room at the top', 32–5; R. Samuel, '"Bastard" capitalism', in Thompson, *Out of Apathy*, 36–8. For criticism, see Crosland, 'Inequalities of wealth', 29–30; W. A. Lewis to H. Gaitskell, 13.1.1955, 4; Lewis Papers, Correspondence Box 5.
148 Meade, *Efficiency*, 41; Crosland, *Future*, 298; see also Jay, *Socialism*, 200–1, 290–1.
149 Crosland, 'Inequalities of wealth', 38.
150 For a detailed discussion of the points made in this and the following two paragraphs, see Jackson, 'Revisionism reconsidered', 419–37.
151 Lewis, 'Socialist economic policy', 173. See 'A property-owning democracy', note to Hugh Gaitskell from Labour Party Research Department, n.d. [*c*.1955], Gaitskell Papers C133; Crosland, 'Inequalities of wealth', 39; Jay, *Socialism*, 290–4; Meade, *Efficiency*, 41–2.
152 Whiting, *Labour Party*, 130–72; Daunton, *Just Taxes*, 279–89; Jackson, 'Revisionism reconsidered', 425–9.
153 Jay, *Socialism*, 291.
154 Lewis, 'Distribution of property', 366; Crosland, *Future*, 404, 516.
155 Meade, 'Next steps in domestic economic policy', LPRD, RD201/November 1948, 4; Meade, *Efficiency*, 55; C. A. R. Crosland, 'How find the savings?', *SC*, August 1953, 176; Lewis, 'Distribution of property', 366; Labour Party, *Homes of the Future* (London, 1956), 21–6; Socialist Union, *Reflections*, 30–1.
156 D. Jay, 'Equity shares and the small saver', LPRD, RE125/December 1956, 1; Jay, *Socialism*, 291.
157 'The control of profits', LPRD, R32/February 1951, 4; Crosland, *Future*, 362–5; N. Davenport, 'Wider share ownership II', *Spectator*, 17.3.1961, 376–8; Meade, *Efficiency*, 55.
158 P. Lamartine Yates, 'The distribution of property', *SC*, January 1956, 25; Jay, 'Equity shares and the small saver', LPRD, RE125/December 1956; Jay, 'Scheme for a public unit trust', LPRD, RE574/June 1959; Jay, *Socialism*, 292–4. The Labour-sympathising financier Nicholas Davenport later claimed that the original idea for this scheme was his, and that Jay had 'appropriated the idea without acknowledgement' in 1962. Davenport appeared unaware that Jay (and Yates) had in fact been arguing for this idea since 1956: Davenport, *Memoirs*, 204.
159 Jay, *Socialism*, 294.
160 'Preliminary memorandum on equality', LPRD, RE36/March 1956, 26.

161 Gaitskell, 'Socialism and nationalisation', 35–6, quote at 36; see also 'Mr Gaitskell on more public ownership', *Sunday Times*, 12.2.1956, 7; Lewis, 'Distribution of property', 366–7; R. Marris, 'The redistribution of wealth', *SC*, April 1956, 12–15.

162 D. Jay, letter to *The Times*, 26.7.1957, 11; his 'Public capital and private enterprise', *Fabian Journal*, 28 (1959), 14.

163 'Bevan hits at state shares in industry', *Sunday Times*, 26.2.1956, 9; *LPACR 1957*, 128–61.

164 Labour Party, *Industry and Society*, 39–40; see also Torrie, 'Ideas, policy and ideology', 220–6.

165 Crosland, *Future*, 496.

Conclusion

A plausible formula?

In this book I have examined the historical development of the ideal of equality and its role in the ideology of the British Left. I have focused on three main themes. The first, and overriding, theme of this book is the sheer historical durability of a particular kind of social democratic egalitarianism. From the Edwardian period to the early 1960s, both left liberals and socialists were profoundly disturbed by the unfair economic inequality that structured British society. The aim of reducing or eliminating that inequality (and not simply poverty) was fundamental to progressive political thought and to the Left's understanding of its political purpose. Although an unremarkable observation in itself, the character of this egalitarianism is more surprising than this bald summary suggests. It did not conform to partisan portrayals of the mean-spirited envy or utopianism purportedly inherent in demands for economic equality, and its theoretical structure cut across certain categories that have often been seen as distinct. I have documented five features of the Left's commitment to equality in support of these claims.

First, the Left contested their opponents' portrayal of the debate about social justice as necessarily polarised between a moderate and socially tolerable ideal of 'equality of opportunity' and a radical and socially ruinous principle of 'equality of outcome'. Any stark distinction between these ideals was shown to be both philosophically and empirically unconvincing by a succession of leading egalitarians, perhaps most notably by R. H. Tawney and Anthony Crosland. They argued that if the aspiration of 'equality of opportunity' was taken seriously, as the ambition to neutralise the impact of individuals' social class background on their life chances, then it would in fact require a significant reduction in inequality of condition. As long as privileged individuals were capable of greatly advantaging their children in terms of education, financial assets and cultural resources, equality of opportunity would remain a sham. It would be 'the impertinent courtesy of an invitation to unwelcome guests, in the certainty that circumstances would prevent them from accepting it'.[1]

Second, although social democrats favoured an expansive principle of equal opportunity in order to enable every individual the opportunity to develop their potential, they were sceptical of principles of social justice that would distribute material resources in proportion to either productive contribution or the scarcity value of particular skills. This meant that social democrats usually saw both a centrist liberal meritocracy and a 'Ricardian socialism', based on the labour theory of value, as unjust. Such social democratic egalitarians characteristically argued that differences in individual productivity were determined by natural and social contingencies that individuals could not control and therefore asserted that the entitlement of all members of the community to a civic minimum was derived from their needs, and from their status as free and equal citizens. In this sense, social democrats envisaged a just society that went beyond the 'bourgeois' understanding of equal opportunity, but avoided the radical Left's ambiguous juxtaposition of a principle of need with the 'deeply bourgeois values about people's ownership of themselves', and 'the product of their own labour', found in the invocation of the labour theory of value as a distributive principle.[2]

Third, social democrats certainly conceded that some inequalities were permissible, not as just rewards for greater productive contribution, but rather as unfair but economically efficient incentive payments. They consistently rejected the idiosyncratic strict economic egalitarianism of Shaw on the grounds that identical rewards would insufficiently motivate highly skilled individuals to perform important jobs and would therefore undermine economic efficiency. As I stressed earlier, there are interesting affinities between this position and the model of 'democratic equality' later expounded by John Rawls.

Fourth, social democrats insisted that individuals must exercise certain responsibilities in return for a fair share of social rights. In the vocabulary of the period discussed in this book, theirs was a 'functional' theory of social justice: rights to income, and other social benefits, were not granted unconditionally, but rather depended on the performance of a social function. There are certainly weaknesses to this view, not least, as we have seen, its gendered character, but it is fascinating to note the consistency with which egalitarians argued for an obligation to work in the early to mid-twentieth century. This finding does not sit easily with the views of certain critics of egalitarianism, who often conjure up images of a doctrine that is far too lax in its prescriptions about social obligations. Clearly, the 'functional' theory of justice was partly intended to meet this latter objection; it was rhetorically significant in that it appropriated opponents' concerns about work and turned them against the wealthy and the privileged. But it also reflected the Left's underlying conviction about social fairness. In return for a just share of the benefits of social membership, social democrats believed that each individual should take a share of the duties (civic, productive, familial) necessary to sustain a prosperous and harmonious community. However, as we saw in the previous chapter, the particular social conditions of post-war Britain made these duties a less pressing concern that they had been in earlier decades. As a result, the obligation to contribute became much less frequently discussed by the Left in the latter half of the twentieth century and, at some point, actually began to be perceived as an exclusively conservative rhetorical device, conjuring up images of Victorian workhouses and oppressive state intrusion into the lives of the poor and vulnerable. The evidence assembled here suggests that this perception underestimates the importance of the obligation to work to the politics of the Left during the rise of British social democracy.

Fifth, the Left saw equality as an ideal that encompassed both economic and social dimensions. It was not an aspiration that focused solely on distributing fair shares of resources at the cost of cultivating a community characterised by egalitarian social relationships and civic participation. A number of political theorists have recently argued that these two egalitarian ideals conflict with one another (sometimes offering supporting citations from texts written in the period discussed in this book). According to their analysis, concerns about resource distribution can crowd out or even undermine the objective of enabling individuals to meet one another as equals in their social and political lives and, according to these commentators, this latter aspiration was the one rightly prioritised by egalitarians in the past.[3] Earlier egalitarian thought cannot offer a straightforward resolution to these contemporary debates, but it does suggest that the apparent antagonism between economic and social equality has been drawn much too sharply by these commentators. When British egalitarians first formulated their ideas, and directed their political energies towards social reforms, they saw material inequalities as the most important influence on the inequalities of status that segregated social classes from each other, and they aimed to eliminate both. The British Left thought that injuries to the social status and self-respect of the workers were principally due to their workplace experiences, their pay packets and the places in which they lived. The absence of a substantive attempt to equalise these economic conditions, the Left argued, would itself make a mockery of any aspiration to treat every citizen with equal respect.

Such is the first theme of this book: the significance of a multi-faceted but coherent social democratic egalitarianism to the ideology of the British Left. In addition to this emphasis on an important continuity in the progressive ideology of this period, a second theme of the preceding chapters has been an important transformation in the Left's conceptualisation of its egalitarian objectives. In the first three decades of the twentieth century, egalitarians aimed both at securing a more equitable distribution of the goods necessary to live a fulfilling life and at bringing about a qualitative transformation in the character of economic relationships, in order to foster a community based on co-operation and mutual service rather than competition and the profit motive. To left liberals and socialists, both of these goals were closely connected: they hoped to dilute, or possibly even eliminate, motives of self-interest in order to promote greater economic equality. A growth in egalitarian attitudes and preferences, they argued, would lead the highly paid to feel motivated to work at least partly by a desire to serve the community, as a result reducing the economic inequality necessary to promote productive efficiency. This understanding of the relationship between the values of equality and community, and the accompanying commitment to the promotion of an egalitarian social ethos, remained important to some egalitarians throughout the entire period examined in this book. In particular, it was granted a fresh lease of life by the social experiences of the Second World War and the post-war interest in the 'organic' character of working-class culture.

However, from the 1930s onwards, some leading figures on the Left began to distance themselves from these communitarian aspirations. These 'revisionists' did not prioritise the qualitative social transformation envisaged by other egalitarians. Indeed, many of them initially drew on Keynesian theory, and the utilitarian argument for equality gleaned from welfare economics, in order to show that greater economic equality would, in addition to its ethical desirability, enhance productive and distributive efficiency. These efficiency arguments appeared most persuasive in the specific economic and political context of the 1930s and 40s, and in the post-war period revisionist social democrats reverted to arguments for equality that were mainly grounded on social justice. However, given their intellectual background in political and economic theories that were premised on the sovereignty of the rational self-interested individual, leading revisionists were hesitant about regarding the alteration of 'selfish' economic behaviour as an important egalitarian goal. Indeed, revisionist politicians in the 1950s and 60s explicitly rejected organicist political discourse and its implications for the pursuit of equality. This was not only for practical reasons, since these revisionists were in fact unclear about the significance of organicism for public policy, but also stemmed from their more libertarian political outlook, since they were wary of placing oppressive social pressures on the individual.

By the 1960s, although egalitarians remained united around the principles of social justice discussed earlier, they were now divided over the role that the concept of community should play in egalitarian thought, and over the political lessons that could sensibly be derived from the social experiences of war and traditional working-class culture. Revisionist thought had palpably shifted away from the philosophical and political idealism that had structured the thinking of earlier generations of socialists and left liberals. The loss of these idealisms had both costs and benefits for the Left and it would be too simplistic to portray this development as either a straightforward story of ground gained or lost.[4] Nonetheless, the critics of revisionism were undoubtedly correct when they observed that at least some of the revisionists were revising the ends as well as the means of socialism.

While the Left's conceptualisation and justification of its egalitarian ideals is the dominant concern of this book, a third theme is the Left's extended debate about the most effective means of implementing equality. The British Left's ideas about egalitarian strategy in this period were not reducible to a straightforward choice between 'socialism' or the 'welfare state'. Prior to the 1930s, egalitarians proposed a diverse range of policies that cut across this dichotomy. While some recommended state ownership of productive assets as the most direct route to equality, others favoured a decentralised, mutualist model of socialism. A third group of egalitarians advocated a mixture of policies, and for practical purposes so did many egalitarians who ultimately favoured socialism, since they saw various forms of state intervention in the economy as staging posts on the way to an eventual socialist settlement. Such policies included a generous welfare system;

strong trade unions; state-provided public services (especially high-quality secondary education free at the point of use); progressive taxation of income and wealth; the diffusion of private property; and indeed some public ownership.

During the 1930s, a pessimistic analysis of the extent to which a capitalist economy could cope with economic redistribution gained ground, and, in particular, an explicitly Marxist model of egalitarian strategy found a receptive audience on the British Left. This had two components: first, the claim that capitalist productive efficiency inevitably required extreme class inequality. Capitalist economies, it was argued, could not function effectively without very large material incentives and the savings of the rich. Second, this Marxist analysis also stressed that capitalists possessed too much economic and hence political power to acquiesce voluntarily in a gradual programme of economic redistribution. Rapid and, if necessary, violent expropriation was the only way to secure an egalitarian society. This second point was never taken all that seriously by the majority of the British Left. Democratic procedures and the protection of a standard set of civil and political liberties were usually taken to be non-negotiable components of a just society. The gradual, democratic route to equality remained the Left's default position. However, the relationship between efficiency and economic inequality posed more difficult questions. The flourishing of Keynesian theory in the 1930s persuaded some egalitarians that in fact substantial redistribution need not have a negative impact on the overall efficiency of an economy based on private property and the market. However, this issue remained a palpable source of ideological tension throughout Labour's period in government during the 1940s, as the wartime vogue for economic planning popularised the anti-market route to equality. It was only during the revisionist period that an egalitarian critique of public ownership and economic planning was fully elaborated. From the late 1940s onwards, revisionists claimed that, given the split between ownership and control at the heart of capitalist enterprises, a far more plausible egalitarian strategy was for the state to pursue collective ownership of capital by purchasing shares in private enterprises, and to equalise the ownership of private property. Importantly, the introduction of a non-selective education system was also accorded a greater role in egalitarian strategy after the War, as a means of advancing both equal opportunity and equality of status.

At the end of the period covered by this book, James Meade set out four analytically distinct egalitarian strategies: a trade union state that relied on a strong labour movement to equalise wages and conditions; a welfare state that employed high direct taxes on incomes to fund generous social benefits; a property-owning democracy that distributed private property equally between every member of the community; and socialism, understood as state ownership of productive assets.[5] Meade thought that the first two strategies would be ineffective if pursued on their own: collective bargaining would eventually become inflationary and the high rates of income tax required to fund social benefits would at some point impede economic efficiency. Moreover, both the welfare state and strong collective bargaining would leave untouched grave inequality in the ownership of property. Meade therefore recommended a hybrid egalitarian strategy as the way forward:

he wanted to deepen the great social achievements of the welfare state and trade union movement by combining measures designed to equalise private property holdings with an increase in the amount of property under social ownership.[6] As Meade recognised, although it is helpful for analytical purposes to distinguish between these different models of egalitarian strategy, the use of such ideal types should not be taken to indicate that the Left has to make a definitive political choice between distinct egalitarian policy regimes. In any actually existing democratic polity, egalitarians will pursue a variety of egalitarian strategies, varying the emphasis between them according to contingent political circumstances. Although this point was not always clearly apparent to the egalitarians discussed in this book, we should not underestimate the complexity of their thinking about egalitarian strategy. Characterisations of earlier egalitarians as straightforward exponents of a 'socialist' or a 'welfare state' solution to the problem of inequality neglect the diversity of the policy tools that they saw as relevant to the pursuit of an egalitarian society.

Overall, it is salutary to recall that the egalitarianism of the British Left was not intended as an exercise in pure idealism. It was aimed at rectifying the demonstrable social injustices of the British class system, and philosophical arguments were therefore ultimately constrained by considerations of political strategy. The usually emollient Hobhouse, driven to something like passion by his debate with Shaw in the pages of the *Nation*, gave a glimpse of this political analysis:

> It is no wonder that 'society' takes kindly to Mr Shaw's revolutionary ideas. 'Society' is safe as long as socialism is in Mr Shaw's hands. Nor is there a more convenient armour against a serious assault than a plausible formula which no one intends to apply to things, which has, in fact, no point of contact with things, but serves simply to discredit anyone who makes a serious attempt to deal with things by attacking existing inequality at the point where it is, in fact, most vulnerable.[7]

The phantom danger of a Shaw-style 'plausible formula which no one intends to apply to things' remains a major objection offered against egalitarianism. However, it should be clear from the preceding pages that such allegations do an injustice to the complex ideas about equality developed, defended and applied by the British Left in the first six decades of the twentieth century.

What's Left?

The end of the period covered by this book, the early 1960s, can usefully be taken as a natural break in the history of the British Left's egalitarianism. In 1964, the Labour Party returned to office, and from that date the social democratic Left increasingly found itself on the back foot. The Labour governments of 1964–70 and 1974–79 introduced significant political initiatives designed to advance an egalitarian agenda, but the work of these governments was ultimately constrained by the formidable political and economic crises that engulfed them. At the same time, and partly as a result of the perceived failures of the Labour governments of the 1960s and 70s, classical social democratic ideology also entered a period of profound crisis, as it was outflanked to the left by a resurgent neo-Marxism and to the right by the arrival of neo-liberalism. Significantly, of course, the emergence of second-wave feminism and movements for racial equality in this period placed other forms of injustice on the Left's political agenda, and issued important correctives to the focus on class-based inequality that had dominated the politics of the Left earlier in the twentieth century. These movements posed searching questions about the nature of the classless community envisaged by traditional socialist ideology, and the extent to which the social experiences of the white working-class male had set the agenda of progressive political thought. Nonetheless, the promotion of greater material equality was still seen as an important criterion of the success or otherwise of Labour in office, and exhaustive empirical research continued to document grave social and economic inequalities.[8]

However, the years after 1979 saw a succession of dramatic setbacks for economic egalitarianism. At an ideological level, the basic assumptions of the Left's egalitarian philosophy were challenged by the New Right's revitalisation of libertarian and desert-based principles of justice, and by Hayek's powerful attempt to reject the entire concept of 'social justice'. Influenced by this thinking, the advocates of Thatcherism proclaimed the reduction of material inequality and relative poverty to be damaging and irrelevant political goals.[9] This ideological commitment was amply borne out in practice by the conduct of the Thatcher government in office. The ferocity of this New Right critique, and its undeniable political success, prompted both progressive political theorists and politicians to reconsider the desirability and feasibility of the Left's characteristic principles of social justice. While the political theorists largely rejected the philosophical ambitions of the Right's legitimation of economic inequality,[10] a new generation of revisionist politicians became increasingly doubtful about the political feasibility of ambitious egalitarian objectives and even rather uncertain about the desirability of egalitarian ideals in the first place. Partly these uncertainties were no doubt the response of the rational office-seeking politician to exceptionally difficult political constraints. For much of the period covered by this book, the Left had assumed that the disadvantaged, the working class, formed a majority of the British population. In contrast, after the social changes of the 1980s, it could plausibly be argued that the social character of Britain was significantly less propitious for egalitarian electoral appeals. But while this quasi-sociological observation was clearly important for the construction of a viable left of centre political strategy, these latter-day revisionists at times seemed to confuse this strategic dilemma with philosophical worries about their foundational value commitments, and indeed they appeared to underestimate the ideological victory for the Right signalled by the anti-egalitarian shift in their thinking. After all, poverty and inequality did not disappear after 1979. Indeed, both increased dramatically.[11]

Seen in this light, my historical analysis carries with it an important political implication. After the political traumas of the 1980s, self-flagellation was for a time the defining characteristic of the British Left's perception of its past. In particular, politicians, historians and social scientists all identified significant shortcomings in the political identity of the Labour Party. Labour has been seen as embedded in a defensive and unimaginative working-class identity; as too close to the trade unions; as insufficiently open to the insights of progressive liberalism; as excessively and incoherently socialist in its economic doctrines; and as congenitally incapable of attracting a broad base of electoral support.[12] In contrast to this rather grim characterisation, this book has added another, less gloomy dimension to our understanding of the traditions and culture of the British Left: an ideological commitment to the ideal of equality. But equality is not one more piece of anachronistic historical baggage to be cast over the side in the pursuit of power; on the contrary, it is the very basis of progressive politics. As Gaitskell noted, if Labour 'were ever to abandon [equality], then I think there would be very little left to distinguish us from the Tories'.[13] In spite of all its ambiguities and difficulties, the tradition of thinking about equality that I have discussed in this book remains the most important we have for understanding what it means to be on the Left in British politics. For if the Left does not strive to narrow economic and social inequality, and to tackle the multiple injustices of a class-riven society, then in what sense does it remain 'the Left'?

Notes

1 Tawney, *Equality*, 150.
2 'Self-ownership, history and socialism: an interview with G. A. Cohen', *Imprints*, 1 (1996), 8.
3 M. Walzer, *Spheres of Justice* (Oxford, 1983), xi–xvi, 3–30, 118–19, 176–7; Wolff, 'Fairness, respect and the egalitarian ethos'; E. Anderson, 'What is the point of equality?', *Ethics*, 109 (1999), 287–337; Miller, *Principles*, 239–44; S. Scheffler, 'What is egalitarianism?', *Philosophy and Public Affairs*, 31 (2003), 5–39.
4 For a balanced overview of the relevant issues, see Plant and Vincent, *Philosophy*, 180–3.
5 This paragraph draws on Jackson, 'Revisionism reconsidered', 438–40.
6 Meade, *Efficiency*, 36–68.
7 Hobhouse, 'Letters to the editor: equality of income', *Nation*, 7.6.1913, 384.
8 E.g. landmark studies such as A. B. Atkinson, *Poverty in Britain and the Reform of Social Security* (Cambridge, 1969); P. Townsend, *Poverty in the United Kingdom* (Harmondsworth, 1979). See also the Fabian Society's assessments of Labour's record in government on equality: Townsend and Bosanquet, *Labour and Inequality*; and N. Bosanquet and P. Townsend (eds), *Labour and Equality* (London, 1980). For an account of Labour's egalitarianism in the 1960s and 70s, see Ellison, *Egalitarian Thought*, 135–200. The history of Labour's egalitarian fiscal policy in this period is recounted in Whiting, *Labour Party*, 173–258, 328–38; Daunton, *Just Taxes*, 290–301.
9 E.g. F. A. Hayek, *The Constitution of Liberty* (London, 1960); Nozick, *Anarchy*; K. Joseph and J. Sumption, *Equality* (London, 1979).
10 E.g. R. Plant, 'Socialism, markets and end states', in J. Le Grand and S. Estrin (eds), *Market Socialism* (Oxford, 1989), 50–77; Plant, 'Social democracy', 176–94; A. Sen, *Inequality Re-examined* (Cambridge, MA, 1992); Cohen, *Self-ownership*; R. Dworkin, *Sovereign Virtue: The Theory and Practice of Equality* (Cambridge, MA, 2000).

11 For critical scrutiny of these ideological developments, see B. Barry, *Why Social Justice Matters* (Cambridge, 2005); Jackson and Segal, 'Why inequality matters'.
12 One important statement of these arguments is David Marquand's justly celebrated *The Progressive Dilemma* (London, second edition, 1999). For a judicious assessment of the self-hating labourism characteristic of the genre, see J. Cronin, *New Labour's Pasts* (London, 2004).
13 *Diary of Hugh Gaitskell*, 542, dictated 14.7.1956.

Select bibliography

Note: The place of publication is London unless otherwise stated.

1 Primary sources

a Manuscripts and personal papers

At the Bodleian Library, Oxford
Labour Party Research Department Archive (microfiche)

At the British Library of Political and Economic Science, London
Brian Abel-Smith Papers
C. A. R. Crosland Papers
Evan Durbin Papers
Fabian Society Papers
Graham Wallas Papers
James Meade Papers
Passfield Papers
R. H. Tawney Papers
Richard Titmuss Papers

At the Modern Records Centre, Warwick University
Victor Gollancz Papers
Socialist Union Papers

At Nuffield College Library, Oxford
G. D. H. Cole Papers

At the Seeley G. Mudd Manuscript Library, Princeton University
W. Arthur Lewis Papers

At University College, London
Hugh Gaitskell Papers

b Official records
House of Commons Debates, Fourth Series (until end of 1908) and Fifth Series
Labour Party Annual Conference Reports

c Newspapers and periodicals
British Journal of Sociology
Daily Herald
Economic Journal
Economica
Encounter
Fabian Journal
Fabian News
Fabian Quarterly
Forward
International Journal of Ethics
Labour Leader
Labour Monthly
Left News
Manchester Guardian
Modern Quarterly
Nation
Nation (New York)
New Leader
New Left Review
New Reasoner
New Statesman
NFRB Quarterly
Observer
Political Quarterly
Socialist Commentary
Socialist Review (volume numbers dropped from August 1922)
The Times
Tribune
Universities and Left Review

d Books, pamphlets, reports and speeches
Abel-Smith, B. and P. Townsend 'New pensions for old', *Fabian Research Series No. 171* (1955).
Abel-Smith, B. and P. Townsend *The Poor and the Poorest* (1965).
Acland, R. *The Forward March* (1941).
Atkinson, A. B. *Poverty in Britain and the Reform of Social Security* (Cambridge, 1969).
Attlee, C. R. *The Labour Party in Perspective* (1937).
Attlee, C. R. *Purpose and Policy: Selected Speeches* (1947).
Barker, E. *Political Thought in England, 1848 to 1914* (second edition, 1928 [1915]).
Bassett, R. *Essentials of Parliamentary Democracy* (1935).
Bendix, R. and S. M. Lipset (eds) *Class, Status and Power: Social Stratification in Comparative Perspective* (1967).
Berle, A. and G. Means *The Modern Corporation and Private Property* (New York, 1932).
Bevan, A. *In Place of Fear* (1952).
Bevin, E. *The Job to be Done* (1942).
Beveridge, W. *Planning Under Socialism and Other Addresses* (1936).
Beveridge, W. *Social Insurance and Allied Services* (1942).
Beveridge, W. *The Pillars of Security* (1943).
Beveridge, W. *Full Employment in a Free Society* (1944).
Booth, C. *Life and Labour of the People in London* (1891–1903).
Bosanquet, N. and P. Townsend (eds) *Labour and Equality* (1980).
Bowley, A. L. and A. R. Burnett-Hurst *Livelihood and Poverty* (1915).
Brailsford, H. N. *Socialism for To-day* (1925).
Brailsford, H. N. *Families and Incomes: The Case for Children's Allowances* (n.d. [1926]).
Brailsford, H. N. *The Levellers and the English Revolution* (1961).
Brailsford, H. N., J. A. Hobson, A. C. Jones and E. F. Wise *The Living Wage* (1926).
Burnham, J. *The Managerial Revolution* (1942).
Burns, C. D. *Government and Industry* (1921).
Burns, C. D. *Industry and Civilisation* (1925).
Burns, C. D. *The Philosophy of Labour* (1925).
Burns, E. *The Only Way Out* (1932).
Burns, E. *Capitalism, Communism and the Transition* (1933).
Burns, E. *Introduction to Marxism* (1952 [1939]).
Burns, R. *Poetical Works of Robert Burns*, ed. W. Wallace (Edinburgh, 1990).
Cecil, H. *Conservatism* (1912).
Central Advisory Council for Education *Early Leaving* (1954).
Chiozza Money, L. *Riches and Poverty* (1905).
Churchill, W. S. *Liberalism and the Social Problem* (1909).
Clark, C. *National Income and Outlay* (1937).
Cole, G. D. H. *The World of Labour* (1913).
Cole, G. D. H. *Self-Government in Industry* (1917).
Cole, G. D. H. *Chaos and Order in Industry* (1920).
Cole, G. D. H. 'Guild socialism', *FT No. 192* (1920).
Cole, G. D. H. *Guild Socialism Restated* (1920).
Cole, G. D. H. *Social Theory* (1920).
Cole, G. D. H. *The Payment of Wages* (second edition, 1928 [1918]).
Cole, G. D. H. *The Next Ten Years in British Social and Economic Policy* (1929).
Cole, G. D. H. *Incentives Under Socialism* (Girard, 1931).
Cole, G. D. H. *A Guide Through World Chaos* (New York, 1934 [1932]).

Cole, G. D. H. *Principles of Economic Planning* (1935).

Cole, G. D. H. *The Simple Case for Socialism* (1935).

Cole, G. D. H. *Money: Its Present and Future* (third edition, 1947 [1936]).

Cole, G. D. H. *A Short History of the British Working Class Movement Volume 3* (1937).

Cole, G. D. H. *Beveridge Explained* (1942).

Cole, G. D. H. *The Means to Full Employment* (1943).

Cole, G. D. H. *Socialist Economics* (1950).

Cole, G. D. H. *The British Co-operative Movement in a Socialist Society* (1951).

Cole, G. D. H. *Is this Socialism?* (1954).

Cole, G. D. H. *A History of Socialist Thought Volume 1: The Forerunners* (1959).

Cole, G. D. H. and W. Mellor *The Meaning of Industrial Freedom* (1918).

Council for the Victory of Socialism *Equality in Education: A Policy for Labour* (n.d. [1958]).

Cripps, S. *Why this Socialism?* (1934).

Crosland, C. A. R. *The Future of Socialism* (1956).

Crosland, C. A. R. *The Conservative Enemy* (1962).

Crosland, C. A. R. *Socialism Now and Other Essays* (1974).

Crossman, R. H. S. 'Socialism and the new despotism', *FT No. 298* (1956).

Crossman, R. H. S. 'Labour in the affluent society', *FT No. 325* (1960).

Crossman, R. H. S. *Planning for Freedom* (1965).

Crossman, R. H. S. (ed.) *New Fabian Essays* (1952).

Dalton, H. *Some Aspects of the Inequality of Incomes in Modern Communities* (1920).

Dalton, H. *Principles of Public Finance* (1929 [1922]).

Dalton, H. *The Capital Levy Explained* (1923).

Dalton, H. *Practical Socialism for Britain* (1935).

Dalton, H. *Call Back Yesterday: Memoirs 1887–1931* (1953).

Dickinson, H. D. *The Economics of Socialism* (1939).

Durbin, E. 'Socialist credit policy', *New Fabian Research Series No. 15* (1934).

Durbin, E. *The Politics of Democratic Socialism: An Essay on Social Policy* (1940).

Durbin, E. *What Have We to Defend? A Brief Critical Examination of the British Social Tradition* (1942).

Durbin, E. *Problems of Economic Planning* (1949).

Engels, F. *Anti-Dühring* [1894], in *The Collected Works of Karl Marx and Frederick Engels Volume 25* (1987).

Fabian Society *Social Security: Evidence Submitted to the Interdepartmental Committee on Social Insurance and Allied Services* (1942).

Floud, J. E., A. H. Halsey and F. M. Martin *Social Class and Educational Opportunity* (1956).

Fox, R. *Communism and a Changing Civilisation* (1935).

Gaitskell, H. *Money and Everyday Life* (1939).

Gaitskell, H. *Recent Developments in British Socialist Thinking* (n.d. [c.1956]).

Gaitskell, H. 'Socialism and nationalisation', *FT No. 300* (1956).

The Diary of Hugh Gaitskell 1945–56, ed. P. Williams (1983).

Glasier, B. *The Meaning of Socialism* (Manchester, 1919).

Glasier, B. *William Morris and the Early Days of the Socialist Movement* (1921).

Glass, D. V. (ed.) *Social Mobility in Britain* (1954).

Gollancz, V. *More For Timothy* (1953).

Gollancz, V. (ed.) *The Betrayal of the Left* (1941).

Gore, C. (ed.) *Property: Its Rights and Duties* (1913).

Green, T. H. *Lectures on the Principles of Political Obligation*, ed. P. Harris and J. Morrow (Cambridge, 1986 [1890]).

Haldane, J. B. S. *The Inequality of Man and Other Essays* (Harmondsworth, 1937 [1932]).

Hardie, J. K. *From Serfdom to Socialism* (1907).

Hayek, F. A. *The Road to Serfdom* (1944).

Hayek, F. A. *The Constitution of Liberty* (1960).

Henderson, H. D. 'Inheritance and inequality: a practical proposal', *'The New Way' Series* XV (1926).

Hobhouse, L. T. *Morals in Evolution* (1956 [1906]).

Hobhouse, L. T. *Liberalism* (Cambridge, 1994 [1911]).

Hobhouse, L. T. *Social Evolution and Political Theory* (New York, 1913 [1911]).

Hobhouse, L. T. *The Labour Movement* (third edition, 1912).

Hobhouse, L. T. *The Metaphysical Theory of the State* (1918).

Hobhouse, L. T. *Elements of Social Justice* (1922).

Hobhouse, L. T. *Social Development* (1924).

Hobson, J. A. *John Ruskin* (1898).

Hobson, J. A. *The Crisis of Liberalism* (Brighton, 1974 [1909]).

Hobson, J. A. *Work and Wealth* (1914).

Hobson, J. A. *Democracy After the War* (1918).

Hobson, J. A. *Taxation in the New State* (1919).

Hobson, J. A. *Problems of a New World* (1921).

Hobson, J. A. *Incentives in the New Industrial Order* (1922).

Hobson, J. A. *The Economics of Unemployment* (1922).

Hobson, J. A. *Wealth and Life* (1929).

Hobson, J. A. *Poverty in Plenty: The Ethics of Income* (1931).

Hobson, J. A. *Confessions of an Economic Heretic* (1938).

Hoggart, R. *The Uses of Literacy* (1957).

Hyndman, H. M. *The Economics of Socialism* (1896).

Hyndman, H. M. *Social Democracy: The Basis of its Principles and the Cause of its Success* (1904).

Jackson, B. and D. Marsden *Education and the Working Class* (1962).

Jackson, T. A. *Dialectics: The Logic of Marxism and its Critics* (1936).

Jay, D. *The Nation's Wealth at the Nation's Service* (1938).

Jay, D. *The Socialist Case* (1938).

Jay, D. *Socialism in the New Society* (1962).

Jenkins, R. *Fair Shares for the Rich* (1951).

Jenkins, R. *Pursuit of Progress* (1953).

Jenkins, R. *The Labour Case* (Harmondsworth, 1959).

Joseph, K. and J. Sumption *Equality* (1979).

Jouvenal, B. de *The Ethics of Redistribution* (Cambridge, 1951).

Keynes, J. M. *The Collected Writings of John Maynard Keynes, Volumes 1–30*, ed. D. E. Moggridge and E. S. Johnson (1971–89).

Labour Party *Labour and the New Social Order* (1918).

Labour Party *Homes of the Future* (1956).

Labour Party *Personal Freedom: Labour's Policy for the Individual and Society* (1956).

Labour Party *Towards Equality: Labour's Policy for Social Justice* (1956).

Labour Party *National Superannuation* (1957).

Labour Party *Industry and Society* (1958).

Labour Party *Learning to Live* (1958).

Labour Party General Election Manifestos, 1900–97, ed. I. Dale (2000).

Lansbury, G. *Your Part in Poverty* (1917).

Laski, H. 'The state in the new social order', *FT No. 200* (1922).

Laski, H. *A Grammar of Politics* (1970 [1925]).

Laski, H. 'Socialism and freedom', *FT No. 216* (1925).

Laski, H. *Communism* (1927).

Laski, H. *The Recovery of Citizenship* (1928).

Laski, H. *Liberty in the Modern State* (1930).

Laski, H. *Democracy in Crisis* (1933).

Laski, H. *The State in Theory and Practice* (1935).

Laski, H. *Parliamentary Government in England* (1950 [1938]).

Laski, H. *Reflections on the Revolution of Our Time* (1943).

Laski, H. *Faith, Reason and Civilisation* (1944).

Laski, H. *Will Planning Restrict Our Freedom?* (Cheam, 1945).

Lerner, A. *The Economics of Control: Principles of Welfare Economics* (New York, 1946 [1944]).

Lewis, W. A. *Principles of Economic Planning* (1969 [1949]).

Lindsay, A. D. *Karl Marx's Capital: An Introductory Essay* (1925).

Lipset, S. M. and R. Bendix *Social Mobility in Industrial Society* (Berkeley, CA and Los Angeles, 1959).

Little, I. *A Critique of Welfare Economics* (Oxford, second edition, 1960 [1957]).

Lloyd George, D. *Better Times: Speeches* (1910).

Lyons, E. *Assignment in Utopia* (1938).

MacDonald, J. R. *Socialism and Society* (1905).

MacDonald, J. R. *Socialism and Government* (1910).

MacDonald, J. R. *The Socialist Movement* (1911).

MacDonald, J. R. *Socialism: Critical and Constructive* (1921).

MacKenzie, J. S. *A Manual of Ethics* (third edition, 1897).

MacKenzie, N. (ed.) *Conviction* (1958).

Magee, B. *The New Radicalism* (1962).

Mallock, W. H. *A Critical Examination of Socialism* (1908).

Mallock, W. H. *The Limits of Pure Democracy* (1918).

Marshall, A. *Principles of Economics* (eighth edition, 1920 [1890]).

Marshall, T. H. *Citizenship and Social Class* (Cambridge, 1950).

Marx, K. *Critique of the Gotha Programme* [1875], in D. McLellan (ed.), *Karl Marx: Selected Writings* (Oxford, 2000).

Masterman, C. F. G. *The New Liberalism* (1920).

Meade, J. *An Introduction to Economic Analysis and Policy* (Oxford, 1936).

Meade, J. *Planning and the Price Mechanism: The Liberal Socialist Solution* (1948).

Meade, J. *Efficiency, Equality and the Ownership of Property* [1964], in J. Meade, *Liberty, Equality and Efficiency* (Basingstoke, 1993).

Mill, J. S. *Principles of Political Economy* [1848], in *The Collected Works of J. S. Mill, Volume 2*, ed. J. M. Robson (Toronto, 1965).

Mill, J. S. *Utilitarianism* [1863], in J. Bentham and J. S. Mill, *Utilitarianism and Other Essays*, ed. A. Ryan (1987).

Mill, J. S. *Autobiography* (1989 [1873]).

Mill, J. S. *Chapters on Socialism* [1879], in J. S. Mill, *On Liberty and Other Writings*, ed. S. Collini (Cambridge, 1989).

Miller, W. *How the Russians Live* (1942).

Milner, E. and D. Milner *Scheme for a State Bonus: A Rational Method of Solving the Social Problem* (Darlington, 1918).

Morris, W. *News From Nowhere* (Cambridge, 1995 [1891]).

Morrison, H. *Looking Ahead: Wartime Speeches* (1943).

Muir, R. *The New Liberalism* (n.d. [1923]).

National Committee for the Prevention of Destitution *The Case for the National Minimum* (1913).

Orwell, G. *The Complete Works of George Orwell, Volumes 1–20*, ed. P. Davison (1998).

Owen, R. *An Address to the Inhabitants of New Lanark* [1816], in *Selected Works of Robert Owen Volume 1: Early Writings*, ed. G. Claeys (1993).

Paine, T. *Agrarian Justice* [1796], in T. Paine, *Rights of Man, Common Sense and Other Political Writings*, ed. M. Philp (Oxford, 1995).

Palme Dutt, R. *Socialism and the Living Wage* (1927).

Pedley, R. *The Comprehensive School* (1964).

Pethick-Lawrence, F. W. 'National finance', *FT No. 229* (1929).

Pickard, B. *A Reasonable Revolution* (1919).

Pigou, A. C. *Wealth and Welfare* (1912).

Pigou, A. C. *The Economics of Welfare* (second edition, 1924 [1920]).

Pigou, A. C. *Socialism Versus Capitalism* (1937).

Pipkin, C. *The Idea of Social Justice* (New York, 1927).

Pollitt, H. *Selected Articles and Speeches Volume 2: 1936–9* (1954).

Priestley, J. B. *Postscripts* (1940).

Rathbone, E. *The Disinherited Family: A Plea for the Endowment of the Family* (1924).

Rathbone, E. *The Ethics and Economics of Family Endowment* (1927).

Rhys Williams, J. *Something to Look Forward to: A Suggestion for a New Social Contract* (1943).

Ritchie, D. G. *Natural Rights* (1894).

Robinson, J. *Introduction to the Theory of Employment* (1937).

Robinson, J. *An Essay on Marxist Economics* (1942).

Robinson, J. *Essays in the Theory of Employment* (Oxford, 1947).

Robinson, J. *Collected Economic Papers Volume 1* (Oxford, 1951).

Robson, W. 'Socialism and the standardised life', *FT No. 219* (1926).

Rowntree, B. S. *Poverty: A Study of Town Life* (1901).

Rowntree, B. S. *The Human Needs of Labour* (1918).

Rowntree, B. S. and G. R. Lavers *Poverty and the Welfare State* (1951).

Rowse, A. L. *Mr Keynes and the Labour Movement* (1936).

Ruskin, J. *Unto this Last* (1862).

Russell, B. *Roads to Freedom: Socialism, Anarchism and Syndicalism* (1918).

'Seven Members of the Labour Party' *The Labour Party's Aim* (1923).

Sharp, A. (ed.) *The English Levellers* (Cambridge, 1998).

Shaw, G. B. 'Socialism and superior brains: a reply to Mr Mallock', *FT No. 146* (1909).

Shaw, G. B. *The Case for Equality* (1913).

Shaw, G. B. *The Intelligent Woman's Guide to Socialism and Capitalism* (New York, 1928).

Shaw, G. B. 'Socialism: principles and outlook', *FT No. 233* (1930).

Shaw, G. B. *Everybody's Political What's What* (1944).

Shaw, G. B. (ed.) *Fabian Essays in Socialism* (1889).

Sidgwick, H. *Principles of Political Economy* (third edition, 1901 [1883]).

Simon, B. *Intelligence Testing and the Comprehensive School* (1953).

Simon, B. *The Common Secondary School* (1955).

Simon, E. D. *The Inheritance of Riches* (1925).

Simon, E. D. *How to Abolish the Slums* (1929).

Sloan, P. *Soviet Democracy* (1937).

Snowden, P. *The Individual Under Socialism* (n.d. [1910]).

Snowden, P. *The Living Wage* (1912).

Snowden, P. *Labour and National Finance* (1920).

Snowden, P. *Socialism Made Plain* (1920).

Snowden, P. *Twenty Objections to Socialism* (1920).

Snowden, P. *Labour and the New World* (1921).

Snowden, P. *The Rich Man's Budget: Mr Churchill's Proposals Exposed* (1925).

Socialist Union *Socialism: A New Statement of Principles* (1952).

Socialist Union *Twentieth Century Socialism* (Harmondsworth, 1956).

Socialist Union *Education and Socialism* (1958).

Socialist Union *Reflections on the Social Services* (1958).

Spencer, H. *The Man Versus The State* (Harmondsworth, 1969 [1884]).

Spender, S. *Forward from Liberalism* (1937).

Strachey, J. *The Coming Struggle for Power* (1932).

Strachey, J. *The Nature of Capitalist Crisis* (1935).

Strachey, J. *The Theory and Practice of Socialism* (1936).

Strachey, J. *What Are We to Do?* (1938).

Strachey, J. *Why You Should Be a Socialist* (1938).

Strachey, J. *A Programme for Progress* (1940).

Strachey, J. *A Faith to Fight for* (1941).

Strachey, J. 'Labour's task', *FT No. 290* (1951).

Strachey, J. *The Just Society: A Reaffirmation of Faith in Socialism* (1951).

Strachey, J. *Contemporary Capitalism* (1956).

Strachey, J. *The Strangled Cry and Other Unparliamentary Papers* (1962).

Tawney, R. H. *The Acquisitive Society* (1937 [1921]).

Tawney, R. H. *Equality* (1931).

Tawney, R. H. *The Radical Tradition* (1966 [1964]).

Tawney, R. H. (ed.) *Secondary Education for All: A Policy for Labour* (n.d. [1922]).

R. H. Tawney's Commonplace Book, ed. J. M. Winter and D. M. Joslin (Cambridge, 1972).

Temple, W. *Christianity and Social Order* (1976 [1942]).

Thompson, E. P. *William Morris: Romantic to Revolutionary* (1955).

Thompson, E. P. (ed.) *Out of Apathy* (1960).

Titmuss, R. M. *Problems of Social Policy* (1950).

Titmuss, R. M. *Essays on the 'Welfare State'* (1963 [1958]).

Titmuss, R. M. *Income Distribution and Social Change: A Study in Criticism* (1962).

Titmuss, R. M. *The Gift Relationship: From Human Blood to Social Policy* (New York, 1997 [1970]).

Townsend, P. *The Family Life of Old People: An Inquiry in East London* (1957).

Townsend, P. *Poverty in the United Kingdom* (Harmondsworth, 1979).

Townsend, P. and N. Bosanquet (eds) *Labour and Inequality* (1972).

Tressell, R. *The Ragged Trousered Philanthropists* (2004 [1914]).

Wallas, G. *Our Social Heritage* (1921).

Webb, B. *The Wages of Men and Women: Should They Be Equal?* (1919).

Webb, B. *My Apprenticeship* (1926).

The Diary of Beatrice Webb Volume 4, 1924–43: 'The Wheel of Life', ed. N. MacKenzie and J. MacKenzie (1985).

Webb, S. 'National finance and a levy on capital: what Labour intends', *FT No. 188* (1919).

Webb, S. 'The roots of labour unrest: an address to employers and managers', *FT No. 196* (1920).

Webb, S. and B. Webb *Industrial Democracy* (second edition, 1902).
Webb, S. and B. Webb *English Poor Law Policy* (1910).
Webb, S. and B. Webb *The Prevention of Destitution* (1911).
Webb, S. and B. Webb *A Constitution for the Socialist Commonwealth of Great Britain* (1920).
Webb, S. and B. Webb *The Consumers' Co-operative Movement* (1921).
Webb, S. and B. Webb *The Decay of Capitalist Civilisation* (1923).
Webb, S. and B. Webb *Soviet Communism: A New Civilisation* (second edition, 1941 [1935]).
Wells, H. G. *This Misery of Boots* (1907).
Williams, R. *Culture and Society, 1780–1950* (1958).
Williams, R. *The Long Revolution* (1961).
Wolfe Howe, M. de (ed.) *The Holmes-Laski Letters: The Correspondence of Mr Justice Holmes and Harold Laski, 1916–35* (1953).
Wollheim, R. 'Socialism and culture', *FT No. 331* (1961).
Wootton, B. *Plan or No Plan* (1934).
Wootton, B. *End Social Inequality: A Programme for Ordinary People* (1941).
Wootton, B. *Freedom Under Planning* (1945).
Young, M. *Big Man, Small World: A Discussion of Socialist Democracy* (1948).
Young, M. *The Rise of the Meritocracy: An Essay on Education and Equality* (1961 [1958]).
Young, M. 'Is Equality a Dream?', First Rita Hinden Memorial Lecture, supplement to SC, January 1973.
Young, M. and P. Willmott *Family and Kinship in East London* (revised edition, 1962 [1957]).

e Articles and chapters

Abel-Smith, B. 'Whose welfare state?', in MacKenzie (ed.), *Conviction*, 55–73.
Attlee, C. R. 'Guild socialism v. municipal socialism: a reply', *SR*, 116 (1923), 213–18.
Ayer, A. J. 'Forward from the welfare state', *Encounter*, December 1956, 75–8.
Beer, S. H. *et al.* 'Fabianism revisited', *Review of Economics and Statistics*, 35 (1953), 199–210.
Bevan, A. 'The fatuity of coalition', *Tribune*, 13.6.1952, 1–2.
Beveridge, W. 'Freedom from idleness', in G. D. H. Cole *et al.*, *Plan for Britain* (1943), 83–100.
Birnbaum, N. 'Politics and "abundance"', *Dissent*, Summer 1958, 238–43.
Birnbaum, N. 'Ideals or reality?', *SC*, September 1959, 5–7.
Blumler, J. 'A look at the Left', *SC*, February 1960, 4–7.
Booker, H. S. 'Lady Rhys Williams' proposals for the amalgamation of direct taxation with social insurance', *EJ*, 56 (1946), 230–43.
Burns, C. D. 'Productivity and reconstruction', *IJE*, 28 (1917–18), 393–401.
Clarke, J. S. 'Social insecurity', *PQ*, 16 (1945), 30–9.
Clarke, R. W. B. 'The Beveridge Report and after', in W. Robson (ed.), *Social Security* (1943), 272–327.
Cole, G. D. H. 'The basis of wages', *NS*, 17.4.1920, 34–5.
Cole, G. D. H. 'The minimum wage', *SR*, 23 (1924), 58–63.
Cole, G. D. H. 'The diffusion of ownership', *NS*, 24.3.1928, 753–4.
Cole, G. D. H. 'Why I am a socialist', in G. D. H. Cole, *Economic Tracts for the Times* (1932), 321–7.
Cole, G. D. H. 'Socialism for radicals', *NS*, 20.11.1937, 846.
Cole, G. D. H. 'Socialism and the welfare state', *NS*, 23.7.1955, 88–9.
Cole, G. D. H. 'Twentieth-century socialism?', *NS*, 7.7.1956, 8–9.

Cole, M. 'Education and social democracy', in Crossman (ed.), *New Fabian Essays*, 91–120.

Crick, B. 'Socialist literature in the 1950s', *PQ*, 31 (1960), 361–73.

Cripps, S. 'The future of the Labour Party', *NS*, 3.9.1932, 255–6.

Crosland, C. A. R. 'Review of *A Critique of Welfare Economics*', *Universities Quarterly*, 5 (1951), 180–3.

Crosland, C. A. R. 'The transition from capitalism', in Crossman (ed.), *New Fabian Essays*, 33–68.

Crosland, C. A. R. 'How find the savings?', *SC*, August 1953, 176.

Crosland, C. A. R. 'National superannuation', *SC*, May 1956, 18–19.

Crosland, C. A. R. 'Aims of social policy', *Fabian Journal*, No. 19, July 1956, 19–24.

Crosland, C. A. R. 'Conditions of welfare', *Encounter*, March 1958, 68–70.

Crosland, C. A. R. 'Leftover left to kill', *Spectator*, 24.10.1958, 555.

Crosland, C. A. R. 'A reply', *SC*, September 1959, 7–10.

Crosland, C. A. R. 'Inequalities of wealth', in Crosland, *The Conservative Enemy*, 28–40.

Crosland, C. A. R. 'The public schools and English education', in Crosland, *The Conservative Enemy*, 167–82.

Crosland, C. A. R. 'Radical reform and the Left', in Crosland, *The Conservative Enemy*, 127–42.

Crosland, C. A. R. 'Comprehensive education', in Crosland, *Socialism Now*, 193–210.

Dalton, H. 'Our financial plan', in H. Morrison *et al.*, *Forward From Victory! Labour's Plan* (1946), 38–51.

Dalton, H. 'Shaw as economist and politician', in C. M. Joad (ed.), *Shaw and Society* (1953), 250–62.

Davenport, N. 'Wider share ownership II', *Spectator*, 17.3.1961, 376–8.

Dickinson, H. D. 'The economic basis of socialism', *PQ*, 1 (1930), 561–72.

Durbin, E. 'The importance of planning', in G. Catlin (ed.), *New Trends in Socialism* (1935), 145–66.

Durbin, E. 'The response of the economists to the ethical ideal of equality', in T. H. Marshall *et al.*, *The Ethical Factor in Economic Thought* (1935), 13–25.

Durbin, E. 'Professor Durbin quarrels with Professor Keynes', *Labour*, April 1936, 188.

Durbin, E. 'The problems of the socialised sector', in Durbin, *Problems of Economic Planning*, 58–90.

Fox, A. 'Chances for children', *SC*, February 1957, 26.

Fox, A. 'Class and equality', *SC*, May 1956, 11–13.

Fox, A. 'Top people', *SC*, December 1958, 20–2.

Gaitskell, H. 'Economics', in N. Mitchison (ed.), *An Outline for Boys and Girls and Their Parents* (1932), 647–90.

Gaitskell, H. 'The economic aims of the Labour Party', *PQ*, 24 (1953), 5–18.

Gaitskell, H. 'Foreword', in E. Durbin, *Politics of Democratic Socialism* (1954 [1940]), 7–14.

Gaitskell, H. 'Public ownership and equality', *SC*, June 1955, 165–7.

Gaitskell, H. 'At Oxford in the twenties', in A. Briggs and J. Saville (eds), *Essays in Labour History* (1960), 6–19.

Glasier, B. 'Socialism and the theory of Marx', *LL*, 15.1.1909, 33.

Glasier, B. 'Final words on Marx', *LL*, 29.1.1909, 65.

Gollancz, V. 'Slow down', *LN*, January 1940, 1415–20.

Gollancz, V. 'Recapture the spirit of socialism', *LN*, June 1941, 1740–6.

Gore, C. 'The quality of justice', in R. Hogue (ed.), *British Labour Speaks* (New York, 1924), 131–51.

Hall, S. 'A sense of classlessness', *Universities and Left Review*, No. 5, Autumn 1958, 26–32.

Hall, S. 'Crosland territory', *NLR*, No. 2, 1960, 2–4.

Hall, S. 'The supply of demand', in Thompson (ed.), *Out of Apathy*, 56–97.

Halsey, A. H. 'Genetics, social structure and intelligence', *British Journal of Sociology*, 9 (1958), 15–28.

Halsey, A. H. 'Inequalities in education', *New Reasoner*, Spring 1958, 102–3.

Halsey, A. H. 'Intelligence and ideology', *NLR*, No. 11, 1961, 9–11.

Halsey, A. H. and L. Gardner 'Social mobility and achievement in four grammar schools', *British Journal of Sociology*, 4 (1953), 60–75.

Hampshire, S. 'A new philosophy of the just society', *New York Review of Books*, 24.2.1972, 34–9.

Henderson, A. 'The character and policy of the British Labour Party', *IJE*, 32 (1921–22), 119–23.

Hinden, R. 'The dying community', *SC*, March 1959, 10–12.

Hinden, R. 'The public ownership debate', *SC*, March 1960, 4–7.

Hinden, R. 'Socialism by half', *SC*, March 1962, 14–17.

Hobhouse, L. T. 'The ethical basis of collectivism', *IJE*, 8 (1898), 137–56.

Hobhouse, L. T. 'The historical evolution of property, in fact and in idea' [1913], in L. T. Hobhouse, *Liberalism and Other Writings* (Cambridge, 1994), 176–98

Hobhouse, L. T. 'The right to a living wage', in W. Temple (ed.), *The Industrial Unrest and the Living Wage* (1913), 63–75.

Hobhouse, L. T. 'The regulation of wages', in R. Cecil *et al.*, *Essays in Liberalism* (1922), 165–75.

Hobhouse, L. T. 'Aristocracy' [1930], in L. T. Hobhouse, *Sociology and Philosophy: A Centenary Collection of Essays and Articles* (1966), 189–206.

Hobhouse, L. T. 'The problem', in J. A. Hobson and M. Ginsberg (eds), *L. T. Hobhouse: His Life and Work* (1993 [1931]), 264–91.

Hobhouse, L. T. 'Liberal and humanist', in *C. P. Scott 1846–1932: The Making of the 'Manchester Guardian'* (1946), 84–90.

Hobson, J. A. 'The influence of Henry George in England', *Fortnightly Review*, 62 (1897), 835–44.

Hobson, J. A. 'Is socialism plunder?', *Nation*, 19.10.1907, 82–3.

Hobson, J. A. 'The new industrial revolution', *Contemporary Review*, 118 (1920), 638–45.

Hobson, J. A. 'Towards social equality', Hobhouse Memorial Lecture 1931, in *Hobhouse Memorial Lectures 1930–40* (1948), 3–34.

Hobson, J. A. 'The socialist case', *MG*, 15.10.1937, 6.

Hobson, J. A. and E. Durbin 'Under-consumption: an exposition and a reply', *Economica*, No. 42 (1933), 402–27.

Horrabin, J. F. 'The class struggle', in L. Anderson Fenn *et al.*, *Problems of Socialist Transition* (1934), 171–92.

Jay, D. 'The economic strength and weakness of Marxism', in G. Catlin (ed.), *New Trends in Socialism* (1935), 103–22.

Jay, D. 'Mr Keynes on money', *The Banker*, April 1936, 10–14.

Jay, D. 'Public capital and private enterprise', *Fabian Journal*, No. 28, July 1959, 9–14.

Jenkins, R. 'Equality', in Crossman (ed.), *New Fabian Essays*, 69–90.

Kalecki, M. 'Political aspects of full employment', *PQ*, 14 (1943), 326–31.

Lamartine Yates, P. 'The distribution of property', *SC*, January 1956, 20–1, 25.

Laski, H. 'The individual and the common good', *Nation*, 13.5.1922, 227–8.

Laski, H. 'The personnel of the English Cabinet, 1801–1924', *American Political Science Review*, 22 (1928), 12–31.

Laski, H. 'A plea for equality', in H. Laski, *The Dangers of Obedience and Other Essays* (London and New York, 1930), 207–37.

Laski, H. 'Some implications of the crisis', *PQ*, 2 (1931), 466–9.

Laski, H. 'Review of *Road to Wigan Pier*', *LN*, March 1937, 275–6.

Laski, H. 'Review of *The Acquisitive Society*', *LN*, September 1937, 514–15.

Lewis, W. A. 'A socialist economic policy', *SC*, June 1955, 171–4.

Lewis, W. A. 'The distribution of property', *SC*, December 1955, 365–7.

Lewis, W. A. 'Underdog-ism', *Observer*, 22.7.1956, 8.

MacKenzie, N. 'Poverty, security and socialism: some afterthoughts on the failure of Beveridge', *Fabian Journal*, No. 15, March 1955, 24–8.

MacRae, D. 'The ideological situation in the labour movement', *PQ*, 24 (1953), 78–89.

MacRae, D. 'Social stratification: a trend report', *Current Sociology*, 2 (1953–54), 7–31.

Marris, R. 'An economist's challenge', *Twentieth Century*, February 1955, 159–67.

Marris, R. 'How unfair are incomes?', *Twentieth Century*, May 1955, 405–15.

Marris, R. 'The redistribution of wealth', *SC*, April 1956, 12–15.

Martin, K. 'A social democrat', *NS*, 30.3.1940, 436.

Meade, J. 'The state and liberty', *Spectator*, 11.1.1935, 55.

Montagu, I. 'The USSR month by month: riches', *LN*, September 1936, 94–7.

Morrison, H. 'Social change – peaceful or violent?', *PQ*, 10 (1939), 4–9.

Oakeshott, M. 'Democratic socialism', *Cambridge Review*, 19.4.1940, 347–9.

Palme Dutt, R. 'Notes of the month: the ILP and revolution', *LM*, September 1932, 533–62.

Palme Dutt, R. 'Notes of the month: a landmark of the British labour movement', *LM*, January 1936, 3–26.

Pollitt, H. 'Mr Orwell will have to try again', *Daily Worker*, 17.3.1937, 7.

Rathbone, E. 'The remuneration of women's services', *EJ*, 27 (1917), 55–68.

Robbins, L. 'Notes on public finances', *Lloyds Bank Review*, 38, October 1955, 1–18.

Robson, W. A. 'The Beveridge Report: an evaluation', *PQ*, 14 (1943), 150–63.

Rothman, S. 'British Labor's "New Left"', *Political Science Quarterly*, 76 (1961), 393–401.

Rowntree, B. S. 'Labour unrest and the need for a national ideal', *Contemporary Review*, 116 (1919), 496–503.

Rowntree, B. S. 'Industrial unrest', in R. Hogue (ed.), *British Labour Speaks* (New York, 1924), 93–107.

Shaw, G. B. 'The simple truth about socialism' [1910], in G. B. Shaw, *The Road to Equality* (Boston, 1971), 155–94.

Shonfield, A. 'Labour and equality', *Listener*, 9.2.1956, 202–4.

Shore, P. 'In the room at the top', in MacKenzie (ed.), *Conviction*, 23–54.

Stapledon, O. 'Socialism and ethics (II)', *LN*, March 1941, 1661–5.

Strachey, J. 'We are all "reformists" now', *NFRB Quarterly*, Summer 1938, 14–19.

Strachey, J. 'The object of further socialisation', *PQ*, 24 (1953), 68–77.

Tawney, R. H. 'Poverty as an industrial problem' [1913], in J. Winter (ed.), *R. H. Tawney: The American Labour Movement and Other Essays* (Brighton, 1979), 111–28.

Tawney, R. H. 'The inequality of incomes', *Highway*, February 1921, 58–9.

Tawney, R. H. 'The minimum wage in Great Britain', *New Republic*, 28.6.1922, 125–7.

Tawney, R. H. 'British socialism today', *SC*, June 1952, 124–30.

Taylor, C. 'Alienation and community', *Universities and Left Review*, 5, Autumn 1958, 11–18.

Taylor, C. 'What's wrong with capitalism? 1', *NLR*, No. 2, 1960, 5–11.

Taylor, C. 'Changes of quality', *NLR*, No. 4, 1960, 3–5.

Thompson, E. P. 'Socialist humanism: an epistle to the Philistines', *New Reasoner*, Summer 1957, 105–43.

Thompson, E. P. 'Revolution again!', *NLR*, No. 6, 1960, 18–31.

Titmuss, R. M. 'The irresponsible society' [1959], in Titmuss, *Essays on 'the Welfare State'*, 215–43.

Titmuss, R. M. 'The limits of the welfare state', *NLR*, No. 27, 1964, 28–37.

Townsend, P. 'Measuring poverty', *British Journal of Sociology*, 5 (1954), 130–7.

Townsend, P. 'A society for people', in MacKenzie (ed.), *Conviction*, 93–120.

Townsend, P. 'The truce on inequality', *NS*, 26.9.1959, 381–2.

Townsend, P. 'The meaning of poverty', *British Journal of Sociology*, 18 (1962), 210–27.

Vaizey, J. 'We call it wallop', *SC*, March 1959, 15–17.

Webb, S. and B. Webb 'What is socialism? XII – the approach to equality', *NS*, 28.6.1913, 364–6.

Williams, R. 'Culture is ordinary', in MacKenzie (ed.), *Conviction*, 74–92.

Williams, R. 'An educated democracy', *SC*, October 1959, 8–10.

Willmott, P. 'Opportunities for all?', *SC*, April 1960, 31–2.

Willmott, P. 'The status seekers', *NLR*, No. 3, 1960, 70–1.

Wilson, T. 'Changing tendencies in socialist thought', *Lloyds Bank Review*, July 1956, 1–22.

Wollheim, R. 'The English dream', *Spectator*, 10.3.1961, 334–5.

Wootton, B. 'Shavian socialism', *EJ*, 39 (1929), 71–7.

Wootton, B. 'Before and after Beveridge', *PQ*, 14 (1943), 357–63.

Wootton, B. 'Return to equality?', *PQ*, 23 (1952), 261–8.

Young, M. 'What might have been', *New Society*, 2.11.1972, 262–4.

Young, M. and P. Willmott 'Institute of Community Studies', *Sociological Review*, 10 (1961), 203–13.

2 Secondary sources

a Books

Addison, P. *The Road to 1945: British Politics and the Second World War* (1975).

Allett, J. *New Liberalism: The Political Economy of J. A. Hobson* (Toronto, 1981).

Anderson, P. *English Questions* (1992).

Archer, R. *et al.* (eds) *Out of Apathy: Voices of the New Left Thirty Years On* (1989).

Backhouse, R. *A History of Modern Economic Analysis* (New York, 1985).

Barker, R. *Education and Politics 1900–51: A Study of the Labour Party* (Oxford, 1972).

Barker, R. *Political Ideas in Modern Britain* (1997).

Barrow, L. and I. Bullock *Democratic Ideas and the British Labour Movement* (Cambridge, 1996).

Barry, B. *Political Argument* (1990 [1965]).

Barry, B. *Why Social Justice Matters* (Cambridge, 2005).

Beer, S. *Modern British Politics* (1969 [1965]).

Bellamy, R. *Liberalism and Modern Society* (Cambridge, 1992).

Bentley, E. *Bernard Shaw* (1967).

Black, L. *The Political Culture of the Left in Affluent Britain, 1951–64: Old Labour, New Britain?* (Basingstoke, 2003).

Bobbio, N. *Left and Right: The Significance of a Political Distinction* (Cambridge, 1996).

Briggs, A. *Social Thought and Social Action: A Study in the Work of Seebohm Rowntree 1871–1954* (1961).

Briggs, A. *Michael Young: Social Entrepreneur* (2001).

Brivati, B. *Hugh Gaitskell* (1997).

Brooke, S. *Labour's War* (Oxford, 1992).

Brown, K. D. *Labour and Unemployment* (Newton Abbot, 1971).

Bullock, A. *The Life and Times of Ernest Bevin Volume 1: Trade Union Leader, 1881–1940* (1960).

Butler, D. and G. Butler *British Political Facts 1900–2000* (Basingstoke, 2000).

Calder, A. *The People's War: Britain 1939–45* (1992 [1969]).

Callaghan, J. *Rajani Palme Dutt: A Study in British Stalinism* (1993).

Chappelow, A. *Shaw: 'The Chucker-out': A Biographical Exposition and Critique* (1969).

Claeys, G. *Machinery, Money and the Millennium: From Moral Economy to Socialism, 1815–60* (Princeton, NJ, 1987).

Clarke, P. *Liberals and Social Democrats* (Cambridge, 1978).

Clarke, P. *The Keynesian Revolution in the Making, 1924–36* (Oxford, 1988).

Clarke, P. *The Cripps Version* (2002).

Cohen, G. A. *Self-ownership, Freedom and Equality* (Cambridge, 1995).

Cohen, G. A. *If You're an Egalitarian, How Come You're so Rich?* (Cambridge, MA, 2001).

Cole, M. *The Life of G. D. H. Cole* (1971).

Collini, S. *Liberalism and Sociology: L. T. Hobhouse and Political Argument in England 1880–1914* (Cambridge, 1979).

Collini, S. *Public Moralists: Political Thought and Intellectual Life in Britain 1850–1930* (Oxford, 1991).

Collini, S. *Absent Minds: British Intellectuals in the Twentieth Century* (Oxford, 2006).

Connolly, W. *The Terms of Political Discourse* (Princeton, NJ, third edition, 1993).

Crick, B. *George Orwell: A Life* (Harmondsworth, 1992).

Cronin, J. *Labour and Society in Britain 1918–79* (1984).

Cronin, J. *New Labour's Pasts* (2004).

Crosland, S. *Tony Crosland* (1983).

Cunliffe, J. and G. Erreygers (eds) *The Origins of Universal Grants* (Basingstoke, 2004).

Daunton, M. *Trusting Leviathan: The Politics of Taxation in Britain, 1799–1914* (Cambridge, 2001).

Daunton, M. *Just Taxes: The Politics of Taxation in Britain, 1914–79* (Cambridge, 2002).

Davenport, N. *Memoirs of a City Radical* (1974).

Dench, G., T. Flower and K. Gavron (eds) *Young at Eighty* (Manchester, 1995).

Drucker, H. *Doctrine and Ethos in the Labour Party* (1979).

Dudley Edwards, R. *Victor Gollancz: A Biography* (1987).

Durbin, E. *New Jerusalems: The Labour Party and the Economics of Democratic Socialism* (1985).

Dworkin, R. *Sovereign Virtue: The Theory and Practice of Equality* (Cambridge, MA, 2000).

Ellison, N. *Egalitarian Thought and Labour Politics: Retreating Visions* (1994).

Elster, J. *Making Sense of Marx* (Cambridge, 1985).

Englander, D. and R. O'Day (eds) *Retrieved Riches: Social Investigation in Britain 1840–1914* (Aldershot, 1995).

Fielding, S. *The Labour Party: Continuity and Change in the Making of 'New' Labour* (Basingstoke, 2003).

Fielding, S., P. Thompson and N. Tiratsoo *'England Arise!' The Labour Party and Popular Politics in 1940s Britain* (Manchester, 1995).

Fitzgibbons, A. *Keynes's Vision* (Oxford, 1988).

Fleischacker, S. *A Short History of Distributive Justice* (Cambridge, MA, 2004).

Foote, G. *The Labour Party's Political Thought* (1997).

Francis, M. *Ideas and Policies Under Labour 1945–51* (Manchester, 1997).

Freeden, M. *The New Liberalism: An Ideology of Social Reform* (Oxford, 1978).

Freeden, M. *Liberalism Divided: A Study in British Political Thought 1914–1939* (Oxford, 1986).

Freeden, M. *Ideologies and Political Theory* (Oxford, 1996).

Freeden, M. *Liberal Languages: Ideological Imaginations and Twentieth-Century Progressive Thought* (Princeton, NJ, 2005).

Freeden, M. (ed.) *Reappraising J. A. Hobson* (1990).

Gaus, G. *The Modern Liberal Theory of Man* (1983).

Giddens, A. *The Third Way and its Critics* (Cambridge, 2000).

Goldthorpe, J. *Social Mobility and Class Structure in Britain* (Oxford, 1987).

Goldthorpe, J., D. Lockwood, F. Bechhofer and J. Platt *The Affluent Worker in the Class Structure* (Cambridge, 1969).

Greenleaf, W. H. *The British Political Tradition Volume 2: The Ideological Heritage* (1983).

Griffiths, G. *Socialism and Superior Brains: The Political Thought of Bernard Shaw* (1993).

Gutmann, A. *Liberal Equality* (Cambridge, 1980).

Halsey, A. H. *No Discouragement: An Autobiography* (Basingstoke, 1996).

Halsey, A. H. *A History of Sociology in Britain* (Oxford, 2004).

Halsey, A. H. and N. Dennis *English Ethical Socialism: Thomas More to R. H. Tawney* (Oxford, 1988).

Halsey, A. H. and J. Webb (eds) *Twentieth Century British Social Trends* (Basingstoke, 2000).

Harris, J. *Unemployment and Politics: A Study in English Social Policy* (Oxford, 1972).

Harris, J. *Private Lives, Public Spirit: A Social History of Britain, 1870–1914* (Oxford, 1993).

Harris, J. *William Beveridge* (Oxford, second edition, 1997).

Harrison, R. *The Life and Times of Sidney and Beatrice Webb, 1858–1905: The Formative Years* (Basingstoke, 2000).

Haseler, S. *The Gaitskellites: Revisionism in the British Labour Party* (1969).

Hawthorn, G. *Enlightenment and Despair: A History of Social Theory* (Cambridge, 1987).

Hazareesingh, S. *Political Traditions in Modern France* (Oxford, 1994).

Howell, D. *British Social Democracy: A Study in Development and Decay* (second edition, 1980).

Howell, D. *British Workers and the Independent Labour Party 1888–1906* (Manchester, 1983).

Howell, D. *MacDonald's Party: Labour Identities and Crisis, 1922–31* (Oxford, 2002).

Howson, S. and D. Winch *The Economic Advisory Council 1930–39* (Cambridge, 1977).

Jay, D. *Change and Fortune: A Political Record* (1980).

Jeffreys, K. *Anthony Crosland* (1999).

Johnson, E. and H. Johnson *The Shadow of Keynes: Understanding Keynes, Cambridge and Keynesian Economics* (Oxford, 1978).

Kenny, M. *The First New Left: British Intellectuals After Stalin* (1995).

Kent, R. A. *A History of British Empirical Sociology* (Aldershot, 1981).

Kloppenburg, J. *Uncertain Victory: Social Democracy and Progressivism in European and American Thought 1870–1920* (Oxford, 1986).

Koselleck, R. *Futures Past* (Cambridge, MA, 1985).

Kramnick, I. and B. Sheerman *Harold Laski: A Life on the Left* (1993).

Kymlicka, W. *Contemporary Political Philosophy: An Introduction* (Oxford, second edition, 2002).

Laborde, C. *Pluralist Thought and the State in Britain and France 1900–25* (2000).

Lavoie, D. *Rivalry and Central Planning: The Socialist Calculation Debate Reconsidered* (Cambridge, 1985).

Le Grand, J. *The Strategy of Equality* (1982).

Leventhal, F. M. *The Last Dissenter: H. N. Brailsford and his World* (Oxford, 1985).

Lowe, R. *The Welfare State in Britain Since 1945* (Basingstoke, third edition, 2005).

Lukes, S. *Marxism and Morality* (Oxford, 1985).

McBriar, A. M. *Fabian Socialism and English Politics, 1884–1918* (Cambridge, 1962).

McBriar, A. M. *An Edwardian Mixed Doubles: The Bosanquets Versus the Webbs* (Oxford, 1987).

MacIntyre, A. *After Virtue* (1985).

MacIntyre, S. *A Proletarian Science: Marxism in Britain, 1917–33* (Cambridge, 1980).

McKibbin, R. *The Ideologies of Class* (Oxford, 1990).

McKibbin, R. *Classes and Cultures: England 1918–51* (Oxford, 1998).

MacNicol, J. *The Movement for Family Allowances 1918–45: A Study in Social Policy Development* (1980).

Marquand, D. *The Progressive Dilemma* (second edition, 1999).

Marshall, G., A. Swift and S. Roberts *Against the Odds? Social Class and Social Justice in Industrial Countries* (Oxford, 1997).

Meadowcroft, J. *Conceptualizing the State: Innovation and Dispute in British Political Thought 1880–1914* (Oxford, 1995).

Miller, D. *Principles of Social Justice* (Cambridge, MA, 1999).

Morgan, K. *Against Fascism and War: Ruptures and Continuities in British Communist Politics, 1935–41* (Manchester, 1989).

Morgan, K. *The Webbs and Soviet Communism* (2006).

Morgan, K. O. *Keir Hardie: Radical and Socialist* (1997 [1975]).

Murray, B. *The People's Budget 1909–10* (Oxford, 1980).

Newman, M. *John Strachey* (Manchester, 1989).

Newman, M. *Harold Laski: A Political Biography* (1993).

Nicholson, P. *The Political Philosophy of the British Idealists* (Cambridge, 1990).

Nozick, R. *Anarchy, State and Utopia* (Oxford, 1974).

O'Donnell, R. M. *Keynes: Philosophy, Economics and Politics* (Basingstoke, 1989).

Otter, S. den *British Idealism and Social Explanation* (Oxford, 1996).

Parkin, F. *Class Inequality and Political Order* (1972).

Pedersen, S. *Family, Dependence and the Origins of the Welfare State* (Cambridge, 1993).

Pedersen, S. *Eleanor Rathbone and the Politics of Conscience* (New Haven, 2004).

Pelling, H. *America and the British Left* (1956).

Pimlott, B. *Labour and the Left in the 1930s* (Cambridge, 1977).

Plant, R. *Modern Political Thought* (Oxford, 1991).

Plant, R. and A. Vincent *Philosophy, Politics and Citizenship* (Oxford, 1984).

Pocock, J. G. A. *Politics, Language and Time* (1972).

Raphael, D. D. *Concepts of Justice* (Oxford, 2001).

Rawls, J. *A Theory of Justice* (Oxford, 1999 [1971]).

Ree, J. *Proletarian Philosophers: Problems in Socialist Culture in Britain 1900–40* (Oxford, 1984).

Reisman, D. *Anthony Crosland: The Mixed Economy* (Basingstoke, 1997).

Reisman, D. *Crosland's Future: Opportunity and Outcome* (Basingstoke, 1997).

Reisman, D. *Richard Titmuss: Welfare and Society* (Basingstoke, second edition, 2001).

Richter, M. *The Politics of Conscience: T. H. Green and his Age* (1964).

Richter, M. *The History of Political and Social Concepts* (Oxford, 1995).

Riddell, N. *Labour in Crisis: The Second Labour Government, 1929–31* (Manchester, 1999).

Ritschel, D. *The Politics of Planning: The Debate on Economic Planning in Britain in the 1930s* (Oxford, 1997).

Roberts, E. A. *The Anglo-Marxists: A Study in Ideology and Culture* (Lanham, MD, 1997).

Rubinstein, D. and B. Simon *The Evolution of the Comprehensive School, 1926–72* (second edition, 1972).

Runciman, D. *Pluralism and the Personality of the State* (Cambridge, 1997).

Runciman, W. G. *Relative Deprivation and Social Justice: A Study of Attitudes to Social Inequality in Twentieth Century Britain* (Harmondsworth, 1972 [1966]).

Sassoon, D. *One Hundred Years of Socialism* (1997).

Searle, G. *The Quest for National Efficiency* (Oxford, 1971).

Sen, A. *On Economic Inequality* (Oxford, 1973).

Sen, A. *Inequality Re-examined* (Cambridge, MA, 1992).

Shepherd, J. *George Lansbury: At the Heart of Old Labour* (Oxford, 2002).

Simhony, A. and D. Weinstein (eds) *The New Liberalism* (Cambridge, 2001).

Skidelsky, R. *Politicians and the Slump* (1967).

Skidelsky, R. *John Maynard Keynes: The Economist as Saviour 1920–37* (1994 [1992]).

Skidelsky, R. *Keynes* (Oxford, 1996).

Skidelsky, R. *John Maynard Keynes: Fighting For Britain 1937–46* (2000).

Skinner, Q. *Liberty Before Liberalism* (Cambridge, 1998).

Skinner, Q. *Visions of Politics Volume 1: On Method* (Cambridge, 2002).

Stansky, P. and W. Abrahams *Orwell: The Transformation* (1994 [1979]).

Stears, M. *Progressives, Pluralists, and the Problems of the State* (Oxford, 2002).

Stedman Jones, G. *Languages of Class* (Cambridge, 1982)

Stedman Jones, G. *An End to Poverty? A Historical Debate* (2004).

Stevenson, J. and C. Cook *Britain in the Depression* (1994).

Sutherland, G. *Ability, Merit and Measurement: Mental Testing and English Education 1880–1940* (Oxford, 1984).

Swift, A. *Political Philosophy: A Beginners' Guide for Students and Politicians* (Cambridge, 2001).

Swift, A. *How Not to be a Hypocrite: School Choice for the Morally Perplexed Parent* (2003).

Tanner, D. *Political Change and the Labour Party, 1900–18* (Cambridge, 1990).

Taylor, M. *Men Versus the State: Herbert Spencer and Late Victorian Individualism* (Oxford, 1992).

Terrill, R. *R. H. Tawney and his Times* (1974).

Thomas, H. *John Strachey* (1973).

Thompson, N. *John Strachey: An Intellectual Biography* (1993).

Thompson, N. *Political Economy and the Labour Party: The Economics of Democratic Socialism, 1884–1995* (1996).

Thompson, N. *The Real Rights of Man: Political Economies for the Working Class 1775–1850* (1998).

Thorpe, A. *Britain in the 1930s* (Oxford, 1992).

Thorpe, A. *The British Communist Party and Moscow 1920–43* (Manchester, 2000).

Thorpe, A. *A History of the British Labour Party* (Basingstoke, 2001).

Tomlinson, J. *Democratic Socialism and Economic Policy: The Attlee Years 1945–51* (Cambridge, 1997).

Toye, R. *The Labour Party and the Planned Economy 1931–51* (Woodbridge, 2003).

Tully, J. (ed.) *Meaning and Context: Quentin Skinner and his Critics* (Cambridge, 1988).

Waldron, J. *God, Locke and Equality* (Cambridge, 2002).

Walzer, M. *Spheres of Justice* (Oxford, 1983).

Warde, A. *Consensus and Beyond* (Manchester, 1982).

Weinstein, D. *Equal Freedom and Utility: Herbert Spencer's Utilitarianism* (Cambridge, 1998).

Wersky, G. *The Visible College: A Collective Biography of British Scientists and Socialists of the 1930s* (1978).
White, S. *The Civic Minimum: An Essay on the Rights and Obligations of Economic Citizenship* (Oxford, 2003).
Whiting, R. *The Labour Party and Taxation* (Cambridge, 2000).
Williams, P. *Hugh Gaitskell* (1979).
Williamson, P. *National Crisis and National Government* (Cambridge, 1992).
Winch, D. *Economics and Policy: A Historical Study* (1969).
Winter, J. *Socialism and the Challenge of War* (1974).
Wood, N. *Communism and British Intellectuals* (1959).
Wright, A. *G. D. H. Cole and Socialist Democracy* (Oxford, 1979).
Wright, A. *R. H. Tawney* (Manchester, 1987).
Zweiniger-Bargielowska, I. *Austerity in Britain: Rationing, Controls and Consumption 1939–55* (Oxford, 2000).

b Articles and chapters

Anderson, E. 'What is the point of equality?', *Ethics*, 109 (1999), 287–337.
Arblaster, A. 'Tawney in retrospect', *Society for the Study of Labour History Bulletin*, 54 (1989), 95–102.
Atkinson, A. B. 'The case for a participation income', *PQ*, 67 (1996), 67–70.
Benn, C. 'Comprehensive school reform and the 1945 Labour government', *History Workshop Journal*, 10 (1980), 197–204.
Bevir, M. 'Fabianism and the theory of rent', *History of Political Thought*, 10 (1989), 313–27.
Bevir, M. 'Welfarism, socialism and religion: on T. H. Green and others', *Review of Politics*, 55 (1993), 639–61.
Bevir, M. 'British socialism and American romanticism', *English Historical Review*, 110 (1995), 878–901.
Bevir, M. 'William Morris: the modern self, art, and politics', *History of European Ideas*, 24 (1998), 175–94.
Bevir, M. 'Sidney Webb: utilitarianism, positivism, and social democracy', *Journal of Modern History*, 74 (2002), 217–52.
Black, L. 'Social democracy as a way of life: fellowship and the Socialist Union, 1951–59', *Twentieth Century British History*, 10 (1999), 499–539.
Blaug, M. 'The formalist revolution or what happened to orthodox economics after World War Two?', in R. Backhouse and J. Creedy (eds), *From Classical Economics to the Theory of the Firm* (Cheltenham, 1999), 257–80.
Brooke, S. 'Atlantic crossing? American views of capitalism and British socialist thought 1932–62', *Twentieth Century British History*, 2 (1991), 107–36.
Brooke, S. 'Problems of "socialist planning": Evan Durbin and the Labour government of 1945', *Historical Journal*, 34 (1991), 687–702.
Brooke, S. 'Evan Durbin: reassessing a Labour "revisionist"', *Twentieth Century British History*, 7 (1996), 27–52.
Clarke, P. 'The progressive movement in England', *Transactions of the Royal Historical Society*, Fifth Series, 24 (1974), 159–81.
Clarke, P. 'The social democratic theory of the class struggle', in J. Winter (ed.), *The Working Class in Modern British History* (Cambridge, 1983), 3–18.
Clarke, P. 'Hobson and Keynes as economic heretics', in Freeden (ed.), *Reappraising J. A. Hobson*, 100–15.
Cohen, G. A. 'Back to socialist basics', *NLR*, No. 207, 1994, 3–16.

Cohen, G. A. 'Self-ownership, history and socialism: an interview with G. A. Cohen', *Imprints*, 1 (1996), 7–25.

Cohen, G. A. 'Socialism and equality of opportunity', in M. Rosen and J. Wolff (eds), *Political Thought* (Oxford, 1999), 354–8.

Collini, S. 'Hobhouse, Bosanquet and the state: philosophical idealism and political argument in England 1880–1918', *Past and Present*, 72 (1976), 86–111.

Collini, S. 'Moral mind: R. H. Tawney', in S. Collini, *English Pasts* (Oxford, 1999), 177–94.

Cooter, R. and P. Rappoport 'Were the ordinalists wrong about welfare economics?', *Journal of Economic Literature*, 22 (1984), 507–30.

Cranston, M. 'Keynes: his political ideas and their influence', in A. Thirlwall (ed.), *Keynes and Laissez-Faire* (1978), 101–15.

Crick, B. 'Shaw as political thinker', in B. Crick, *Crossing Borders: Political Essays* (2001), 188–205.

Dancy, J. 'From intuitionism to emotivism', in T. Baldwin (ed.), *The Cambridge History of Philosophy 1870–1945* (Cambridge, 2003), 695–705.

Fielding, S. 'Labourism in the 1940s', *Twentieth Century British History*, 3 (1992), 138–53.

Francis, M. 'Mr Gaitskell's Ganymede: re-assessing Crosland's *Future of Socialism*', *Contemporary British History*, 11 (1997), 50–64.

Freeden, M. 'Rights, needs and community: the emergence of British welfare thought', in A. Ware and R. Goodin (eds), *Needs and Welfare* (1990), 54–72.

Freeden, M. 'The stranger at the feast: ideology and public policy in twentieth-century Britain', *Twentieth Century British History*, 1 (1990), 9–34.

Freeden, M. 'The coming of the welfare state', in T. Ball and R. Bellamy (eds), *The Cambridge History of Twentieth-Century Political Thought* (Cambridge, 2003), 7–44.

Geras, N. 'The controversy about Marx and justice', *NLR*, No. 150, 1985, 47–85.

Goldthorpe, J. 'Intellectuals and the working class in modern Britain', in D. Rose (ed.), *Social Stratification and Economic Change* (1988), 39–56.

Goldthorpe, J. 'A response', in J. Clark, C. Modgil and S. Modgil (eds), *John H. Goldthorpe: Consensus and Controversy* (1990), 399–438.

Harris, J. 'Some aspects of social policy in Britain during the Second World War', in W. Mommsen (ed.), *The Emergence of the Welfare State in Britain and Germany* (1981), 247–62.

Harris, J. 'The transition to high politics in English social policy 1880–1914', in M. Bentley and J. Stevenson (eds), *High Politics and Low Politics in Modern Britain* (Oxford, 1983), 58–79.

Harris, J. 'Political ideas and the debate on state welfare, 1940–45', in H. Smith (ed.), *War and Social Change* (Manchester, 1986), 233–63.

Harris, J. 'Political thought and the welfare state, 1870–1940', *Past and Present*, 135 (1992), 116–41.

Harris, J. 'War and social history: Britain and the home front during the Second World War', *Contemporary European History*, 1 (1992), 17–35.

Harris, J. 'Contract and citizenship', in D. Marquand and A. Seldon (eds), *The Ideas that Shaped Post-War Britain* (1996), 122–38.

Harris, J. 'Political thought and the state', in S. Green and R. Whiting (eds), *The Boundaries of the State in Modern Britain* (Cambridge, 1996), 15–28.

Harris, J. 'Ruskin and social reform', in D. Birch (ed.), *Ruskin and the Dawn of the Modern* (Oxford, 1999), 7–33.

Harris, J. 'Labour's political and social thought', in D. Tanner, P. Thane and N. Tiratsoo (eds), *Labour's First Century* (Cambridge, 2000), 8–45.

Heinemann, M. 'The People's Front and the intellectuals', in J. Fryth (ed.), *British Fascism and the Popular Front* (1985), 157–86.

Hickson, K. 'Equality', in R. Plant, M. Beech and K. Hickson (eds), *The Struggle for Labour's Soul: Understanding Labour's Political Thought Since 1945* (London, 2004), 120–36.

Jackson, B. 'The uses of utilitarianism: social justice, welfare economics and British socialism, 1931–48', *History of Political Thought*, 25 (2004), 508–35.

Jackson, B. 'Revisionism reconsidered: "property-owning democracy" and egalitarian strategy in post-war Britain', *Twentieth Century British History*, 16 (2005), 416–40.

Jackson, B. 'The conceptual history of social justice', *Political Studies Review*, 3 (2005), 356–73.

Jackson, B. and P. Segal 'Why inequality matters', *Catalyst Working Paper* (2004).

Lamb, P. 'Laski's ideological metamorphosis', *Journal of Political Ideologies*, 4 (1999), 239–60.

Lowe, R. 'The Second World War, consensus and the foundation of the welfare state', *Twentieth Century British History*, 1 (1990), 152–82.

Lowe, R. 'The rediscovery of poverty and the creation of the Child Poverty Action Group, 1962–68', *Contemporary Record*, 9 (1995), 602–11.

Lukes, S. 'Socialism and equality', in L. Kołakowski and S. Hampshire (eds), *The Socialist Idea* (1977), 74–95.

McKibbin, R. 'Nothing more divisive', *London Review of Books*, 28.11.2002, 3–6.

Miller, D. 'In what sense must socialism be communitarian?', *Social Philosophy and Policy*, 6 (1989), 51–73.

Miller, D. 'Equality and market socialism', in P. Bardhan and J. Roemer (eds), *Market Socialism: The Current Debate* (New York, 1993), 298–314.

Neavill, G. B. 'Victor Gollancz and the Left Book Club', *Library Quarterly*, 41 (1971), 197–215.

Otter, S. den '"Thinking in communities": late nineteenth-century liberals, idealists and the retrieval of community', in E. H. H. Green (ed.), *An Age of Transition: British Politics 1880–1914* (Edinburgh, 1997), 67–84.

Paul, D. 'Eugenics and the Left', *Journal of the History of Ideas*, 45 (1984), 567–90.

Plant, R. 'Democratic socialism and equality', in D. Lipsey and D. Leonard (eds), *The Socialist Agenda: Crosland's Legacy* (1981), 135–55.

Plant, R. 'Socialism, markets and end states', in J. Le Grand and S. Estrin (eds), *Market Socialism* (Oxford, 1989), 50–77.

Plant, R. 'Social democracy', in D. Marquand and A. Seldon (eds), *The Ideas That Shaped Post-War Britain* (1996), 165–94.

Plant, R. 'Crosland, equality and New Labour', in D. Leonard (ed.), *Crosland and New Labour* (Basingstoke, 1999), 19–34.

Plowright, J. 'Political economy and Christian polity: the influence of Henry George in England reassessed', *Victorian Studies*, 30 (1987), 235–52.

Reisman, D. 'Crosland's *Future*: the first edition', *International Journal of Social Economics*, 23 (1996), 3–55.

Roemer, J. 'Egalitarian strategies', *Dissent*, Summer 1999, 64–74.

Scheffler, S. 'What is egalitarianism?', *Philosophy and Public Affairs*, 31 (2003), 5–39.

Stapleton, J. 'Localism versus centralism in the Webbs' political thought', *History of Political Thought*, 12 (1991), 147–65.

Stears, M. 'Guild socialism and ideological diversity on the British Left, 1914–26', *Journal of Political Ideologies*, 3 (1998), 289–305.

Stears, M. 'Needs, welfare and the limits of associationalism', *Economy and Society*, 28 (1999), 570–89.

Stears, M. and S. White 'New liberalism revisited', in H. Tam (ed.), *Progressive Politics in the Global Age* (Cambridge, 2001), 36–53.

Stedman Jones, G. 'The determinist fix: some obstacles to the further development of the linguistic approach to history in the 1990s', *History Workshop Journal*, 42 (1996), 19–35.

Tanner, D. 'The development of British socialism, 1900–18', in E. H. H. Green (ed.), *An Age of Transition: British Politics 1880–1914* (Edinburgh, 1997), 48–66.

Thompson, N. 'Hobson and the Fabians: two roads to socialism in the 1920s', *History of Political Economy*, 26 (1994), 203–20.

Tomlinson, J. 'The limits of Tawney's ethical socialism: a historical perspective on the Labour Party and the market', *Contemporary British History*, 16 (2002), 1–16.

Tuck, R. 'The contribution of history', in R. Goodin and P. Pettit (eds), *A Companion to Contemporary Political Philosophy* (Oxford, 1993), 72–89.

Vaizey, J. 'Whatever happened to equality? 3: Equality and fairness', *Listener*, 16.5.1974, 629–31.

Van Parijs, P. 'Competing justifications of basic income', in P. Van Parijs (ed.), *Arguing for Basic Income* (1992), 3–43.

Veit-Wilson, J. H. 'Paradigms of poverty: a rehabilitation of B. S. Rowntree', *Journal of Social Policy*, 15 (1986), 69–99.

Waters, C. 'J. B. Priestley', in S. Pedersen and P. Mandler (eds), *After the Victorians* (1994), 209–26.

Weinstein, D. 'The new liberalism of L. T. Hobhouse and the re-envisioning of nineteenth-century utilitarianism', *Journal of the History of Ideas*, 57 (1996), 487–507.

Weinstein, D. 'The new liberalism and the rejection of utilitarianism', in Simhony and Weinstein (eds), *The New Liberalism*, 159–83.

White, S. 'Needs, labour and Marx's conception of justice', *Political Studies*, 44 (1996), 88–101.

White, S. 'Rights and responsibilities: a social democratic perspective', in A. Gamble and A. Wright (eds), *The New Social Democracy* (Oxford, 1999), 166–79.

White, S. 'Rediscovering republican political economy', *Imprints*, 4 (2000), 213–35.

Wolff, J. 'Fairness, respect and the egalitarian ethos', *Philosophy and Public Affairs*, 27 (1998), 97–122.

Wolff, J. 'Training, perfectionism and fairness', *Journal of Applied Philosophy*, 21 (2004), 285–95.

Yeo, S. 'A new life: the religion of socialism in Britain, 1883–96', *History Workshop Journal*, 4 (1977), 5–56.

Young, M. (interviewed by P. Hennessy) 'The 1945 general election and the post-war period remembered', *Contemporary Record*, 9 (1995), 80–98.

c Unpublished theses

Bevir, M. 'British socialist thought 1880–1900' (DPhil, Oxford University, 1989).

Bryan, D. E. H. 'The development of revisionist thought among British Labour intellectuals and politicians, 1931–64' (DPhil, Oxford University, 1984).

Howell, D. 'The restatement of socialism in the Labour Party 1947–61' (PhD, Manchester University, 1971).

Nuttall, J. 'Psychological socialism: Tony Crosland and the politics of the mind' (DPhil, Oxford University, 2001).

Peters, J. N. 'Anti-socialism in British politics, c.1900–22: the emergence of a counter-ideology' (DPhil, Oxford University, 1992).

Robinson, S. J. 'R. H. Tawney's theory of equality: a theological and ethical analysis' (PhD, Edinburgh University, 1989).

Stears, M. 'Socialism and pluralism: a study in British inter-war ideology' (DPhil, Oxford University, 1997).

Torrie, C. 'Ideas, policy and ideology: the British Labour Party in opposition, 1951–59' (DPhil, Oxford University, 1997).

Van Trier, W. 'Everyone a king: an investigation into the meaning and significance of the debate on basic incomes with special reference to three episodes from the British inter-war experience' (PhD, University of Leuven, 1995).

Index

Note: 'n.' after a page reference indicates the number of a note on that page; books are listed under the names of their authors or editors

Milton Keynes UK
Ingram Content Group UK Ltd.
UKHW021841020124
435344UK00014B/62